The Complete Guide to Fruit and Vegetable Growing

General Editor: Roy Hay

S. Millar Gault
John Wright
Susan M. Passmore
Harry Baker
Margaret Leach

Photographic contributors include
Ernest Crowson AIIP, FRPS and
The National Fruit Trials

The Complete Guide to

FRUIT & VEGETABLE GROWING

Ward Lock Limited · London

First published in Great Britain in 1978 by
Ward Lock Limited
116 Baker Street, London W1M 2BB
A member of the Pentos Group

This book was designed and produced
for the publisher by
George Rainbird Ltd
36 Park Street, London W1Y 4DE

House Editors: Karen Goldie-Morrison, Alastair Dougall
Designer: Alan Bartram
Illustrators: Paul Buckle and Terri Lawlor
Indexer: Betty Dewhurst

Text filmset by Jolly & Barber Ltd
Rugby, Warwickshire, England

Printed and bound by
Dai Nippon Printing Co Ltd
Hong Kong

British Library Cataloguing in Publication Data
A complete guide to fruit and vegetable
    growing.
    1. Vegetable gardening. 2. Fruit-culture
    I. Hay, Roy II. Royal Horticulture Society
    635   SB322

ISBN 0-7063-5597-0

Contents

Acknowledgments

The publishers would like to thank the following people for all their valuable help and assistance: Elspeth Napier, Audrey Brooks, John Swabey and Andrew Halstead. Especial mention must also be made of Ernest Crowson whose photographic expertise was much valued.

The table on bottling by the quick water bath method on page 179 is reproduced from *Home Preservation of Fruit and Vegetables*, Bulletin 21, Ministry of Agriculture, Fisheries and Food, H.M.S.O. The winemaking table on page 201 is reproduced by permission of *Do-It-Yourself* magazine.

Photographic acknowledgments

Vegetable colour
A-Z Botanical Collection Ltd – Plates 57, 111, 150.
Heather Angel MSC – Plate 103.
Ardea Photographics, J. L. Mason – Plate 170.
Dr Alan Beaumont – Plate 67.
Pat Brindley – Plates 10, 32, 39, 41, 42, 76, 80, 84, 96, 98, 101, 106, 137, 138.
Ernest Crowson AIIP, FRPS – Plates 2–9, 13–20, 22–31, 44–7, 49–52, 55–6, 58–61, 63–6, 72–4, 78–9, 82, 85–92, 95, 97, 99, 100, 104, 107–8, 112–5, 117–20, 122–5, 127–30, 133, 135–6, 141–2, 144, 146–9, 152–60, 162–5, 167–9.
Brian Furner – Plates 48, 62, 66, 68, 70, 109–10, 145.
Hurst Gunson, Cooper, Taber Ltd. – Plates 83, 94.
Bernard Alfieri, Natural History Photographic Agency – Plates 139, 143.
Harry Smith Horticultural Photographic Collection – Plates 1, 12, 33, 34, 43, 53, 54, 69, 71, 77, 93, 121, 131, 132, 134, 161, 166.
Spectrum Colour Library – Plates 81, 116.
Thompson and Morgan – Plate 21.
Tom Wellsted – Plates 11, 102, 105, 126, 140, 151.

Fruit colour
A–Z Botanical Collection Ltd – Plate 167.
Heather Angel MSC – Plates 2, 57, 172.
Harry A. Baker – Plates 63, 66, 91, 96, 121, 168.
J.G. & I. M. Barrett, 'Felstar Wines,' – Plate 85.
Colour Library International – Plates 88, 90.
R. J. Corbin FLS – Plates 102, 104.
Ernest Crowson – Plates 4–5, 7, 9–14, 16, 18–21, 23–6, 29–31, 33–4, 36, 38–42, 46–7,
50, 61, 64–5, 67, 72, 77, 81, 83–4, 86–7, 92–3, 94–5, 97, 100, 101–5, 116, 119, 150, 156–7, 159–60, 164, 169–71.
Brian Furner – Plates 45, 71, 98, 99, 162, 174.
J. C. Hayon – Plates 142, 147, 173.
Dr. Alan Legge – Plates 48–9.
National Fruit Trials (Ministry of Agriculture, Fisheries and Food) – Plates 6, 8, 17, 22, 27, 32, 35, 51–55, 60, 62, 68, 73–6, 78, 108–11, 113–5, 117–8, 120, 123–4, 126–7, 129–34, 138–40, 114–5, 149, 151–2, 154–5.
New Zealand Fruit Growers' Federation Ltd – Plate 56.
The Royal Horticultural Society – Plates 69–70, 135, 158.
Donald Smith – Plates 28, 37, 103, 136–7.
Harry Smith Horticultural Photographic Collection – Plates 3, 15, 43–4, 79–80, 107, 112, 122, 125, 128, 141, 143, 146, 148, 153, 161, 163.
Spectrum Colour Library, R. T. Way – Plate 166.
Louis Trémellat – Plates 1, 82, 89, 106, 165.

Black and white photographs
Barnaby's Picture Library – pp. 12–13 (Lensart), p. 23 (N. Westwater), pp. 90–91 (P. Rosser), p. 177.
Fisons Ltd – p. 168, a and b.
Imperial Chemical Industries Ltd – pp. 169, b and c, 171 a, 172 c, 173 a, 175 a.
Murphy Chemical Ltd – pp. 168 c, 169 a and d, 170 a.
The Royal Horticultural Society – pp. 171 c and b, 172 a and b, 173 b, 174 a, 175 b, 176 a.

Bibliography

The ABC of Preserving Prepared by the Ministry of Agriculture, Fisheries and Food and the Central Office of Information.

Les Beaux Fruits de France Georges Delbard, Édition Delbard, Paris 1947.

Catalogue of British Pears National Fruit Trials.

Dictionary of Gardening The Royal Horticultural Society, Ed. Fred Chittenden, Clarendon Press, Oxford 1956.

Encyclopedia of Garden Plants and Flowers Consultant Ed. Roy Hay Reader's Digest, London 1971.

The Fruit Garden Displayed The Royal Horticultural Society.

Fruit Pests, Diseases and Disorders The Royal Horticultural Society, Wisley Handbook 27.

The Gardening Year Consultant Ed. Roy Hay, Reader's Digest, London 1972.

The Grafter's Handbook R. J. Garner, Faber 1967.

The National Apple Register of the UK Muriel W. G. Smith, Ministry of Agriculture, Fisheries and Food, London 1971.

Plant Varieties and Seeds Gazette H.M.S.O. 1976.

The Vegetable Garden Displayed The Royal Horticultural Society 1975.

The Practical Gardening Encyclopedia Ed. Roy Hay and Roger Davies, Ward Lock, London 1977.

The Complete Handbook of Fruit Growing Roy Genders, Ward Lock, London 1976.

The Complete Book of Vegetables and Herbs Roy Genders, Ward Lock, London 1972.

Foreword

As the standard of living of a nation rises the diet of its people tends to change. To the basic energy-giving cereal foods and cheap root vegetables, meat or fish are added and, later, fruit and more tasty vegetables. The diet of many people has been influenced in recent years through the availability of cheap foreign travel and swift transport of perishable produce by air. Also the advent of deep-freezing has changed the pattern of modern diet.

Gone are the days when people ate fruits and vegetables only in their appropriate season. Some think this is a pity, recalling that people were content enough to eat swedes, turnips, beetroot and kale and even dried haricot beans in winter. They enjoyed the first new peas or beans, radishes and fresh ripe tomatoes and looked forward to the first strawberries and raspberries.

Frozen and canned produce, 'convenience' foods as they are called, are now so common that a generation has grown up that has never really tasted fresh vegetables gathered and cooked in peak condition.

But in recent years, people are more and more appreciating the flavour and probably better nutritional value of fresh produce. Who would have thought twenty or thirty years ago that such exotic items as globe artichokes, peppers and aubergines and avocados would be found in every street market or that every cookery book would be rich in recipes in which they are an essential ingredient. Foreign travel, if it has not broadened the mind, has certainly widened the appreciation of many unusual fruits and vegetables.

But these good things have to be paid for. Only a super optimist would believe that they are ever going to be any cheaper so it makes sense for all the reasons set out above to grow as many of our own fruits and vegetables as we can.

The amount of garden space devoted to food crops is obviously a matter to be decided by personal circumstances and preferences. Although it is usual to grow these crops in one part of the garden, screened from the ornamental part by a low hedge of roses or such like, it is quite possible to integrate fruits and vegetables with the flowers and shrubs nearer the house. Fruits against walls, tomatoes and sweet corn judiciously planted among the flowers; an edging of beetroot or carrots to a rose bed; New Zealand spinach among shrubs; all these and many more may be grown to ease the housekeeping bills.

The choice of crops to grow depends on the tastes of the family. If nobody likes parsnips then there is no point in growing them. If there is a preference for runner beans, and there is a deep freeze available, it would pay to grow large quantities of runner beans even at the expense of winter crops like kale or savoys.

This book has been designed to give as much advice as is needed for anyone living in a temperate climate to grow the fruits and vegetables suited to his soil and situation. The influence of climate is of profound importance – often a controlling factor in the successful production of various crops. This has been kept firmly in mind by the authors and it is something that every reader should study seriously. No book can tell a gardener exactly what would be the best crops to grow in his particular garden. There are areas where because of climatic factors – shortness of the growing season, danger of late or early frosts – certain crops are not worth risking. Or, in such areas, some cultivars may be more likely to succeed than others – 'Bramley's Seedling' apple for example is very susceptible to frost damage and should never be planted where frosts at flowering time are normally to be expected.

Anyone moving to a new locality, or deciding for the first time to grow food crops would be wise to supplement the information given in this book by seeking local intelligence. The members of a local horticultural society or even some of the old residents in the public bar of the inn are usually brimming with information about cultivars that do well in the neighbourhood and only too willing to pass it on. They may of course be a bit out of date and the new comer while following local custom should experiment gently with new cultivars and techniques. Gardeners are notoriously conservative but it pays to listen to local garden lore and build upon it cautiously.

This book consists of five sections, the first being an introduction to fruit and vegetable growing, in which such matters as soil cultivation, tools, crop rotation and weed control, are discussed.

The vegetable section begins with a discussion of each vegetable, its particular cultivation needs and its susceptibility to attack by pests or diseases. There is also a monthly calendar of work in the vegetable plot. The dictionary of vegetable cultivars is followed by colour photographs illustrating the cultivars and cross-referenced with the text.

Fruit cultivation deals with the very wide range of factors involved in the successful production of fruit. Apart from the suitability of a site for growing the different fruits there is the question of the choice of fruits and of their cultivars, the suitability of the different rootstocks on which various fruits are grafted for different soils or situations. Pruning and training trees in restricted forms is also dealt with as is the puzzling problem of choosing cultivars which will pollinate each other. There is a calendar of monthly operations in the fruit garden.

In the dictionary of fruit cultivars, the description of each cultivar includes its origin if known, its cropping potential, hardiness or susceptibility to disease, and other important characteristics.

The section also includes charts showing flowering periods and compatibility groups for apples, pears, plums and cherries.

The section on pests and diseases of fruits and vegetables covers all the main troubles that affect these crops in temperate climates.

Every reader obviously must decide for himself the planning of the fruit and vegetable plots. Not only must the balance between the ornamental and the kitchen garden be decided, the balance between long term crops, i.e. tree fruits, and short term crops like strawberries and raspberries, also needs consideration. So to with vegetables: the only really long term vegetable however is asparagus. The point to bear in mind is the length of time you are likely to stay in one place; if you might move in say five or ten years it is probably not worth while planting tree fruits. Your interest would probably be better served by planting gooseberries, raspberries, currants, loganberries, blackberries and the like.

Another important factor to be considered when planning a kitchen garden is whether home preserving will be actively carried on – deep freezing, bottling, jam making and so on. The fifth section on home preserving merits careful study because, depending on the size of the family and its likes and dislikes, it is often wise to choose crops that can be preserved and used when the shop article is scarce and expensive. It may be better to keep plenty of soft fruits, sweet corn, beans, peas, globe artichokes and young carrots in the deep freezer than quantities of main crop potatoes, turnips and swedes. These at least may be bought in good condition in the shops. Soft fruits are usually expensive as they are labour intensive crops and often appear in the shops in poor condition.

Horticulture has been bedevilled by synonymy – the same cultivars being known by several names not only in Britain but in overseas countries. Now the EEC countries have set up a system whereby the vegetable cultivars are being sorted out and this problem of synonyms is being resolved. The cultivars mentioned in this book and their synonyms are right up to date according to the EEC lists at the time of going to press.

Unfortunately there is no similar register of fruit cultivars but where possible known synonyms are shown.

ROY HAY

PREPARING THE GARDEN

Preparing the Soil

The Soil

Without the soil we cannot live, therefore it is wise to manage it to the best of our ability, knowing that by doing so it will in due time reward us with better crops. Few who garden can choose their soil, and we are therefore obliged to take that which is available and do our best to improve it. Even the poorest of soils can be brought into 'good heart' given time, resulting in higher yields of improved quality.

When taking over a garden, and every 3 or so years afterwards, it is advisable to have the soil analysed. This may be done by sending samples away – local authorities sometimes undertake soil analyses – or doing your own tests with the very reasonably priced kits now available.

Types of Soil

Soils are very variable in different areas of the country and can alter from garden to garden and sometimes even in one garden. Rocks, broken down by various agencies, sometimes over millions of years, have provided the mineral basis for soils, a process completed by the constant addition of decomposed vegetation and animal remains. For our purpose, soils can roughly be classified by texture, usually determined by the size of the soil particles.

– Clay

Clay soils are heavy to dig and to cultivate. This is because they are made up of particles so small that water cannot pass through readily. In wet winters, therefore, there is a tendency to waterlog, leaving this type of soil sticky and wet, very cold in the spring and, consequently, slow to warm up. Further difficulties arise in summer because clay soils shrink as they dry, creating cracks which result in further drying. In a drought this can cause considerable damage to crops. Such soils can usually be improved by digging in quantities of organic matter, such as strawy manure or partially decayed leaves during late autumn and winter. On these clay soils making a seed bed at a texture sufficiently friable may be quite difficult, but if some weeks before a dressing of lime at 230 to 240g. per sq. m. (8oz. per sq. yd) is spread on the surface, the soil will break down that much easier. Likewise, dressings of sand, peat and gypsum can further improve an intractable soil, without building up its lime content.

– Chalk

Alkaline chalk soils, derived from chalk hills, are particularly common on downland and are generally very deficient in organic matter, thus needing large quantities of humus-forming material to be worked in during cultivation. Such soils, often shallow, seldom require lime and under good cultivation will produce good crops, especially brassicas, beans and peas.

– Sand

Sandy soils are altogether different from clay. The particles are coarse and do not stick together, but though being easy to work, water drains rapidly and often wastefully through them, especially during summer. Such soils require large quantities of farmyard manure or compost to enrich them and help prevent the wastage of soluble plant foods. This is important because plant foods, being soluble drain through too rapidly for the plant roots to make full use of them. In very wet winters this excessive drainage may be aggravated by autumn cultivation. On these light soils cultivation is better left until spring.

– Peat

Peat soils, high in organic matter, are generally confined to badly drained low-lying areas such as bogs and fens. However, when well drained, such soils can be highly fertile and produce bumper crops. Peaty soils can also be found on high moorland when they are often badly drained and very acid, and by their elevation, isolation and exposure they are of little value for the production of vegetables. However, vegetables may be grown in such a situation with adequate shelter, drainage and heavy applications of lime. When well cultivated, peaty soils often produce very fine crops of celery, onions and potatoes.

– Loam

This is without doubt the soil most desired by most gardeners. Loam soils, with their proper balance of sand and clay particles, and fertility derived from a frequently high humus content (shown by a high population of earthworms) usually have sufficient body to retain plant foods without excessive leaching. Loams warm up more quickly in spring, because they are dark in colour, thereby leading to earlier and stronger seed germination. Beneficial bacteria are likely to be more active in such soils, thus increasing the fertility and producing stronger healthier plants and good crops.

– Silts

Composed of very fine particles, these are inclined to be sticky and less easily drained. After rain, the soil surface often compacts into a hard, cement-like crust as drying takes place, making cultivation difficult. Any surface cultivation is therefore best carried out before complete drying has occurred and a surface dressing of a humus-forming material such as peat may lessen compaction.

– Alluvial soils

These are generally found in valley bottoms, and are caused by the deposition of soil particles carried by rivers and streams from higher land. Very often such soils are highly fertile, especially when well drained. Where flooding is not a danger such land is capable of growing fine crops.

Soil Improvement

Good soil structure has long been recognized by gardeners, as a fundamental requirement for fertility. Without such a structure, the fertilizers you apply, particularly those which are inorganic in origin may to a large extent be wasted, this wastage occurring because the soil cannot retain them sufficiently long for plant roots to make the best use of them. This holding capacity is very largely dependent upon the humus in the soil, resulting from the break-down of applied compost, leafmould, farmyard manure or peat.

As already indicated, heavy soils are most readily improved by such materials as very strawy manure, like that from riding or racing stables, partially decayed leaves or rough peat. Autumn cultivation can also be beneficial in breaking down the soil by the pulverizing action of frost and weathering by wind over winter. Fertility is more easily maintained on soils that are sandy and light by the use of cow or pig manure, though this is only likely to be obtainable in rural areas. Today most gardeners use home made compost very successfully but it must be available in reasonable quantities. On light, sandy soils, clay was formerly spread on the surface to stop 'wind blow' and help moisture retention. Expense has

made this practice virtually obsolete, but where circumstances permit, amateur gardeners may find it still of value.

No digging as a practice, has been much publicized by some gardeners in recent years. Sowing and planting takes place in compost spread thickly on the soil surface. Followers of this technique consider the earthworm to be more efficient than the spade in taking organic matter to a greater depth and providing natural aeration of the soil. The main disadvantage is, perhaps, the need to produce large quantities of compost, for often it is difficult to obtain the necessary materials in sufficient quantities from a small garden. Compost heaps also take up room in small gardens. Thus, in my opinion a spade or digging fork, if properly used, will aerate the soil very satisfactorily, while the labour of digging, will not be any greater than that expended on gathering the material for large quantities of compost.

Mulching with compost, peat or leafmould can be beneficial to all crops particularly runner beans or tomatoes by its reduction of water loss by evaporation. Mulching also avoids damage to surface roots, especially those of crops like sweetcorn, and hoeing, which may cause root and stem damage when carelessly done, is unnecessary as weeds are smothered by the mulch, while materials used add in time to the humus in the soil. Some of the mulch will have been taken down by worms, while all that is still left on the surface after the crop has been cleared can be dug into the soil.

Many gardeners find straw, so long as it has not been treated with a hormone spray used by some farmers, very effective as a mulch when applied to a depth of 13 to 15cm. (5 to 6in.). Those gardeners with a lawn find it is a useful way to dispose of the mowings. In this case however only a thin layer should be applied at one time, as when put on thickly the mowings are apt to heat and turn into a greasy, smelly mess. Sawdust is another material which is better not applied thickly, unless very well weathered. Peat is of course very good indeed but more expensive.

The most modern method of mulching is to use strips of black polythene either between the rows or, in the case of potatoes, over the plants, cutting holes to enable the plant to come through. This form of mulch does not add anything to the fertility of the soil, but does suppress weeds and helps to retain moisture.

Mulches should generally be applied in spring, after the soil has had time to get warmed up. Do not wait till high summer as by then it will have dried out. Retention of moisture is of great importance so that if dry, the soil should be given a good soaking of water before the mulching material is applied. Although mulching is best done in spring there are exceptions, asparagus for one, mulching usually being carried out when the tops are cut down in late October or early November. Then a dressing of well-rotted compost or manure should be applied.

Turning over the soil by digging is still to my mind the best way to improve it, especially if you can at the same time incorporate bulky organic material to augment the supply of plant nutrients. This turning over, shatters the surface, thereby introducing air and admitting rain.

Digging is good exercise, but if you are not used to it, it is tiring work so take it in easy stages. It is best to start towards the end of October and

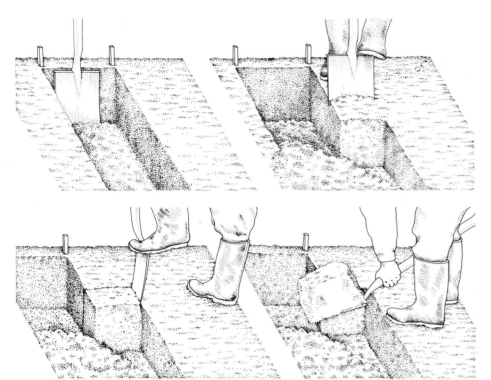

Single digging
First trench dug 30cm. (12in.) wide to depth of spade (top left). Cutting the spit (top right). Inserting spade vertically (bottom left), lift spadeful of soil (bottom right), and place in first trench. Place a little manure in each newly dug trench.

carry on during November and December when the weather is suitably cool and the soil is not too wet. Heavy soils will then get broken down by frost and can be worked down in spring into what gardeners call a fine tilth.

Depth of cultivation varies according to the locality, being dependent to some extent on the nature of the subsoil. Bringing up chalk, gravel or impervious clay to the surface may impair the soil for sowing seeds until it has mellowed. The top layer or spit is the most important for growing crops, and where this is very shallow it can be deepened by working in organic matter and breaking up the subsoil with a digging fork. Nowadays deep trenching and double-digging are no longer popular and, except for odd exceptions, are not really necessary.

A good spade is still the best digging tool except in heavy soils, where a digging fork may be easier to handle, and is certainly the better tool for breaking up subsoil.

In single digging, the soil is inverted to one full depth of the spade, this depth being achieved by inserting the spade almost vertically. The digging may be too shallow if the spade is allowed to slant too much. Any organic matter is placed in the trench, worked in with a fork, if greater depth is required, and the next spit turned over to fill the previous trench and make another. If the soil is very heavy, by digging it in autumn and leaving it in rough ridges a greater volume is exposed to the effect of frost. Much unnecessary moving of soil can be avoided if the plot is divided equally down the middle. Then soil removed by making a trench at the end of one half is transferred to the adjacent half to fill in the last trench when digging is finished. Otherwise, if the whole plot were to be dug at once, soil from the opening trench would

have to be taken in a wheelbarrow to the other end of the plot: very fatiguing work.

Where a new vegetable garden is being created, or perhaps when a lawn is being converted to vegetable growing, it is wise to skim off surface turf and place it grass side downwards on top of the forked up subsoil. The turf should be well chopped, any other organic matter added and then covered with the top spit. The turf from the first trench should be left with the soil for the completion of the last trench.

Tools
The cultivation of a vegetable garden can only be carried out in a proper manner with the aid of tools. A glance in a garden shop window will reveal a wide range of tools, which may confuse the beginner, however not all are essential.

It is wise to purchase good tools; cheap ones turn out to be expensive in the long run, being inefficient and easily broken. Therefore buy the best tools you can afford, getting the most essential first. Some – especially smaller tools such as a trowel, hand fork or knife may well solve a family problem where a Christmas or birthday present is required.

All tools should be looked after and not left lying around to get rusty or endanger children. Any soil adhering to them should be removed by scraping and washing, and they should be rubbed over with an oily rag when dry. All tools should be kept under cover in a shed or garage.

– Apron
Once used by all professional gardeners, the amateur will still find an apron very useful for the protection of clothing, and, when equipped with a kangaroo-type pocket, for holding small tools, twine etc.

– Broom
A garden always looks more attractive when it is kept tidy and this applies particularly to paths. A stiff broom, generally known as a bass broom, is ideal for this purpose.

– Dibber
These are most useful for transplanting brassicas and leeks from a seed-bed; that is, bare root plants. They are frequently home made from a broken off wooden fork or spade handle. Retain a foot or so of the stem attached to the handle and sharpen the end. Steel-pointed dibbers are even better, especially for use on heavy soils.

– Forks
Various types of fork are available, the most essential being the four-pronged digging fork which is particularly useful for turning over heavy soil or for breaking up the second spit when double digging is done. Choose this tool on the same basis as the spade, ensuring no flaw is present in any of the tines. Stainless steel digging forks keep cleaner. They are usually made smaller and lighter and so are useful for breaking up soil for a seed bed, for incorporating fertilizer dressings or for lifting root crops. Not so essential but useful where potatoes are grown, is the flat-tined or potato fork which is not so liable to damage the tubers as the digging fork. For loading and turning farmyard manure or compost, the manure fork with its slender, curved tines is ideal but is of little value for soil cultivation. Long handled manure forks are useful for gathering hedge trimmings for the bonfire or waste vegetable matter, coarse herbage or straw for the compost heap.

– Gloves
Not all gardeners favour the wearing of gardening gloves but many find they afford valuable protection when pruning and protect the hands when using fertilizers, or mixing up fungicides and insecticides. They are usually made in hide, pigskin, chrome leather or a washable fabric.

– Handfork
Small but useful tools, especially for lifting plants without causing damage to the roots, or for pricking over soil between plants in frames or cloches, and may be used instead of a trowel for planting in heavy soils.

– Hoes
Many hoes, some quite elaborate in design are available; the Dutch hoe which is available with blades of different sizes is particularly useful. The 15cm. (6in.) wide blade is large enough for most purposes, especially on heavy soils. The Dutch hoe is used by working backwards, pushing the hoe forward just under the surface, to loosen and aerate the soil, and kill off weeds. The handle should be set at an angle which allows the tool to be used comfortably without undue stooping. The Dutch hoe is particularly valuable in spring when soil has been set by winter rain, especially amongst growing crops as its use helps to retain moisture and keep down weeds.

The draw hoe is another first class tool for killing weeds, particularly when they have attained some size or grow in heavy soil which has become too firm for the Dutch hoe to operate freely. Again different blade sizes are available, the 15cm. (6in.) size being perhaps as useful as any for general use. It can be used for drawing out seed drills; shallow and flat ones for peas or beans, deep ones for potatoes, or the shallow ones used for small seeds. Hoes with triangular heads

Garden tools:

1 Spade	4 Draw hoe	7 Dutch hoe (large blade)
2 Flat-tined potato fork	5 Onion hoe	8 Dutch hoe (small blade)
3 Rake	6 Digging fork	9 Garden trowel and handfork
		10 Steel-pointed dibber

are available just for making seed drills but cannot be used for other work like the draw hoe. The small-bladed short-handled hoe is especially useful for weeding among seedlings or other small valuable plants. It looks like a miniature draw hoe and is used in like manner. The commercial grower often knew it as an onion hoe, although he used it for other crops as well, but today it is far less used, having been superseded by chemical weedkillers.

In larger gardens the wheel or planet hoe used to be very popular as it could be pushed through large areas of crops and kill weeds more quickly and easily than was possible by hand hoeing. The well-designed modification of this hoe in aluminium and steel, the high wheel cultivator, has replaced the original wooden frame.

– Labels
Available nowadays in plastic as well as wood, labels are essential if you wish to keep a good record of your cultivars. The practice of placing empty seed packets on sticks is untidy and unreliable.

– Miscellaneous
Small essentials are a good knife, secateurs, and a diary or notebook and pencil, for keeping any records on your own and notes from visits to other gardens, where other cultivars or methods arouse your interest.

– Lines
A good garden line, preferably on a strong metal or wooden reel, is essential for drawing out drills neatly and accurately, thus making the best use of the garden space available. A measuring rod can be made from a 1.8 to 3m. (6 to 10ft) length of straight timber, 5 by 5cm. (2 by 2in.), can be

marked off by saw cuts every 8 or 15cm. (3 or 6in.).

– Rake
For preparation of seed beds, good rakes are essential. They can be bought in varying sizes and numbers of teeth in wood or metal. For the initial breaking down of the soil I prefer the wooden hay rake. This is useful also for removing rubbish and stones, clearing up hedge bottoms or, carefully handled, for turning over onion and shallot bulbs when drying.

– Rotary tiller
Manufactured in various sizes and power, these tools are designed to save heavy manual labour. To use them properly you must plan your vegetable garden so that the machine can work comfortably through the rows. While not substitutes for the spade, still in my view the best tool for garden cultivation, they are ideal for controlling weeds, cutting them up and churning them into the soil. Set to work at shallow depths rotary cultivators can quickly produce a fine tilth as long as the soil is in the right condition and not saturated, as after heavy rain. These cultivators are also useful for destroying waste trash from early crops. Not only does this prevent loss of moisture from the soil, but the quicker break-down of the debris greatly assists preparation for sowing or planting second crops.

– Spade
A good spade remains an essential tool for all gardens. Even where rotary cultivators and the like are used corners still have to be turned over by hand. Choose a spade with a handle length to suit your height – too large a one will make work more arduous – and, if you can afford it, one with

a stainless steel blade. At one time all spade, fork, and shovel handles were made of ash wood.

Nowadays tough plastic handles in part or full are fitted to most tools. Whichever type of handle you choose make sure there are no splinters or rough projections liable to tear the hands.

– Sprayers
Many small spraying and dusting machines are now available for the application of fungicides or insecticides in the vegetable garden. In some areas such machinery can be hired.

– Trowel
This is most useful for setting out plants which have been started off in pots, a job for which a dibber is quite unsuitable. Trowels are frequently available in cheap versions but you will be better served by one with a stainless steel blade. If you measure the length of combined handle and blade, usually around nine inches, it can also be useful as a guide to the required distance between your plants, as you plant.

– Water Can and Hose
Most gardeners will find it is necessary to use water in the garden, if not at all times of the year, most certainly in spring and summer, and where crops are grown in greenhouse or frame a hose is almost essential. A hose will save a great deal of walking, but be prepared for a ban on the use of hoses in very dry weather in some areas, and find out whether it is necessary to buy a licence to use a hose. Cheap hoses are likely to have a short life so it is better to buy a good quality plastic hose which will last for several years.

Water cans are available in 5 or 10 l. (1 or 2 gal.) sizes. Choose one you can carry comfortably when full. Plastic cans are very durable, lighter and easier to keep clean than a metal one. Buy a strong one, with at least two roses; a fine one for watering seedlings and a coarser one for outdoor garden use. If you have a greenhouse a long spout or an extension helps to reach across a wide staging, and if you grow plants on high shelves, one of the small shelf cans is much easier to manipulate.

– Wheelbarrow
A barrow is useful in most gardens. Wooden barrows have largely been replaced by metal or plastic ones. If possible, choose one with a rubber-tyred wheel. These are easier to push and less likely to damage paths than those shod with metal. If possible, keep your barrow under cover especially in winter.

Rotation of Crops
Few gardeners will dispute that some sort of rotational cropping is worthwhile, if not essential. Proper rotation will ensure a slower build up of pests and diseases and other inhibitors to maximum growth.

For instance, overcropping small gardens with potatoes has led to potato cyst eelworm becoming a curse which can only be starved out by a complete absence of tubers to act as host, which may take up to 7 years.

Club-root too is a major disease in many gardens, particularly where brassicas are grown on the same plot year after year, and especially if no effort has been made to reduce soil acidity. If, in addition to liming, brassicas are kept off the affected area for a few seasons, damage from the disease is likely to be less. Likewise white rot disease of onions can be prevented by growing this crop on a different site every season.

Another reason for rotation is the nutritional one, since some groups of plants take large quantities of plant food of a particular type from the soil. For instance, brassicas and some of the quicker growing salad crops need a great deal of nitrogen and thereby deplete the soil of this particular element. Slow growing root crops, on the other hand, such as carrots and beetroot need less immediate nitrogen and are thus suitable to follow brassicas. As is well known, legumes like peas and beans are able to fix and utilize atmospheric nitrogen with the help of nodule forming bacteria found on their roots. They too need less nitrogen applied as fertilizer although some is often necessary, especially in the early part of the season. By rotation residual plant foods can be better used economically. This makes sense in another respect too: most root crops grow best on land heavily manured for the previous crop: otherwise they tend to split and 'fang'.

Against crop rotation some people cite the success of well-known exhibitors who appear never to change the site, particularly with leeks and onions. What must be remembered is that these are specialist growers who have acquired by experience a unique knowledge of their crop and, in consequence, can take precautions to combat pests and diseases, and who usually incorporate some fresh soil or compost each year.

Three-Year Rotation   FIRST YEAR

PLOT ONE	PLOT TWO	PLOT THREE	PERMANENT CROPS
beans: runner, broad, dwarf	seed bed for brassicas	early potatoes	compost heap
celery	brussel sprouts	beetroot	asparagus
leeks	cabbage	carrots	rhubarb
onions	cauliflower	parsnips	globe artichokes
peas	kales	swedes	jerusalem artichokes
tomatoes	sprouting broccoli		seakale
	turnips		herbs
Cultivation			
Deep or double dig autumn or winter. Apply compost, FYM, or peat.	Single dig or Rotovate. Apply lime if necessary. Apply general purpose fertilizer.	Single dig. Apply general purpose fertilizer.	
SECOND YEAR	SECOND YEAR	SECOND YEAR	
plot three	plot one	plot two	
THIRD YEAR	THIRD YEAR	THIRD YEAR	
plot two	plot three	plot one	

This is only a suggested method of allying cultivation with cropping.
Lettuce, shallots and spinach may be included where room is available.

Four-Year Rotation   FIRST YEAR

PLOT ONE	PLOT TWO	PLOT THREE	PLOT FOUR	PERMANENT CROPS
early potatoes	broad beans	seed bed for brassicas	beetroot	asparagus
maincrop potatoes	dwarf beans	brussel sprouts	carrots	rhubarb
celery	runner beans	cabbage	parsnips	globe artichokes
onions	peas	cauliflower	chicory	jerusalem artichokes
leeks could follow	tomatoes	kales	salsify	herbs
early potatoes		sprouting broccoli	spinach beet	seakale
		turnips		compost heap
Cultivation				
Deep or double dig autumn or winter. Apply compost, FYM or peat.	Single dig. Apply general purpose fertilizer.	Single dig or rotovate, applying lime to surface if necessary. Apply general purpose fertilizer a fortnight in advance of planting	Single dig. Apply general purpose fertilizer in advance of sowing seeds.	
SECOND YEAR	SECOND YEAR	SECOND YEAR	SECOND YEAR	
plot four	plot one	plot two	plot three	
THIRD YEAR	THIRD YEAR	THIRD YEAR	THIRD YEAR	
plot three	plot four	plot one	plot two	
FOURTH YEAR	FOURTH YEAR	FOURTH YEAR	FOURTH YEAR	
plot two	plot three	plot four	plot one	

Many gardeners arrange a particular crop in a permanent site for a special reason and consequently take some extra trouble to ensure its food requirements are catered for. In this connection I think of runner beans, which may be grown to separate the vegetable garden from the lawn or flower garden, to hide such necessary appurtenances as the compost heap or garden shed, or even to avoid being overlooked by neighbours. The Jerusalem artichoke is also frequently grown on a permanent site as a barrier; nevertheless, even they grow better if replanted annually, especially if the previous crop is cleared of all tubers – not an easy task – and a good dressing of compost incorporated in the pre-planting cultivation.

Permanent crops should be sited in such a way that basic rotation is unhampered. Asparagus is a favourite in many households, and will crop for many years, so it should be placed at one side or end of the plot. Rhubarb and perennial herbs should be allotted a similar position.

The planning of crop rotation is simplified by grouping similar crops together for reasons already stated and for ease of cultivation. This allows for 3 main groups; brassicas or greens, pulses which include beans and peas, and root crops. Potatoes may of course be included with root crops if they are to be grown in a limited number or as early cultivars. If, however, you intend to grow maincrops also, which normally require a fairly large amount of space allotted to them, then you have to think of a 4-year rotation.

The suggested rotations on page 17 are for general guidance only and should be amended according to personal requirements. In general there is an interval of 2 years in the 3-year diagram, and 3 years in the 4-year one before the crop is repeated, thus breaking continuity of cropping and lessening the chances of a carry over of disease.

In the 3-year plan, plot 1 allows for deeper cultivation with application of compost for crops which need this treatment. Plot 2 does not require such deep cultivation, for brassicas enjoy a firm root run; if lime is required these are the crops which need it most. Plot 3, which rounds off this plan, caters for root crops which will benefit from the residues of previous crops but will not induce the roots to fork. If sufficient compost is available and not required on plot 1 it can be allocated to the potato crop.

The 4-year plan is designed for gardeners who wish to grow potatoes. If you wish to grow enough to take up one plot you can combine plots 1 and 2 for purposes of cultivation, especially if sufficient manure or compost is available. If not, you can place the compost in a trench before planting potatoes, simply placing the seed tubers on it before covering over. Potatoes are ideal in many ways in a newly started garden, not only smothering weeds but indirectly improving soil structure through the necessary operations of planting, hoeing, earthing up and digging the crop. Having allotted one plot to potatoes you can revert to the 3-year plan for other crops with the exception of course of the early potatoes in the root crop section.

By keeping to the overall plan, inter-cropping and catch-cropping, your work should become less arduous and rewarded by high yields of fine quality.

The Compost Heap

The application of fermented animal and vegetable matter, known as compost, to the soil, was first advocated at the beginning of the century. The principle is better understood today, and often inorganic nitrogen is applied to satisfy the needs of the bacteria that break down the vegetable matter. It is not always fully appreciated what a considerable amount of material is needed for compost. This can be a problem in some gardens.

Compost can be made from almost any organic waste material. Weeds, crop debris such as pea and bean haulm, lawn mowings, vegetable kitchen waste, torn up rags and newsprint, waste straw and dead leaves may all be used. Avoid cabbage and Brussels sprouts stalks – they take too long to rot – as well as diseased material, man-made fibres which will not rot or woody prunings such as from roses, which should be burnt. Place the material to be composted in a layer, firm by treading and moisten with water if dry. Animal manure can be placed in another layer on top, but a proprietary activator can be used or sulphate of ammonia at 15 to 20g. per sq. m. ($\frac{1}{2}$oz. per sq. yd). Each layer can be about 30cm. (12in.) thick and may then be covered with 2.5cm. (1in.) of top soil. Another layer of waste material may be added as available, adding ground chalk or limestone at 115 to 120g. per sq. m. (4oz. per sq. yd). Water well and cover with another layer of soil. Build up as waste is available, adding either manure or sulphate of ammonia to each alternate layer until a height of 1.5m. (5ft) is attained, topping off with a layer of soil. Turning will be necessary and watering if dry, a month or so after completion. Cover over with soil again after turning when it can be left until required for digging in.

Cast up seaweed has been used for years by commercial growers, especially in the production of early potatoes. If you live near the coast it is worth while digging seaweed in or putting it on the compost heap. Proprietary seaweed manures, either dry or liquid are readily available. They are usually quick acting, and in addition to the major elements also contain valuable trace elements.

Green manuring, the digging in of growing plants, is another worthwhile way of increasing humus in the soil, especially now that supplies of farmyard manure are hard to get and compost may be hard to make. Green manuring can, in theory, be carried out on vacant land at any time but for practical reasons early spring or very early autumn when crops have been cleared, are the times usually chosen.

Mustard, rape and Italian ryegrass can all be used for this purpose, seed being sown on lightly raked ground at 30 to 40g. per sq. m. (1oz. per sq. yd), and well raked in. When the plants have grown 30cm. (12in.) high they should be dug in, together with a dressing of a nitrogenous fertilizer at 15 to 20g. per sq. m. ($\frac{1}{2}$oz. per sq. yd) to assist breakdown if the ground is to be used for a crop of vegetables. Mustard used as green manure may well reduce incidence of scab on potatoes, as may fresh lawn mowings in the drills.

Fertilizers

Many amateur gardeners are puzzled about fertilizers, wondering why they are necessary, which are best, and when they should be used. Farmyard manure is now very difficult to obtain, particularly in towns and compost is seldom available in sufficient quantity. In nature, few soils are sufficiently fertile to contain the essential elements for vegetable growing: all crops require supplies of nitrogen, phosphate, potash, magnesium and calcium, as well as the minor elements. These they take up in solution from the soil. Apart from the nutrients taken off by the crops themselves, losses occur from leaching into the drainage. Such deficiencies have then to be made up by the application of manures and fertilizers.

Even when manure or compost is freely available, it is advisable to supplement them both with fertilizers. Generally these are best worked into the soil by fork, rake or hoe a fortnight or so before planting or seed sowing takes place. Nitrogenous fertilizers promote quick vigorous growth in vegetables. Supplies must be adequate to grow leafy crops such as brassicas, celery and lettuce. Phosphatic fertilizers are essential for seedling development, and for stimulating and encouraging a good root system. Root crops in particular benefit greatly from phosphates. Potash fertilizers not only aid balanced growth in vegetables but also improve quality.

Organic Fertilizers

– Dried blood

This is a quick acting, nitrogenous organic fertilizer normally used only as a top dressing on a valuable crop such as greenhouse tomatoes where it is usually applied at 30 to 70g. per sq. m. (1 to 2oz. per sq. yd). It can also be used dissolved in water at 30 to 40g. to 5 l. (1oz. to 2 gal.) when it is even quicker acting.

– Hoof and horn meal

This is made from the ground up hooves and horns of animals, and is useful as a slow release nitrogenous fertilizer. Outdoors, it should be applied well in advance of crop requirement, either in winter or early spring at 65 to 70g. per sq. m. (2oz. per sq. yd).

– Bonemeal

Made from ground up dried bones, this is much valued by amateur gardeners because of its long sustained supply of phosphate with a little nitrogen. At one time anthrax could be contracted from bonemeal, but there is no fear of that today, but as with other fertilizers it is advisable to wear gloves especially if your hands have any cuts or scratches. 65 to 70g. per sq. m. (2oz. per sq. yd) can be considered an average dressing.

– Fishmeal

Manufactured from dried and ground waste fish and fish residues, this is a valuable slow acting fertilizer principally containing nitrogen and phosphate. Modern methods of manufacture have improved its smell, which is, nevertheless, still quite strong. From 65 to 140g. per sq. m. (2 to 4oz. per sq. yd) are usually applied.

– Seaweed fertilizers

These have become popular in recent years, both in liquid and powdered form. They are available with potash and a range of trace elements.

– Hop manure

This is made from residual waste from breweries and is a suitable substitute for farmland manure.

– Concentrated organic manures

These are available under proprietary names and are advertized in horticultural journals. Usually rich in plant foods they are also easily handled.

Inorganic Fertilizers

– Sulphate of ammonia

This is a nitrogenous fertilizer and being a soluble salt is quickly available to plants. For vegetables, the soil must be adequately supplied with lime since sulphate of ammonia tends to acidity. It is frequently used in general purpose mixtures. Use it during spring and summer at the rate of 30 to 40g. per sq. m. (1oz. per sq. yd), 10 to 14 days before planting or sowing, or as a top dressing during the growing periods.

– Nitrate of soda

This is a soluble salt derived from natural deposits and is a very quick acting nitrogenous fertilizer. It is particularly useful for applying in spring to crops which require a tonic after overwintering, e.g. spring cabbage. A top dressing of up to 30 to 40g. per sq. m. (1oz. per sq. yd) soon shows an effect especially as the weather improves. It can nevertheless be used into early summer.

– Nitro chalk

This is a nitrogenous fertilizer combined with calcium and unlike sulphate of ammonia does not further acidify soils which are deficient in lime. Very quick acting and sold in granular form, it can therefore be easily applied at the rate of 30 to 40g. per sq. m. (1oz. per sq. yd) throughout the growing season from spring to autumn. It is used a great deal for top-dressing brassicas.

– Superphosphate

This is the best known phosphatic fertilizer and is used both in compounds and by itself. Adequate phosphate is essential for a good root system thereby encouraging high yields in root crops, and it is also used to supply phosphate in compound fertilizers. May be worked into seed beds before sowing at up to 65 to 70g. per sq. m. (2oz. per sq. yd).

– Sulphate of potash

This is the best known potash fertilizer. Adequate potash is necessary with nitrogen and phosphate for balanced growth; it helps to sustain balanced growth and winter hardiness. There must never be a potash deficiency for potatoes and tomatoes. This fertilizer may be bought straight or in compound mixtures. Use it straight at 30 to 40g. per sq. m. (1oz. per sq. yd).

– Muriate of potash

This was once regarded by gardeners as somewhat inferior to sulphate of potash and only to be used if sulphate was unobtainable. This opinion has been largely invalidated by the superior products now available. It is cheaper than sulphate of potash and has become the main potash constituent of concentrated compound fertilizers. If applied straight, use it at the same rate as sulphate of potash.

– Lime

Lime is principally used as a corrective to soil acidity and as said earlier, aids the cultivation of heavy soils. However it should not be over-used. Lime is not generally required on chalky soils and, on other soils, it is possible to find out whether it is really necessary by using a soil testing kit. These kits are on sale in garden shops and garden centres. More detailed soil analyses are obtainable in the UK, through some advisory services, which not only give the pH of your soil but will usually advise as well on major nutrient element requirements.

The pH scale mentioned above indicates the alkalinity or acidity of the soil. Neutrality is expressed as pH 7, any figures above that indicate alkalinity, any below the degree of acidity. Most vegetable crops grow best within the range pH 6.5 to 7. Green crops, such as brassicas, beans and peas, grow most successfully on alkaline soils so lime should be applied to that section of the garden reserved for brassica crops, when analysis shows acidity. Obviously amounts will vary according to the degree of acidity, but as a guide, ground chalk or limestone at the rate of 185 to 190g. per sq. m. (6oz. per sq. yd) of soil will be adequate. Calcium carbonate such as ground chalk or limestone is unlikely to harm plants or soil in the way lime or hydrated lime can do, before they are converted to calcium carbonate. Lime should be applied to the surface of the soil as soon as digging or other cultivation has been completed. Applied as suggested in crop rotation, each area will have been treated in turn; this should be ample for the next 3 or 4 years before re-testing the soil to see whether more lime is necessary. On most soils, replacement is necessary due to constant leaching and crop requirements for calcium. Lime is not a plant food in itself, but is essential for the full release of other plant foods. It is also useful as a soil conditioner on heavy clay soils, improving and maintaining structure, and on acid, peat soils vegetable growing would be quite impossible without it.

Seed Sowing

Every gardener knows that most vegetables start by seed being sown, even though transplanting later follows. The wise gardener takes great care to ensure he gets a first class seed bed. The soil must not be too moist or stick to the feet. Often, with help from sun and wind, soil can be dried out by forking over lightly early in the day. Preliminary raking to remove stones and clods and to level is best done with the wide hay rake. For fine seeds the requisite fine tilth is made with a metal or wire rake. Firming by treading must be done with great care, taking due regard of prevailing weather conditions.

To get the drills straight a garden line should be stretched very tightly. These should be drawn out sufficiently deep for the size of the seeds to be sown. In very dry weather the drills should be soaked with water and allowed to drain off for an hour or two before sowing. Sowing should always be done evenly and not too thickly, especially with crops such as carrots and onions where it is not desirable to thin.

Where thinning is necessary in a crop such as lettuce this should be done as soon as the seedlings can be handled, any gaps being filled by carefully lifting surplus plants and transplanting.

Brassica crops and leeks are usually sown in a seed bed, as thinly as possible, so as to get good sturdy plants, which in due course are transplanted to their cropping quarters. Transplants should not be too large or hard when lifted from the seed bed. In dry weather, it is worthwhile soaking the seed bed the day before lifting, and using at all times a fork to loosen the plants. Another good precaution is to cover the lifted roots to prevent further drying out. Leeks and

Preparing seed bed

1 Treading to firm ground prepared by forking
2 Raking to get fine tilth.

3 Standing on footboard to protect bed, draw out drills to depth required.
4 Sowing seeds.

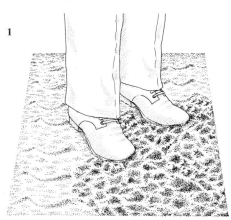

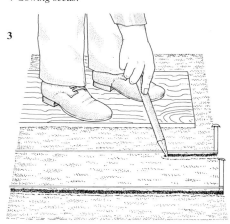

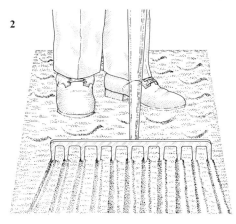

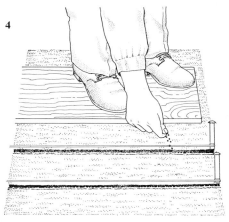

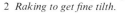

brassicas are usually planted with a dibber. However, large plants with big roots may be planted better with a trowel, as one has to do with plants from pots. Whichever method is used planting should be firm, the exception being leeks, which, in their deep holes should only be watered in. All newly planted seedlings should be well watered.

Pelleted Seeds

Today some vegetable seeds are available encased in easily dissolved pellets. They can be bought by the amateur gardener, as well as the commercial grower. The main advantage is that awkwardly shaped seeds, difficult to sow thinly by mechanical means, such as those of carrots, lettuce and parsnips can now be accurately spaced at regular intervals outdoors, or under glass as in the case of winter lettuce. Often thinning or transplanting can now be eliminated altogether. Although the pellet case is quickly softened by moisture, germination can be disappointing and erratic especially in dry weather. Irrigation is almost essential for success with pelleted seeds; the soil surface should not be allowed to dry, until adequate germination is assured. Germination may also be slower than with 'natural' seeds.

F_1 Hybrids

Many cultivars of vegetable are nowadays listed in catalogues as being F_1 hybrids. Such hybrids, characterized by evenness of type and performance, are the first generation obtained by crossing often inbred selected parent lines. Seed saved from F_1 hybrids will not breed true in the next generation, so fresh seed must be bought each year. F_1 hybrids are particularly valuable for commercial production for their greater uniformity and hybrid vigour. Plants from open pollination are far less even and often mature over a longer period, which the amateur may prefer. In this respect he may well wish to buy packets in which cultivars are mixed.

Successional Cropping

This has different interpretations. I tend to regard it as the provision, over a period of time, of successive crops of such vegetables as beetroots, carrots, cabbage, cauliflower, peas and lettuce, of which cabbage and lettuce can be available over most of the year. Skill in such cropping lies in knowledge of the maturing dates of varieties chosen for succession related to the correct sowing dates. Seed catalogues are a good guide for a start until experience of local conditions has been built up and recorded.

– Beetroot

By successional sowings a continuous supply of small tender roots can be kept up for the greater part of the year. The first sowings around mid-March should be of a cultivar such as 'Boltardy', which has been bred for early sowing and, as the name indicates, is less likely to bolt to seed. Fortnightly sowings after these early sowings can then be made from mid-April until July. 'Little Ball' is ideal for these later sowings; a larger sowing of this cultivar near the end of June will provide a supply of roots for winter storage. To augment this a sowing of 'Cheltenham Green Top' in mid-May will provide a long-rooted cultivar with longer-keeping qualities. In northern, colder areas the earlier sowings may require cloche protection.

– Carrot

These may be sown in late March or early April in the open; if earlier supplies are required protection will be needed. 'Amsterdam Forcing' or a selection such as 'Amstel' are ideal. To keep up the supply 'Nantes' is suitable or one of its selections, and monthly sowings can be made up to the end of July. Where attacks from carrot-willow aphid are prevalent, the April–May sowings should be omitted. For storage purposes 'Autumn King' or 'St Valery' can be sown in June. It is possible to leave later sowings in the ground to be lifted as necessary, using a light covering of straw in severe weather.

– Cabbage

The sowing of suitable cultivars at the correct time ensures a supply of this valuable vegetable most of the year. A sowing under glass in January–February, from which the plants are transplanted outdoors in March, can be followed by outdoor sowings of the same cultivars in March–April. 'Golden Acre', or one of its selections, is ideal where a ball-headed cultivar is required, and 'Hispi', an F_1 hybrid, has produced very early crops.

To provide cabbages for use in autumn and during winter, sowings on a seed bed in May of 'Christmas Drumhead' and 'January King' will provide drumhead-type heads, while the old cultivar 'Winnigstadt' is still worth growing where a tight, pointed head is required.

Spring cabbage, so called because it comes into use in spring is sown in early August in southern gardens, although it is necessary to sow it in July in more northern areas. 'April', 'Harbinger' and 'Wheeler's Imperial' are suitable where small-headed cultivars are appreciated. If larger types are required 'Durham', 'First Early Market' or 'Offenham' can be relied upon.

In recent years ball-headed cabbages suitable for winter storage have gained in popularity and a sowing in early March of a 'Langendijk' selection, 'Holland Winter White', should fit the bill.

– Cauliflower

To provide cauliflowers over a long season sowings at different times are required, and a selection of cultivars from particular groups is chosen. A very wide range has been developed, especially for the commercial grower and many of these are suitable for amateur gardeners also. Summer cultivars can be sown in late September or early October and overwintered in cold frames for planting in spring. Another sowing can be made under glass in January or February, or in a seed bed March to April. Suitable cultivars are 'All the Year Round', 'Alpha', 'Snowball' and 'Dominant'.

Cultivars for sowing in a seed bed from April to early May are: 'Barrier Reef', 'Boomerang', 'Kangaroo' and 'Manly'. The winter cauliflower (broccoli) group are sown from mid-April to mid-May. This includes the 'Roscoff' cultivars which in the UK can only be grown successfully in relatively frost-free areas such as the Channel Islands, south-western areas of England and certain coastal areas such as Pembroke (Dyfed); selections of the cultivar 'English Winter', 'Adam's Early White', 'St George', 'Late Queen', and 'June Market' (the latter particularly useful in colder northern areas); and 'Walcheren Winter–Thanet'. 'Roscoff' types are available in a wide selection of cultivars, maturing from November until late April.

Sprouting broccoli is sown at the same time as winter cauliflower. The hardiest type is 'Purple Sprouting' which is available in early and late cultivars and matures, depending on the weather, from February to April; White Sprouting matures in March and April; 'Italian Sprouting', usually known as Calabrese, should be sown in situ June or July for gathering in autumn; an April sowing in situ or transplanted will provide an earlier supply.

– Pea

A succession of peas fresh from the garden from June to September is the laudable aim of many gardeners and there are different ways of achieving this. Being a believer in simple methods whenever possible, I prefer to choose a cultivar such as 'Onward', one of our most reliable peas, making sowings in succession from mid-March until the end of June. If a row is sown when the previous row has germinated a regular supply can be ensured. However, as 'Onward' requires 90 days from sowing to picking, you may extend the cropping period by sowing a round-seeded cultivar such as 'Feltham First' or the hardy 'Hurst Beagle' in February, following on with 'Kelvedon Wonder' made at the same time as your first sowing of 'Onward'. The season can be extended at the latter end also by sowing 'Kelvedon Wonder' in late June or early July.

An alternative method is to sow a range of cultivars; there are many to choose from: 'Early Onward', 'Recette', 'Show Perfection' and 'Miracle' may be relied upon. Where cloches are available earlier crops may be obtained. 'Little Marvel' is a suitable dwarf cultivar for this purpose.

– Lettuce

This valuable crop can be produced all the year round by growing several of the wide selection of cultivars now available. Some of these are bred for particular conditions, such as heated greenhouses, cold greenhouses, cold frames and cloches, while others are for sowing in the open in spring and summer, and others again for sowing in autumn. There are 3 distinct types, cabbage, cos and the loose leaf type of which 'Salad Bowl' is typical, producing fresh young leaves in abundance if kept picked; it can be sown from April to the end of July.

One of the least troublesome ways of obtaining a succession during summer, especially in a small garden, is to sow mixed cultivars with different maturing dates. By sowing fortnightly from March to mid-July an added supply period is obtainable, which can be further extended by sowing towards the end of August or beginning of September suitable cultivars such as 'Imperial Winter', 'Valdor' and 'Winter Density'.

Earlier cutting of lettuce is made possible by sowing under glass in January, and transplanting in February to the open ground; suitable cultivars are 'Hilde-Fortune', 'Hilde-Suzan' and 'Unrivalled'. For those who appreciate 'Webb's Wonderful', a curly, very crisp, large lettuce, sowings can be made at fortnightly intervals from March to July, and similar sowings can be made of my own particular favourite the dwarf compact cos-type 'Little Gem', which can also be sown early and grown under cloches. To produce lettuce out of season, that is to say in winter, heated or cold glass is required and suitable cultivars must be chosen. 'Kwiek', sown in August, matures during November–December in a cold house. 'Kloek', sown in August, will do likewise in slight heat or, sown in September, will mature in March in heat. 'Kordaat', sown in August, matures in November in heat, or, if sown in October, will mature in March in heat.

Another method of successional cropping is to follow on a cleared crop with another. Early potatoes are frequently followed by cabbages sown later from July to August. Where room is available, turnips and leeks are other useful crops for winter storage. Maincrop potatoes may be followed by winter lettuce. Broad beans may be followed by sowings of round beet and carrots either for storing, in the case of beet, or for use as required in the case of carrots.

Generally, it is better to use quick growing cultivars for these secondary crops so as not to interfere with the main crop of the following season. It is also important to have cleared ground available to prepare for these crops.

Catchcropping

This can be very worthwhile, especially in small gardens. Where crops such as broad beans, spring cabbage, peas and early potatoes have been grown as early maincrops and harvested, land becomes free in late June or early July. This is available for re-cropping but at this time of year soil is apt to dry out very quickly, so moisture must be conserved as much as possible in order to ensure the quick and successful germination of the succeeding crops. After clearing any haulm or debris from the previous crops the surface should be run through with a hoe to provide a nice tilth for sowing and also to help the conservation of moisture. If very dry weather conditions prevail, thorough watering of the drills after they have been drawn out will be of further assistance.

July sowings of several vegetables will provide useful late crops; these should be completed by the third week in July in southern gardens, and in the first week in northern and later areas. It is important to sow early, quick-maturing cultivars such as: beetroot 'Little Ball'; carrots 'Amsterdam Forcing' and 'Nantes'; cauliflower 'Snowball', sown *in situ* and thinned 30 to 36cm. (12 to 15in.) apart; kohlrabi *in situ* and thin to 15cm. (6in.) apart; lettuce 'Little Gem' *in situ* thin to 10cm. (4in.) apart; onion 'White Lisbon'; pea 'Kelvedon Wonder', a cultivar more resistant to mildew for a late sowing; spinach 'Longstanding Round'; dwarf bean 'The Prince' or, if you prefer the stringless pencil-podded type, try 'Sprite'; radish 'Cherry Belle', or mixed cultivars which give an extended season of use; turnip 'Golden Ball' is of outstanding flavour for winter use sown at this time; 'Manchester Market' is also useful; spring greens or collards, which can often be used during the winter months, are produced by an *in situ* sowing at the end of July in close rows 30cm. (12in.) apart. The cabbage cultivar 'First Early Market 218' is excellent for this purpose if plants are thinned to 8 or 10cm. (3 or 4in.) apart.

Intercropping

This is particularly important in small gardens, as, by filling up spaces in crops which only require space in their early stages, a considerable addition can be made to the vegetable supply. In the heyday of the large private garden, lettuce, a crop in almost constant demand during the summer, was nearly always planted or sown in conjunction with broad beans and peas, following on in succession and in conjunction with the major crop. Nowadays, lettuce can be obtained in mixed cultivars, which ensures a spread over of maturity and lessens the likelihood of waste.

The mixed packet idea has also been extended to radishes, also ideal for intercropping, as they germinate quickly, take up little space and can be cleared before any interference with the major crop takes place. Quick germination may also render this crop ideal for use as a 'marker' in crops which are slower in germination such as onions, parsley or parsnips. A few seeds of radish dropped thinly in the same row, are useful as indicators, allowing a hoe to be pushed through between the rows to check germinating weeds. Many gardeners prefer to sow runner beans in pots and plant out later, and radishes can be broadcast in a wide band along the area, the beans planted in due course in a double row on the outside edges.

Brussels sprouts are a major crop which also require a good deal of space between plants. This space can be intercropped with an early non-bolting beet, early carrots and turnips, all of which will be ready for use before being smothered by the sprout leaves.

Protected Cultivation

Cultivation of vegetables in heated glasshouses has suffered a decline since the days when asparagus was forced, dwarf beans and early potatoes were grown in large pots and carrots and other vegetables were grown on hotbeds made up in frames. Nowadays, large areas of glass are devoted to such crops as tomatoes and cucumbers, and more recently aubergines, capsicums and lettuce.

Where a heated greenhouse is available it is useful for sowing seeds of crops, which, when hardened off, can be planted outside and mature earlier than those from outdoor sowings. Use of a heated structure, perhaps a shed, not necessarily a glasshouse, can also be made for forcing crops such as chicory, seakale and rhubarb during winter months. In such structures it is necessary to exclude light and this can also be done under the staging in a glasshouse.

Cold greenhouses and cold frames may be used in the same way as heated ones, but plants will of course be later because of lower temperatures. Portable cold frames and cloches may be used in the garden to protect lettuce and carrots as growing crops, or seedling plants of cauliflower and lettuce for transplanting. Walk-in polythene structures are an innovation in protected cultivation which have attained popularity commercially because of lower costs. Although they are much shorter lived, they can be used for the production of the above mentioned crops.

Cloches in many shapes, sizes and heights are now available in glass and plastic materials. Glass is probably best but is more expensive, more easily broken and being heavier, is more difficult to handle. Those made from plastic have to be well anchored, otherwise they are likely to be blown off the crop during winter gales. These cloches are usually run in continuous rows and raise soil and air temperatures sufficiently to forward and protect crops. They are useful in northern gardens enabling gardeners to grow the less hardy crops, such as sweet corn or tomatoes.

Another development is the polythene tunnel, which is much cheaper and easier to handle than cloches. The tunnels consist of a long narrow strip of clear polythene film stretched over wire hoops placed at regular intervals. The film is kept in position over the hoops by other thinner wire hoops. Ventilation is provided by lifting up one side of the plastic, and if both sides are brought together at the top, rain or irrigation can get in to water the crop. Ready-made kits can be purchased but many practical gardeners make their own.

Cultivation under Cloches

Cloches are a great advantage in northern areas and in colder gardens where it is not possible to get such early crops as further south. Strip cropping, by moving the cloches from one row to another as required, is a good way to exploit them fully. With the usual exception of root crops, which should be grown on land manured for a previous crop, plenty of organic matter must be worked into soil where cloches are to be used for protection. This will lessen the task of watering as the soil will be more retentive of moisture and nutrients.

With a little planning cloches can be used during the greater part of the year. Broad beans and peas from late October and early November sowings can be overwintered until April, as can cauliflowers and lettuce. A start can then be made with dwarf beans, marrows, sweet corn, tomatoes and ridge cucumbers. When these no longer require protection, aubergines, capsicums and melons can be grown.

Tomatoes can be laid on straw in September and covered to ripen, as can onions before storing. Late crops of dwarf beans, lettuce and endive may also be grown under cloches to extend the season.

Cloches are valuable also in spring, when they may be used to dry out the soil to permit seed sowing. Ventilation requires some attention, so in winter, to prevent the funnelling through of cold winds, the ends of the cloches should be blocked by a pane of glass. In very hot summer weather, the removal of an occasional cloche in the row combined with the open ends should give adequate ventilation.

Irrigation

A ready supply of water is of paramount importance in the production of high quality vegetables. When water is limited growth can be so restricted that hard, woody growth and less palatable produce is inevitable.

Methods of cultivation suggested in this book, such as the annual breaking up of part of the garden to incorporate organic material, will both help to conserve soil moisture and ensure adequate drainage. Drainage always is important, vital where irrigation is to be used. Shallow cultivation to the same depth every year can create a hard pan of consolidated soil preventing proper drainage. This is all too frequently a legacy left by builders after altering or constructing houses. The use of bulldozers and other heavy machines, especially during the winter months does much damage to soils in new gardens, especially on clay subsoils.

Heavy soils are more retentive of water than those of a light sandy nature, so that more rain or irrigation is required by the latter, and a greater supply of organic matter in order to retain moisture.

The good soil structure which is so essential for good plant growth can be harmed by the impact of large water drops. In normal rainfall the water drops are smaller than those supplied by artificial sprinklers and less damaging to the soil and the plants. Water should be applied in a fine spray, especially when establishing seedlings or young plants.

In small gardens a water can is useful especially for establishing freshly transplanted plants. If these are planted by dibber, leave a hole close to the stem when the roots are firmed and fill it up with water once or twice. This is much more effective than splashing the water around to be wasted by evaporation.

A perforated flat polythene hose, which throws out a very fine spray, may be laid amid crops or close to the row, ensuring the plants get the benefit while the operator walks on the dry paths between.

Trickle irrigation equipment which has been used under glass particularly for tomatoes can also be used outside for row crops such as runner beans. No loss occurs from evaporation and there is little if any damage to the soil. Sprinklers of various kinds and sizes are also available. I prefer the oscillating type which sprays a square or rectangular area and is more accurate and effective than the circular types.

Plants which are not allowed to suffer from water shortage respond by better leaf growth, which is obviously an advantage in crops such as cabbage, celery and lettuce where leaves and stems are the edible parts of the plant. In root crops regular watering must be maintained as a sudden influx of water after a dry period causes splitting. Watering produces larger roots and a milder flavour. However watering must be judicious as carrots are less coloured and sweet when watered excessively.

Maincrop potatoes are best watered when formation of the first tubers takes place, indicated in some cultivars by the plants flowering. Earlies however should be encouraged to make rapid growth from the start as by watering before stress occurs, edible-sized tubers are produced more quickly. Incidentally, irrigated crops of potatoes suffer less from scab. Tomatoes have been found to produce smaller but more highly flavoured fruits when allowed to suffer from mild water stress. Larger, finer looking fruits, though somewhat insipid in flavour, are produced more abundantly under conditions free from water stress.

Runner beans respond to watering from the early stages. This encourages growth, flowering, and rapid pod swelling. Contrary to popular belief, it has no effect on the non-setting of flowers, which is due to a lack of insect pollinators.

Peas mainly benefit from irrigation when the peas have set, and again about 10 days later when they begin to swell.

Seeds do not germinate readily in dry soil, so give the drills a thorough soaking either the previous day or some hours before sowing. During very hot weather transpiration losses can be counteracted by frequent light sprayings of the foliage. Heavy spraying is wasteful. In some seasons the soil is well supplied with moisture in spring, but where the winter has been dry, irrigation will be required before crops can be established. Many gardeners will, by keeping a close watch on their crops, be able to decide whether irrigation to avoid water stress is required. If you are unable to decide, a small hole one spit deep can be taken out and the soil at the bottom examined. If it is moist there will be no cause for alarm but in many seasons it will be dry, a sure indication that more water is required. The soil can be examined again after watering to see whether enough water has been put in. Overlapping, which occurs particularly when water is applied by spraying in circular areas, is less harmful in amateurs' gardens than in commercial establishments. The commercial grower prefers a crop which matures evenly, resulting in easier harvesting and clearance of the area. The amateur, however, prefers a crop which turns in unevenly and so provides a succession of kitchen purposes.

Vegetables without a Garden
If you do not have a garden it is still possible to grow a few herbs and vegetables provided you have a window box, patio or yard. A window box may be used for growing herbs – chives, parsley, sage, thyme, or mint – which can be picked fresh as required. A good compost should be used to fill the box, and you will have to ensure the usual precautions necessary for window boxes: that they are permitted and safely fixed.

You may also grow salad vegetables such as lettuce. The cultivar 'Little Gem' is ideal as the plants only require 8cm. (3in.) or so of soil and, by thin sowing, you can thin gradually, and, when a little size has been attained, use the thinnings, leaving some plants to develop fully. As room is cleared a few more seeds may be sown. 'Salad Bowl' is another cultivar which provides you with salad material over a long period, as long as you ensure the plants have enough moisture to keep them growing and in good health. If your window box is of reasonable size and depth, bush tomatoes are another possibility as this type require no pruning, staking or tying, though watering and some feeding will be required to keep up production. A cultivar such as 'Pixie' may be planted 30cm. (12in.) apart, so you should be able to grow 4 plants in an average window.

Depending on taste, other vegetables can be tried, such as spring onions or round beet. Tubs can be used while tomatoes can be grown in pots about 20cm. (8in.) in diameter. Climbing French beans are ideal for growing in a large tub or half-barrel as their continuous bearing habit is an asset, and problems of non-setting, which sometimes occur with runner beans, normally do not arise. If you would like to create a talking point with your friends, try the cultivar 'Violet Podded Stringless'. This bean has attractive purplish foliage and flowers and produces tender, violet-blue pods. Framed on a tripod of bean rods or bamboo canes, quite a spectacular effect can be created in a yard or patio not unduly shaded by buildings or trees.

Such an area is also suitable for the modern development of growing bags filled with peat-based compost, a method which has proved quite successful for a range of crops. Vegetables grown successfully in this way are ridge cucumbers, the cabbage 'Hispi', onions of the 'Ailsa Craig' type, aubergines, dwarf beans, dwarf runner beans, Chinese cabbage, bush marrows, several cultivars of tomatoes, including bush tomatoes, and lettuces, the cultivar 'Salad Bowl' being excep-tionally good. In this type of culture it must be borne in mind that compost soon becomes denuded of plant nutrients, so that regular feeding with a liquid fertilizer is necessary. I have no doubt that crops other than those mentioned can be grown by this method, so further experimentation, according to taste and local conditions, would be worth a try.

Weed Control
This is particularly important in the vegetable garden, where so many of the crops are grown from seed. Competition from weeds, especially while the vegetables are small, has a lasting harmful effect, so every effort should be made to control them right from the start. Weeds can be harmful in other ways too; they act as reservoirs for virus diseases and as hosts for fungus disease like club root.

Although most established crops can overcome weeds, or at least hold their own, it is still important to destroy weeds before a crop of viable seeds is produced. Some weeds, annual nettle, chickweed, and shepherd's purse, must be got rid of very quickly, as they flower and set seeds very early. To some extent, advantage may be taken of the facility with which many annual weeds germinate by allowing them to do so and then hoeing them off or forking them in with the fertilizer dressing which is often applied a week or two before sowing or planting. Weed elimination by hoeing in slow germinating crops can be started earlier if a marker crop like radish is also sown.

Some gardeners, however, find constant use of the hoe somewhat tedious and prefer to use a herbicide such as paraquat-diquat. Used as a spray before sowing or planting all annual weeds will be cleared, and it will temporarily inhibit the growth of many perennials by killing off the top growth. This is done without causing any harm to the soil.

This herbicide may also be used to control weeds in crops which are widely spaced, such as beans, Brussels sprouts and peas, but care must be taken to prevent the liquid from splashing on to foliage as damage will be quite severe.

Propachlor will not kill existing weeds but deals effectively for 6 weeks after application with germinating weeds. It can be used immediately after sowing of all brassica crops or after planting out. In the case of onions it can be used after sowing and after germination until 3 or 4 leaves have been produced. Leeks also can be kept clear in the early stages of their growth by this method.

Granular weedkillers such as Casoron G are easily applied and will effectively control both annual and perennial weeds. Couch, a very persistent weed in asparagus beds can be controlled by dalapon.

It must be emphasized that paraquat-diquat mixtures are available to the amateur only in granular form. Even so, all herbicide containers should be given a 'poison' label and locked in a safe place. Label instructions must always be read, understood and followed, to ensure chemical weedkillers do the job they are supposed to do, and that accidents do not occur.

VEGETABLES

Vegetable Cultivation

Angelica

A robust hardy perennial and native of northern and central Europe, naturalized in some parts of the UK as a garden escape. Very ornamental, it may attain a height of 2.4m. (8ft). Well known for its candied leaf stalks. Thrives best in shady, moist places which are well drained. The life of the seeds is short, so they should be sown as soon as they are ripe in August or September. Sow in stations 60cm. (2ft) apart with the same distance between the rows. Self-sown seedlings sometimes are found around established plants.

PESTS AND DISEASES
Generally trouble-free.

Artichoke, Chinese

A herbaceous perennial from the temperate regions of the Far East.

A vegetable with limited appeal, it may be grown in a sunny border in rows 38cm. (15in.) apart with 23cm. (9in.) between the tubers and 10cm. (4in.) deep. Planting is best done in March in light well drained soil; add some compost or peat if the soil is heavy to ensure a good crop.

Cultivation in summer is simple; keep the plants clear of weeds. Tubers can be lifted when the foliage has dried out, generally in late October and November; however they are best left in the soil and dug as required as the tubers deteriorate rapidly when lifted. They can be stored in sand or peat if it is inconvenient to leave them in the ground. It is wise to wash lifted tubers well before the soil gets dry, otherwise they are hard to clean. Keep them covered to avoid the discoloration which occurs if exposure to light is allowed for any length of time.

PESTS AND DISEASES
Generally trouble-free.

Artichoke, Globe

A herbaceous perennial native of southern Europe.

The globe artichoke is one of our most handsome plants, with attractive grey foliage and violet-blue flowers, and will enhance any garden large enough to contain it comfortably. As a vegetable, it is the immature flower heads or chokes which are eaten, the delicate and distinctive flavour of which is highly appreciated by connoisseurs, though considered an acquired taste by some.

Established plants occupy a considerable amount of room, so if you do not know whether you really like them or not, enough plants may be obtained from a specialist grower to make a modest planting in the flower or shrub border. If in due course you find its culinary qualities are not appreciated you will still have an attractive plant in the garden.

To grow globe artichokes, a reasonably fertile soil and an open position away from the shade of trees is required. The soil should be well drained and have a normal dressing of compost or farmyard manure incorporated into it before planting. A heavy dressing is not only extravagant but likely to cause soft growth making the plants vulnerable in a severe winter.

Propagation is possible by 3 methods: seed, division or from suckers. Seed is the least satisfactory, as the plants show considerable variation and many are poor when compared with named varieties. Propagation by suckers removed from established plants ensures similarity to the parent plant. By scraping the soil away from the parent

plant, 2 or 3 suckers with a piece of root attached can be removed with a sharp knife. These should be planted in April when the growths are about 30cm. (12in.) in length after trimming back the tops of the leaves and removing any decaying or damaged tissue.

Planting should be firm but not deep, allowing 60 to 75cm. (2 to 2½ft) between the plants but at least 90cm. (3ft) between the rows. Water in if the weather is dry and, if necessary, provide light shade with the aid of a few twigs near the plant. Summer cultivation is easy, involving the occasional use of a hoe to keep down weeds, and, if necessary, watering. This is a crop that responds to adequate moisture, especially if enriched with liquid manure. First year plants are later in producing their heads than established plants, so that by making a fresh planting annually, a succession can be kept up. Globe artichokes deteriorate after 3 or 4 years, being most productive in the second and third, so after a cropping in the fourth year, the plants should be destroyed.

Large heads should be encouraged by limiting the number of growths to 3 or 4 and removing the lateral buds, so leaving the terminal or king bud to be gathered. Clean up the plants before winter, cutting off all flowering stems close to the roots and shortening the longer leaves. Some bracken, straw or litter should be placed around the plants and held in place by soil in cold gardens during the winter months, however this is not usually necessary in warmer regions. This protective material should be removed in spring when mild weather becomes prevalent, generally about the end of March. Fork the bed, working in a light dressing of a general purpose fertilizer.

Gathering should take place when the flower head is fully developed, but with the green scales close and tight. If left until the violet-blue flower coloration has begun to show, the head will be uneatable.

PESTS
Aphids, particularly in May and June, and slugs.
DISEASES
Generally trouble-free.

Artichoke, Jerusalem

A hardy herbaceous perennial, native of North America. This is a useful plant for planting as a screen in summer, to obtain privacy or to hide the compost heap. It will grow in any soil provided it does not get waterlogged. Though some rate it highly as a root vegetable, it is not to everyone's liking so cannot be recommended for small gardens.

A member of the sunflower family, its yellow flowers are seldom seen in the UK except in long hot summers. It repays better cultivation than it generally receives, often being left to fend for itself instead of being lifted each year, resulting in very poor tubers. Where appreciated, it should be planted early in the season in February or March on land that has been well dug and dressed with compost. Select medium-sized tubers and plant 30 to 38cm. (12 to 15in.) apart, 76cm. (2½ft) between rows and 15cm. (6in.) deep.

During summer simply keep down weeds by occasional hoeings. In early winter the stems may be cut down to the ground and the tubers lifted for use as required. The Jerusalem artichoke, especially on good soil, can grow to the considerable height of 2.4 to 3m. (8 to 10ft). This may be a

disadvantage in an exposed garden where it may be necessary to fix a wire between posts to which the stems can be tied for support. Tubers are not produced until late in the season and they are not generally worth lifting until November.

If the ground is required the crop may be lifted from late November onwards and stored in soil or sand. However, stored in this manner they do not keep as well as potatoes. It is better to lift in February, select and replant for next year's crop and use the largest tubers in the kitchen. Make sure all tubers are lifted, as any that are left will grow and become a nuisance the following season.

PESTS AND DISEASES
Generally trouble-free.

Asparagus

A hardy herbaceous perennial, native of Europe, including the UK.

Although widely appreciated, asparagus has been somewhat neglected in smaller gardens. It will grow on most soils unless they be acid peats, chalky or very heavy clay. The main draw-back to cultivation is the length of time required before you can begin to cut the crop, at best 2 to 3 years, but from then the plants will crop for at least 25 years: beds have been known to thrive for half a century. This is, therefore, a crop to grow when you have settled down to a permanent residence. The ground should be thoroughly prepared, especially as, in addition to the time it will be occupied, asparagus has an enormous root system which requires double digging and the incorporation of such organic materials as farmyard manure or compost. Wild plants are often found near the sea-coast and, therefore, some growers feel it has a liking for seaweed and that salt is appreciated. Those who are able to incorporate seaweed, particularly when well composted in their soil preparations, will not regret so doing but, as with applications of salt, it is not essential for success.

What is necessary is good drainage and reasonable lime content, so if your soil tends to be acid, apply ground chalk or limestone 65 to 95g. per sq. m. (2 to 3oz. per sq. yd), during the preparatory operations. Weeds should be cleared, in particular couch grass or bindweed which are difficult to eradicate afterwards without damaging the asparagus plants. This is best taken care of in the previous season, if possible, to ensure total eradication.

Traditionally in private gardens asparagus was grown in beds of 3 rows, often raised by throwing up soil from pathways either side, providing a greater depth of soil and better drainage.

Recent research has shown that yield per acre is greatly increased by closer spacing than was formerly the practice. Trials carried out at Luddington Experimental Station showed the best spacing to be at 30cm. (12in.) apart in rows 30cm. (12in.) apart. A space of 76cm. (30in.) is left as a path between each block of three rows. Yields up to 1.93 tonnes to the acre have been obtained in these trials compared with a little over half a tonne which was normal in the past. The beds are on the flat, not raised.

Asparagus plants may be raised from seed but the best growers plant 1 year old crowns. Sowing may be done on good fertile soil during March or early April in drills 5cm. (2in.) deep, 46cm. (18in.) apart. In order to produce good 1 year old crowns for planting, thin to 15cm. (6in.) apart. Germination is slow, but a few radish seeds dropped in at the same time will germinate quickly and indicate where the seed rows are, thus facilitating hoeing between the rows. Raised in this way the young plants can be transferred to the permanent site the following year in March or April, just before new growth commences. The planting of older crowns is sometimes recommended on the grounds of quicker production, but I am convinced that carefully lifted 1 year plants, properly planted re-establish themselves more quickly and give better results. Plant in a prepared trench taken out 30cm. (12in.) wide and 20cm. (8in.) deep. Replace soil to a depth of 8cm. (3in.) in the bottom in ridge or mound formation, and spread the roots out over this when planting, covering with 8cm. (3in.) of soil. Care must be taken to ensure the roots are not allowed to dry out while planting; this is more likely to happen when unpacked from another source. Hoeing to keep down weeds will fill up the remainder of the trench gradually during the first season.

When soil preparation has been properly carried out assistance from fertilizers should not really be required until the second year after planting when a good general fertilizer should be applied at 90 to 95g. per sq. m. (3oz. per sq. yd) in early March; a good practice which should be followed annually.

No asparagus should be cut until the third year after planting and then only for a limited season, confined to a 6 week period. This may be extended in following years by 2 weeks but should in most districts finish by the end of June. All shoots appearing after that should be allowed to grow so as to build up buds for the following seasons crop. In very windy situations a few bamboo canes along the rows linked with string will prevent young growths from 'blowing out'. The practice of cutting green foliage is deprecated. If required for ornamental purposes, a few plants in the flower garden will provide the necessary material.

In autumn asparagus foliage becomes yellow and stems should then be cut down before ripe berries fall and give rise to unwanted seedlings. Shears can be used for this, cutting close to the ground, and the foliage burned. On heavy soils several inches of soil can be mounded over the row; on light soils this may be deferred until March. Formerly when farmyard manure was in plentiful supply, a layer was spread over the crowns before covering with soil. To harvest, cut the strongest growths when 8 or 10cm. (3 or 4in.) above ground, pushing the knife down close the growth so that around 10cm. (4in.) of white stem is severed below the surface. A sharp knife, with serrated edge, should be used as wild hacking will damage later growths. If not immediately required the shoots can be stood in water which should be changed daily. Standing in iced water, followed by storage in a refrigerator at 0 to 4°C. is also recommended.

PESTS
Asparagus beetle and slugs.
DISEASES
Violet root-rot and rust.

Asparagus Pea
An annual native of southern Europe which is also known as the winged pea, because of its short 4-winged pods, which, eaten young, have a delicate flavour to some suggestive of asparagus. This is a very attractive plant; the brownish-red flowers bloom for a considerable time so it is well worth growing in the flower garden.

Seeds may be sown in April under glass and the seedlings planted out in May, 30cm. (12in.) apart, or outdoors early in May when the seedlings should be thinned down to the same distance. Sowing 2 or 3 seeds at the appropriate distance will result in a considerable saving of seed, and the surplus seedlings can be removed when fit to handle. Light, well drained soils are most suitable and a sunny position is preferable to a shaded one. It requires little attention apart from hoeing and watering if drought conditions prevail. A few short twigs will support the plants if it is desired to keep them clear of the soil. In good soil a height of 46cm. (18in.) is reached. The whole pod is eaten and pods should be picked when 2.5cm. (1in.) long and still young. Regular picking encourages further production.
PEST AND DISEASES
Generally trouble-free.

Aubergine or Egg-Plant
A tender annual originating in the tropics and a popular crop in many warmer countries. In the UK it is now more appreciated than formerly when it was sometimes grown as an ornamental plant. In the UK it can only be grown outdoors in very sheltered gardens in a good summer and generally it will require greenhouse or cloche protection. Seeds should be sown under glass in February or March in John Innes seed compost or one of the soilless composts in a minimum temperature of 16°C. (about 60°F.).

As soon as the seedlings can be handled, transplant them into 5cm. (2in.) pots or soil blocks. When they are well rooted transfer to 18 or 20cm. (7 or 8in.) pots of John Innes 3 or to a border under glass if available. For culture under cloches delay the sowing until March so as to prevent the plants starving and getting checked before planting out.

The soil outside should be made fertile with compost and warmed up for some days by putting the cloches in place before planting 60cm. (2ft) apart in late May in warm areas or in June where less congenial conditions generally prevail. When the plants are 15cm. (6in.) high pinch out the tops and limit the number of fruits to 4 or 5. When these have formed stop lateral growths. The plants must never be allowed to suffer from lack of moisture and liquid manure is especially beneficial when the fruits are swelling. A stake to each plant is usually necessary and daily syringing through and under the foliage will help to discourage red spider. Fruits should be picked while the polish and bloom is retained. Although I have grown varieties with white and variegated green fruits, those with deep purple-black fruits are more popular.
PESTS
Red spider mite, especially when grown in pots under glass.
DISEASES
Generally trouble-free.

Balm
A hardy, easily grown perennial also known as lemon balm. Native to southern Europe, it has become widely naturalized in northern Europe. Seeds should be sown outside in April, thinning or transplanting the seedlings 30cm. (12in.) apart each way. A plant which grows freely in any reasonable soil, when established, it seeds freely and self-sown seedlings can become a nuisance. The leaves have a strong lemon fragrance when crushed or handled but the flavour is less strong. The leaves are sometimes used in pot-pourri and summer drinks with borage.
PESTS AND DISEASES
Generally trouble-free.

Basil, Sweet
A half hardy annual, originally from South-east Asia that has been cultivated in Europe for about 2000 years. It has been credited with the ability to repel flies.

Seeds should be sown in a greenhouse in spring at a temperature of 13°C. (55°F.). Sowing in pots or soil blocks facilitates a good start when the plants are hardened off and planted out. A sheltered position with good soil should be chosen, and planting at the end of May or early in June should eliminate the danger of frost. Plant 20cm. (8in.) apart in rows 30cm. (12in.) apart. Sweet basil grows to about 60cm. (2ft) high. Where basil is valued for flavouring, a few plants may be lifted and placed in pots or containers and kept in a greenhouse. The plants should be cut back hard for this purpose, or bush basil, *Ocimum minimum*, grown; this only reaches a height of 15 to 30cm. (6 to 12in.). Pinching out the tops induces 'bushiness', and so more leaves.
PESTS AND DISEASES
Generally trouble-free.

Bay
Despite being a native of the Mediterranean region, this tree is surprisingly hardy in cooler countries. In warm, sheltered gardens, when allowed to grow naturally, it can grow over 9m. (30ft) high and can be used as a main feature in herb gardens of sufficient size. It is often grown in tubs, more for ornamental effect than for culinary purposes and can be trained into various shapes. Tub plants can be moved into a cool greenhouse in winter. The sweet bay can be propagated by cuttings in late summer in a propagating frame. Leaves can be picked as required for flavouring various dishes, or as an essential constituent of bouquet garni.
PESTS AND DISEASES
Generally trouble-free.

Bean, Broad
A hardy annual, much favoured because it thrives on most soils and is comparatively easy to grow, providing one of the earliest crops. There are signs of its increasing popularity, especially of green-seeded varieties which are more attractive in colour and are found to be superior for freezing, now an important aspect of this crop. For convenience broad beans may be classified in 3 groups, longpod, Windsor and dwarf. Long-pods are hardy, crop heavily and look more impressive, Windsors are of better flavour, while the dwarf strains are suitable for growing under cloches to get an earlier crop.

Where the soil has been well manured for a previous crop little more preparation beyond breaking the soil down to a fine tilth will be required. In sheltered well drained gardens an earlier crop can be obtained by a sowing in early November. Some gardeners have found by experience this early sowing unprofitable and prefer to wait until February. Where an autumn sowing is desired apply beforehand a dressing of sulphate of potash 15 to 20g. per sq. m. ($\frac{1}{2}$ oz. per sq. yd).

Broad beans are generally grown in double rows, which should be taken out as a flat-bottomed trench 5cm. (2in.) deep. Sow the seeds 23cm. (9in.) apart, with the same distance between the rows. A space of 60cm. (2ft) will be required between each pair of rows. Cover the seeds over to a depth of 5cm. (2in.). Before sowing, examine seeds for the round exit holes of the bean beetles, and discard those affected.

Spring sowings can be made from February onwards, as soon as soil conditions allow, with a second sowing towards the end of March if a succession is required. Later sowings do not as a rule crop so freely and are liable to be attacked by black-fly. To counteract this, remove the tops of the plants as soon as plenty of flowers have formed; this also helps to ensure well filled pods. These tops can be boiled and buttered – they look like spinach, but have a 'beany' taste. General cultivation consists of keeping the ground clear of weeds, while the removal of the tops generally ensures that the plants do not require support. Some gardeners enjoy them picked young and cooked whole with the pods. Usually they are allowed to develop more fully.

In very cold, northern gardens where ground cultivation cannot be undertaken until April, broad beans may be sown in a greenhouse or frame in February or March where a little heat is available. Boxes 13cm. (5in.) or 15cm. (6in.) deep will be required and old potting compost is quite satisfactory. The seedlings transplant very well, if lifted with a trowel and may be planted out after hardening off, in mid-April. A dwarf cultivar such as 'The Sutton' may be sown in February or even earlier in sheltered areas and can be left under cloches until late March or early April when the cloches should be opened a little to allow bees entrance for pollination. The broad bean has an attractive flower, white with black spots, which is wonderfully fragrant.

PESTS
Bean aphid or blackfly.
DISEASES
Chocolate spot.

Bean, climbing French

For convenience I will include some climbing beans in this group because of their growth habit, although they do not all have the white self-fertile flowers which are characteristic of the dwarf French. Their need for support makes them less popular than they deserve. They have a considerable advantage in the length of the cropping season, particularly when the beans are picked when young and tender. They are more reliable than runner beans; the problem of the non-setting of pods does not arise.

The necessary supports vary according to cultivar, however, none need such a strong structure as runner beans. Generally a cultivar such as 'Blue Lake White Seeded' can be supported on strings stretched between 2 wires 1.8m. (6ft) apart, the bottom one just above ground level. These wires must be kept reasonably taut with wooden poles. Double rows, 30cm. (12in.) apart are best. These should be drawn out 5cm. (2in.) deep and the seeds sown about 15cm. (6in.)

apart. A few extras should be sown which, if carefully lifted, can be used to fill gaps; alternatively, sow thicker than required and thin out the seedlings. A space of 1.5m. (5ft) will be required between each pair of double rows. Sowing around mid-May should be suitable for most gardens: a little earlier in warm, sheltered gardens, later in northern and colder areas.

PESTS AND DISEASES
Except for chocolate spot, same as broad beans; also bean anthracnose.

Bean, dwarf French

A tender annual, often known as the kidney bean from the shape of the seeds, although some cultivars have round seeds. White-flowered dwarf French beans, like those of climbing French are self-pollinated. This is a popular and valuable vegetable which, in the heyday of the large private garden was highly prized for early forcing in pots in warm greenhouses. Nowadays, such methods are only considered practical in exceptional cases, and early crops are more likely to be forwarded under continuous cloches or polythene tunnels. Dwarf bean seeds are apt to rot in very cold soil so it is important to put the protective cover in place some weeks before sowing to warm it up. This is a crop which appreciates a deeply dug, well-drained soil which warms up quickly and which has been enriched by the addition of compost during digging. If you live in an area where horse manure or used mushroom compost is available, these are most useful additives. Dwarf beans benefit considerably from a nitrogenous fertilizer at 30 to 35g. per sq. m. (1 oz. per sq. yd) applied while breaking down the soil to a fine tilth before sowing the seeds.

For the earliest crop under protection, sowing can begin at the end of March in sheltered areas, but mid-April will be better in exposed or cold gardens. A double row may be sown 20cm. (8in.) or so apart with seeds staggered at 13cm. (5in.) apart and 5cm. (2in.) deep. If a hard frost occurs, place some protective material, such as straw or bracken, over the cloches at night. Ventilate during the day when weather is warm, and by mid-May tunnels may be opened up. Protection may be removed by the end of May. Unprotected sowings may be made towards the end of April except in colder areas where they should be delayed until May. Single rows are probably best and may be 46cm. (18in.) apart. Seeds can be dropped in pairs 23cm. (9in.) apart, taking away the weaker plants in due course. Drawing a little soil up to each side will provide some support for the plants and this can be supplemented if necessary by a few twigs. Regular hoeing to control weeds and watering to keep the soil moist are the usual cultivation requirements.

Picking should be started while the pods are young and tender, as they are then more appreciated in the kitchen and continuous cropping is encouraged. July sowings can be made to extend the season; but generally the plants will require protection in September.

PESTS AND DISEASES
The same as climbing French beans.

Bean, Haricot

The haricot bean is grown in the same manner as the dwarf French. The pods should not be picked while green but left until they are fully ripe. The

plants can be lifted at the end of summer and hung up in an airy place under cover to ripen fully if bad weather has been a hindrance. Seeds may be thrashed out and should be kept dry in storage until required.

PESTS AND DISEASES
The same as French beans.

Bean, Runner

The runner bean is a half-hardy perennial plant from Mexico and South America with tuberous roots which can be stored in frost-proof conditions during winter months. It is, however, so easily raised from seed that no useful purpose is served by over-wintering the roots.

This is a very popular vegetable in the UK from the Midlands southwards but is of no value in colder areas. A most beautiful plant, noted for its bright scarlet flowers, it may be used as a background to borders, or as a screen to hide some unsightly object. Though frequently known as 'Scarlet Runner', there are also bicoloured, white and pale pink flowered cultivars. Commercial growers sometimes grow this crop in bush form by pinching back the climbing growths. Dwarf non-trailing forms are also available and are particularly suited to small gardens.

The runner bean, often allocated a permanent site, requires a strong structure because when fully grown, a row presents a large surface area to the wind. This applies particularly on allotments which are frequently exposed. If possible then, a sheltered site should be selected; this also encourages insect pollinators. When well grown, runner beans yield a very heavy crop so the labour of taking out a trench is worth while. The trench should be 60cm. (2ft) wide and 2 spits deep. Break up the bottom with a digging fork where possible. Manure or compost should be incorporated as the work proceeds, in time to let the soil settle. Many growers on heavy soil find it is worth while to open a trench in autumn and to use this for household scraps or any garden rubbish which will rot down and turn into humus. Refilling can be done gradually as long as it is completed several weeks before sowing or planting takes place. If, when completed, the surface of the trench is kept lower than the surrounding area, watering later on in periods of drought will be made easier. A dressing of 2 parts superphosphate to one part sulphate of potash should be applied at 56g. per sq. m. (2oz. per sq. yd) during the soil preparation.

Only in very favoured areas can runner beans be sown before mid-May and germinate successfully. If an earlier start is desired, sow under cloches during the last week in April. The cloches should have been placed in position a few weeks before in order to warm up the soil. An alternative method is to sow in pots or boxes, which is useful if seed is in short supply because, started off in a greenhouse or frame, germination should be trouble-free. Boxes at least 13cm. (5in.) deep are required. Old potting soil, to which has been added damp peat or leaf mould, is ideal. Pots are a little more trouble, but less disturbance is caused to the plants when planting takes place. Use 9 or 13cm. ($3\frac{1}{2}$ or 5in.) pots, placing 2 seeds in each and remove the weaker plant a few days after germination. All plants should be well hardened off before planting out towards the end of May or early June when frost is no longer a danger. It must be remembered that young

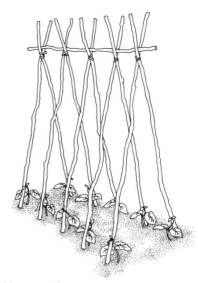  

Staking runner beans
3 methods: staking with bean poles (left), with netting supported by posts (centre), and (right) with canes in wigwam formation, 75cm. (2½ft.) between plants.

runner bean plants are very tender and susceptible to frost damage.

Where a late supply is required, a sowing in mid-June in colder areas, or late June in more favoured districts, can be very profitable; early sowings are usually exhausted by late September. Seeds should be sown 5cm. (2in.) deep and at least 23cm. (9in.) and preferably 30cm. (12in.) apart. Double rows are usual and these should be 46cm. (18in.) apart. If more than one double row of runner beans is required 1.5m. (5ft) will be needed between the pairs of rows. If the plants are to be supported by poles or canes, the seeds should be sown directly opposite each other in the rows, unless poles are placed in position first. This is especially desirable when planting from pots or boxes.

STAKING

Bean poles should be inserted in the soil opposite each other, one to each plant, so that they will be about 30cm. (12in.) apart. Cross the poles over about 1.8m. (6ft) above ground level and run some thin poles along the top of the cross-over. When lashed together with strong string, a stable structure will result, strong enough to withstand autumn winds. The beans sometimes require a little attention when the cross-over is reached to keep the shoots on the upward path. Pinch out the tips when the top of the pole has been reached.

Alternative methods of support can, of course, be used, such as upright canes fixed to wires stretched between poles or netting of various sorts or stout 2.4m. (8ft) poles may be set 1.8m. (6ft) apart so that there is 1.8m. (6ft) showing above ground. 10 beans may then be sown or planted round the pole, about 60cm. (2ft) away from it. Strings are then attached to the top of the pole and anchored with bent wire loops in the ground beside each plant. However, where supports are a problem, crops can be grown on the bush system by sowing the beans in single rows 15cm. (6in.) apart in rows 60cm. (2ft) apart. Pinch out the tips of the plants when they begin to run up and repeat as necessary. Good crops can be produced but the pods are less likely to be

straight and are apt to get splashed with soil and also damaged by slugs in wet weather. A straw mulch will keep the beans clean.

Treatment during summer consists of controlling weeds and keeping the surface soil loose until the plants have made some growth. Mulching with strawy manure before the soil dries out or after a good watering smothers weeds and helps to retain moisture. This is a crop which should not be allowed to suffer from lack of water, so, if necessary, give a thorough soaking when the flower buds are seen.

The beans should be harvested regularly while tender and before the seeds start swelling; if necessary they may be kept upright in a little water for a day or two in a cool place or if there is a surplus, frozen. To harvest a white-seeded cultivar for use when dried, leave all the pods on the plants until thoroughly ripened. In late or wet seasons, pull up the plants and hang them in a dry airy shed to finish off. To save seeds for next season, treat the pods in a similar manner.

PESTS

Bean aphid or blackfly and slugs and snails.

DISEASES

Bean anthracnose and root rot.

Bean, Soya

A tender annual, thought to have originated in China where it has been a staple food for a long time. It has also become popular in parts of the USA, and had aroused some attention in the UK because the cultivar illustrated, 'Fiskeby V' is credited with being suitable for temperate climates. Many growers have been disappointed with its performance however, and in colder areas it will require starting off in pots and planting out after the danger of frost is over. Whether the resultant crop will be worth-while remains to be seen. Perhaps in time it will become acclimatized or cultivars will be bred which are more suitable. In certain northern European countries where warmer weather conditions prevail, better crops may be forthcoming.

PESTS AND DISEASES

Generally trouble-free.

Beetroot or Red Beet

Red beet, beetroot or garden beet are various names applied to this biennial plant which has long been favoured as a component of salads and is now also recognized for its qualities as a vegetable. This is a crop which should not be sown on ground which has been freshly manured but on a site which has been manured for a previous crop. Few gardeners grow long beet nowadays and find the globe varieties meet their requirements very much better, especially in the kitchen. However, a long type of beet keeps better in storage, so where roots are valued late in the season, a sowing of long beet should be made towards the end of May or early in June. Roots from earlier sowings tend to get too large and coarse, consequently, where this type is to be grown, the ground should be dug one spit deep. Where soil is poor or has not been manured for the previous crop a general purpose fertilizer should be worked in during the preparation of the seed bed at the rate of 90g. per sq. m. (3oz. per sq. yd). When forked over, tread the soil lightly, levelling off with a rake before drawing the drills out. These should be 2.5cm. (1in.) in depth and 30cm. (12in.) apart, allowing at least 8cm. (3in.) between rows for a long variety. Strains of beet resistant to bolting may be sown as early as mid-March, especially if the site is sheltered, or earlier in the month where cloche protection can be given. This very early type can be sown for succession up to mid-April when the normal cultivars can be sown. Beet are, in fact, small clusters of seeds. They are easily handled and can be dropped into the drill at 10cm. (4in.) intervals, thinning these in due course to a single plant. The long maincrop cultivar should be allowed 15cm. (6in.) and thinned also to single plants; this can be done at the rough leaf stage. Sowings can be made at intervals to supply a succession of young roots which should not be allowed to grow beyond the size of a tennis ball before pulling. Those from early sowings are pulled as required.

A last sowing should be made in early July. This will provide roots for use in winter, especially in mild climatic areas where a little straw or bracken will ensure sufficient protection.

Hoeing to keep weeds in check must be carried out carefully to avoid damage to the roots.

In colder areas the roots should be lifted for storage when large enough for household requirements and before severe frosts set in. Generally October is the time for lifting and this must be done carefully with a fork. Try to ensure that the roots are not damaged or bruised; any damaged while being lifted or by pests should be discarded. Tops should not be cut off but removed by twisting off by hand so that colour is not lost through bleeding. Lift if possible on a dry day so that the soil can be shaken from the roots, which can be stored in a cool dry frost-proof place. Boxes may be used in conjunction with sand or dry peat to contain the roots or a clamp can be made in the open in a sheltered position near a building or a hedge.

PESTS
Leaf mining fly.
DISEASES
Violet root rot.

Beet, Leaf
A hardy biennial native of southern Europe, the leaf beet, especially the variety 'Perpetual Spinach', is much used as a substitute for spinach and has also been called spinach beet. Although slightly inferior in quality to spinach, *Spinacia oleracea*, the leaf beet is a much more prolific and accommodating plant. It will grow on most soils but will repay manuring with a higher production of more succulent leaves. The root is of no culinary value.

When the soil has been well prepared, sowing may take place in late March or early April in drills 38cm. (15in.) apart and 2.5cm. (1in.) deep. In due course the plants should be thinned down 15 to 20cm. (6 to 8in.) apart; half this distance at first. Eventually remove every second plant. If not required immediately, the leaves will freeze very well. These should be gathered as soon as they have attained usable size; this encourages further cropping. If well looked after one sowing will keep in production for most of the season, however a further sowing in August will provide a late winter supply.

'Silver or Seakale' is also used as a substitute for spinach by stripping the leaves off the stems and mid-ribs. The mid-ribs may then be cooked separately as seakale. This plant also appreciates well cultivated soil supplied with organic materials. It makes a very handsome addition to the garden especially if not allowed to suffer from lack of moisture. More room is required if manure is provided and seeds should be sown in April in drills 46cm. (18in.) apart. Thinning gradually when fit to handle, the plants can ultimately be left at 25cm. (10in.) or so apart. Leaves should be pulled off rather than cut.

PESTS
Leaf mining fly.
DISEASES
Generally trouble-free.

Borage
A hardy annual native of southern Europe which has become naturalized in the warmer parts of western Europe. It attracts bees and has brilliant blue flowers. Seeds can be sown in rows 60cm. (2ft) apart, sowing in stations 38cm. (15in.) apart and thinning down to one plant in due course. It

will seed freely especially on light soils and maintain itself by self-sown seedlings. The leaves, which have a subtle cucumber flavour, may be used in drinks or chopped up and added to salads.

PESTS AND DISEASES
Generally trouble-free.

Broccoli, Sprouting
The sprouting broccolis require the same cultural conditions as winter cauliflower, see p. 30.

The most commonly grown and hardiest type is the purple, although the white is considered by some to be more delicate in flavour. Though not so widely grown commercially, this is a valuable vegetable in winter and early spring when green vegetables are likely to be scarce. The central head may be cut first and will be succeeded by a number of side shoots. Early and late selections of both colours are available and mature from March to April. All of these are suitable for home freezing.

Perennial broccoli is favoured by some gardeners and can be grown from seed sown in April and planted out 90cm. (3ft) apart in June. A central head is produced in spring with several smaller heads surrounding. In a well cultivated fertile soil it will carry on for some years.

PESTS AND DISEASES
The same as cauliflower.

Brussels Sprouts
A biennial plant, supposedly developed by the Belgians around their capital city and certainly grown in Belgium for a long time, possibly 8 centuries. This is an important crop in the UK, grown in quantity commercially and one of the most popular vegetables for winter use grown by gardeners. It may be grown on any well drained, medium to heavy soil, especially if well manured for the previous crop. It is important to carry out the necessary cultivation some considerable time before planting so that the soil has time to settle, as firm planting is essential for this crop. Loose soil which has been recently dug with fresh compost or manure added is a sure recipe for inferior, loose-blown sprouts. A supplementary dressing at the rate of 90 to 95 g. per sq. m. (3oz. per sq. yd) of 2 parts (by weight) superphosphate to one of sulphate of potash should be worked in before planting.

Seed sowing should be done on a firm seed bed in rows spaced at least 15cm. (6in.) apart in shallow drills round about mid-March, sowing the seeds thinly to ensure sturdy plants. When fit to handle these may be thinned to 2.5cm. (1in.) apart to prevent thin drawn up plants. A further sowing in April will provide a later batch of plants to extend the picking season. The young plants should be well watered on the day before transplanting. In cold northern areas Brussels sprouts are sometimes sown under cloches or in a frame to ensure good plants for transplanting before the end of May. Plants raised in this fashion should be hardened off before transplanting.

Transplanting should take place towards the end of May or early in June. It is worth loosening the plants with a fork so as to retain a good root system and plant at 76cm. (30in.) apart each way, making sure each plant is very firm; water afterwards if the soil is dry. If showery weather is chosen for planting much time will be saved.

Summer cultivation consists of hoeing to keep weeds down and the surface soil loose; also some growers draw soil up to the stems when the plants have become established. In autumn the lower leaves turn yellow and these should be removed and placed on the compost heap. As the sprouts become ready, picking should be started systematically from the bottom. They are usually parted from the stem quite easily by downward pressure, if not, a sharp knife may be used. In order to forward sprout formation market growers sometimes carry out an operation known as 'cocking'. This is simply removing the growing tip of the plant early in September, not the sprout top, which is often used at the end of the season after all the sprouts have been picked. In seasons when a severe winter has caused a scarcity of green vegetables, I have found the young green growths which are produced in April very useful. This then is a crop which can provide food from September to April and is therefore worthy of good cultivation.

In small gardens of limited space catch crops can be grown between the rows, using quick maturing cultivars of such vegetables as carrot, lettuce, summer spinach, radish, red beet and turnip, which must be cleared before the sprout plants close the rows.

When clearing, the stumps should be burned, especially if affected by club root, or taken to the compost heap.

PESTS
Aphids, cabbage root fly and flea beetles.
DISEASES
The same as cauliflower.

Cabbage
This hardy biennial is regarded by some authorities as being indigenous to Europe and western Asia but thought by some to have been brought northwards by the Romans. It is found growing wild in coastal areas of the UK. It has been in cultivation for a long time and has given rise to a large number of varieties, strains and selections. It is therefore possible to supply this vegetable at any time of the year. For convenience, cabbages can be arranged in 4 groups. Spring-sown for summer use, summer-sown for use in autumn and winter, early autumn-sown to turn in during spring and often called spring cabbage, and a type which has acquired popularity in recent years, which can be used all winter and stored if required.

Cabbages will thrive on any well drained soil in good condition, especially if it has been well manured for a previous crop. This is not always possible, so a general purpose fertilizer may be required, especially for spring-sown plants at 90 to 95 g. per sq. m. (3oz. per sq. yd) rate. Lime may also be required if there is any tendency to acidity, as this is a condition unsuitable for brassicas.

Cabbages for summer use must be sown in spring on a well prepared seed bed about 1.5cm. (½in.) deep in late March or early April. In cold northern gardens this may be done in a cold frame or under cloche protection in early March. The young plants should be ready for planting in May or early June. Water well the day before transplanting if the ground is dry, and plant firmly 46cm. (18in.) either way. If necessary, water again after planting and hoe carefully until such time as the plants cover the soil. See that they do not suffer from lack of water and watch out for pests and diseases.

Cabbages for use in autumn and winter may be sown on a prepared seed bed in late April or the first 2 weeks in May. By this time of year dry weather may necessitate a thorough soaking of the seed drills a few hours before sowing in order to ensure good germination. Sow in drills about 1.5 to 2cm. ($\frac{1}{2}$ to $\frac{3}{4}$in.) in depth and transplant in late June or July on land well manured for a previous crop. If a dibber is used when planting, make a hole close to the plant while firming, which may be filled with water if dry weather is prevalent. A planting distance of 46cm. (18in.) between plants and 60cm. (2ft) between rows is suitable. Regular hoeing is beneficial and keeps down weeds.

Cabbages for winter storage have recently become a feature of supermarkets and shops in the UK. These may be grown from seeds sown in March and transplanted in June 46cm. (18in.) between plants and 60cm. (2ft) between the rows. Very firm, ball-headed cabbages are produced which are excellent for cooking, for winter salad or coleslaw. Ready to cut from October to December, the heads may be stored in a cool, airy shed where they will keep in good condition for several weeks, only requiring the removal of the outer leaves before use.

Autumn-sown cabbage for use in spring, familiarly known as spring cabbage, is the type many appreciate most of all for the young tender hearts which are ready for cutting when green vegetables are scarce in most gardens. This is a crop which, as a rule, is planted to follow an earlier, cleared crop. If following early potatoes, little cultivation will be necessary, other than forking through to level, treading to firm and raking with a wooden rake.

Seed should be sown in a seed bed during the last week in July for northern gardens, while those in the south will find the second week in August more suitable. Transplanting is done from mid-September to mid-October; late planting impairs the chance of the plants getting well established before winter. Planting distances will vary according to the variety and its use. For hearting cabbage of the larger varieties, 46cm. (18in.) either way is reasonable, but if spring greens or collards are required, double up on the plants in the row so that every second one can be cut when needed. An alternative method for collard production is to sow a suitable cultivar thinly the last week in July, *in situ*, thinning the plants to 8 to 10cm. (3 to 4in.) apart when fit to handle. From this sowing, collards should be available from December probably until April.

The crop should be hoed when soil is suitable, and at least once before winter sets in; at the same time, pull up a little soil to the plants for protection. This helps drain surplus water away from the plants in wet areas. Early in the new year hoe the soil to stimulate growth, which may be further encouraged by a dressing of sulphate of ammonia at 67g. per sq. m. (2oz. per sq. yd) at the end of February or beginning of March. Some growers prefer nitro-chalk at the same rate, others advocate nitrate of soda.

PESTS
Cabbage aphid, birds, cabbage root fly maggots, flea beetle and cabbage white caterpillars.
DISEASES
Club root, damping off and leaf spot.

Cabbage, Chinese

An annual, also known as Chinese leaves, presumably a native of China where it has been known for centuries, which only arrived in Europe in the last century. Well described as an aristocratic cos lettuce, it has a delicate flavour when cooked or eaten raw in salads. It requires soil well laden with organic matter so as to retain moisture and should be sited to obtain a little shade at noon, such as would be provided by runner beans.

This is a crop which is liable to bolt if sown early. Transplanting also induces bolting so *in situ* sowings are required and these not before July. The seeds are large enough to ensure thin sowing and the plants should be allowed 30cm. (12in.) at least when well grown. As the plants grow quickly, a few small sowings should be made frequently to avoid wastage. Thinnings can be used in the kitchen.

Closely related, and also called Chinese cabbage, is *Brassica chinensis* which is a loose leafed type with edible greenish-white stalks more likely to be found in Chinese restaurants than in gardens.
PESTS AND DISEASES
Generally trouble-free.

Cabbage, Red

There is only a limited demand for this crop in the UK where it is generally grown for pickling, although it is an excellent vegetable when cooked.

In northern gardens it is usually sown during August, and overwintered in the seed bed, in a frame or under cloches when weather becomes severe. These plants can be put in their cropping situation when soil and weather conditions are suitable between March and late April, to get as long a growing season as possible. Firm planting is essential, and at least 60cm. (2ft) each way between plants and rows is required. Land in good heart is required, and, as with other cabbages, soil acidity may be corrected by an application of ground chalk or limestone. In southern gardens an open ground sowing in a seed bed in March will suffice, although heads may be somewhat smaller than those from an autumn sowing. The heads should be ready for pickling in August or September but should be cut before bad weather sets in.
PESTS AND DISEASES
Red cabbage is affected by the same pests and diseases as cabbage.

Cabbage, Savoy

This biennial plant, botanically related to the Brussels sprout, is in appearance much more like the cabbage, differing mainly in having crimped leaves with a more sturdy habit. An important crop, particularly in colder northern gardens, where its ability to withstand severe weather in winter is an advantage, not only for supply purposes but because flavour is considered to improve after frost. That there is a close relationship between Savoy and cabbage is evident from the popular cultivar 'January King' which is classified as both by some seed growers.

This is a crop which can be grown on any reasonable soil which is not waterlogged. However it appreciates similar conditions as cabbage sown for autumn cutting, that is land well manured for a previous crop with a 90 to 95g. dressing per sq. m. (3oz. per sq. yd) of 2 parts

superphosphate to one of sulphate of potash. Early crops are not usually required but can be produced from an April sowing. More valuable as a late crop, seeds should be sown in a seedbed in May. Transplanting on firm ground can be carried out in July or early August at least 46cm. (18in.) apart and 60cm. (2ft) between the rows. Some flexibility is required because of varietal differences in size.
PESTS AND DISEASES
The same as cabbage.

Calabrese

Calabrese, also known as green Italian sprouting broccoli has become very popular, much of it being cooked after freezing, for which purpose it is particularly suitable. Not hardy like sprouting broccoli it is best sown *in situ* in June and July in rows up to 60cm. (2ft) apart. When ready to handle, the seedlings can be thinned down to 38cm. (15in.) apart in the row. Keep the plants clear of weeds and ensure they do not suffer from shortage of moisture. The central head should be cut first and side shoots will then provide the bulk of the crop. These can be cut about 15cm. (6in.) in length, during autumn months.
PESTS AND DISEASES
The same pests and diseases as cauliflower.

Cardoon

A perennial native of southern Europe, the cardoon is generally grown in the UK as an annual from seed. Seldom seen in gardens except as an ornamental plant and held in higher regard by some gardeners than its near relation the globe artichoke for this purpose. However, as a vegetable it requires a good deal of room, and, unless you have a particular taste for it, the labour required seems hardly worth while. The blanched stems are used either boiled, in soups, or eaten raw in autumn and early winter.

Good soil conditions are required, so take out a continuous trench 46cm. (18in.) wide and as much deep; dig in a good layer of farm-yard manure or compost and return soil so as to be under the normal level by a few centimetres. This will allow for good soakings of water during dry weather. I have found that best results followed from starting with plants raised in pots sown in a cool greenhouse in late April and hardened off for planting in late May. 60cm. (2ft) is required between the plants which must not suffer from lack of moisture while growing and benefit from liquid manure at weekly intervals.

Blanching may be begun in September and is easier to manage if a good strong stake is provided for each plant. The process generally requires 6 to 8 weeks, the leaves being drawn close together and tied near the tops of the plants. Strips of corrugated cardboard can then be wound round the stems working from the bottom upwards; use gloves as cardoons are very prickly. A little soil banked round the bottom will exclude light. An alternative method is to thatch with straw, but care must be taken to ensure the plants are dry. Cardoons are not hardy, so additional protection in severe weather may be required.
PESTS AND DISEASES
Generally trouble-free.

Carrot

A biennial plant grown as an annual, which grows wild in the UK and Europe and is reputed to have been cultivated for 2000 years. Large areas where the soil is a deep sandy loam or fenland peat are used by commercial growers for production of this crop, a sure indication that if you have a heavy soil you will have to lighten it by adding compost, peat and even sand. By use of protection, frames, cloches or plastic tunnels, carrots may be produced early in the season, followed by sowings at intervals, and a main crop grown for winter storage, so that this root vegetable will be available all the year round. Indispensable as a vegetable, the carrot also possesses decorative foliage. Heavier soils should, if possible, be well dug the previous autumn, preferably following a crop which has been well manured in order to prevent the forked roots which usually occur in freshly manured soils. On very light soils a dressing of well-rotted compost, as long as it is thoroughly mixed with the top soil, will be beneficial in dry seasons. The soil should be cultivated on a dry day, working it into a fine tilth and incorporating a dressing of a general purpose fertilizer at 90 to 95g. per sq. m. (3oz. per sq. yd). Rake the soil level after gently firming, and sow the seeds evenly and thinly in rows 23 to 30cm. (9 to 12in.) apart and 2cm. (¾in.) deep. Some varieties of carrot are obtainable as pelleted seed, which renders thin sowing easier, so that plant thinning may not be necessary.

In sheltered gardens in the south of England, carrots may be sown in February under protection, followed by outdoor sowings in March. These can be followed by further monthly sowings according to requirements up to the end of July, except in very late, cold areas. Some gardeners do not sow in April and May and thereby avoid attacks of the carrot willow aphid.

The crop should be kept clear of weeds by careful hoeing and thinning of the plants, carried out when the rough leaf has appeared. Short varieties should be left at 5cm. (2in.) apart, intermediate at 10cm. (4in.). Evenings are the best time for this operation or a dull day, particularly if it is showery. Firm the soil afterwards and apply water if necessary; these precautions are required to defeat carrot fly.

Carrots are much appreciated as young tender roots so early sowings should be pulled as soon as a usable size has been attained. Those for winter storage should be lifted in October, loosening the roots with a fork so as not to cause damage. Twist or cut off the foliage, discarding any damaged or diseased roots. Store in sand or soil in boxes or against the wall in a cool, frost-proof shed. Where such accommodation is lacking, an outdoor clamp can be made, stacking the roots in pyramidal form, and covering with a layer of straw and soil. In districts where more favourable climatic conditions prevail and the soil does not become too wet, July sowings may continue to be lifted as required. If severe weather threatens, cover with some bracken or straw.

PESTS
Aphids and carrot fly.

DISEASES
Violet root rot.

Cauliflower

This biennial brassica, usually grown as an annual, is one of our most popular vegetables. An important vegetable commercially, much work has been done by breeders in different parts of the world resulting in several strains and a wide range

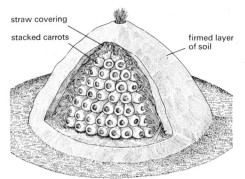

Storing carrots
Cross-section of outdoor clamp. Having cut off tops, carrots are stacked and covered with straw. The pyramid is then covered with soil, which is firmed.

straw covering
stacked carrots
firmed layer of soil

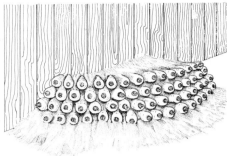

Carrots stored in sand against inside wall of shed.

of cultivars which ensure supplies most of the year. Some of these cultivars are available to amateur gardeners who will benefit from their better quality curds.

Cauliflowers may be divided into 4 groups, summer cauliflower which is ready for cutting from late May to July, autumn cauliflower, from late July to December, winter cauliflower, frequently called broccoli, and sometimes confused with sprouting broccoli, from January to May, and Roscoff cauliflower which is much more specialized and can only be grown in the mild coastal areas of south west England.

Summer cauliflower is a demanding crop to grow and is only worth planting in a highly fertile soil which is either unlikely to dry out or can be irrigated. The soil should be deeply dug in autumn, enriched with farmyard manure or compost and, if required, given a dressing of ground chalk or limestone. A dressing of a general purpose fertilizer worked in by hoe or rake just before planting should ensure the plants are not short of nutrients. If after planting growth appears slow, a light dressing of a nitrogenous fertilizer sulphate of ammonia or nitrate of soda at 30–35g. per sq. m. (2oz. per sq. yd) will accelerate growth. Cauliflower cultivars in this group may be sown up to late September or early October, pricked out about 10cm. (4in.) apart in a cold frame, hardened off in spring and planted out when danger of frost is over. Where a limited number of plants are required, they may be pricked off in 9cm. (3½in.) pots or soil blocks, thus ensuring less root disturbance and the chance of producing small premature heads or buttons. Cauliflowers occasionally produce 'blind' plants which, lacking a growing tip, are useless and must be discarded. These seem less likely to result from spring sowing, which can be carried out in January or February where autumn sowing is impractical. Sow in a frame or greenhouse in a temperature of 10°C. (50°F.) and prick off into small pots or the more modern containers.

Harden off the plants and transfer to the cropping quarter in late March, if you have a very sheltered garden, or April. Transplant at 46 to 60cm. (18 to 24in.) apart either way and plant firmly. Regular hoeing keeps down weeds and the curds, when seen, can be protected by breaking down a couple of leaves over them.

Autumn cauliflower requires similar cultural conditions to the summer group but the seeds are sown in a well prepared seed bed from the end of April to mid-May. Later sowing around mid-May is considered to reduce the incidence of blindness, particularly in Australian raised cultivars. Plant out at 60cm. (2ft) apart either way.

Winter cauliflower is not reliably hardy in exposed northern gardens in very severe winters, but survives normal winters, especially when grown on firm soil. Thus it is usual to plant on soil where a previous crop, such as peas, has been hoed off but which has not been disturbed by cultivation. A 2 to 1 mixture of superphosphate and sulphate of potash should be applied and hoed in before transplanting at 90 to 95g. per sq. m. (3oz. per sq. yd). Dressings of nitrogen should not be applied to this crop, as soft growth is apt to suffer damage in severe winters.

Seeds should be sown in a seed bed mid-April to mid-May and transplanted at least 60cm. (2ft) either way as ground becomes available in June and July. Puddling in may be necessary in hot dry weather. The roots are dipped in a slurry of soil and water and then planted firmly with a dibber. Hoeing to keep down weeds is desirable but once established, the crop must be grown hard to come through the winter, so heavy applications of water should not be made.

PESTS
Birds, cabbage root fly and flea beetle.

DISEASES
The same as cabbage, and also club root and damping off.

Celeriac

A biennial in which the roots have been bred by selection rather than the leaf-stalks, so much so that it is often called turnip-rooted celery. It is not very popular in the UK although it is easier to grow than celery, if soil is well enriched. It is really a root vegetable with a similar flavour to celery, though the tops are edible if cooked.

Celeriac is a crop which appreciates good cultivation so that the addition of manure or compost is indispensable, unless a good dressing has been given for the previous crop. In such a case a supplementary dressing of a good general fertilizer at 60 to 70g. per sq. m. (2oz. per sq. yd) will be advantageous to the crop. An open sunny site is best, unshaded by buildings or trees.

Seeds should be sown in March as advised for celery, the seedlings transferred to a cold frame, and hardened off and planted out in May or early June in cold districts. Plant out at 30cm. (12in.) between the plants, 46cm. (18in.) between the rows, taking care not to bury the plants, and firm them well.

Summer cultivation consists of keeping the plants clear of weeds, ensuring adequate moisture in dry weather and the removal of side shoots as they appear. The latter, if allowed to develop, spoil the shape of the roots. Some of the older leaves may also be removed as the roots develop. The roots may be lifted for use as required until the danger of frost arises, or by November, when they should be lifted and stored. Celeriac stores well in sand or peat in a dry shed after leaves have been removed.

PESTS AND DISEASES
The same as celery although celeriac is not so liable to attack.

Celery

A hardy biennial European native and an important commercial crop grown in areas with peaty soil and a high water table, thus ensuring the plants never suffer from moisture stress. The soil must also be very fertile, achieved by the addition of well rotted farmyard manure and a complete fertilizer. Few gardens can provide these conditions but the good cultivation necessary to grow celery successfully provides almost ideal conditions for following crops which benefit from deep cultivation.

Celery requires a trench at least 46cm. (15in.) wide and 30cm. (12in.) deep. Work a good layer of manure or compost into the bottom, returning the soil so that it comes to within 8 to 10cm. (3 to 4in.) of ground level. It is easier to grow only one row of plants in each trench; if more than one is required, 1.2m. (4ft) of space from centre to centre will be necessary for earthing up.

Seed should be thinly sown in March in a pot in a greenhouse or propagating frame where a temperature of 15.6°C. (60°F.) is available. When fit to handle, prick off the seedlings in boxes. Remove to a cold frame when established, where they should be hardened off for planting late in May. A later sowing in late March or early April may be pricked out in a frame or under a cloche to provide a successional supply. Celery seedlings should never be allowed to suffer from lack of water. Sowing too early and dryness result in plants bolting. Seed which has been treated against *Septoria* (celery leafspot) should be obtained. Alternatively, plants may be bought from a local nursery, although this restricts one's choice of cultivar.

Plants should be lifted with as many roots as possible after a good watering the previous day, and planted from 20 to 25cm. (8 to 10in.) apart unless required for show purposes when 30cm. (12in.) will be necessary. Unless weather is showery settle the plants in well with a good watering, and water generously in dry summer weather. When established, a light dressing of superphosphate up to 65 to 70g. per sq. m. (2oz. per sq. yd) will help the plants along. Bad leaves and side growths should be removed from the base of the plants and a loose tie under the leaves helps to keep the stems together. Earthing up is necessary to blanch celery, otherwise it is inedible. This should not be commenced until the plants

are over 30cm. (12in.) high and it is often a good plan to have a clearing attack on slugs beforehand. Only 15cm. (6in.) of soil should be applied, taking care that none gets into the centre of the plant. Some gardeners tie round a piece of black polythene or sheet of newspaper to prevent this. A second earthing will be required about 3 weeks later and then the final one, which, if the process started in mid-August, will take place in October. 6 weeks are generally required for thorough blanching before the crop can be used. Some protection with straw or bracken may be required in severe weather to keep the crop as long as possible.

Ridges should be sloped away neatly at the final earthing, covering up all the stems but not the leaves. This will ensure that rain runs off the ridge, rather than into it, therefore preventing heart rot.

Self-blanching celery has become very popular as, although it may not attain the quality of blanched celery, it provides an earlier crop without the labour of making trenches and earthing up. Fertile soil is required for this crop too, so a generous application of well rotted manure or compost is required and should be well dug in. If sown too early, this type is apt to bolt. Therefore, sow towards end of March, prick off seedlings in boxes and harden off in a cold frame.

Plant out in late May or early June, retaining all possible roots. A trowel is more suitable for planting than a dibber. Single row planting is not advisable for this type of celery, so plant in a block with 23cm. (9in.) between the plants either way. Self-blanching celery must not suffer from lack of moisture, so thorough weekly soakings are necessary unless the weather is wet. Basal growth should be removed, and some straw tucked in around the plants around the outside of the block assists blanching. Being less hardy than trench celery, this crop should be used as soon as ready and will be at its best in August and September.

PESTS
Celery fly, leaf miner, slugs and snails.
DISEASES
Celery leaf spot.

Chervil

An annual with a short life formerly grown in large private gardens where its flavour, suggestive of aniseed, was valued as a flavouring for soups and salads. As these gardens have declined so has the culture of chervil in the UK but it is still popular in continental countries. It can be sown *in situ* during August and September in a sunny spot for use during winter. For summer use it may be sown from February to April in a shady border which should be kept moist in hot dry weather, when it is apt to run quickly to seed. Sow in rows 30cm. (12in.) apart, thinning seedlings to a few centimetres apart.
PESTS AND DISEASES
Generally trouble-free.

Chicory

A hardy European perennial which grows wild in many parts of England and is conspicuous because of its beautiful blue flowers. Generally found in areas of chalky soil, it is sometimes grown in gardens as an ornamental plant. In continental Europe the cultivated forms of this plant have been developed for use in salad.

Chicory is grown as a biennial, and should be sown in early June in northern gardens, and mid-June in southern areas, lifting the roots in autumn from October to mid-November and inducing next year's growth. This must be done in complete darkness for the Witloof types which produce the 'chicons' frequently seen in good greengrocers during winter and spring.

This is an easily grown crop on any reasonably fertile soil which preferably should have been manured for a previous crop. The seeds should be sown thinly in drills 1.3cm. (½in.) deep and 30cm. (12in.) apart, thinning the seedlings to 25cm. (10in.) apart when fit to handle, or sow in stations at this distance and reduce to single plants. Keeping weeds under control by hoeing and cutting out flowering stems should any appear is the only necessary cultivation in summer. In light soils, irrigation may be required in periods of drought and a mulch will also assist.

When lifting time arrives, the roots should be heeled in, covering with soil to prevent freezing. Forcing can be done by lifting roots as required, cuttings off the tops within an inch of the crown, and cutting back the tap root also so as to be more convenient for placing in pots or boxes. Place the roots close together with fairly moist soil or peat as packing and place in a shed, greenhouse or convenient place indoors where the temperature will be around 10 to 13°C. (50 to 55°F.). Absolute darkness is essential and this can be assured if you have a deep box in which you can cover up the crowns completely with peat or sand to a depth of 15 to 18cm. (6 to 7in.). The 'chicons' will be ready to use when 15 to 20cm. (6 to 8in.) long, that is when the tips can be seen breaking through, when they should be broken off when required.

Sometimes secondary chicons or leaves are produced, and although inferior in size are useful salad material.

'Chicons' can be produced *in situ* on a well drained site by cutting back the tops in September and covering with a ridge of soil, naturally a much slower method, and one which may interfere with cultivation but produces a good quality crop.

One of the difficulties of growing blanched Witloof chicory is to persuade it to make those close fat buds or 'chicons'. Too often the leaves splay out and are only fit for salad. One way is to plant the roots in a pot of sand, fill another pot of the same size with sand, place a piece of cardboard over it, invert it and place it on top of the pot containing the roots. Then the cardboard is pulled out. One must by experience learn to judge when the 'chicons' have grown large enough to cut because once the pot of sand is removed, it cannot be replaced.

New cultivars are now available which make 'chicon' production easier and cleaner as no covering soil is required. Sow April to May; thin to 3in (8cm).
PESTS AND DISEASES
Generally trouble-free.

Chili Pepper, Sweet Pepper, Capsicum

Natives of South America, which are grown as annuals, although some may be perennial in hot tropical countries. Commonly known as 'sweet' peppers, these have been popular for a long time in many countries and have become more so in recent years in the UK.

This is a crop which requires a long growing season, so early sowing is necessary. March is the most suitable month, and a greenhouse or propagating frame which can maintain a temperature of 16 to 18°C. (60 to 65°F.) is required. Sowing may be direct into small pots, soil blocks or in a seedtray, using John Innes Seed Compost or a soilless compost. In the latter case the seedlings will have to be pricked off into pots or soil blocks when 2 or 3 leaves have formed. Cultivation afterwards depends on whether the crop is to be grown in pots or planted out under protection; the plants do well under large barn cloches, especially if planted in trenches.

Plants to be grown in pots must be potted on before becoming pot-bound, into 18 or 20cm. (7 or 8in.) pots, using a good compost such as John Innes 3. Towards the end of May the plants will not require artificial heat, especially in warmer areas, and should receive a daily syringing in hot weather. A moist atmosphere should be maintained to discourage red spider mite. A short stake is generally necessary and some growers pinch off the early flowers. Feeding with a liquid fertilizer every week, after fruits commence swelling, is very beneficial. The fruits of 'sweet peppers' are usually used when green so can be picked at that stage.

Chilis, or hot peppers, may be grown in smaller pots; 13cm. (5in.) are suitable, especially if required for ornamental purposes. In this case the fruits which may be red or yellow are allowed to ripen. Chilis for culinary purposes are used in curry, pickles or sauces and, if required for chili vinegar, are used when green.

Good results have been obtained commercially by planting out capsicums under glass, or protecting them by cloches or polythene tunnels. The two latter methods are convenient for amateur growers who can plant out in May in sheltered areas and later in the month in exposed parts. This is a tender plant so it is imperative to avoid the check which frost would impose. In sheltered gardens it is possible to plant out of doors in June, but in general most gardeners will get better results from protecting this crop. Growing in a single row, under cloches, plants should be spaced 46cm. (18in.) apart. Eventually the cloches will have to be raised to clear the large bushy plants which can attain a height of 1 to 2m. (4ft.). In periods of drought care must be taken to ensure an adequate supply of moisture.

PESTS
Red spider mite and aphids.
DISEASES
Generally trouble-free.

Chives

A hardy perennial which has a very wide range in the northern hemisphere with considerable diversity of forms, some of which can attain a height of 60cm. (2ft). It has been grown throughout Europe for many years and imparts a mild onion flavour to soups and salads. In Scotland, chives are used to flavour mashed potatoes as they get past their prime in May and June.

A plant that will grow easily in most soils provided it has adequate moisture. Chives can be grown from seeds sown in March or April but quicker results are obtained by dividing the clumps of narrow, pencil-like bulbs. This can be done in spring or autumn, planting the small clumps in rows 30cm. (12in.) apart with 15cm.

(6in.) between the plants. Division should take place every 3 years, otherwise the plants deteriorate and should be replanted on a fresh site.

Though evergreen, chives make a useful and pleasant edging to the herb or vegetable garden and are very decorative if allowed to flower. The close heads of rosy purple flowers are edible and look very much like common thrift (*Armeria maritima*). Chives can be grown in pots for bringing into the greenhouse for forcing, where early material is required, and these can also be placed on the window-sill. A window-box is another suitable site especially if chives are planted in good soil and not allowed to dry out.

PESTS
Generally trouble-free.
DISEASES
Rust.

Chives, Chinese

A convenient English name for a species of *Allium* which has been cultivated in China for two thousand years. Useful for the same culinary purposes as chives, this plant can be grown from seed. Unless the seed heads are cut off self-sown seedlings spring up in sufficient numbers to be a nuisance. The flower heads when fresh may be sprinkled in a salad.

PESTS
Generally trouble-free.
DISEASES
Rust.

Corn Salad, Lamb's Lettuce

A hardy annual native of Europe, one English name given because it is found growing wild in corn fields. The wild plant has been superseded by cultivated varieties which are useful for salad, especially in the winter months. Much more popular in Europe than in the UK. An easily grown plant which can be sown in mid-August, and up to the end of September if successional supplies are required. Sow in drills 15 to 23cm. (6 to 9in.) apart and thin to 10cm. (4in.) apart. A number of short growths are formed which can be cut off close to the base when required for salad. If preferred, separate leaves can be pulled off like spinach. If summer supplies are required sowings can be made from February onwards. In frosty weather the crop can be protected by a covering of straw or bracken.

PESTS AND DISEASES
Generally trouble-free.

Cress

An annual native of Persia, and a plant of very rapid growth which is grown and cut in the seed leaf stage for use as a salad. This is a crop of commercial importance, generally associated with mustard grown in the same way. It is not good practice to sow the two crops together as cress takes 3 or 4 days longer to germinate. Not much in demand in summer when plenty of other salad materials are readily available, it is most appreciated in the period between November and May. It can of course be grown all the year round but this is best done under protection as, if sown outdoors, either watering or rain will spoil the quality of the crop by spattering it with soil. Cress can be grown anywhere, especially where a temperature of 13°C. (55°F.) can be maintained in frame, greenhouse or even on a kitchen windowsill. However, continued production over

a period of time is a little more difficult and, for general purposes, best carried on in trays or boxes which can be filled with moist soil, bulb fibre or compost which has already been used for growing plants. Soil containing some humus to retain moisture is best while manures or fertilizers are unnecessary.

A depth of 5cm. (2in.) is ample over some drainage material and a fine even surface which should be made firm, smooth and level. Soak the soil before sowing; sow the seed evenly and give a light spray. Cover with a piece of wet hessian which should be sterilized with metaldehyde or by boiling. It should then be kept moist by a gentle spray. When the seedlings are over 2.5cm. (1in.) high remove the cover and expose to full light. Cut the crop when seed leaves are fully developed either with a sharp knife or scissors and use within 3 or 4 days. After cutting, discard the soil and make up afresh for the next crop.

PESTS AND DISEASES
Generally trouble-free.

Cress, American

A perennial native of Europe, and also known as land cress, which would seem a more appropriate name for a plant foreign to the American continent. It is useful for winter salads, with a flavour much like watercress but more pungent unless grown on very moist soil. It is also similar in appearance though somewhat smaller in leaf. I have found this crop most easily grown if sown in August or September in rows 23cm. (9in.) apart, thinning plants to around 10cm. (4in.). Remove the tops of the plants as required for salads, some 8 weeks after sowing. In warmer districts, this plant succeeds best in a shaded aspect.

PESTS
Flea-beetle, so cannot be recommended for late spring or summer cultivation.
DISEASES
Generally trouble-free.

Cucumber

A tender plant grown as an annual and credited as having originated in India or the East Indies. It produces fruits which are very popular, in particular for salads. Cucumbers can be divided into two types, the greenhouse or frame cucumber, which can only be grown with success when protected by glass, and the ridge cucumber. Ridge cucumbers generally have more knobbly or spiny skins and can be grown out of doors as they do not require the high temperatures and humid conditions required by the greenhouse type. The fruits of most cultivars of ridge cucumber are much shorter than the long, slim, greenhouse varieties but their flavour is similar.

For frame cucumbers, March is the best time to start seed sowing. The seeds are sown singly in 8cm. (3in.) pots, using a seed compost either John Innes or soilless. Press the seeds in on edge and place in a propagating frame in which a temperature of 18 to 21°C. (65 to 70°F.) can be maintained, when germination should take place in 3 days. When this occurs, transfer the plants to a shelf in full light still keeping a temperature of 15.6°C. (60°F.). Meantime, a bed should have been made up in the greenhouse with soil made rich in humus by the addition of strawy horse manure, if possible. Plant 60cm. (2ft) apart on a slight mound or in boxes or large pots if more convenient. Train the main stem vertically to a cane or string over horizontal wires fixed 25 to 40cm. (10 to 12in.) from the glass. When the plant reaches the top wire, it should be stopped by pinching to induce the development of side or lateral growths. These can be trained horizontally along the wires and stopped at 2 leaves. The fruits are produced on these side shoots, so stopping and loose tying to the wires requires a good deal of attention, as growth can be very rapid if the weather is warm. Some thinning may be necessary also to prevent overcrowding. This rapid growth creates a need for food and roots will appear on the surface. These should be lightly top dressed with a rich compost.

Cucumbers must never be allowed to suffer from lack of moisture at the roots, and occasional watering with a liquid fertilizer is helpful. Ventilation is only required in very hot weather when the temperature has soared above 27°C. (80°F.) and this can be obviated to some extent by light shading of the glass. Cucumbers revel in the steamy atmosphere which arises from high temperatures and damping down.

Cropping can be ensured if the fruits are cut before becoming too large; those surplus to requirements can be kept if placed in water, stem end downwards, in a cool shed.

Where heat is not available, seeds can be sown in late April and planted a month later in a cold house or in a frame. For frame cultivation it is best to place one plant in the centre of each light on a slight mound of good compost placed over a mixture of soil and compost or well rotted manure. Pinch out the growing point when 6 leaves have formed, so that side shoots are induced. Select the 4 best, removing any others at source and peg lightly so that they grow towards each corner, when the growing points should be removed.

Nowadays, some emphasis is attached to the removal of male flowers to prevent pollination and the resultant bitter fruits with seeds. I have never known this happen but I suppose the possibility exists if cucumbers are grown with tomatoes and ventilators are left open, allowing insects to enter. However modern hybrid cucumbers produce all female flowers so offending males or their pollen present no problem.

Ridge or outdoor cucumbers have become more popular with the introduction of new and improved varieties in recent years. Seeds can be sown as advised for frame cucumbers towards the end of April, for planting out towards the end of May or in early June. Ridge cucumbers require a warm situation, fertile soil and adequate moisture and may be something of a disappointment in a cold wet summer unless some protection can be given. Seeds may be sown *in situ* in sheltered gardens about mid-May. The ground should be well prepared in advance by adding plenty of humus in the form of compost, well rotted manure or peat. Holes can be taken out 30cm. (12in.) square at 90cm. (3ft) intervals, filled with compost and, after firming, covered with soil. 2 or 3 seeds can be sown at each of these stations, retaining the strongest plant in due course. Some protection by cloche or panes of glass will assist considerably in getting the plants well established. Where the gherkin cultivars are grown for pickling, a trench should be taken out 30cm. (12in.) wide, filled with compost and covered with soil; the seeds of this type can be sown at intervals of 60cm. (2ft). When the plant has produced 6 leaves, pinch out the growing tip to encourage the production of side growths. Further training is not required but moisture must be supplied in dry weather and this can be aided by mulching. Fruits can be kept clear of the soil by using tiles, pieces of slate or wood if considered necessary. Young plants should be watched for slugs, especially in showery weather. Fruits should be picked while young so as to ensure continued cropping. Gherkins in particular should be taken off when 8cm. (3in.) long.

PESTS
Red spider mite, especially under glass and woodlice.

DISEASES
Anthracnose, gummosis, root rot, grey mould and powdery mildew.

Dandelion

A hardy perennial native of Europe, more often regarded in the UK as a weed than as a vegetable. Many gardeners, especially on the continent, appreciate improved strains of this plant which have thicker, more succulent leaves. May be blanched for salad under an upturned flower pot which has had the drainage hole blocked or covered. The leaves may also be cooked. Sow the seeds in April in drills 30cm. (12in.) apart, thinning the plants down to 20cm. (8in.). In view of its gregarious habits, it is better to remove any flower heads which form. Carefully lift the roots in November, and trim and force as recommended for chicory, to get leaves in winter months. Any left on the growing site can be blanched again in spring under upturned pots.

PESTS AND DISEASES
Generally trouble-free.

Endive

A plant cultivated as an annual for some centuries but of unknown origin. Once cultivated for salad in late autumn and winter before the range of lettuce extended through the year. Its flavour has a distinctive touch of bitterness.

There are two groups of endive, those with curled leaves, also known as staghorns, and those with plain leaves, known as Batavian. Both require good, well drained, medium soil, well supplied with organic matter, to prevent moisture stress. A general fertilizer may be applied at 90 to 95g. per sq. m. (3oz. per sq. yd) some days previous to sowing. Sow in drills 30cm. (12in.) apart in June, for an early crop. The main crop should be sown in July or August at the same distance. The plants should be thinned to 30cm. (12in.) for curled varieties and 38cm. (15in.) for Batavian. Keep the ground between plants weeded until they close the rows. Water if necessary.

Endive must be blanched to be edible. Various methods may be used to exclude light, but only the number of plants required should be treated, for they must be used quickly when blanched. An easy method is to invert a sufficiently large flower pot over each plant; a tile placed over the drainage hole will exclude light. Curled cultivars should be used first, while Batavian, for a supply in winter, can be lifted with a ball of soil placed in deep boxes of soil and placed in a shed or a frame from which light is excluded. Lifting should be done before plants have been touched by frost.

PESTS AND DISEASES
Generally trouble-free.

Fennel

A graceful, feathery, hardy perennial and native of southern Europe which has now become naturalized in many parts of Europe including the UK. Growing up to 1.5m. (5ft) in height, it produces yellow flowers in flat umbels which are followed by seeds with an aniseed like flavour. The bronze leaved form is, also, a most decorative plant. Easily grown in a variety of conditions, as long as it receives some sun, it grows particularly well where drainage is good and moisture is available.

When well established self-sown seedlings appear, these may be used for establishing a new bed, planting about 46cm. (18in.) apart either way. When required for use in the kitchen, some stems should be cut back to encourage young growths, as these are better for flavouring purposes. Some gardeners remove the flower stems for the same purpose which precludes seedlings also.

PESTS AND DISEASES
Generally trouble-free.

Fennel, Florence

An annual plant of Italian origin, also known as finocchio, which grows to about 60cm. (2ft) and may be distinguished from the common fennel by its swollen stem bases. These are delicious cooked whole or sliced raw in salads, while the leaves may be used as those of common fennel.

Florence fennel prefers a sunny situation in light or sandy soil that is well drained and reasonably fertile. Before sowing the seeds *in situ* in April or May, work in a light dressing of a complete fertilizer. Sow seeds in shallow drills 50cm. (20in.) apart, thinning seedlings to 23 to 30cm. (9 to 12in.) when large enough to handle. Keep plants watered when growing, especially in dry weather.

As the stem bases begin to swell, they may be blanched by placing paper collars around them, though this is not essential. They may be gathered as required when large enough.

PESTS
Slugs.

DISEASES
Generally trouble-free.

Garlic

A hardy perennial and strongly flavoured member of the onion family held in considerable esteem by gourmets. Where used with discretion, garlic brings out the flavour of many other ingredients.

It is easily grown on any good garden soil, though it prefers light, well drained conditions, rather than heavy soils which become very hard in hot weather and impair the formation of the bulbs. The garlic bulb consists of several segments which are joined together at the base, and enclosed in a white papery skin. The segments usually separated for planting, may be planted in sheltered gardens in November but in February or March in more exposed areas. A sunny site should be selected and if the soil has been well cultivated and manured for a previous crop, the garlic should respond by producing large bulbs. Plant in rows 30cm. (12in.) apart with 15 to 20cm. (6 to 8in.) between segments. Planting may be done by a dibber or by taking out a drill, in either case 5 cm. (2in.) is sufficiently deep. Keep free of weeds during summer and harvest when the foliage turns yellow, generally late July or August, when weather is dry. Leave soil on the roots. Hang up the bulbs in the open air for sun, wind and rain to clean and polish them. Store them in a warm dry place, such as the bottom of an airing cupboard.

PESTS
Generally trouble-free
DISEASES
White rot.

Good King Henry, Mercury or Perennial Goosefoot

A hardy perennial and native of Europe. It was very popular at one time in Lincolnshire where it became known as Lincolnshire spinach.

A plant easily raised from seed sown in spring *in situ* where it may be thinned to 30cm. (12in.) apart or lifted from a seed bed and planted. When established in good soil it produces young growth, somewhat like kale in appearance but more like asparagus in flavour when cooked. A neglected vegetable in the UK but popular in Germany (where it is known as Gemeiner Gänsefuss).

PESTS AND DISEASES
Generally trouble-free.

Horseradish

A very hardy, perennial, European native which is grown for its long penetrating pungent roots, which in the main are used as a condiment.

Generally this plant is left to fend for itself in some neglected corner where it will grow very well and probably take over completely, however, where the condiment is especially appreciated it is worth growing better roots which show an improvement in flavour.

Young roots or thongs can be planted in good soil in March, 30cm. (12in.) apart either way. Roots with a single crown are best and should be at least 20cm. (8in.) long and straight. Some growers plant at an angle of 45°, although I have always put them in straight, and some inches down the dibber hole. Make firm and keep down weeds. Roots can be lifted in autumn and stored in sand for use when required. It is advisable to clear the bed every 2 years, removing as much of the root as possible.

PESTS
Generally trouble-free.
DISEASES
Leaf spot and white blister.

Kale, Curly or Borecole

Hardy biennials which are popular in northern areas and in the UK. This is indicated by the traditional synonyms which invariably call the curled type 'Scotch'. Curly Kale is valued in northern districts because of its ability to withstand the most severe winter weather; indeed some gardeners think its quality is improved by frost. It is often planted to follow potatoes and sometimes between the rows of maincrop potatoes. If following a crop which has been cleared, it is usually best to hoe through the soil and plant without making it loose by digging.

Seeds should not be sown too early: towards the end of April or even into May in southern gardens. Planting distances can vary according to cultivar, the plain leaved sprouting Kales will require 60cm. (2ft) apart either way, while the curled varieties can be planted a little closer

between the plants. Hoeing during the growing season to check weeds is generally the only cultivation required until March, when a light dressing of nitro-chalk 15 to 20g. per sq. m. (1oz. per sq. yd) will accelerate growth.

Kales would be more popular in the kitchen if the young growths were picked rather than the old tough leaves. Remove the growing point when a good supply of side growths appear in the leaf axils, these, being young and tender, will be more appetizing.

PESTS
Flea beetle.
DISEASES
Damping off and violet root rot.

Kohlrabi

A hardy biennial which finds more favour in some parts of the continent, such as Austria and Germany, than in the UK. A cabbage with a swollen bulb-like stem, it is very useful in hot dry summers where it is much easier to grow than the turnip. Although kohlrabi stands drought well, more succulent roots will be produced from soil in good heart, especially if well manured for a previous crop. Being a brassica, it appreciates lime. A useful plant for catchcropping where its nutty flavour finds favour. It may be sown from early April to early August either in rows 38cm. (15in.) apart or in a seed bed for transplanting. Thin out or transplant at 25cm. (10in.) apart and hoe when required, taking care not to damage the stems and young bulbs. The plants should be pulled for use as required but should never be allowed to get beyond golf ball size. It is unfortunate that kohlrabi does not really store well, though it may be kept in peat for a few weeks. A late sowing of the purple-skinned cultivar can be left *in situ* all winter, for use until spring.

PESTS AND DISEASES
Generally trouble-free.

Leek

A hardy biennial, it has been the national emblem of Wales since the sixth century. It is popular in the northern parts of the UK, its hardiness making it valuable in severe weather, while production is simple in any reasonable soil.

Leeks, although easily grown, will thrive when planted on deeply dug soil which has been well manured for the previous crop. For culinary purposes, leeks are generally planted where an earlier crop has been cleared during the current season. Exhibitors and those who require early supplies, generally sow under glass in January or February, but for kitchen use, an outdoor sowing on a seed bed in March or April will suffice. The earlier sowing should produce larger plants; a great advantage when transplanting. This will take place in late June when ground has been cleared and levelled, after a light forking. If weather is dry the seed bed should be soaked before the plants, which should be around 20cm. (8in.) in height, are lifted with a fork. Lift carefully, discard any weaklings, and lightly trim the plants, taking off long roots so the plants drop easily into the holes, and leaf tips, to prevent worms pulling them into the soil. Plant in rows 23cm. (9in.) apart with at least 30cm. (12in.) between the rows in holes 15cm. (6in.) deep made with a dibber. Lower a plant in each hole, but do not fill with soil; just let some water trickle in from a can. This will anchor the plant and give it

a start. Some gardeners take out a deep drill and plant 23cm. (9in.) apart, drawing soil up to the plants when hoeing. Others, who prefer small leeks, sow thinly in rows as in a seed bed and do not transplant, but pull up soil to the plants to blanch the stems. Regular hoeing to aerate the soil and keep down weeds should be attended to, taking care not to nick the plants. In dry weather the plants will benefit greatly from a good watering, especially if enriched with a liquid fertilizer. Leeks, being exceptionally hardy, can be left where growing and dug up as needed unless the ground is required, when they should be dug up and heeled in behind a north wall or hedge.

PESTS
Thrips, in warm, dry areas.
DISEASES
Rust.

Lettuce

An annual which has been credited with various countries of origin. Nowadays there is a wealth of cultivars and, where glass is available, good management and selection enable the gardener to produce lettuce all the year round. The numerous cultivars may for practical purposes be grouped into types as the cabbage type, cos type and the leaf or non-hearting type.

The cabbage type can be divided further into butterhead cultivars, curly crisp cultivars, forcing cultivars and those hardy enough to withstand winter outdoors.

Good lettuce can only be grown on soil which is rich in organic matter and has been well cultivated by deep digging during autumn or winter. It is essential that the soil should not dry out rapidly as the plants require moisture continuously, in order to heart up well. Lettuces are apt to bolt quickly otherwise. In practice, lettuces are required regularly, particularly in hot summer weather, so it is often convenient to make small sowings as catch crops between other crops where sufficient room is available. If your soil is in good heart and been left rough it should be broken down and levelled, working in a general purpose fertilizer at 90 to 95g. per sq. m. (3oz. per sq. yd), preferably some days before sowing or planting. Frequently in gardens production of lettuce is wasteful because of excessive and infrequent sowings. Drills 1.3cm. ($\frac{1}{2}$in.) deep should be drawn 30cm. (12in.) apart, and, if small sowings sufficient to cater for requirements are made fortnightly, wastage can be cut out. The first outdoor sowings can be made early in March, as soon as a good tilth can be produced, and continued up to the end of July. When the first true pair of leaves are formed, the seedlings should be thinned according to the cultivar. 'Little Gem', for example, requires 13cm. (5in.) or so, whereas 'Webb's Wonderful' requires 30cm. (12in.). Pelleted lettuce seed is available which makes thin sowing and singling much easier. In April, transplanting thinned seedlings can be done successfully in moist weather, from the earliest sowings. Later on, especially in warmer areas, transplanting is a waste of time, as the plants invariably bolt instead of hearting up. It is quite possible to produce lettuce earlier if a sowing can be made in a cool greenhouse or frame in mid-February when, after hardening off, planting out may be done towards the end of March.

Even earlier supplies can be obtained by sowing thinly under cloches in January in sheltered gardens or February in colder conditions, thinning the plants in due course. The winter hardy lettuces can be useful for filling a gap in the supply but are rather coarse when compared with other types. They are not suitable for sowing in spring or summer but very successful crops may be produced by planting and overwintering with the protection of cold frames. In reasonably sheltered gardens, seeds should be sown towards the end of August or early in September in drills 30cm. (12in.) apart. Thin during October. If lifted carefully, the thinnings can be transplanted about 23cm. (9in.) apart. A nitrogenous fertilizer applied in March along the row 14g. (½oz.) per dozen plants will hasten growth considerably.

The production of lettuce under glass in winter, now a very important branch of commercial horticulture, requires facilities and techniques beyond the range of the amateur gardener, who, however, can grow lettuce in a heated house during winter, if sufficient room is available at temperatures of 15.6°C. (60°F.) by day and 10°C. (50°F.) by night. Seed is usually sown in trays from September to December and pricked off into soil blocks or peat pots, which, when rooted through, are placed in the soil bed 2.5cm. (1in.) or so deep and 20 to 25cm. (8 to 10in.) apart. Careful watering is required, and, as a rule, this is better applied to the roots than over the plant, but the soil must be kept reasonably moist. Some cultivars also do well grown in polythene tunnels.

Cultivation in frames is quite feasible for some amateur gardeners, and, as for outside cultivation, the soil should be well supplied with organic matter. The old, well-tried cultivar 'May King', can be sown early in August outside and transplanted 30cm. (12in.) each way in the frame. Small sowings in October and February in pots in the frame may be transplanted to give headed lettuces in spring.

Cos lettuces are especially popular, and modern cultivars are self-folding, so the practice of tying is no longer necessary. The larger growers require at least 30cm. (12in.) either way, but 'Little Gem' will succeed very well with 13cm. (5in.) between plants.

The non-hearting or American types such as 'Salad Bowl' may be sown from early April to July, removing a few leaves from each plant at any one time as required.

PESTS
Root and other species of aphid, slugs, cutworms and other caterpillars.
DISEASES
Damping-off, downy mildew, grey mould and certain viruses.

Marrow

A popular half-hardy annual of unknown origin which is easily grown in moist, humus-rich soil, well supplied with moisture and sited in a sunny position. Grown mainly in the open by amateurs, commercial growers produce early crops under protection in considerable quantities.

There are 2 types of marrow, bush and trailing, the former being more useful for small gardens, especially if early fruits are required as it is suitable for frame or cloche cultivation.

If the ground where marrows are to be grown was dug over in winter, it is advisable to mark stations for the bush plants 90cm. (3ft) either way. Take some soil out and fill up with manure or compost, digging it in well before replacing the soil on top and marking it with a stick. Plants may be grown in pots or soil blocks, and sown during the second or third week in April in a heated greenhouse. These should be hardened off and planted towards the end of May when severe frost should no longer be a danger. If this is inconvenient, good crops may be grown by direct sowing in early May. Place 2 or 3 seeds on their edge about 2.5cm. (1in.) deep, removing the weaker plants so as to leave 1 at each station in due course. An inverted pot may be used to protect the small plants from frost at night; this should be removed in the morning. Trailing marrows may be accommodated if desired; it is really a matter of siting. The wigwam method, whereby seeds are sown in stations about 75cm. (2½ft) apart each way and grown up supports, is useful in small gardens. Another method is to plant or sow trailing marrows outside maincrop potatoes and allow the plants to trail up between the rows. A fence may be used also with perhaps an occasional tie to keep the plant in place. The compost heap is another suitable place for planting and the plants will do well if not allowed to dry out. Little attention is required during summer as weeds are generally smothered by the foliage, but watering will be necessary in very dry weather. Fruits should be kept picked when they attain 20cm. (8in.) in length by twisting off carefully to keep the plants fruiting. However, where fruits are wanted for storage, allow some to attain full size. When properly ripened they can be hung up in a dry, frost-proof shed. When marrows are grown under protection, hand pollination may be necessary to ensure fruits. Outside, pollination is done by insects. The female flower can be recognized by the embryo fruit behind the flower. This is absent in the male. Inside, pollination is done by picking a male flower, removing the petals and pushing the pollen covered core into the centre of the female flower.

Courgettes require the same conditions as marrows but cultivars especially suitable for producing small fruits in quantity have been bred and should be grown for this purpose. These cultivars can be grown more closely, about 60cm. (2ft) apart between plants and production can be advanced by cloche protection in the early stages of growth. The fruits should be picked when from 10 to 15cm.(4 to 6in.) in length. This must be done regularly as fruits allowed to grow will just be ordinary marrows. The plants must be kept watered; liquid manure will assist greatly in keeping up production.

PESTS
Slugs.
DISEASES
Cucumber mosaic virus, grey mould and powdery mildew.

Mint

Hardy perennial herb with strongly aromatic foliage having a strong association with new potatoes and green peas, while mint sauce is a traditional accompaniment in the UK to lamb. Several species and varieties are grown of which spearmint is probably the most popular in the UK.

Plants do not thrive in dry conditions, so when a new bed is made, the soil should be deeply dug and organic matter added. If the plants grow well the bed can remain for 3 to 4 years. Young plants for a new bed can be grown from divisions or cuttings. The easiest method is to remove young stems from the outside of the bed and dibble these in the newly prepared bed 23cm. (9in.) apart either way with the growing point just under soil level. This can be done in February or March and the bed kept clear of weeds, especially in the first year.

Where mint is required in winter some plants can be lifted, placed in large pots or a box, covered with soil, put in a glasshouse with a temperature of 15 to 16°C (60°F.) and kept reasonably moist. Mint can also be grown in a container placed in a position handy for the kitchen. In the garden of limited space it may be necessary to curb its spreading habit by growing in a bottomless container, such as an old dustbin, raised a few inches above soil level. Spearmint, *Mentha spicata* is not known to occur as a wild plant but believed to be the result of a cross between *M. longifolia*, the horse mint and *M. suaveolens*, the round-leaved mint. A very vigorous herbaceous perennial, it produces long invasive runners, especially if grown in good soil which is also moist. Spearmint should be cut back regularly to encourage flowerless growths from the roots; cut back stems in late autumn and top dress with some old well-matured compost or manure.

Bowles mint, *Mentha × villosa alopecuroides*, is known under various names, French mint, apple mint, round-leaved mint, fan-tail mint, woolly mint or *Mentha rotundifolia* 'Bowles' variety. It is a plant of rampant growth even on dry soils where it grows better than other mints and can attain a height of 90cm. (3ft). The large, 8cm. (3in.) leaves are almost round in shape, very woolly and are more resistant to rust than spearmint.

PESTS
Generally trouble-free.
DISEASES
Rust.

Mushroom

The growing of mushrooms, despite the scientific advances of recent years, remains an unpredictable business. A visit to the horticulture section of a good library will inform you that books have been devoted to the culture of this crop, so only general guidance can be given in this work.

Mushrooms do not require daylight so can be grown in a cellar, garage or shed where a temperature of around 10 to 13°C. (50 to 55°F.) can be maintained. Making up the compost in which mushroom spawn is planted is the most time consuming part of the operation unless prepared compost is bought. Formerly compost was made from stable manure, but today if you are able to get fresh horse manure this will have to be augmented by using wheat straw, as this composts best. If you cannot get horse manure you will have to use one of the proprietary activators. Soak the straw thoroughly with water until it reaches saturation point. Make a 15cm. (6in.) layer of the shaken out straw, sprinkling the activator on top, and adding further layers with activator. Add horse manure or dry poultry manure if possible, as this improves the quality of the compost. The compost heats up in a few days when the heap should be turned, bringing the outside to the middle, and vice versa, shaking the straw as you do so, and adding water where the straw has dried out. Gypsum may be added at this stage, 1 part by weight to 100 parts of straw; this prevents the compost turning sticky. Two more turnings at weekly intervals will be necessary to bring it into a brown friable condition, without any objectionable smell, and moist without being wet. Take the temperature with a soil thermometer, which, if below 27°C. (80°F.) will be ready for making up the bed or putting in boxes or trays. Where boxes are being used, make the compost firm by pressing it down with a brick to an even depth of 23cm. (9in.). The temperature may rise at first but when it drops back to 21 to 24°C. (70 to 75°F.), the mushroom spawn should be inserted 5cm. (2in.) into the compost, 23 or 25cm. (9 or 10in.) apart. The spawn should be broken up into 2cm. (¾in.) pieces. Grain spawn, generally scattered on the surface, is becoming more popular, though it is best used when some experience has been gained.

The compost should not be watered; the surface can be kept moist by covering with black polythene. In a week's time the mycelium should be developing through the compost, and in another week's time, soiling or casing can be done. This is a 4 to 5cm. (1½ to 2in.) cover of sterilized soil which should not be firmed but should be moist. If moisture is required, only sufficient to moisten the casing should be applied through a fine rose, so as to avoid water penetrating into the compost. In a few weeks mushrooms should begin to appear and when large enough should be picked with an upward twisting movement. If holes are left, fill with some casing soil. When thriving, mushrooms often produce in flushes at weekly intervals and continue to do so for two months when the exhausted compost can be removed. This is valuable material for mulching or building up the organic matter in the soil. Boxes must be disinfected before further use; indeed everything connected with the growing of this crop must be kept scrupulously clean.

PESTS
Mushroom flies.

DISEASES
Unhygienic conditions may cause mushroom diseases.

Mustard

An annual, native of Europe, and a plant of very rapid growth. Seeds are white, so that this plant is usually known as white mustard and grown and cut in the seed leaf stage for salad, in the same manner as cress. Cultivation is identical, except that mustard should be sown 3 or 4 days later. Frequency of sowing should of course be allied to requirements. Brown mustard, *Brassica juncea*, is not recommended, being rather hot.

PESTS AND DISEASES
Generally trouble-free.

Onion

A biennial bulbous plant of unknown origin. Growing large exhibition onions requires a high state of fertility which is kept up by using a permanent bed enriched annually for the purpose. Arguments arise in consequence, some considering this a dangerous practice because of disease and pests. The solution is quite simple: if you like to produce large onions, grow them in a permanent bed until it becomes troublesome. I know of one which has been producing wonderful onions for over half-a-century. Large onions are criticized also, generally by people who have never grown them, as unfit to eat, in fact they can be of better flavour than many small onions.

Onions should be grown on an open sunny site, preferably on a medium type loam; heavy soil will require good cultivation to assist drainage, while light sandy soils will require moisture-holding organic matter. Cultivation should be carried out in the autumn by deep digging, incorporating a good dressing of farmyard manure or compost. Leave the soil as rough as possible on the surface, dressing with lime if it is found to be on the acid side. In February, the bed can be prepared by forking, treading to make it firm and raking to make it as level as possible. Before sowing or planting, a fertilizer dressing may be worked in, being careful to avoid highly nitrogenous formulas. A dressing of 3 parts superphosphate to 1 part sulphate of potash applied at 120 to 125g. per sq. m. (4 oz. per sq. yd) or a proprietary fertilizer low in nitrogen should be applied before planting or sowing.

Sowing in spring should be undertaken as early in the season as it is possible to get a nice tilth – mid-February in southern gardens and up to the end of March in northern parts. Shallow drills under 2.5cm. (1in.) in depth should be drawn out 30cm. (12in.) apart. Sow the seeds thinly (pelleted seeds are an aid to this), cover and firm well.

Many gardeners like to sow onions in the autumn for planting in the spring, using cultivars specially suited for this purpose. This method is well suited for those with light soils apt to dry out in summer or where onion fly attacks are rife. In this case, sowings can be made in a seed bed which does not require a previous dressing of fertilizer and is sited in a sheltered place. The seedlings are left unthinned and lifted in early March, planting them 15cm. (6in.) apart in rows 30cm. (12in.) apart. Trowel planting is best, allowing room for the roots and ensuring the base of the onion is just under ground level. Sowing usually takes place in August; earlier in the month for northern gardens, later in those further south. For very early onions, Japanese cultivars are now available which, if sown in August, can be pulled in June and early July. These are not transplanted, so should not be sown in a seed bed. They should be sown in rows 30cm. (12in.) and thinned out to 5cm. (2in.) apart in spring. This type is unsuitable for sowing in spring.

Where manure is difficult to obtain and results from seed-sowing have proved unsatisfactory, onion sets are usually the answer, especially in cold northern gardens or where rainfall is high. These are immature bulbs which have had their growth interrupted while small. Plant on soil which has been prepared with a dressing of fertilizer as already recommended. Unpack the sets on arrival and spread out in a cool place until planting can take place in March or April 10 to 15cm. (4 to 6in.) apart in rows 30cm. (12in.) apart. Plant so that the tip of the bulb just appears. Onions from sets rarely suffer from attack by mildew or onion fly.

Some gardeners like to raise their plants under glass and should plant out as recommended for autumn sown onions but in mid-April, after the plants have been well hardened off.

Summer cultivation consists of hoeing carefully so as not to cause damage, and weeding by hand close to the plants. Sown onions should be thinned in stages, leaving the plants 10 to 15cm. (4 to 6in.) apart; the latter distance for 'Ailsa Craig' type onions. Thinnings may be used for salad, so should not be wasted. By August bulbs will show signs of ripening naturally, and this can be hastened by bending over any tops which remain upright. A fortnight later the bulbs may be loosened with a fork and lifted carefully, placing them in a sunny place, to dry off. When this has been achieved store them in a dry, cool, airy shed in flat-bottomed trays or polythene nets.

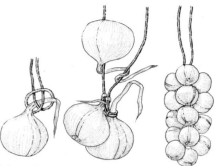

Tying onions.

If the onions have been made up into ropes or bunches, these can be hung up on the rafters of a shed.

—salad onions

While thinnings may be used for salads, it is necessary to cater for this requirement at other periods of the year by special sowings of a suitable cultivar such as 'White Lisbon'. This cultivar may be sown in March or April, or, in northern gardens, in mid-July, while further south, sowings may be made up to late August. From these, onions of pencil thickness can be pulled from March onwards. Onions for salad may be sown more thickly than those for bulb production, and it is usual to sow according to requirements when making the spring sowing, to extend the supply available from the autumn sowing.

Where it is desired to pickle onions the best results will be obtained by sowing the small, white, Silverskin type of onion for this purpose. Small onions of any type can be pickled, but will not be of such fine appearance or so mild in flavour. A soil of moderate fertility is best and the seeds should be broadcast on a bed, not more than 90cm. (3ft) in width, and kept clear of weeds. Cover the seeds lightly; do not thin the seedlings. Seed may be sown in March and the onions harvested when large enough in July.

PESTS
Onion fly maggots and onion eelworm.

DISEASES
Neck rot, onion mildew, onion smut and white rot.

Onion, Ever-Ready

This has been much confused with the Welsh onion *Allium fistulosum*. Like chives, but much stronger in growth and more pungent in flavour, this is an easily grown plant. Dense tufts are formed which can be split up at any time, except during very dry weather, and replanted. Planted in good soil, growth is very rapid, so plenty of onion flavoured foliage is available. Flowers are seldom seen on this plant.

PEA 37

PESTS AND DISEASES
Generally trouble-free.

Onion, Tree
The tree onion is an interesting variation in the onion family which produces small, extremely pungent bulbs instead of flowers on the top of hollow stems. The plant may be propagated by these as the stems, if left unsupported, bend over and the bulbs soon start to root where they touch the soil. Propagation can also be done by division of the underground bulbs, although it is easier to insert the whole clump of top bulbs 30cm. (12in.) apart. The small onions can be picked as required for use or for pickling.
PESTS AND DISEASES
Generally trouble-free.

Onion, Welsh
This hardy plant, also known as the Japanese bunching onion and onion leek, has been much confused in the UK with the ever-ready onion, *A. cepa* var. *perutile*. This has occurred to such an extent that the latter plant is generally supplied if the Welsh onion is ordered. The Welsh onion flowers freely, producing blooms which open first on the apex of the flower head. These produce seed each year, after which the plant dies back, to reappear again early in the following year. The leaves are tubular.
PESTS AND DISEASES
Generally trouble-free.

Parsley
A biennial herb, native of Sardinia and said to have been in cultivation for nearly 500 years. It is now extensively cultivated and can also be grown in window boxes.

This plant succeeds best on fertile, well drained soil, and is frequently grown in conjunction with onions, in the belief that it wards off onion fly.

Where an early supply is required, a sowing under glass in February in a temperature of 13°C. (55°F.) will provide seedlings which can be pricked off in boxes or Jiffy pots. Duly hardened off, these should be planted out in April. Parsley is much used in some households in small quantities, so it is a good idea to plant in a handy position for picking, not too far away from the kitchen. Where, however, the precaution of a second outside sowing in July has been taken and some of the plants protected with a cloche, the early sowing of the plants may not be so important. The first outdoor sowing should be made late in March or early in April, and as germination is exceedingly slow (6 weeks is quite common) it is sensible to drop a few seeds of radish into the drills before covering. They germinate quickly in the rows and indicate where weed seeds are germinating so that they can be removed before they interfere with the parsley seedlings that come up later. Thin the seedlings in due course to 15cm. (6in.) apart, removing every second plant as they close up, to prevent overcrowding. Keep the plants clear of weeds and see that they do not dry out in periods of drought. A light dressing of a nitrogenous fertilizer should be applied when watering or in showery weather. Constant picking as required, by taking a few outside leaves from each plant, is a better practice than denuding a single plant at one time.

Being a biennial, parsley runs quickly to seed in its second year, especially from the March to April sowing and the plants are best removed when this occurs. The later July sowing should keep a supply going until the next crop is ready, but if any flower stems form, remove them. Parsley is sometimes dried in a hot oven and rubbed down for winter use. Surplus leaves can be deep frozen for use in times of scarcity; better colour is retained by this method.
PESTS
Maggots of carrot and celery fly.
DISEASES
Generally trouble-free.

Parsley, Hamburg Turnip-Rooted
Known generally in the UK as Hamburg parsley, this vegetable has attained more popularity on the continent, particularly in Germany where it is known as 'Hamburger Schnitt'. Seeds should be sown in late March or early April in drills 64mm. (¼in.) in depth and 36cm. (15in.) apart. Seeds may be sown in stations 23cm. (9in.) apart and the seedlings in each thinned to 1 when large enough to handle. Like other root crops cleaner, better shaped, more useful roots are produced when grown on soil manured for a previous crop. The roots resemble small parsnips in colour and shape. The foliage, more parsley-like in appearance, remains on the plant during the winter and can be used for flavouring.

In Germany, the roots are boiled but they can also be grated raw and used in salads.
PESTS
Carrot fly maggots.
DISEASES
Canker.

Parsnip
A hardy biennial, and a native of Europe which grows wild in the UK, this is essentially a crop which should be grown on land manured for a previous crop. Deep digging is necessary; the parsnip is a deep-rooted plant but shorter rooted varieties are available and these may be grown where the soil is shallow. A dressing of a general purpose fertilizer should be worked in at 50 to 60 g. per sq. m. (2oz. per sq. yd) during the preliminary cultivations of forking and raking. Where there is a deficiency of lime, a dressing should be applied after digging, though not at the same time as the fertilizer.

Parsnips have long been considered as a crop which should be sown as early in the season as a reasonable tilth can be attained in the soil, but in southern gardens at least, sowing in May will produce good roots for culinary purposes, while in northern gardens, March sowings may be necessary. Sow in drills 2.5cm. (1in.) deep and 38cm. (15in.) apart. As the seeds are easily handled, 3 or 4 may be sown in stations 15cm. (6in.) apart. Parsnip seed is notoriously slow in germination, but a few radish seeds dropped between stations will give an early indication of where the drills are and allow a preliminary run through with the hoe, so that the young seedlings are not overwhelmed by weeds when they germinate. Thin the seedlings down to 1 plant per station when large enough to handle. Parsnip seed, in addition to being slow, usually only retains good germination for one season so it is unwise to rely on old seed and better to buy afresh each year. On very stony soils it is advisable to bore a few holes along the drill with a crowbar. This should be rotated to get a width of 8 to 10cm. (3 to 4in.) by 46cm. (18in.) in depth. Some old potting compost or screened soil may be used to fill up the holes, in which, after settling, 3 or 4 seeds can be sown and eventually thinned to a single plant. Little attention is required during the summer months except occasional hoeing to keep weeds in check, taking care not to damage the roots. You can get over this by mulching with a suitable material, such as peat or compost. Parsnips are usually left in the soil until required for the kitchen, being quite hardy. If you have any left when it comes to March, it is advisable to lift them and store in soil or sand in a cool place; this checks a start into fresh growth.
PESTS
Maggots of celery fly.
DISEASES
Parsnip canker.

Pea
A hardy annual which has been cultivated for so many thousands of years that its origin seems to be unknown. With strong claims to be our oldest vegetable, it still remains very popular and is an important crop for commercial growers.

Peas appreciate good soil and will withstand drought better where plenty of organic matter is available. I have always had good results from peas when grown following a previous crop of potatoes for which the ground was well manured. Deep digging is worth while, as it enables the roots to penetrate downwards for moisture and nutrients, and helps to prevent drying out in very hot weather. If well manured, further fertilizer may not be required; in any case this crop caters for its own nitrogenous requirements by extracting them from the air, so that only phosphate and potash will be required. A mixture of these can be made either in equal proportions or doubling the superphosphate and applying at 30 to 35g. per sq. m. (2oz. per sq. yd) run, forking into the soil before drawing out the drill to ensure direct contact is not made between seeds and fertilizers. Acid soils should be dressed with ground chalk or limestone after digging has been done.

Seeds can often be sown towards the end of February in sheltered gardens, when soil conditions become suitable, but in cold areas, March is the more likely month. Flat drills, 15cm. (6in.) wide and 5 to 8cm. (2 to 3in.) deep can be drawn out with a hoe and the seeds sown thinly along the rows. More precise methods are followed by some gardeners who place them in the drill at 5 to 8cm. (2 to 3in.) apart, allowing 2 or 3 rows in each drill. Cover the seeds with the soil removed from the drill.

In cold gardens a round-seeded variety should be sown at first, being hardier. Wrinkled-seeded or marrowfat peas, which have a much better flavour, should be sown from early March onwards. Where autumn or winter sowings are made, it is usual to sow a round-seeded variety in November or December and it is an advantage if these sowings can be afforded cloche protection. Drills are usually spaced in accordance with the height of the cultivar. There are many pea cultivars available but to my mind it is better to select a limited number which not only suit your requirements but are known to succeed in your particular area. Most gardens today have only limited space, so repeated sowings at regular intervals of a good maincrop can be preceded by an early cultivar such as 'Kelvedon Wonder'. The same cultivar may be sown according to district in June or July to end the season as it is resistant to mildew, a particularly troublesome disease late in the year.

As soon as the young plants are 5cm. (2in.) high they should be carefully hoed to keep weeds down and the plants should be supported by small twigs. Taller cultivars will require further support; pea sticks are ideal for this. These are now difficult to obtain so 10 or 13cm. (4 or 5in.) mesh wire-netting or plastic netting should be put in place when two pairs of leaves have formed. In dry weather a good soaking of water, when the peas are coming into flower, followed by another when the young pods can be seen, works wonders with the crop. This moisture can be further conserved by applying a mulch.

Peas should be picked from the bottom of the plant upwards as the pods become filled and before becoming old and 'corny'. This should be done regularly as it encourages the development of the later pods. When finished, the haulm should be hoed off and conveyed to the compost heap. Sugar pea or mangetout varieties relieve you of the task of shelling as the pods are eaten. These should be picked when young, before the peas have developed to such an extent inside the pods as to raise large bumps. Methods of cultivation are the same as outlined.

PESTS
Aphids, pea moth caterpillars and pea thrips.
DISEASES
Damping-off, downy mildew, grey mould and root rot.

Potato

The wild potato is native to the highland areas of South America, but many superior tubering forms have been developed since it was first brought into cultivation. Though a half hardy perennial it is grown as an annual for its tubers.

A plant that will produce a crop on any well cultivated soil, but which will amply repay a good dressing of farmyard manure or compost applied in the previous autumn. This should be well dug in, as the potato appreciates a deep, fine tilth rather than lumpy soil which is apt to lose moisture. A proprietary fertilizer or a good general compound, should be applied just before or during planting, in close proximity to the seed tubers but not in actual contact with them.

The quality of the seed tubers is important and it is usual to buy fresh tubers each season from a reliable source where crops are inspected for health and certified as true to variety. Tubers should, however, be examined on arrival in case they have been damaged by frost, bad handling or have become affected by disease. Blight may go undetected in the early stages and develop to show signs of rot during transit. Affected tubers should be removed. Good results may also be obtained from home produced tubers, especially those taken from a crop of fresh tubers; these are generally known as 'once grown'. Saving tubers longer than this leads to a considerable deterioration in cropping ability and should only be practised for some exceptional reason, such as keeping an uncommon or scarce cultivar.

Normally, early and second early cultivars are grown in order to produce early crops. Tubers of large egg size or about 56g. (2oz.) in weight are selected when harvesting the crop, and can be placed in a tray. Left outside or in an open shed

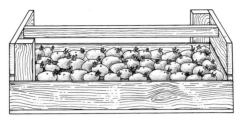

A wooden potato box with corner blocks filled with sprouted tubers.

the tubers turn green, and though useful for seed purposes are then inedible. Storage in a frost-free shed, preferably with some ventilation, is necessary before this danger arises in late autumn. 'Sprouting' or 'chitting' is carried out by setting up the tubers, rose end upwards, in trays in January or February. Commercial growers use special trays designed for this purpose which, however, are generally on the large side for small growers, so that seed trays or boxes may be used. Tomato trays are sometimes obtainable and, as these have corner blocks, are most useful. Corner blocks are essential if the trays are stacked, as they ensure that the tubers sprout in light conditions, and produce good sturdy sprouts of about 4cm. (1½in.) in length. Stacking in a light, frost-proof shed is best, though a greenhouse may be used. In the latter, control of temperature and of aphids will be required during warm spring days. Larger tubers may be cut into two with a sharp knife between the eyes at the rose end some weeks before planting, retaining one eye at least

on each portion. The two halves should be kept pressed together until planting takes place.

For early crops it is most important to choose a sheltered position or one which can be protected from frost which retards and reduces the crop. On light soils, particularly in warm gardens, planting may begin in early March when soil and weather conditions are suitable. This applies particularly where extra early crops can be produced under a protective cover such as cloches. Less sheltered gardens will provide more suitable conditions later in March or April, the latter month being most suitable for general planting.

Generally, planting takes place in drills, taken out by spade or draw-hoe up to 15cm. (6in.) deep. These drills may be 60cm. (2ft) apart for early crops, placing the sprouted tubers at 30cm. (12in.) apart. If grown under cover, these distances can be closed up by 8cm. (3in.) either way. More room is required for maincrop cultivars, for which the distance between tubers should be extended to 38cm. (15in.), and between drills to about 70cm. (28in.) to a maximum of 86cm. (34in.), if room is available, for varieties which produce very strong haulm. After planting, the drills should be filled in with soil.

Some gardeners with limited room now cover an early variety with 90cm. (3ft) wide black plastic sheeting, unrolled along the drill. Anchored in the soil on either side and at the ends, slits are eventually cut in the plastic to allow growths to come through. This method not only suppresses weeds but enables the young tubers to be harvested as soon as the desired size has been attained. The plastic is replaced so that those of

Planting potatoes
Draw out drills 15cm. (6in.) deep with draw hoe (top left), place sprouted tubers 30 or 38cm. (12 or 15in.) apart (top right), rake soil over drill into slight mound (bottom left), and (bottom right) fork between rows.

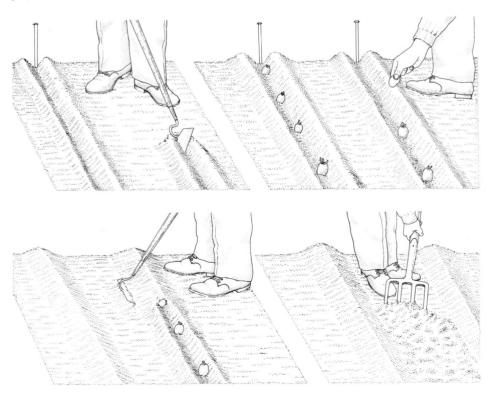

smaller size can grow on. This may also be done to afford protection from late frosts as it is the general custom to earth up the plants as growth proceeds. Some growers now regard this as unnecessary but it has some advantages; it disturbs seedling weeds, helps to cover up young tubers, prevents greening and makes harvesting easier.

Earthing up potatoes
Hoe between rows to kill weed seedlings (top), and then pull up soil with draw hoe (centre). Earthing up completed (bottom).

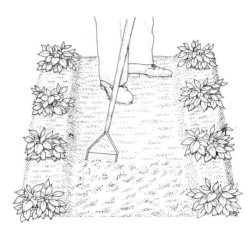

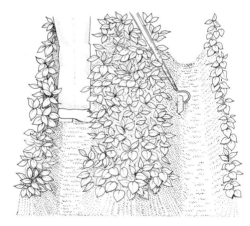

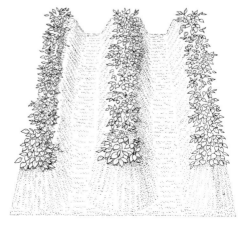

Early potatoes may be harvested in July and lifted for immediate use as required. Maincrop cultivars are allowed to grow until October or when the haulm has died down and the skin on the tubers has set firmly. Care must be taken during lifting, as damaged tubers will not keep in store. Tubers should be allowed to dry on the ground for a few hours before storing, either in a shed or in clamps in the open. Storage in the dark is essential; in the light, tubers will green and become inedible. Small quantities can be stored in boxes or any suitable container and accommodated in a cool, frost-proof shed. Larger quantities can be stored in a clamp prepared on the ground. If well drained, some soil can be taken and covered with straw on which the potatoes should be placed in a ridge-shaped mound. This should be covered with straw held in position by a couple of spadefuls of soil. The potatoes should be allowed to sweat for a week or two when the straw should be covered with at least 15cm. (6in.) of soil. In cold areas and in severe weather it may be necessary to augment this with more soil or straw to keep the tubers safe.

PESTS
Colorado beetle, potato cyst eelworm, slugs and wireworm.

DISEASES
Blight, dry rot, potato scab, powdery scab, wart disease and leaf roll and mosaic virus diseases.

Pumpkins and Squashes
These are half-hardy annuals, native to tropical America and require similar growing conditions to marrows.

Some are very ornamental in appearance, particularly when ripe and the flesh is generally firmer than that of marrows. A long season of growth is required, so starting off in pots helps to give more time to produce mature fruits.

Where large pumpkin fruits are desired, it is generally necessary to limit the number to two on each plant. Much of the surplus growth should be removed, taking care to leave several leaves. Keep well watered and regularly fed once the fruits have set. As the fruits grow they should be placed on a tile or slate and moved frequently so as to be of good shape and even colour. Allow to ripen well before cutting, when the stem should be retained. The fruits will store well in a cool dark shed.

PESTS
Generally trouble-free.

DISEASES
Grey mould.

Radish
The radish has been cultivated for centuries in China and Japan and may have originated there. Although an annual plant, the winter radish should be considered a biennial in habit. A rich, fertile and friable soil is required, while for early crops a warm sheltered position is a great asset, ensuring quick production, a vital factor with regard to quality. Slow grown radishes are liable to be hot, unpleasant and indigestible. In small gardens, radishes are seldom allotted their own plot but are grown as a catch crop where room is available amongst a slower growing crop, or as markers for slow germinating crops. Outdoor sowings may be made in early March in sheltered positions and may be protected by a sprinkling of straw. Sowing may be earlier in frames, under plastic tunnels or cloches. Seed should always be sown thinly in shallow drills allowing 15cm. (6in.) between the rows. In clean soil, especially in frames, thin broadcasting of seed may be done in conjunction with another crop. In summer months it is essential to choose a moist, shady spot behind a north wall or hedge and water regularly, otherwise the result will be poor. Being a quickly produced crop, little attention apart from watering or damping over is required between sowing and pulling. Birds often pull out the young germinating seedlings, which may have to be protected by a net. Radishes should always be used while young.

The winter radish differs completely from the type already described, producing much larger and longer roots, but somewhat more pungent in flavour. Like other root crops, this type of radish is best sown to follow another crop for which the soil was well manured. The soil may be prepared by forking over, treading and raking to a fine tilth. Sow in rows 23 to 30cm. (9 to 12in.) apart, thinning the seedlings to 15cm. (6in.) apart. This radish is liable to bolt if sown too early, so in northern gardens this should be done around mid-July, and up to a month later in southern gardens. The roots are hardy and may be used from the ground as required, or stored in sand in a cool place behind a north wall if this is more convenient.

The roots may be used in salad during winter months but if found to be too pungent are excellent cooked as turnips.

PESTS
Flea beetle.

DISEASES
Common scab.

Rhubarb
A hardy perennial plant which originated in China and Tibet where its root was used medicinally some thousands of years ago. In the 19th century its stalks were first used when forced, as a fruit, and it has now become a familiar sight in gardens. Thriving in any good soil, especially heavy, it responds readily to manuring although it is often planted in a neglected corner of the garden. Rhubarb is somewhat unusual in that its stems are used as a fruit, but it is always classed as a vegetable for show purposes and is generally referred to as such in books.

The thick, fanged roots are an indication that the plant requires deep soil, and being a permanent crop, this should be deeply dug and well manured. For the same reasons permanent weeds must be removed, so that a dirty piece of land would be better prepared by the planting of a cleaning crop such as potatoes; any weeds left may then be cleared while lifting.

Rhubarb may be raised from seed quite easily, but it is better in practice to grow a named cultivar, which can be planted in October, February or March. Planting distances vary according to cultivar, at least 90cm. (3ft) each way being required in good soil; possibly another 30cm. (12in.) will be required by strong growing maincrop cultivars.

Established roots should be divided so that one good crown on each set can be seen, these should be planted firmly so that the buds are only covered with soil to a depth of 5cm. (2in.). No stalks should be pulled during the first year, to allow the plants to get thoroughly established, and only a limited number in the second year. As the plants increase in size, heavier pullings can take place early in the season but later growths should be left to build up buds for the following year. In established beds, strong plants can be forced *in situ* by covering with some receptacle such as an empty bin or barrel which has had the top and bottom removed. The crop should be covered with strawy manure, leaves or bracken and the top replaced. Covering particularly an early cultivar with these materials in December will forward the crop without the assistance of any receptacle.

An earlier crop may be produced by lifting 3 year old roots specially grown for the purpose which have been left unpulled, to build up good crowns. The roots may be dug up as soon as the leaves die down, generally in November, and are left exposed on the ground for a few weeks before being brought indoors. Under the stage of a warm greenhouse is probably the best place, packing the roots in tightly with old potting soil or moist peat, keeping the roots moist and covering over with sacks, old carpets or other material to exclude light. A temperature of 13 to 16°C. (55 to 60°F.) is suitable; too high a temperature will produce flabby stalks with poor colour. Pack roots in boxes in a boiler house, garage or shed if a greenhouse is unavailable. Forced roots should be discarded; they are not worth replanting.

Rhubarb will benefit from a top dressing of a general purpose fertilizer annually, either when pulling has ceased or in spring. If manure or compost can be spared, a spring dressing will assist in building up the crowns. Some varieties flower; indeed rhubarb in flower is quite attractive. For culinary purposes, however, this should be discouraged and the flowering shoots cut out at the base. Pulling is done by pushing down inside the stalk at the base and pulling outwards with a slight twist, when it will come away complete. Stalks should not be cut, neither should all be removed at one time.

PESTS
Generally trouble-free.
DISEASES
Crown rot.

Sage

An evergreen aromatic sub-shrub popularly grown as a herb and valuable for ground cover and garden effect. A native of southern Europe where it grows in arid, stony situations. It succeeds best in well drained 'chalky' soils. Common sage prefers a sunny position and may be grown in a large pot or container. For this purpose the broad-leaved form is best for it seldom flowers, and hence has to be propagated from cuttings or layers. Cuttings taken with a heel during the summer may be rooted fairly easily in a frame. Growths round the outside of a plant will take root where they come into contact with the soil; this may be encouraged by placing soil over some of the more pendulous growths. The tips of the plants may be removed to make them bushy; older plants may be cut back in April to prevent them becoming leggy. By an annual pruning, the plants may be kept in shape and last for several years before renewal is required. Sage may also be grown from seed but seedlings are inferior to the broad-leaved form as they expend most of their vitality in flowering. There are other forms: 'Alba', with white flowers, 'Icterina', with leaves edged yellow, 'Purpurascens', with leaves and stems suffused purple, and 'Tricolor', splashed and suffused white, purple and pink. All of these are valuable for effect in a herb collection or the garden but are not favoured to the same extent in the kitchen.
PESTS AND DISEASES
Generally trouble-free.

Salsify

A hardy biennial, native of northern Europe, which is mainly grown for its long tapering roots. When cooked, these have a delicate, sweet flavour. It is sometimes known as the 'vegetable oyster', although, despite this eulogy, it is seldom seen in gardens.

Salsify tends, even more than other root crops, to produce forked roots, so that a light, fertile soil is best for its cultivation. This should not be freshly manured; if the site was well manured for the previous crop, good results should follow.

Where the soil is heavy or stony, individual stations can be prepared for each root by means of a crowbar. Fill these stations with a prepared compost, sowing 2 or 3 seeds in each, thinning in due course to 1 plant per station. Seeds are usually sown in April but may also be sown in May if required. Sow in shallow drills, 38cm. (15in.) apart, thinning the plants down to at least 15cm. (6in.) apart, leaving the strongest. Hoeing to check weeds is the only cultural attention required during summer, except in periods of drought, when watering will be required and, if material is available, mulching to assist the crop.

Salsify is quite hardy, so may be left in the soil and lifted as required, or lifted and stored in sand. By late October or November, the roots will be ready for use and should be lifted carefully, as damaged roots are apt to bleed.

Being a biennial, salsify produces flower stems in the second year and if roots are left unlifted, these young tender growths may be cut when 15cm. (6in.) long and used as asparagus. An alternative method is to clean up the plants, removing any leaves, and ridge up the soil over the plants to a depth of 15cm. (6in.). The result will be blanched growths which may be used in salads much in the same manner as chicory. Salsify leaves are also useful as an addition to salad.
PESTS AND DISEASES
Generally trouble-free.

Scorzonera

A hardy biennial from southern Europe which is seldom seen in gardens. It was used at one time as a cure for snake bite, and known as viper's grass. It is grown for its black-skinned, white-fleshed roots, which though quite different in appearance to salsify, require similar cultivation, except for the time of sowing. Plants from early sowings tend to flower prematurely, and therefore should be delayed until May. Roots may be lifted in October but, as they are brittle, some care is required. Some growers are known to give their plants another year to attain greater size. The young growth produced in spring may be eaten, as with salsify.
PESTS AND DISEASES
Generally trouble-free.

Seakale

A hardy perennial European native which was commonly grown in the larger private gardens for forcing in winter. The decline of these gardens has led to a decline in the cultivation of a vegetable relatively easy to grow but which has to be blanched to become edible, and does not have a long shelf life. Where forcing is a problem through lack of facilities, 'natural' seakale can be grown. This is not forced in heat but covered up outside and allowed to develop naturally. It is considered by some to be better in quality.

'Natural' seakale is grown on a permanent bed until the crop shows signs of deterioration. An open sunny site with fertile, well-drained soil is best. This should be deeply dug, incorporating a good dressing of well-rotted farmyard manure or compost. Where the soil is acid, it should have a surface dressing of lime.

Propagation by 'thongs', which are really root cuttings, produces a crop more quickly than growing from seed. Propagation by seed is readily done but 2 years are required to produce a crop; this time is halved by the thong method. However, seeds may be sown in March or April, the seedlings thinned to 15cm. (6in.) apart, then lifted, and planted out the following April. An alternative method is to lift every second seedling for replanting, leaving the others *in situ*. The 'thongs' are taken from side roots, preferably of finger thickness, although pieces of pencil thickness may be used. Each thong should be from 10 to 15cm. (4 to 6in.) in length, and should be cut straight across from the main root. A slanting cut at the rooting, and generally thinner end, enables the operator to place it correctly so that the newly formed eyes will be near the surface. The thongs are then usually tied in small bundles and laid in sand until planting time. By then eyes will have formed and may be seen quite easily. Generally, several are produced and should all be rubbed off except the strongest, as the best produce comes from single crowns.

In early April distances may be adjusted according to the method of forcing adopted. The old practice was to plant the thongs or sets in triangular fashion, 15cm. (6in.) between sets, and 75cm. (30in.) between the respective stations. These were covered by seakale pots, a receptacle now outmoded because of lack of demand and expense. Large flower-pots, or boxes may be used instead. These should be in place in November, and packed around with stable litter or decaying leaves or a mixture of both. Light must be totally excluded and boxes or pots of sufficient height used to get good blanched growth up to 20 or 23cm. (8 or 9in.) in length. Cut off, with a little piece of crown, at the base before the flower head at the apex shows.

A method which can extend the supply is to plant in a row 30cm. (12in.) apart, or even two rows and in January, preferably when the soil is in friable condition, dig along on either side and cover the crowns to a depth of 20 or 23cm. (8 or 9in.). Plenty of soil must be kept on the side so that the young growth is induced upwards. When the blanched growths get close to the surface the soil cracks. Then the soil can be removed carefully and the crop cut. When cleared, return the soil to its former position, just leaving the crowns covered. If available, a dressing of manure or, failing this, a complete fertilizer can be lightly forked in to help build up the crowns for the next season's crop. During summer keep clear of weeds, remove any flowering stems and keep the number of growths down to 2, to get good sizeable crowns.

The earliest seakale is produced by lifting the crowns as soon as the leaves have died down. The thongs should be removed from the main root which may then be stored in sand until required for forcing. This may be done in the same manner as rhubarb, packing the crowns in an upright position under the stage of a warm greenhouse or in large pots or boxes, using any old potting soil or leaf mould or any reasonable material which is handy. A temperature of 13°C. (55°F.) is quite high enough for good produce, and there must be total exclusion of light. The crop should be ready for cutting in 4 or 5 weeks. Small batches of crowns introduced at regular intervals will keep up a supply until available by the 'natural' method described earlier. When forced the crowns are of no further use and may be allowed to dry out for the bonfire.

PESTS AND DISEASES
Generally trouble-free.

Shallot
A perennial plant, native of Israel, which although closely allied to the onion botanically, is quite different in its habit of growth. Traditionally, shallots should be planted on the shortest day, in December, and lifted on the longest, in June. In practice however, planting is normally carried out in February , although the shallot is a very hardy plant and stands up well to severe weather.

Shallots require soil which is in good heart, deeply dug and manured for a previous crop. The soil should be forked over before planting, a light dressing of a general fertilizer worked in, and the surface consolidated by light treading. If made too firm, many of the bulbs push themselves out of the soil when growth starts and have to be replanted.

Planting should be done in shallow drills 30cm. (12in.) apart with the sets 15cm. (6in.) apart. Cover the sets with soil so that only the tip can be seen. When growth starts, little more attention is required beyond keeping the plants clear of weeds and occasional hoeing. Take care not to damage the bulbs and remove soil if necessary so that the bulbs are exposed to the sun. By the end of July, leaves will turn yellow and the clusters of bulbs can then be lifted and allowed to dry off on the surface for a few days. Ensure proper ripening by turning over gently once or twice and store in trays or bundles in a cool, well-ventilated, frost-proof shed. Sort the bulbs over when convenient, throwing out any showing signs of decay, and select those required to plant next year which should be around 2cm. (¾in.) in diameter. Large bulbs are ideal for kitchen use and small ones for pickling.

Shallots have a more delicate flavour than onions, and the leaves while green may be used in salad, or for flavouring.

DISEASES
Trouble-free, with the exception of a virus disease which results in degeneration of the stock.

PESTS
Generally trouble-free.

Sorrel
The common sorrel is a widespread European native, which thrives on acid soils; indeed it is indicative of this type of soil. *Rumex scutatus*, a hardy herbaceous perennial from central and southern Europe has become naturalized in the UK. A broad-leaved form French sorrel, is best for cultivation and is valued by some for soup and salads. It can be sown in March or April in drills 46cm. (18in.) apart, thinning the plants to 30cm. (12in.). In the autumn it can be propagated by division. To produce large succulent leaves, grow on good soil which is inclined to be acid and remove all flowering stems. The plants generally last in good condition for at least 4 years.

PESTS AND DISEASES
Generally trouble-free.

Spinach
A hardy annual known as prickly spinach or spinage. These names are derived from the prickly or spiny seeds and not from the leaves. The round-seeded spinach, *Spinacea oleracea* var. *inermis*, provides this vegetable during the summer months.

Spinach is a crop which requires well manured, well cultivated soil; for winter spinach, good drainage is also necessary. This crop can be sown in August and September in rows 30cm. (12in.) apart and just over 1.3cm. (½in.) in depth. The seedlings should be thinned when fit to handle; in the first place to about 8cm. (3in.) apart. Alternate plants may then be taken out when closing up in the row and will then be large enough to use after cutting off the roots. Hoe through after thinning to ensure freedom from weeds.

For summer crops, sowing may be started in February, as soon as the soil is in good condition and the weather is co-operative. The first sowings in February and March are best carried out on a sheltered but unshaded site. Later sowings appreciate a little shade in hot weather, such as may be provided by runner beans or peas, and adequate moisture, so that irrigation is a great help. Sowing should be discontinued after August, all sowings being in rows 30cm. (12in.) apart, thinning early to 23cm. (9in.) between the plants. Regular sowings should be carried out according to requirements and the leaves picked as they become large enough.

There is some confusion regarding this crop, brought about by other crops such as spinach beet, seakale beet and New Zealand spinach, which are grown as substitutes. All these are dealt with in their own right in this book.

PESTS
Generally trouble-free.

DISEASES
Downy mildew and cucumber mosaic virus.

Spinach, New Zealand
A tender annual native of New Zealand, which, although not a true spinach botanically, is a useful substitute in hot dry weather. Plants may be sown under glass towards the end of March in 8cm. (3in.) pots, thinning down to one plant when fit to handle. When hardened off they may be planted out towards the end of May or early June at 90cm. (3ft) apart each way. In all but very cold areas however, an outdoor sowing early in May will be less trouble. The seeds are hard and germinate more readily if soaked in water overnight, then 2 or 3 should be sown at each station, 90cm. (3ft) apart and 1.3cm. (½in.) deep. Remove the surplus plants to leave the strongest plant at each position, and hoe to clear weeds between them. They will soon spread over the soil, smothering any weeds which try to compete for space.

New Zealand spinach appreciates a warm situation but produces more succulent growths where plant nutrients are available and moisture is not lacking. This is a 'cut and come again' plant, so growths can be cut off regularly as required, the leaves being removed more readily afterwards.

PESTS AND DISEASES
Generally trouble-free.

Swede
A hardy biennial, sometimes known as Swedish turnip and rutabaga and still confused with the turnip. However, the swede is quite distinct, having smooth, glaucous leaves which are allied to the cabbage and arise from a distinct stem. The roots are larger than those of the turnip, have a different flavour and a more colourful, yellow flesh. It is undervalued in southern parts of the UK where its culture may be difficult; in northern regions, where cooler, moister climatic conditions suit it much better, it is highly appreciated as a winter vegetable.

The swede requires the same conditions as the turnip, a fairly fertile soil which is adequately limed and retentive of moisture. Hot, dry soils are quite unsuitable; the foliage gets attacked badly by mildew and the roots become fibrous and tough. In northern districts, sowing is carried out in May in drills 38 to 46cm. (15 to 18in.) apart, the plants being singled down to around 25cm. (10in.). In southern gardens, sowing should be delayed until mid-June, when, to ensure a good germination, drills 2cm. (¾in.) deep should be well watered before sowing. In dry weather, the seedlings should be watered in the evenings, this also helps to discourage flea-beetles which thrive in dry weather. Summer cultivation consists of hoeing to control weeds and watering, if possible, in very dry weather.

Being hardy, swedes will stand in milder areas and can be lifted as required. In cold areas roots may be lifted by the end of October. Remove the tops and store in a clamp or in boxes of sand in a cool shed.

PESTS
Flea beetle.

DISEASES
Brown heart, club root and downy mildew.

Sweet corn
An annual plant of American origin. It is a variety of maize, and sometimes also called sugar corn.

Sweet corn succeeds very well on soils suitable for general crops, especially if well manured for the previous crop. An open site where the crop will get the full benefit of the sun should be chosen. During the soil preparation a general purpose fertilizer should be worked into the surface soil at 90 to 95g. per sq. m. (3oz. per sq. yd) after having been deeply dug some time previously. It is a somewhat tender plant and care has to be taken that frost does not severely check the young seedlings. In exposed places where an early start is required, seeds may be sown under cloches towards the end of April or early in May. I prefer sowing in peat pots or soil blocks, 2 seeds to each, removing the weaker seedling in due course. Sweetcorn does not like to be disturbed by transplanting. Plant in late May and arrange in a block of short rows to ensure pollination by the wind. Planting distances will vary according to variety but generally 38cm. (15in.) between plants and 60 to 75cm. (24 to 30in.) between the rows will suffice.

A direct sowing may also be made in mid-May, placing seeds in each station at the same distances as recommended above, and later removing the weaker plant. This will provide a successional crop. Cold northern gardens will find pot-sown plants more satisfactory, however, because of the shorter summer season. During the summer in warmer areas, simply hoe carefully to destroy weeds, drawing up some soil to the plants to help stabilize them against the wind. There is no point in removing suckers or side growths. Good watering will be required in very dry weather. If available, a good mulch after watering will help conserve the moisture.

Sweet corn should be harvested when the silk at the end of the cob has turned dark brown and the cob feels full and well developed. You may confirm this by opening the sheath and pressing a seed; if it is milky the cob can be removed by a sideways twist and jerk. It is generally considered that the shorter the time between picking and cooking the better the flavour and the more tender the seeds.

PESTS
Frit fly: Plants grown in pots and planted out are not damaged.
DISEASES
Generally trouble-free.

Tarragon
A moderately hardy herbaceous perennial of which there are 2 forms which are similar in appearance but distinctive in flavour. True or French tarragon, *Artemisia dracunculus* var. *sativa*, has a flavour unlike any other herb and is held in high regard in 'haute cuisine'. The original home of French tarragon is not certain, but it is thought to have been southern European Russia. It grows up to 90cm. (3ft) high in soil which is well drained, provided with humus and in a sunny position. This plant requires some protection in colder areas, which can be provided by a sprinkling of straw or bracken. Replanting is best done in spring when the young growth is seen, as seed is not produced. Replanting is necessary every 4 years. Russian tarragon, *A. dracunculus* var. *inodora*, is a much hardier and more vigorous plant which may reach up to 1.8m. (6ft) in height. It is not worth planting in a vegetable garden since what little flavour it possesses is unpleasant.

Russian tarragon is sold as seed, though may be available as a pot plant, whereas French tarragon, the most suitable culinary type, is only available as a pot plant and is increased by cuttings. Thus care should be taken to distinguish between the types when buying this plant to avoid disappointment.
PESTS AND DISEASES
Generally trouble-free.

Thyme
Thyme must be one of the oldest and most popular herbs in UK gardens, where it has been grown for several hundred years. The common or French thyme, *Thymus vulgare*, is derived from a species common in the western Mediterranean

region. A stiffly compact shrub 23cm. (9in.) high and evergreen, its neat appearance and delightful aroma, especially when the leaves are rubbed, are an asset in any garden.

Golden thyme is a bright yellow-green leaved form of similar habit, but slightly milder flavour; of ornamental value in a herb garden. Plants can be raised easily from seeds sown in a warm corner in April and planted out 15cm. (6in.) apart as an edging, or in a bed with 30cm. (12in.) between rows. It prefers a light, well-drained soil. When new growth is required for kitchen use, the plants may be cut back after flowering.

Caraway thyme, *T. herba-barona*, is a native of Corsica and Sardinia with an aroma strongly resembling caraway plus thyme. The growths form a loose mat in which, as it comes into contact with the soil, roots are produced; propagation, therefore presents no problem.

Lemon thyme, *T. citriodorus*, forms a loosely open bush 30cm. (12in.) high. Its broad leaves have a lemon scent. Not quite as hardy as common thyme, it may succumb in a hard or wet winter. Like common thyme, this plant can be readily propagated from cuttings in a cold frame in late summer or by division in March or April. Lemon thyme is preferred by some for its milder, fruitier flavour.
PESTS AND DISEASES
Generally trouble-free.

Tomato
A short-lived perennial native of South America which, when it first arrived in Europe, was grown as an ornamental plant and known as the 'Love-apple'. Its popularity as a vegetable has only been attained in the present century, and allied to this, some decline in quality has taken place in commercially grown tomatoes. The amateur grower has an advantage by growing varieties of good quality and allowing the fruits to ripen before picking. Many grow their crops in small greenhouses under cloches or outside in warmer areas. In northern gardens it is better to grow in a greenhouse. Even under cloches growing outside is a gamble which seldom pays off.

The most successful crops are grown in heated glasshouses and with the glass going down almost to soil level. In such houses, the plants are directly planted in the soil and this should be fertile, well-drained and properly prepared by adding well-rotted manure or compost. Large quantities of manure should not be added as excessive leaf production may result. If tomatoes have not been grown previously, you should get a good crop for a few seasons.

Later, soil sterilization becomes necessary, and though few amateurs are able to use steam, the method usually employed by the commercial grower, a chemical sterilizer, either a proprietary one or formalin, may be used according to directions. As this operation is carried out when the soil is fairly dry, it is essential to flood at least twice afterwards to ensure that the subsoil becomes thoroughly moistened so as to carry the crop through the summer. Do this work during the winter months so as to allow a month to elapse before planting the crop. If the soil is acid, lime should be added and a proprietary tomato base fertilizer hoed in before planting.

Tomato seeds may be sown early if a heated greenhouse or propagating frame is available, but generally it is unwise and uneconomical to do so

before mid-February when the hours of daylight will be increasing. A temperature of 18°C. (65°F.) is required to ensure quick germination when it can be lowered to 15.6°C. (60°F.). Professional growers use various techniques, such as sowing in sand over peat, or, in sterilized soil, but amateurs in general follow the more orthodox method of sowing in seed-trays and pricking off into pots or soil-blocks. Some opt out of those preliminaries and buy plants from a local grower. Seeds may be sown singly in soil blocks but are better sown spaced out singly about 2.5cm. (1in.) apart in a seed tray of John Innes seed compost or one of the soilless composts. A few days after germination, when the seed leaves have opened out fully, they should be pricked out in pots or soil blocks, handling the plants carefully by the seed leaves, and avoiding any pressure on the stems. Set out the plants on a greenhouse stage where there is ample light. This produces well-developed plants, which, when the first truss begins to show, will be ready for planting out. Remove any plants which are affected by virus disease, or which appear bushy or fern-like in appearance (sometimes known as 'jacks'), these should be destroyed to ensure they are not planted out. Planting should be carried out before the plants get pot-bound and care must be taken to ensure that the roots are not dry. Distances vary according to circumstances, a double row may be given 46cm. (18in.) apart either way, but if you have to walk between, 76cm. (30in.) may be required between the next 2 rows. If the root ball is set slightly lower than the surrounding soil, it may be kept easily supplied with water, which is necessary until the roots are re-established. Plants grow quickly so must be supported soon after planting with a wooden stake with a length of thick fillis string attached. The other end is tied to a wire running along at a convenient height and connected to the rafters. As the plant grows it is twisted round the string so that it remains upright.

Tomatoes, especially under glass, are grown as cordons on a single stem so that side shoots have to be removed at the earliest stage possible to avoid stem damage. When the plants are well established a thorough soaking of water will be necessary, and liquid feeding when the second truss has begun to set. Proprietary feeds are available and should be used according to instructions. Setting can be assisted by lightly spraying the plants with water during the morning on bright days and by maintaining a buoyant atmosphere by intelligent use of the ventilators. While tomatoes appreciate warmth, they do not like a steamy atmosphere, so ventilation is required when 24 to 27°C. (75 to 80°F.) is reached. A little ventilation in the morning helps to dry the atmosphere, and in very hot weather, light shade is helpful, especially in small greenhouses. This protects the plants and reduces the loss of moisture by evaporation. In hot weather a small crack of air all night helps to keep a buoyant atmosphere. Many amateur growers seem keen on defoliating their plants, often to excess. Strong growing plants may require an odd leaf taken off not only to expose the fruit to more light but also to allow air circulation to be improved. Old leaves which show obvious signs of deterioration near the base of the plant may be taken away, and others as the fruits show signs of ripening.

Pick fruits as they ripen by snapping them off from the main stem and retaining the calyx. Where the greenhouse is to be used for a following crop, such as chrysanthemums, the plants should be stopped in mid-August to allow most fruits time to ripen before removal.

RING CULTURE

This method of cultivation has been carried out with great success by many amateurs and can be used under glass or outdoors. It is most effective where soil-borne diseases have made direct planting difficult. A bed of aggregate 15cm. (6in.) deep is required and it may be necessary to remove 15cm. of soil to accommodate this. Clinker is now difficult to obtain but .65cm. ($\frac{1}{4}$in.) gravel is very satisfactory and should be washed to clear it of dust. Bottomless containers in whalehide or plastic, 23 or 25cm. (9 or 10in.) in diameter should be filled with a good compost such as John Innes 3 in which the plants are grown. Water the plants in the rings until the roots reach the aggregate which should be kept moist. The plants develop a double root system; the feeding roots fill the container, while those in the aggregate draw the moisture they require from the gravel. Feeding is applied through the rings. Once fruit has formed, a proprietary liquid fertilizer should be used once a week. In hot dry weather, the aggregate should be soaked every day. The aggregate should be sterilized chemically before being used again.

PEAT BAGS

Polythene bags filled with specially prepared peat with plant nutrients added have been used very successfully indoors, and out, for a wide range of crops, including tomatoes. They can be used in small greenhouses, on balconies, or patios. Care must be taken to prevent waterlogging, and after the first few weeks liquid feeding becomes necessary.

OUTDOOR CULTIVATION

Satisfactory crops of tomatoes are only produced outdoors in the warmer areas of the UK. Even in the milder districts a warm sheltered border near to a wall or fence is preferable. The soil should be well dug and improved by adding compost or manure. Before planting a general purpose fertilizer at 90 to 95g. per sq. m. (3oz. per sq. yd.) should be applied. Seeds should be sown in late March or early April and, after pricking off in pots, may be grown in a cold greenhouse or cold frame, where the plants may be kept sturdy. Harden off and plant out in late May or early July, according to climatic conditions. Protection, with cloches or an inverted pot for the first few nights will ensure an undamaged start. Outdoor tomatoes are best grown as single cordons and require to be planted 38 to 46cm. (15 to 18in.) apart. Bush types require 15cm. (6in.) more between plants with a further 15cm. (6in.) between rows in open ground. Watering is only required in very dry weather.

Excepting bush cultivars, to obtain a good crop of ripe fruits it is necessary to restrict the plant to 4 or 5 trusses. The top growth should be taken out at a leaf or so beyond the topmost truss. Each plant will require the removal of side shoots and a good strong stake, which should be placed in position at planting time.

Bush tomatoes neither require staking nor pinching. Mulching with straw prevents the fruits becoming soiled. If cloches are available, place them in position in September, both to forward the plants and increase the crop. The cordon plants may also be cut away from the stakes, laid down on straw and protected with cloches to extend the season. Further prolongation, by picking late fruits which are just colouring and placing in a drawer wrapped in paper, will supply fruits until late in the year.

PESTS

Potato cyst eelworm.

DISEASES

Blight, when grown outdoors, blossom end rot, blotchy ripening, leaf curl, greenback, cladosporium or leaf mould, corky root, fusarium and verticillum wilt and various virus diseases, in particular tomato mosaic.

Turnip

A biennial of uncertain origin. 'The Neep', as it is known in Scotland, prefers cool, moist growing conditions, so it is better suited to northern gardens. In warmer, drier areas, especially where plenty of organic matter is present in the soil, early and late crops present no great problem, but except in a wet season, summer crops are exceedingly difficult to grow.

The earliest crops of outdoor turnips are generally grown on land that has been well manured in the previous season, supplementing this with a dressing of general purpose fertilizer at 90 to 95g. per sq. m. (3oz. per sq. yd). The soil should have been deeply dug and limed if necessary during autumn or winter, and fertilizer applied during the seed bed preparation. Drills 2cm. ($\frac{3}{4}$in.) deep and about 30cm. (12in.) apart should be drawn out in which to sow the seeds thinly, eventually thinning the plants when fit to handle to 10 to 13cm. (4 to 5in.) apart.

Seed sowing is governed by weather but except in very sheltered situations this is rarely practicable until late March. Earlier sowings will have to be made under the protection of frames or cloches. Successive sowings may be made during April but, unless irrigation is available, it is usually a waste of time to sow again until late July, for winter storage purposes. Turnip tops seem to have lost popularity to some extent, but are a valuable standby crop in severe winters. For this purpose, a sowing from the middle to the end of August may be made, leaving seedlings unthinned, providing thin sowing has been practised.

Early turnips should be pulled while young, and not allowed to grow above golf-ball size. For storage, roots should be lifted carefully with a fork in late October. Twist off the tops and store in sand or soil in a cool shed or outdoor clamp, whichever is most convenient.

PESTS

Flea beetle.

DISEASES

Generally trouble-free.

Watercress

A hardy perennial aquatic herb found growing wild in the UK and grown commercially in beds. The strains in cultivation are improved forms of the native plant and 2 main types are grown. The green type is grown in summer, and the brown in winter or spring. The plant grows best in hard water containing lime, usually from natural springs or artesian bores. Watercress may be grown from seed, pricking the seedlings off in trays when they should be planted out beside running water. Few gardens however possess streams and have to substitute a trench in which a bunch of watercress, which will have embryo roots, may be planted out 10 to 15cm. (4 to 6in.) apart and kept well watered. Make the trench about 60cm. (2ft) wide and some centimetres below the natural soil level. Plant in spring and cut back if the plants flower, when young growths will be produced for use in autumn.

PESTS AND DISEASES

Generally trouble-free.

Monthly Calendar of Work

A calendar of monthly operations in the vegetable garden can only be regarded as a brief reminder of seasonal operations and for general guidance. A rigid timetable just cannot be applied, because climatic conditions and those brought about by soil and situation, vary considerably and affect plant growth. The gardener must therefore adapt advice according to local conditions and take some measure of responsibility in coming to decisions. This is in particular necessary with regard to household requirements; there is no point in producing crops which never get eaten.

January

The hours of daylight in January are few and weather is often rather inclement for working in the open. It is however a good time to read seed and plant catalogues and lists and make a note of requirements.

There is often a large number of cultivars of some kinds of vegetables available and it may be wise to take advice from a local horticultural society, local expert or from the press. Many papers publish weekly articles which may be helpful regarding the best cultivars. For your main growing it is generally better to grow those which have proved successful in past years. Novelties however should not be neglected. Many are the result of scientific breeding programmes over many years, though they should be judged by results in your own garden.

Work with nature rather than against her. Keep off your garden when it is very wet, especially on heavy soil. Where digging was possible in the autumn, now will be a good time to apply lime, if it is needed, in the form of ground chalk or limestone.

Those vegetables left in store such as beet, carrots, potatoes, onions, swedes and turnips, should be examined regularly, particularly onions, and any showing signs of decay should be removed to prevent damage spreading. Where celery, Jerusalem artichokes, leeks and parsnips are grown, some should be lifted when required, especially if severe weather is imminent. Where severe frost is likely to lie, a little protection with bracken or straw will not only safeguard the crop but will also ensure easier lifting. Brussels sprouts can still be picked and winter cabbages and savoys cut as required. If you have a warm, dark, frost-free place in a greenhouse, garage or shed, chicory, rhubarb and seakale may be forced.

Cauliflower plants for spring planting, if overwintered in a cold frame, should be ventilated except when weather is severe. If a heated greenhouse is available a few tomato seeds may be sown, and also onions of the 'Ailsa Craig' type, excellent both for cooking and exhibition. A diary is useful for forgetful gardeners and this is a good month to transfer relevant information on sowing dates from last year and to plan out the cropping of your vegetable garden. 'Seed' potato tubers should be obtained and an early cultivar set up in a light, frost-free structure. On fine days, clear any spent crops by digging the soil over if it is not too wet and incorporating manure or compost.

February

If digging in manure or compost, was not completed by January, it should be done as soon as conditions of soil and weather allow. This is especially necessary in warm, sheltered areas where sowing and planting some crops can be started. Some days before sowing or planting, where the soil has been dug or cultivated in preparation, a dressing of a general purpose fertilizer can be applied and worked in by fork or hoe.

If you like Jerusalem artichokes and shallots, plant them now. Broad beans and a summer or round-seeded variety of spinach may be sown now.

If potato seed tubers were not set up in January this should be attended to, so as to encourage short sturdy sprouts, ready for planting in late March or early April.

Beet, carrots, potatoes, onions, swedes and turnips still in store should be inspected and sprouts rubbed off. Parsnips still in the ground are better if lifted now, to check the start of fresh growth; store them under a north wall and protect with a covering of earth or sand to prevent them drying out. Celery and Jerusalem artichokes can also be lifted for use. If any Brussels sprouts remain, these can still be picked or, if over, the tops can be cut for use. Savoys may also be cut.

March

March is, weather permitting, a busy month in the vegetable garden, especially if wind has dried out the soil surface and provided conditions to get a nice tilth for seed sowing. Several sowings may be made, so that preparation of the soil for seed beds is of considerable importance.

Crops which should be sown are lettuces, onions, parsley, parsnips, peas and radishes with successional sowings of broad beans and spinach.

August sown onions can be transplanted from seed bed to cropping site. Onion sets and garlic may be planted and that excellent salad plant chives, split up and replanted.

If any of the leek crop remains lift now to prevent new growth, especially in southern gardens and 'heel in' behind a north wall or hedge. On a seed bed Brussels sprouts, cabbages and leeks should be sown for planting out. Celery for planting in trenches, self-blanching celery and celeriac should be sown under glass. Hoeing when soil conditions are favourable can be commenced on the spring cabbage crop to keep down weeds, and encourage growth; work in a nitrogenous fertilizer dressing – nitrate of soda or sulphate of ammonia are suitable. Autumn-sown lettuce and spinach will also benefit from similar treatment.

If you are willing to take a gamble, a planting of early potatoes can be made towards the end of the month, especially if you have a nicely sheltered corner or you can protect a low growing cultivar with cloches. Straw also helps and can do so also for early rhubarb *in situ* which may be further aided by large pots or boxes.

Asparagus established in rows or beds will appreciate a dressing of a good general fertilizer when soil can also be mounded over the crowns.

April

With the advent of April, better weather conditions are expected and all too frequently sedentary workers seize this chance to get on with the garden work to such an extent that sore backs and frayed tempers result. If work was carried out as advised much of the preparatory work would be done, so that seed sowing and planting could go forward in a rational manner, benefiting both the crop and the gardener. Early cultivars of potato should be planted early in the month, maincrops towards the end. Globe artichokes, autumn sown cauliflowers and onions from sets should be planted now, if this was not done last month. Further successional sowings of lettuce, peas, radishes and spinach can be made. Sow early root crops, beetroot, carrots, onions for pickling, onions for salad and turnips as well as further sowings of cabbage and cauliflower for planting later.

Plant asparagus on well prepared soil which should have been made ready in advance, in order to prevent any drying out of the crowns and roots by quick planting. If you possess a greenhouse and appreciate sweet corn, a sowing in pots in the last week will produce an early crop. Runner beans and marrows may also be given a similar start in life; a cold frame will suffice if greenhouse room is unavailable. Tomatoes for outside planting are generally best sown early in the month.

A general fertilizer applied to the area where brassicas are to be planted can be raked or hoed in.

Sprouting broccoli, spring greens and turnip tops will be ready to gather. Asparagus, in established plantings, should now start to provide succulent spears.

May

Although better weather conditions are expected in April, a late frost may do considerable harm. Low-lying areas, being frost-pockets, are particularly vulnerable, and early potatoes, a crop particularly susceptible to serious injury at this time, should not be planted. Where shade prevents the early morning sun reaching the frosted growths, damage can be less severe, while some gardeners have found spraying with water also lessens the effect. Where crops are only grown on a small scale other means of protection such as covering with straw or bracken are feasible. Frost warnings are a useful guide to those willing to take protective measures.

Seed sowing of French and runner beans should now be carried out; those with heavy soils will find the latter part of the month better. Direct sowings of marrows, outdoor cucumbers and sweet corn may be made at the end of this month.

Kales, Savoys, winter cabbages and winter cauliflower (broccoli) should be sown in a seed bed. Sowings in succession where further supplies are required may be made of beetroots, carrots, lettuces, peas, radishes and turnips.

Planting of Brussels sprouts should be done as soon as the plants are large enough. Young tomato plants, if hardened off, can be planted out and also marrows, outdoor cucumbers and sweet corn, raised in pots under protection.

Earlier sown crops such as beetroots, carrots, lettuces, onions, parsnips and turnips can now be thinned. Place stakes or netting in place for peas and also stakes for runner beans. Early potatoes can be earthed up and maincrop varieties protected, as they appear, with a little soil.

Some new season crops such as radishes should be ready to pull, also spring onions for salad. All left-over vegetable waste should be cleared and placed on the compost heap. The stumps of Brussels sprouts, cabbage and cauliflower can be burned when sufficiently dry. Hoeing should be continued as regularly as possible amongst all crops unless they are mulched. Mulching not only smothers weeds but retains moisture and is particularly valuable for beans and peas.

Pests must be controlled, in particular, blackfly on broad beans, cabbage root fly, carrot fly, onion fly, and flea-beetle, applying the appropriate insecticides (see Pests section). Broad beans in full flower should have the tops pinched out. These, if free from blackfly, may be cooked like spinach.

June

In this month the gardener will begin to gain some reward for his labour as broad beans and peas will begin to be ready for gathering. Cabbage, cauliflower, lettuce, onions and radishes should also be available.

Celery to be grown in trenches should be planted, taking care that the plants are well supplied with water. Where the trench was prepared in advance, the ridge top can be used for lettuce as a catch crop so long as not too many are sown at one time. It is a waste of time to transplant lettuce at this season, as they usually run to seed, especially if the weather is hot. Self-blanching celery and celeriac should also be planted, and tomatoes, marrows, cabbage and, if required, more Brussels sprouts. June is the best month to sow swedes, a very useful standby in winter, but difficult to grow in hot, dry areas. Later sowing in a dull spell of weather may be tried.

Successional sowings of beetroot, carrots, lettuces, runner beans and dwarf beans may be made, also a last sowing of peas. Thinning of beetroot, carrots, lettuces and onions may be carried out; thinnings of the latter are a very useful and tasty addition to the salad-bowl.

Regrettably the time has now come to stop cutting asparagus; remaining growth is needed to build crowns for next year's crop.

A dressing of nitrogenous fertilizer, such as nitrate of soda or sulphate of ammonia, helps such crops as beetroot, carrots, onions and parsnips after they have been thinned. Keep a close watch, as last month, for insect pests on your crops and apply insecticides as necessary. Celery fly must be added to the list, and a preventive spray is worth while (see Pests section). Earthing up of maincrop potatoes may now be completed.

July

In the second half of the year vacant pieces of land begin to appear and may be used for further successional sowings of beet, carrots, lettuces, dwarf beans and kohlrabi. Turnips to provide roots for winter storage should also be sown during July and an *in situ* sowing of 'Hungry Gap' kale will provide a useful standby crop next April, especially welcome after a severe winter and during a scarcity of green vegetables. Lifting of early potatoes will be in full swing; the cleared ground can be used for planting cauliflower, cabbage, sprouting broccoli, kales and leeks. In northern gardens cabbages for spring cutting should be sown, and also spinach, beet and parsley. The latter will provide a supply during winter and spring, especially if it can be protected with a cloche during severe weather.

Runner beans should now be at the top of their supports and have the tops pinched out. This crop, and celery, celeriac and marrow, should not be allowed to suffer from a shortage of water.

Tomatoes will be growing fast and require tying and the removal of side growths, except for the bush varieties which should be allowed to grow naturally.

Earthing up of maincrop potatoes, if not already attended to, should be completed and a precautionary spray given with a fungicide against potato blight. In early districts garlic and shallots can be harvested. Cauliflower now producing curds should have these protected by breaking over some leaves to keep the curd white and unspoiled by sun. At the end of the month onions sown last August should have their tops bent over to encourage ripening.

August

Frequently soil in gardens has become very dry by this time so before sowing seeds give the drills a thorough soaking. Cabbages for spring cutting are a case in point and should be sown early in the month. Red cabbage also, whether appreciated for pickling or as a vegetable, gives best results from being sown at this time, especially if given frame or cloche protection during severe winter weather.

Onions are always appreciated in the kitchen, so where early bulbs are required or difficulty is experienced with production from spring sowing, a cultivar suitable for spring planting should be sown by the middle of the month; also one suitable for pulling early for salad. Those sown the previous year will have completed their growth, and can be lifted, and left on the ground for a week. Turn the roots so that they are fully exposed to the sun.

Tomatoes will now have produced the 4 or 5 trusses of fruits required for a full crop and should be stopped beyond the last truss, and side shoots removed. To control blight, a fungicidal spray should be applied according to directions. Runner beans will now be in full bearing and should be gathered as soon as large enough for use, any surplus may be deep frozen or preserved in salt. If necessary continue watering to keep the plants cropping.

September

In many areas harvesting of potatoes may be begun this month. Where infected with disease, the haulm should be cut off and removed for burning. Allow a week for skins to set, and on a dry day get on with the lifting. When the tubers are dry, remove them to a place of storage. Harvesting of spring-sown onions and those grown from sets should also be carried out by lifting carefully and laying out to dry, turning over once or twice so as to expose the bulbs fully to the sun. If the weather turns wet, drying will have to be done under glass or in a shed before the bulbs are fit to store.

Tomato plants can now be cut free from their stakes, laid down on straw and covered with cloches. Pick fruits as they colour, or even green, and place them in a shallow dish. Put one ripe fruit among them and the green ones will ripen. Keep them in a warm place, but not in full sun or the fruits will shrivel. If a greenhouse is available, the whole plant can be pulled up and the fruits will continue to ripen there. Beet should be lifted before the roots become too large and coarse, and put into storage; carrots likewise, before the splitting of the roots is brought on by wet weather.

Celery now requires more attention and may require spraying with a fungicide to prevent leaf-spot. Celery fly may also require control by spraying with an insecticide or, where a slight attack only has been made, by crushing the maggots by hand. Watering is usually required at this time of year. Remove any suckering growths from the base, tie the plants with soft string or raffia and give the first earthing up. Celeriac may also require sucker or side shoot removal, and plenty of water plus liquid manure. Self-blanching celery should now be ready for use.

Cabbages for spring cutting should be planted, and sowings made of lettuce to withstand the winter, as well as spinach and also turnips to provide turnip tops, a neglected but useful crop when green vegetables are scarce, especially in a severe winter.

October
Potatoes not lifted last month should be taken up and stored; also beetroot and carrots when they are large enough, as frost may occur in cold areas. Planting of spring cabbage should be completed where necessary and winter lettuce thinned, or seedlings transplanted.

The asparagus row or bed may be tidied up by cutting down the dying foliage which should be burned. Some more soil may be applied to the celery and some protective material arranged to protect self-blanching celery in case of severe frost. Celeriac may be lifted and stored in sand when it is large enough. Onion bulbs should be thoroughly ripened by this time and ready to tie into ropes for storage in a dry, airy but frost-proof place.

Runner beans will now be over; any edible pods should be picked. The first of the Brussels sprouts will be ready for use. Cauliflowers should be protected from frost by covering their curds with their own leaves.

A good deal of land will now be vacant and should be turned up roughly, especially if it is heavy. Manure or compost can be incorporated if required. Brassica stumps should be cleared away and burned.

November
The remarks made last month about digging vacant land again apply. Double digging of a portion and incorporating manure is an advantage, but not where it is intended to grow root crops in the following year. On light soils in a sheltered garden it is a useful gamble to make sowings of a round-seeded pea and a hardy long-pod broad bean early in the month. Cloches can assist in severe winters but these might be better used for an early spring sowing when the odds are somewhat better.

Clear up and remove yellow leaves from Brussels sprouts or other green crops and take them to the compost heap.

Globe artichokes also should be tidied by cutting down and removing stems and any dead or decaying leaves. In areas where winter cauliflower require some protection it helps to heel them over by removing soil on one side, pushing the plants over and covering up the stem with the soil which you removed. Preferably the plants should face north.

December
If you like hard work and healthy exercise you can continue to double dig the ground where you intend to grow root crops. It will be of advantage to the crop but do not add any manure and leave the application of fertilizer until the spring. Digging should only be done when the soil is not too wet.

In severe weather celery will require protection with bracken or straw. Roots stored in outside clamps will require additional soil to keep them from harm; those stored in a shed should be examined and any decayed or damaged specimens removed.

Rhubarb, chicory and seakale may be forced under a greenhouse stage or anywhere where heat is available and light can be excluded. If you are entertaining friends over the festive season you may ensure a good supply of vegetables, not only the essential Brussels sprouts and potatoes but perhaps also cabbage, savoys, carrots, beet, onions, shallots, Jerusalem artichokes, leeks, swedes and turnips.

COLOUR PLATES

1 **Angelica**
Angelica archangelica

2 **Artichoke, Chinese**
Stachys affinis

Artichoke, Globe
Cynara scolymus
3 Gros Vert de Laon
4 Roscoff Blue

Artichoke, Jerusalem
Helianthus tuberosus
5 White

1

2

3

4

5

6

7

8

9

Asparagus
Asparagus officinalis
6 Argenteuil
7 Connover's Colossal

8 **Asparagus Pea**
Tetragonolobus purpureus

Aubergine
Solanum melongena ovigerum
9 Mammoth

10 **Balm**
Melissa officinalis

11 **Basil, Sweet**
Ocimum basilicum

10

11

12

13 △

14 △

15

16

17 △

18 △

19

20

Bean, Dwarf French
Phaseolus vulgaris
17 Glamis
18 Kinghorn Wax
19 Remus
20 Sprite

Bean, Haricot
P. vulgaris
21 Comtesse de Chambord

21

22

23

24

25 △

26 △

27

28

Bean, Runner
Phaseolus coccineus
22 Enorma
23 Sunset

Bean, Soya
Glycine max
24 Fiskeby V (autumn)

Beetroot
Beta vulgaris var. *esculenta*
25 Burpees Golden
26 Cheltenham Green Top
27 Cylindra
28 Detroit – Little Ball

29

30

31

32

33 △

34

Beet, Leaf
Beta vulgaris var. *cycla*
29 Perpetual Spinach
30 Rhubarb Chard
31 Silver or Seakale

32 **Borage**
Borago officinalis

Broccoli, Sprouting
Brassica oleracea var. *italica*
33 Purple
34 White

35   36

37 △   38   39 △

40
41

Cabbage, Chinese
Brassica pekinensis
42 Pe-tsai

Cabbage, Red
B. oleracea var. *capitata rubra*
43 Niggerhead

Cabbage, Savoy
B. oleracea var. *bullata* subvar. *subauda*
44 Ice Queen
45 January King
46 Savoy King

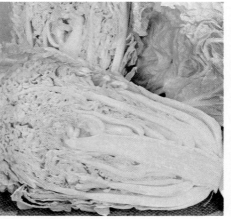

42

43

44 △

45

46

Calabrese
Brassica oleracea var. *italica*
47 Italian Sprouting

48 **Cardoon**
Cynara cardunculus

Carrot
Daucus carota sativus
49 Autumn King
50 St Valery
51 Early French Frame
52 Nantes   Champion Scarlet Horn

47

48

49 △

50 △

51

52

Cauliflower

Brassica oleracea var. *botrytis*

53 Autumn Giant
54 English Winter – Reading Giant
55 Newton Seale
56 Snowball

Celeriac

Apium graveolens

57 Invictus

53 △

55

54 △

56 △

57

Celery
Apium graveolens
58 American Green – Greensnap
59 Giant White
60 Giant Red
61 Golden Self-blanching

58 △

59 △

60

61

62

63

62 **Chervil**
Anthriscus cerefolium

Chicory
Cichorium intybus
63 Witloof

Sweet Pepper, Capsicum
Capsicum annuum
64 Bell Boy

Chili Pepper, Capsicum
C. annuum
65 Friedsdorfer Red
66 Friedsdorfer Yellow

67 **Chives**
Allium schoenoprasum

68 **Corn Salad**
Valerianella locusta

69 **Cress**
Lepidium sativum
Mustard
Sinapis alba

64

65 △

67

68 △

66

69

70

70 **Cress, American**
   Barbarea praecox

Cucumber
   Cucumis sativus
71 Burpee Hybrid
72 Crystal Apple
73 Patio Pik
74 Telegraph Improved

Endive
   Cichorium endivia
75 Batavian Green
76 Green Curled

71

72 △

73 △

74

75

76

77 △

78

79 △

80

77 **Fennel**
   Foeniculum vulgare

78 **Fennel, Florence**
   F. vulgare dulce

79 **Garlic**
   Allium sativum

80 **Good King Henry**
   Chenopodium bonus-henricus

81

82 △

81 **Horseradish**
Armoracia rusticana

Kale, Curly
Brassica oleracea var. *acephala*
subvar. *laciniata*
82 Dwarf Green Curled
83 Pentland Brig

Kohlrabi
B. oleracea var. *gongyloides*
84 Purple Vienna
85 White Vienna

Leek
Allium porrum
86 Giant Winter – Royal Favourite
87 Winter Crop

83

84

85

86

87

88 △

89 △

90

91 △

92 △

93

94

Marrow
Cucurbita pepo
95 Early Gem
96 Golden Zucchini
97 Long Green Trailing
98 Long White Bush
99 Tender and True
100 Vegetable Spaghetti

95

96

97 △

98 △

99

100

101

102

103

104 △

101 **Spearmint**
Mentha spicata

102 **Bowles Mint**
M. × villosa allopecuroides

103 **Mushroom**
Psalliota campestris

Onion
Allium cepa
104 Ailsa Craig – Mammoth
105 Brunswick

105

106

107 △

108 △

109

110

111

Onion (continued)
106 Express Yellow O-X
107 Stuttgart
108 White Lisbon

109 **Onion, Ever-ready**
   Allium cepa var. *perutile*

110 **Onion, Tree**
   A. cepa var. *aggregatum*

111 **Onion, Welsh**
   A. fistulosum

Parsley
Petroselinum hortense
112 Moss Curled

113 **Parsley, Hamburg Turnip-Rooted**
P. crispum 'Tuberosum'

Parsnip
Pastinaca sativa
114 Avonresistor
115 Tender and True

112

113

114

115

116 △

117

118 △

119

120 △

121

Pea
Pisum sativum
116 Feltham First
117 Kelvedon Wonder
118 Onward
119 Purple Podded
120 Sleaford Three Kings
121 Sugar Dwarf Sweet Green
(Mangetout)

122 △

123 △

124

125 △

Potato
Solanum tuberosum
122 Arran Pilot
123 Desirée
124 King Edward VII
125 Pentland Hawk and Pentland Ivory
126 Pink Fir Apple

126

127 △

128 △

129 △

130

131

132

133

134 △

135 △

136

137

138

139 △

140 △

141 △

142

143

Rhubarb
Rheum rhaponticum
139 Timperley Early

140 **Sage**
Salvia officinalis

Scorzonera
Scorzonera hispanica
141 Giant Russian

Salsify
Tragopogon porrifolius
142 Sandwich Island

143 **Seakale** (in summer)
Crambe maritima

144

145

146

147

148

Shallot
Allium ascalonicum
144 Dutch, Giant Yellow

145 **Sorrel, French**
Rumex scutatus

Spinach
Spinacia oleracea
146 Dominant

147 **Spinach, New Zealand**
Tetragonia tetragoniodes (expansa)

Swede
Brassica napus var. *napobrassica*
148 Magnificent

149

150

151

Sweetcorn
Zea mays
149 Kelvedon Glory

150 **Tarragon, French**
Artemisia dracunculus var. *sativa*

151 **Thyme, Golden**
Thymus vulgaris

152 △

153

154 △

155

156 △

157

158

Tomato

Lycopersicon lycopersicum

152 Findon Cross
153 French Cross
154 Gardener's Delight
155 Golden Boy
156 Kirdford Cross
157 Maascross
158 Marmande

159 △

160 △

161 △

162 △

163

164

165

Tomato (continued)
159 Peach
160 Pixie
161 Roma
162 Sonata
163 Tangella
164 Tigerella
165 Tiny Tim

166 △

167 △

168

169

Turnip

Brassica rapa var. *rapa*

166 Golden Perfection
167 Milan White
168 Purple Top Milan
169 Purple Top White Globe

170 **Watercress**

Nasturtium officinale

170

Angelica *Angelica archangelica*
UMBELLIFERAE **1**

Artichoke, Chinese *Stachys affinis* LABIATAE **2**

Artichoke, Globe *Cynara scolymus* COMPOSITAE
– *Gros Camus de Bretagne* large heads of good
flavour but not always readily available.
– *Gros Vert de Laon* a vigorous cultivar, growing
up to 90cm. (3ft) in height, with pale green heads;
highly regarded by many connoisseurs. **3**
– *Large Round French Green* fine round heads;
not quite such a vigorous grower as 'Gros Vert de
Laon'.
– *Roscoff Blue* sharper pointed heads, purplish in
colour. **4**

Artichoke, Jerusalem *Helianthus tuberosus*
COMPOSITAE
Probably the best known cultivar is the 'Pink' or
'Purple-skinned', but the 'White' is of more
delicate flavour and better shape. **5**
– *Fuseau* white-skinned and the easiest to deal
with in the kitchen. However it is not always
readily available.

Asparagus *Asparagus officinalis* LILIACEAE
– *Argenteuil* a later French cultivar of excellent
flavour. **6**
– *'Connover's Colossal'* still the most popular
variety. Introduced from the USA, it is an
excellent asparagus with thick, greenish-white
shoots. **7**
– *Martha Washington* a cultivar from the USA
with resistance to rust. F_1 hybrid pedigree strains
bred from selected male and female plants and
local strains may be found in those parts where
the crop is grown commercially.
– *Paske's Regal* a cultivar which has come to the
fore in recent years, producing a good crop of
large succulent heads unsurpassed for flavour.

Asparagus Pea, Winged Pea
Tetragonolobus purpureus LEGUMINOSAE. **8**

Aubergine, Egg Plant *Solanum melongena*
ovigerum SOLANACEAE
– *Burpee Hybrid* an early, tall growing hybrid,
producing a continuous crop of medium-sized,
oval, dark purple fruits.
– *Early Long Purple* large, dark purple, oval
fruits with firm flesh.
– *Large-Fruited Slice-Rite No. 23* an F_1 hybrid
which produces very large, oblong, black fruits.
– *Mammoth* a standard cultivar with deep purple
fruits. **9**
– *Moneymaker* an F_1 hybrid and a very
productive early cultivar with dark purple fruits
up to 15cm. (6in.) in length.
– *Small Fruited Purple* a very bushy plant, which
produces several fruits. Very suitable for growing
in window boxes, pots, or peat bags.
– *Short Tom* a prolific, early F_1 hybrid with fruits
up to 13cm. (5in.) in length.

Balm, Lemon Balm *Melissa officinalis*
LABIATAE **10**

Basil, Sweet *Ocimum basilicum* LABIATAE **11**

Bay *Laurus nobilis* LAURACEAE **12**

Bean, Broad *Vicia faba major* LEGUMINOSAE

– *Aquadulce* and *Aquadulce Claudia, Aquadulce
Extra Longpod, New Mammoth* long-podded
Seville types, recommended for autumn and early
winter sowing. Very hardy cultivars, with long
handsome pods which mature early, but should
not be sown after the end of January. Earlier
maturity is achieved by sowing seed imported
from a warmer region such as North Africa. **13**
– *Aquadulce Extra Longpod* see Aquadulce
Claudia.
– *Colossal* see Conqueror.
– *Conqueror, Colossal, Exhibition Longpod* a very
long-podded cultivar of excellent flavour, also
good for exhibition. **14**
– *Dreadnought, Giant Exhibition Longpod* a very
long-podded cultivar of excellent quality,
recommended for exhibition.
– *Exhibition Longpod* see 'Conqueror'.
– *Giant Exhibition Longpod* see 'Dreadnought'.
– *Imperial Green Longpod* a green-seeded
longpod; a very heavy cropper.
– *Imperial Green Windsor* an improved form of
Windsor, with up to 7 green beans per pod of
excellent flavour; suitable for main or late crops.
– *Imperial White Longpod* considered to be one
of the longest podded and heaviest croppers;
excellent for exhibition.
– *Imperial White Windsor* an improvement in the
white-seeded form of Windsor bean.
– *Masterpiece Green Longpod* a long-podded
cultivar with green seeds. Useful for exhibition
and has excellent flavour. Suitable for freezing.
– *Meteor* a heavy producer of early maturing
medium length pods, highly recommended for
flavour and deep freezing.
– *New Mammoth* see 'Aquadulce Claudia'.
– *The Sutton* an excellent cultivar for small
gardens, and very useful for growing under
cloches as it only grows to 38cm. (15in.) in height.
A very bushy grower, each plant producing 3 or 4
stems, with a cluster of 13cm. (5in.) pods on each.
It is best grown in a single row because of this,
and is useful for successional cropping. **15**

Bean, Climbing French *Phaseolus vulgaris*
LEGUMINOSAE
– *Blue Lake White Seeded* a strong grower with
fleshy, stringless pods of good flavour; bears a
prolific crop. Suitable for under glass or freezing.
– *Coco-Bicolour* a distinctive cultivar, with very
broad green pods, which, if cooked whole while
young, have an excellent flavour. The distinctly
marked seeds are useful for drying as haricots.
– *Earliest of All* has all the merits of dwarf beans
combined with the advantages of the climbers: an
extended season and easier picking. Suitable for
growing on bushy pea sticks in single rows 90cm.
(3ft) apart. Can also be grown for harvesting, the
white seeds being used as haricots.
– *Guernsey Climbing* see 'Veitch's Climbing'.
– *Romano* a heavy cropper, has stringless, high
quality fleshy pods which freeze well.
– *Veitch's Climbing, Guernsey Climbing* this
cultivar is cultivated under glass in the Channel
Islands and is also suitable for cultivation
outside.
– *Violet Podded Stringless, Bunyard's Blue Coco*
a most distinctive cultivar of vigorous growth, so
bean poles or strong canes are required for
supports. The plants should be 23cm. (9in.) apart
and they attain a height of 2.4m. (8ft). The stems
and leaves are an attractive purplish-blue colour
as are the flowers and pods. The tender pods are

fleshy and distinctive in flavour and become
bright green when immersed in boiling water for
2 minutes. Suitable for freezing, it crops freely
without setting troubles. **16**

Bean, Dwarf French *Phaseolus vulgaris*
LEGUMINOSAE
Considerable advances in continuous cropping
cultivars have been made by plant breeders.
Stringless cultivars suitable for freezing are now
much more popular.
– *Black Prince* recommended for July sowing,
provides a late crop under glass or plastic.
– *Canadian Wonder* a well tried cultivar for
maincrop, matures later and is more suitable for
cold, exposed gardens than earlier maturing
cultivars.
– *Chevrier Vert* a most useful cultivar tolerant to
virus and resistant to anthracnose. It produces a
heavy crop of medium length, dark green pods.
These can be used in 3 stages when green
(Haricots verts), i.e. pods and beans in young
state, in the intermediate stage (Haricots
flageolets), i.e. beans only, used fresh, and when
ripe and dry for use in winter (Haricots secs), i.e.
beans only, but dried.
– *Earligreen* useful for early crops and
successional sowings. Compact in habit, it bears a
good crop of very fleshy pods. When ripe, its
white seeds can be used as haricots; suitable for
freezing.
– *Flair* an early, disease-resistant cultivar with
oval pods, which are very fleshy and stringless;
suitable for freezing.
– *Glamis* a very heavy cropper raised by the
Scottish Horticultural Research Establishment.
It is especially suitable for the more rugged
conditions of exposed and northern gardens.
The fleshy pods are stringless. **17**
– *Kinghorn Wax* a reliable wax-podded bean
with golden pods which are slightly curved. Beans
are white-seeded, have an excellent flavour and
are good for freezing. **18**
– *Masterpiece* one of the most popular cultivars
with long pods which mature early. If picked
young it will continue to crop over a long period
and may be cooked whole. Good for forcing and
suitable for freezing.
– *Phenix Claudia* a heavy cropper with early,
long, dark green pods of good flavour which
retain their colour when cooked. Suitable for
freezing and stringless.
– *The Prince* a very popular early cultivar which
produces an immense crop if kept picked. Very
long pods make it an exhibitor's favourite. Good
for forcing under cloches and for freezing.
– *Processor* a heavy cropping cultivar from the
Continent. The round fleshy pods are stringless,
white-seeded and excellent for freezing.
– *Remus* a cultivar of recent introduction which
carries its pods above the foliage, ensuring easier
gathering. The long, straight pods do not come
into contact with the soil and are of good flavour;
useful in salads as a raw vegetable. **19**
– *Royalty* a heavy cropper especially if picked
young. Of very good quality, it has stringless,
purplish-blue pods which turn green after 2
minutes in boiling water. Grows well in cool
weather.
– *Sigmacropper* a new variety which produces a
very heavy crop.
– *Sprite* a cultivar with dark green pencil pods
which are stringless and excellent for freezing. **20**

– *Tendergreen* an early variety with fleshy round pods produced over a long season if picked hard; stringless and good for freezing.

Bean, Haricot *Phaseolus vulgaris* LEGUMINOSAE
– *Brown Dutch* a brown-seeded cultivar which ripens early.
– *Comtesse de Chambord, White Rice Kidney* a cultivar with short pods on a branching plant. The small white seeds are of good quality when dried out, but in a bad season are inclined to ripen late. **21**
– *Granda* a cultivar which can be used green but is more useful when dried for winter use.
– *White Rice Kidney* see 'Comtesse de Chambord'.

Bean, Runner *Phaseolus coccineus* LEGUMINOSAE
– *Achievement, Cookham Dene* a good general purpose cultivar of high quality, good colour and suitable for freezing.
– *Best of All* see 'Streamline'.
– *Cookham Dene* see 'Achievement'.
– *Crusader* a long-podded cultivar which sets well and produces large clusters of broad, fleshy pods of good quality which are suitable for freezing.
– *Enorma* a very fine cultivar with long, slender deep green pods of excellent quality. Much valued by exhibitors, it is also suitable for freezing. **22**
– *Erecta* see 'White Emergo'.
– *Fry* a white-flowered, self-pollinating, white-seeded, stringless bean from Holland, which is of good flavour and crops and freezes well.
– *Goliath* see 'Prizetaker'.
– *Hammonds Dwarf Scarlet* a true dwarf form, growing about 41 to 46cm. (16 to 18in.) high, which requires no support from stakes. Suitable for cloche cultivation if early crops are required. The short pods, 20 to 23cm. (8 to 9in.) long, are of good quality and suitable for freezing.
– *Hammonds Dwarf White* similar to above in habit, but white-flowered and white-seeded. Very useful for small gardens, it can be grown as recommended for bush cultivars; no pinching is necessary.
– *Kelvedon Marvel, Kelvedon Wonder* an early cultivar, shorter in pod and growth. Very useful for bush cultivation; prolific, of good quality and suitable for freezing.
– *Kelvedon Wonder* see 'Kelvedon Marvel'.
– *Prizetaker* a long-podded cultivar producing a heavy crop of good quality; useful for exhibition and freezing.
– *Prizewinner* large, fleshy pods of good flavour and quality, but surpassed in length by 'Achievement' and 'Enorma'.
– *Streamline* a cultivar with a good constitution which is popular because of its reliability in producing a good crop of long pods.
– *Sunset* a most distinctive cultivar with pale pink, self-pollinating flowers. An early maturing variety of recent introduction, which is very short-jointed and excellent for growing without support by pinching back the growths. Produces a good crop of medium length pods of excellent flavour. **23**
– *White Achievement* a white-flowered and white-seeded form of 'Achievement', with all the excellent qualities of that cultivar. The seeds may be dried in the same way as haricots and used as a substitute for butter beans.

– *White Emergo* a white-seeded and white-flowered variety which produces a heavy crop of fleshy pods of good length suitable for freezing.

Bean, Soya *Glycine max* LEGUMINOSAE
– *Fiskeby V* the cultivar best capable of withstanding cooler climates, though yet to become fully acclimatized. **24**

Beetroot, Red Beet *Beta vulgaris* var. *esculenta* CHENOPODIACEAE
– *Avonearly* a cultivar bred primarily for early cropping but which does not show the tendency of older cultivars of running to seed when sown early; in other words it is bolt-resistant.
– *Boltardy* for early sowing and resistant to bolting. The flesh colour is good; a useful cultivar for early shows.
– *Burpees Golden* a cultivar with rich golden flesh and good flavour which does not 'bleed' like the red. A dual purpose vegetable because the leaves can be cooked like spinach. **25**
– *Cheltenham Green Top* a long cultivar of good quality and one of the best varieties for storage purposes; an old, well-known standard cultivar. **26**
– *Cheltenham Mono* a new cultivar even better in colour than the above and equally good for storing until spring. It has been bred to avoid the need for singling the clusters of plants which develop from ordinary beet seed. It is 'monogerm', so only single plants usually grow from each seed.
– *Crimson Globe* see 'Detroit'.
– *Cylindra* equal in quality to the globe-shaped cultivars. Roots are cylindrical, 13cm. to 15cm. (5 to 6in.) long and 5cm. (2in.) across, a convenient size for cooking. Suitable for freezing. **27**
– *Detroit, Crimson Globe, Globe, Model Red Globe, Perfect, Ruddigore* a fine globe beet, with deep red flesh from which numerous selections have been made.
– *Detroit-Crimson Globe Improved* a good selection for April sowing.
– *Detroit-Little Ball* a selection especially useful for sowing in succession during summer, particularly in July when it produces blood red, globe-shaped roots. Good for use in autumn and early winter. **28**
– *Early Green Top Bunching* see 'Egyptian Turnip Rooted'.
– *Egyptian Turnip Rooted, Early Green Top Bunching* a round flat-rooted beetroot useful for early crops on shallow soils but of inferior quality for later crops.
– *Globe* see 'Detroit'.
– *Model Red Globe* see 'Detroit'.
– *Perfect* see 'Detroit'.
– *Ruddigore* see 'Detroit'.
– *Snowhite* a new cultivar, white-fleshed, non-bleeding and dual purpose as the leaves and stems may be cooked like spinach. Flavour of root earthy and sweet.

Beet, Leaf *Beta vulgaris* var. *cycla* CHENOPODIACEAE
– *Perpetual Spinach* much used as a spinach substitute, it is a prolific and accommodating plant. **29**
– *Rhubarb Chard* a cultivar with long, bright red stems and crumpled dark green leaves. It may be cooked like 'Silver or Seakale'. It is also worth growing as an ornamental plant, for flower

arrangement or for displays of vegetables at shows. **30**
– *Silver or Seakale* a handsome plant with broad, silvery-white mid-ribs. **31**

Borage *Borago officinalis* BORAGINACEAE **32**

Borecole see Kale, Curly.

Broccoli, Sprouting
Brassica oleracea var. *italica* CRUCIFERAE
– *Purple* the most commonly grown and hardiest type. **33**
– *White* considered to be superior in flavour to the above. **34**
Early and late selections of both types available.

Brussels Sprouts *Brassica oleracea* var. *bullata* subsp. *gemmifera* CRUCIFERAE
– *Achilles* an F₁ and reliable, heavy cropper; medium-sized sprouts which keep for a long time and freeze well. **35**
– *Bedford* an open-pollinated or standard variety, of which 'Ashwell's Strain', 'Fillbasket', 'Market Rearguard' and 'Winter Harvest' are all reliable selections which grow well on most soils and cover the season.
– *Citadel* a late F₁ hybrid, easy to pick and to freeze.
– *Focus* an F₁ hybrid which produces fine quality sprouts over a long period; suitable for freezing.
– *Peer Gynt* an F₁ hybrid which suits small gardens, being dwarf in habit. At its best in October, when it is good for exhibition; freezes well. **36**
– *Perfect Line* a mid-season F₁ hybrid which produces a good crop of solid, medium-sized sprouts.
– *Prince Askold* a late, semi-tall cultivar which crops heavily, producing dark green, very solid sprouts of medium size which freeze well.
– *Red* see 'Rubine'.
– *Roodnerf* an open-pollinated or standard variety which has a number of selections: Early Button, with small, walnut-sized sprouts, is especially suitable for freezing; 'Stickema Early', also freezes well and is of good quality; 'Vremo Inter', is excellent up to February.
– *Rubine, Red* an open pollinated or standard variety, has reddish sprouts considered by some gardeners to be of high quality, but generally regarded as a novelty suitable for display.
– *Sigmund* a late-maturing F₁ hybrid which produces very firm sprouts early to mid-season, much the same time as 'Peer Gynt'.
– *Topscore* a very uniform F₁ hybrid which produces very firm sprouts early to mid-season. much the same time as 'Peer Gynt'.

Cabbage *Brassica oleracea* var. *capitata alba* CRUCIFERAE
– *April* a small pointed head compact cultivar, autumn sown for use in spring, ideal for close planting. Not liable to bolt.
– *Autumn Pride* an F₁ hybrid for use in autumn and winter, with large, solid, flat heads of good quality, which retain their condition for a long time.
– *Babyhead* see 'Vienna'.
– *Christmas Drumhead* a well known, hardy dwarf compact cultivar for use in autumn and winter.
– *Durham* autumn sown for use in spring, this is

an early maturing variety with heads of medium size. 'Elf' is a selection of high quality.

– **Evesham Special** see 'Offenham'.

– **First and Best** see 'Offenham'.

– **First Early Market 218** a large-headed variety, autumn sown for use in spring, which produces heads quickly. 'Early Giant' is a selection. Excellent for *in situ* sowing for collards. **37**

– **Golden Acre, June Giant, Primo** a medium to large ball-headed cabbage which may also be sown under glass in January or February where early supplies are required. 'May Express' and 'Progress' are selections.

– **Harbinger** autumn sown for use in spring; a small, conical, pointed-hearted variety of fine quality; very early.

– **Hispi** an F_1 hybrid, is the earliest summer pointed-head cabbage. Uniform in size, it can be planted closer than most; about 25cm. (10in.) apart. Ideal for sowing under glass in January to get an early crop. **38**

– **June Giant** see 'Golden Acre'.

– **June Star** an F_1 hybrid ball-head with very uniform, dark green heads. May be sown under glass. **39**

– **Langendijk 4 – Holland Winter White** a selection grown for winter storage. **40**

– **Myatts Early Offenham** see 'Offenham'.

– **Offenham, Evesham Special, First and Best, Myatts Early Offenham** autumn sown for use in spring; hardy with large, conical heads on short stems, better known in the selection 'Flower of Spring', which has a large heart and little outside leaf. 'Spring Bounty' is another selection of compact habit.

– **Primata** an F_1 hybrid ball-head which matures early, especially if sown under glass.

– **Primo** see 'Golden Acre'.

– **Vienna, Babyhead** a cultivar with small, round heads, which has the advantage of standing a long time without splitting.

– **Wheeler's Imperial** autumn sown for use in spring; a dwarf, dark green compact cabbage, medium in maturity and of fine flavour.

– **Winnigstadt** for use in autumn and winter; despite its age, still a very popular cultivar, with very tight, pointed heads. Darkish green in colour and much favoured by exhibitors for shows in August to October. Very good for shredding in salads. It does well on any reasonably good soil. **41**

– **Winter Monarch** for use in autumn and winter; an F_1 hybrid which stands a long time without splitting and comes in during the difficult months of December to February.

Cabbage, Chinese, Chinese Leaves
Brassica pekinensis CRUCIFERAE

– **Nagoaka** an F_1 hybrid, a uniform grower, producing large, tight cylindrical heads.

– **Pe-tsai** pale green, long, slender hearts. **42**

– **Sampan** an F_1 hybrid less liable to bolt. Shaped like a rugby football and outstanding for its solid hearts.

– **Tip Top** an F_1 hybrid similar to 'Nagoaka', but later in maturing.

Cabbage, Red *Brassica oleracea*
var. *capitata rubra* CRUCIFERAE

– **Langendijk Red Medium** a very uniform cultivar which matures in late autumn.

– **Niggerhead,** a fine cultivar for pickling. **43**

– **Ruby Ball** an F_1 hybrid from USA, has aroused

interest having received the high award of a gold medal in the All America Trials. Uniform in habit; maturing early, solid, ball-shaped with a high reputation for quality.

Cabbage, Savoy *Brassica oleracea*
var. *bullata* var. *subauda* CRUCIFERAE

– **Best of All** an early, large, solid-hearted cultivar, useful for exhibitions and shows in August and September.

– **Celtic** an F_1 hybrid between hardy Savoy and winter storage type cabbage. Very hardy and vigorous, it keeps in good condition without splitting from November to February. Should be useful in exposed areas.

– **Ice Queen** an F_1 hybrid which, by sowing at different times, can be early to late in season. As the name implies, it is very hardy and of good quality. **44**

– **January King** well known for its quality and great hardiness. Generally matures in December, but will stand to April. Indispensable in bad winters. **45**

– **Ormskirk** an old favourite available in a number of selections: 'Early', 'Medium', 'Late', and 'Rearguard', the latter standing until April. Generally hardy and medium in size.

– **Savoy King** an F_1 hybrid which is early, light green, with very solid hearts of excellent quality. **46**

– **Winter King** a new strain; very dark green; very resistant to frost.

Calabrese, Green Italian Sprouting Broccoli
Brassica oleracea var. *italica* CRUCIFERAE

– **Autumn Spear** can be cut from September to November.

– **Empress Corona** an F_1 hybrid matures early and crops heavily during August and September.

– **Green Comet** an F_1 hybrid, has a large central head but few side shoots.

– **Italian Sprouting** recommended for flavour and the home freezer. **47**

Cardoon *Cynara cardunculus* COMPOSITAE **48**

Carrot *Daucus carota sativus* UMBELLIFERAE

– **Amsterdam Forcing-Amstel** an early stump-rooted selection of finger size, excellent for sowing under protection for early crops, or for succession; suitable for freezing.

– **Autumn King, Norfolk Giant** a large stump-rooted variety, suitable for storage or winter use. **49**

– **Autumn King–Concord** a selection with dark flesh and red core, recommended for successional sowings.

– **Berlicum** good for winter storage; high colour and smooth skin; favoured by pre-packers.

– **Chantenay Red Cored, Early Market Horn, Maincrop, Stump Improved, Rooted Scarlet Stump Intermediate** a well known and popular stump-rooted variety favoured for maincrop.

– **Chantenay Red Cored–Favourite** a popular selection of good quality and fine shape; good for exhibition in short carrot classes.

– **Early French Frame** a very early maturing carrot with round roots, ideal for forcing in a frame. **51**

– **Early Market Horn** see 'Chantenay Red Cored'.

– **Little Finger** a slender-rooted carrot ideal for forcing in frames for early protection.

– **Maincrop Stump Improved** see 'Chantenay Red Cored'.

– **Norfolk Giant** see 'Autumn King'.

– **Nantes–Champion Scarlet Horn** a good selection for cloche cultivation; stump-rooted; little core; deep red; ideal for successional sowings; suitable for freezing. **52**

– **St Valery** a long, pointed carrot; bright red; small core; very popular for exhibition in long-rooted classes. **50**

– **Scarla** a stump-rooted maincrop which keeps well in winter. Good colour; almost coreless.

– **Stump Rooted Scarlet Intermediate** see 'Chantenay Red Cored'.

Cauliflower *Brassica oleracea* var. *botrytis*
CRUCIFERAE

– **All the Year Round, Le Cerf** a favourite summer cauliflower, but, though being easy to grow, it compares unfavourably with more recently produced cultivars or selections. It may also be sown outside, when it matures later and is suitable for freezing.

– **Alpha** a summer cauliflower which has several selections: 'Climax', 'Perfection' and 'Polar Ice' are recommended for quality.

– **Autumn Giant** a variety with well protected curds. Selections are: 'Autumn Protecting', which matures from November to December, 'Majestic' and 'Superlative Protecting', which mature in November. **53**

– **Barrier Reef** an autumn cauliflower; the product of an Australian breeding programme; dwarf habit; pure white curds which are deep and uniform and thus very popular. Selection 'Wombat' matures late September.

– **Boomerang** an autumn cauliflower; of similar habit to 'Barrier Reef'; matures October, November.

– **Le Cerf** see 'All the Year Round'.

– **Dominant** a dark-leaved variety of summer cauliflower which withstands dry, warm weather well; a reliable cultivar.

– **English Winter** a winter cauliflower. Selections are: 'Adam's Early White', 'June Market', 'Late Queen', 'Progress', 'Reading Giant' **54**, and 'St George'.

– **Flora Blanca** an autumn cauliflower, similar to 'Autumn Giant'. 'Torina' is a selection, which matures from September to December.

– **Kangaroo** an autumn cauliflower; of dwarf habit; pure white curds; matures from September to October.

– **Manly** an autumn cauliflower; similar to above in habit; matures late October.

– **Mechelse** a typical summer cauliflower, short-legged, and open-leaved, so the curd is unprotected. The selection 'Classic' matures early, has fine-grained, pearly curds, and is suitable for forcing, especially under plastic tunnels.

– **Newton Seale** a winter cauliflower; comes in from mid-March to April; frost-resistant and worth a trial in maritime gardens. **55**

– **Roscoff** a winter cauliflower. Selections commercially available include 'Asmer', 'Trevean' and 'Seale-Hayne'.

– **Snowball** a summer cauliflower; the selection 'Polaris' is even earlier than 'Mechelse-Classic', with solid well-protected curds and 'Arcturus' which is later and recommended for its high quality. **56**

– **Walcheren Winter** a winter cauliflower.

Selections: 'Manston', 'Thanet' and 'White Cliffs'. 'Thanet' comes in end of April followed by 'White Cliffs', with 'Manston' towards the end of May.

Celeriac, Turnip-rooted Celery
Apium graveolens UMBELLIFERAE
– *Alabaster* roots of good quality and flavour.
– *Giant Prague* good quality roots of fine flavour.
– *Globus* good quality roots suitable for freezing.
– *Invictus* a very fine cultivar; large smooth roots and very neat foliage. **57**

Celery *Apium graveolens* UMBELLIFERAE
– *American Green* a self-blanching cultivar; pale green stems, crisp and of good flavour when well grown; 'Greensnap' is a selection. **58**
– *Avonpearl* a new self-blanching cultivar from the National Seed Development Organization, Cambridge.
– *Giant Pink* a trenching cultivar. Selections 'Mammoth' and 'Unrivalled'. Heavy sticks of good length, pale pink in colour, excellent flavour and good for exhibition.
– *Giant Red* a good late trenching variety which will keep into the New Year. Very dark red sticks. **60**
– *Giant White* a well known trenching variety valued for use from October to December. Selections are: 'Mammoth', 'Solid White' and 'White Ice'. **59**
– *Golden Self blanching* very early, crisp and nutty. **61**
– *Latham Self blanching* a good grower of fine flavour.

Chervil *Anthriscus cerefolium* UMBELLIFERAE **62**

Chicory *Cichorium intybus* COMPOSITAE
– *Brussels Chicory* see 'Witloof'.
– *Mitado* a new cultivar from Holland which produces 'chicons' naturally; for forcing from November to February.
– *Normata* as above but for forcing from November to December.
– *Pain de Sucre, Sugar Loaf* resembles a well grown cos lettuce and does not require blanching. Best results are obtained by sowing in June or July.
– *Plumato* similar to 'Mitado' and 'Normata' in habit but for forcing from September to November.
– *Red Verona* may be sown from May to August and, if forced, produces compact red heads of a slightly bitter flavour.
– *Sugar Loaf* see 'Pain de Sucre'.
– *Tardivo* 'folds in' naturally; for forcing from February to April.
– *Witloof, Brussels Chicory* the cultivar usually grown for 'chicon' production. The roots are merely planted in a box or pot of sand, soil or peat, and placed in a dark, warm place. **63**

Chili Pepper, Sweet Pepper, Capsicum
Capsicum annuum SOLANACEAE
– *Bell Boy* an F₁ hybrid is a maincrop green or sweet pepper which has given excellent results commercially, cropping heavily and being resistant to tomato mosaic virus. **64**
– *Canape* an F₁ hybrid green pepper is early with slightly elongated fruits, very suitable for polythene tunnels and resistant to tomato mosaic virus.

– *Cayenne* a recommended chili or hot pepper cultivar.
– *Chili* a recommended hot pepper cultivar.
– *Friedsdorfer Red* grown normally for decorative purposes or for cutting. The fruits may be used in pickles. **65**
– *Friedsdorfer Yellow* as above, but fruits yellow when ripe. Useful for Christmas decoration; fruits may be used in pickles. **66**
– *New Ace* an F₁ hybrid, is the earliest green pepper; a very high yielder when grown in heat and resistant to tomato mosaic virus.
– *Rumba* a new F₁ hybrid green pepper from Holland, very useful for cropping in autumn, giving a high yield.
– *World Beater* a well tried cultivar, producing dark green fruits which turn deep red, with a mild sweet flavour.

Chinese Leaves see Cabbage, Chinese.

Chives *Allium schoenoprasum*
LILIACEAE/AMARYLLIDACEAE **67**

Corn Salad, Lamb's Lettuce *Valerianella locusta*
VALERIANACEAE
– *Large leaved Italian* a popular cultivar. **68**
– *Large Seeded English* a strong grower.
– *Verte de Cambrai* frost resistant; popular in France.

Cress *Lepidium sativum* CRUCIFERAE **69**

Cress, American *Barbarea praecox* CRUCIFERAE **70**

Cucumber *Cucumis sativus* CUCURBITACEAE
– *Baton Vert* an F₁ hybrid ridge cucumber; prolific and of good flavour, maturing early.
– *Burpee Hybrid* an F₁ hybrid; a heavy cropping ridge type with dark green, good quality fruits of equal size. **71**
– *Burpless Tasty Green* an F₁ hybrid; a ridge type which resembles greenhouse cultivars in its high quality fruits; crops heavily and is resistant to downy and powdery mildew.
– *Butcher's Disease Resisting* popular greenhouse type; crops heavily; fruits somewhat ribbed; grows well in heated or cold houses or in frames.
– *Conqueror* an easy growing greenhouse type, which succeeds well in cold houses or in frames; well shaped, dark green fruits.
– *Crystal Apple* a ridge type, unusual in its apple-shaped fruits and its pale yellow colouring. It is juicy, crisp, and excellent for salad. As it is more digestible than most it deserves greater popularity. **72**
– *Femdan* an all female flowered F₁ hybrid greenhouse type.
– *Green Spot* an F₁ hybrid similar in appearance to 'Butcher's Disease Resisting'; a vigorous and heavy cropper.
– *Hokus* regarded by some as the best gherkin.
– *Japanese Climbing* grows well on netting if sheltered by a sunny wall and may also be grown in a cold greenhouse.
– *King George* an exhibitor's favourite; very fine appearance; keeps its colour well.
– *Marion* an F₁ hybrid ridge type; genetically bitter-free and resistant to virus disease; a strong grower.
– *Nadir* an F₁ hybrid; a long-fruited ridge; good flavour and prolific in habit.
– *Patio Pik* an F₁ hybrid ridge type; an unusual

cultivar which can be sown or planted more closely, taking up very little room; crops heavily; good quality. **73**
– *Perfection* a ridge cultivar producing a good crop of 13 to 15cm. (5 to 6in.), long fruits, especially if kept cut.
– *Petite Pepino* a more digestible ridge type, especially if used immediately after picking. Regarded by some as better than 'Crystal Apple', standing up better to bad weather.
– *Sigmadew* a pale, almost white cultivar which grows best under glass and has superb flavour.
– *Telegraph Improved* a popular cultivar of good appearance; reliable under glass or in frame. **74**
– *Venlo* a cultivar used by commercial growers to produce gherkins for the pickle trade, for which purpose it is excellent, as it provides a heavy crop of small fruits.
– *Virgo* an all female-flowered cultivar, suitable for heated or cold houses; resistant to leaf spot and gummosis; a good cropper.

Egg Plant see Aubergine.

Endive *Cichorium endivia* COMPOSITAE
– *Batavian Green* for use in late autumn and winter. **75**
– *Green Curled, Moss Curled* for use in late summer and autumn **76**
– *Moss Curled* see 'Green Curled'.

Fennel *Foeniculum vulgare* UMBELLIFERAE **77**

Fennel, Florence *Foeniculum vulgare dulce*
UMBELLIFERAE **78**

Garlic *Allium sativum*
LILIACEAE/AMARYLLIDACEAE **79**

Good King Henry, Mercury or Perennial Goosefoot *Chenopodium bonus-henricus*
CHENOPODIACEAE **80**

Green Italian Sprouting Broccoli see Calabrese.

Horseradish *Armoracia rusticana* CRUCIFERAE **81**

Kale, Curly or Borecole
Brassica oleracea var. *acephala* subvar. *laciniata*
CRUCIFERAE
– *Cottagers* a very free-growing, plain leaved type; very hardy and prolific; variable in colour.
– *Dwarf Green Curled, Dwarf Green Curled Scotch* a dwarf Scottish cultivar. **82**
– *Dwarf Green Curled Scotch* see 'Dwarf Green Curled'.
– *Frosty* a densely curled cultivar of attractive appearance.
– *Hungry Gap* should be sown *in situ* in July in drills 46cm. (18in.) apart. Thin plants to 30cm. (12in.) apart. A valuable cultivar in cold areas, coming in during April and May.
– *Pentland Brig* a new variety bred in Scotland, the result of crossing a plain-leaved with a curled type; produces freely from February to April. **83**
– *Tall Green Curled, Tall Scotch Curled* the very hardy curled Scottish variety.
– *Tall Scotch Curled* see 'Tall Green Curled'.

Kohlrabi *Brassica oleracea* var. *gongyloides*
CRUCIFERAE
– *Green Vienna* see 'White Vienna'.
– *Primavera White* early and quick growing, it

can be planted more closely than those mentioned below.
- *Purple Vienna* the standard purple cultivar. **84**
- *White Vienna, Green Vienna* also a standard; very pale green bulbs. **85**

Lamb's Lettuce see Corn Salad.

Leek *Allium porrum*
LILIACEAE/AMARYLLIDACEAE
- *Autumn Mammoth – Walton Mammoth* a well tried selection for early use.
- *Giant Winter – Royal Favourite* a handsome, late, long-standing cultivar which is hardy and of good size. **86**
- *Lyon-Prizetaker* mild-flavoured; long, thick, white stems; a popular selection for the kitchen or exhibition.
- *Malabar* a quick grower for use in autumn; medium length stem and dark foliage.
- *Mammoth* very thick white stems; much in favour for exhibition.
- *Marble Pillar* a long-stemmed cultivar with solid, white stems; useful for exhibition.
- *Mont Blanc* a long-stemmed cultivar of superb quality; good for culinary use or for exhibition.
- *Musselburgh* a thick-stemmed, very hardy cultivar much favoured in Scotland for its reliability.
- *Pot Leek* an early, short, extremely thick-stemmed cultivar, up to 13cm. (5in.) blanch; the type popular in Northern England for competitions.
- *Swiss Giant* a long-stemmed, strong growing cultivar.
- *Winter Crop* as its name implies, stands well through the winter months; large white stems; one of the finest leeks of recent years. **87**
- *Yates Empire* a maincrop cultivar which stands well into April; long, thick white stems; a fine variety.

Lemon Balm see Balm.

Lettuce *Lactuca sativa* COMPOSITAE
- *All the Year Round* a well known, mid-season cabbage type cultivar.
- *Arctic King* a cabbage type for autumn sowing outside; a very hardy quick maturing cultivar.
- *Aurelia* a cabbage type for growing outdoors in summer; resistant to top-burn; medium green in colour.
- *Avoncrisp* a curly, crisp heart cultivar, most suitable for cropping in autumn.
- *Avondefiance* a cabbage type for growing outdoors in summer; dark green, mildew resistant; good for June to early August sowing.
- *Blondine–Premier* a forcing selection for sowing in October and January in cold frames for transplanting in the open or under the protection of cloches or frames. **88**
- *Buttercrunch* a medium size, dark green cos lettuce; crisp and long standing.
- *Continuity* a cabbage type for growing outdoors in summer; outside leaves tinged reddish brown; compact; good quality; does well on light soil and stands well. **89**
- *Grand Rapids* a non-hearting lettuce, with curled, fringed leaves, which may be grown under glass for use during the winter months or sown outside for summer or autumn use; good flavour.
- *Great Lakes* a very crisp, large, solid, dark green lettuce; suitable for late sowing.

- *Hilde* a cabbage type which may be sown under glass in January for transplanting in February, and onwards to July for succession: also good for frame or cloche cultivation. 'Fortune' and 'Suzan' are recommended selections.
- *Imperial Winter* a cabbage type for autumn sowing outside; very hardy; an excellent large variety.
- *Kloek* a forcing cultivar; sown in mid-October in slightly heated greenhouse, will turn in late March to early April.
- *Knap* a forcing cultivar; good for cutting mid-April under glass.
- *Kordaat* considered one of the finest cultivars for forcing during winter.
- *Kwiek* suitable for growing in a cold greenhouse; sown in late August will mature November and December; good quality.
- *Little Gem* a semi-cos lettuce; crisp; unequalled for flavour; medium size; hearts well, without any waste and grows well under cloches.
- *Lobcross* a cos lettuce, good for spring and summer sowing; solid hearts.
- *Lobjoits Green Cos* a very large-headed lettuce; rich, dark green; self-folding and crisp; stands well and does not bolt readily. **90**
- *May King, May Queen* a forcing cultivar; matures quickly in frame or greenhouse. Sown in October to March will supply lettuce March to June.
- *May Queen* see 'May King'.
- *Mildura* suitable for sowing in spring and summer; resistant to mildew.
- *Minetto* a small, crisp heart lettuce, pale coloured and attractive in appearance. Stands well in hot weather.
- *New York* see 'Webbs Wonderful'.
- *Pennlake* a smaller version of 'Great Lakes', very uniform in habit; good quality; good for spring and summer sowing.
- *Salad Bowl* a non-hearting cultivar, which may be sown from early April until July. The curled, fimbriated leaves may be picked as required, and are especially useful in dry weather, not being inclined to bolt. The plant keeps producing if only the bottom leaves are removed. **91**
- *Tom Thumb* the smallest lettuce; very early; only suitable for April sowing; handy for cloche or frame culture.
- *Unrivalled* a cabbage type; a good all round cultivar which is very popular and may be sown under glass or in succession outdoors from January to July. **92**
- *Valdor* a new cultivar for sowing in September; withstands severe weather well and produces large heads; may also be grown in a cold frame.
- *Valmaine* a tall growing, dark green cos lettuce which is very good in hot weather; comes in for late summer.
- *Webbs Wonderful, New York* a large crisp heart; very popular; slow to run to seed; pale in colour; inside leaves whiter; very crisp with good flavour. **93**
- *Windermere* a crisp heart; an ideal lettuce for hot, dry conditions: smaller, earlier and more compact than 'Great Lakes'; stands well, matures quickly, and can be sown in succession from March to July. An October sowing in cold frames will heart up in the following May.
- *Winter Density* a very popular cos lettuce for autumn sowing which only requires 15cm. (6in.) between each plant. Unlike the other hardy

cultivars mentioned, it can also be sown in spring and early summer for outside crops. **94**

Marrow *Cucurbita pepo* CUCURBITACEAE
- *Aristocrat* an F$_1$ hybrid suitable for courgettes; dark green fruits which are borne upright, making picking easier; at best when flower fades.
- *Covent Garden* a bush cultivar; heavy cropping; deep green fruits; ideal for young fruits of good quality.
- *Diamond* an early F$_1$ hybrid; suitable for courgettes; very prolific; dark green fruits.
- *Early Gem* an F$_1$ hybrid bush cultivar; very uniform in habit; early; produces heavy crop of long, dark green fruits of good quality; suitable for freezing. **95**
- *Emerald Cross* an F$_1$ hybrid suitable for courgettes; grey green fruits; may also be grown as an early marrow.
- *Golden Delicious* a trailing cultivar; produces a good crop of fruits with hard, orange-yellow skins and bright yellow thick flesh; keeps well for winter storage.
- *Golden Zucchini* suitable for courgettes; golden yellow fruits; may also be grown as a small marrow. **96**
- *Green Baby* suitable for courgettes; dark green, long, slender fruits.
- *Green Bush* an F$_1$ hybrid; very early; abundant producer; medium to dark green fruits.
- *Little Gem* a trailing cultivar from South Africa; round fruits the size of an orange, which should be used while green and may be cooked whole; useful for tripod training.
- *Long Green Bush – Improved Green Bush* a very popular bush selection, producing a large crop; medium-sized, striped, green fruits, good for frame or cloche cultivation and for exhibition.
- *Long Green Bush – Small Pak* a shorter fruited form of above selection; excellent quality; ideal for exhibition.
- *Long Green Trailing* large fruits, very dark green in colour; requires good cultivation; good for exhibition where large fruits are required; a good winter storage cultivar. **97**
- *Long White Bush* a popular cultivar with creamy, white fruits, freely produced and maturing early. **98**
- *Long White Trailing* similar to 'Long Green Trailing' but with creamy white fruits which store well for winter use.
- *Prokor* an F$_1$ hybrid; an early, prolific bush cultivar, dark green, medium sized fruits; a very quick grower.
- *Sleaford Gem* an F$_1$ hybrid; compact bush cultivar; dark green fruits flecked with pale green; very productive over a long period.
- *Table Dainty* a trailing cultivar; small, dark green fruits with pale green stripes; excellent quality and good for exhibition.
- *Tender and True* a bush cultivar; very distinctive, round mottled green fruits of very good quality, produced early. **99**
- *Vegetable Spaghetti* an easily grown trailing cultivar; white or yellow fruits, 20cm. (8in.) long; when mature, the fruits should be boiled and the scooped-out flesh will have the appearance of spaghetti. **100**
- *Zucchini* suitable for courgettes; early, long slender dark green fruits of good flavour.

Mercury see Good King Henry.

Mint (Spearmint) *Mentha spicata* LABIATAE **101**

Mint, Bowles *Mentha* × *villosa alopecuroides*
LABIATAE **102**

Mushroom *Psalliota campestris* AGARICACEAE
White mushrooms because of their appearance
are most popular. Brown mushrooms resist
disease better, grow more vigorously and are
considered better in quality.
There is now a cream variety which shares the
qualities of both. **101**

Mustard *Sinapis alba* CRUCIFERAE **69**

Onion *Allium cepa* LILIACEAE/AMARYLLIDACEAE
– *Ailsa Craig* for spring sowing; probably the
largest onion except for selections; popular with
exhibitors and for culinary use; large, globe-
shaped, straw-coloured bulbs with a mild flavour.
'Mammoth' and 'Improved Mammoth' are
selections which are most suitable for exhibitors
where large bulbs are required. **104**
– *Barletta, Cocktail, Pearl Pickler* a quick
maturing pickling cultivar; small 2.5cm. (1in.)
bulbs; a selection 'Barla', with small, pure-white,
globe-shaped bulbs matures quickly and is
considered to be an improvement.
– *Bedfordshire Champion* one of the best known
cultivars for spring sowing; crops and keeps well;
globe-shaped, straw-coloured bulbs; good
flavour.
– *Bedfordshire Champion – The Sutton Globe* a
selection which crops and keeps well, and ripens
early.
– *Brunswick* a cultivar for spring sowing;
medium-large; semi-flat; deep red colour; keeps
well. **105**
– *Cocktail* see 'Barletta'.
– *Dura* a cultivar for spring sowing; globe-
shaped bulbs; a remarkably good keeper.
– *Express Yellow O – X* a Japanese F₁ hybrid for
sowing *in situ* in autumn; may be pulled from
mid-June; golden brown bulbs. **106**
– *Extra early Kaizuka* a Japanese cultivar for
sowing *in situ* in autumn; flat-shaped; for early
pulling mid to late June; pale, straw-coloured
bulbs.
– *Hyduro* a Dutch F₁ hybrid for spring sowing;
stores well.
– *Hygro* a Dutch F₁ hybrid for spring sowing;
uniform and attractive in appearance; yields
heavily.
– *Imai Early Yellow* a cultivar for sowing *in situ*
in autumn; matures late June to mid-July; semi-
globular, straw-coloured bulbs.
– *The Kelsae* an exhibition type onion for spring
sowing grown in Scotland and northern areas, as
it matures quickly.
– *Nocera* a pickling cultivar; small silver skin,
also used as a cocktail onion.
– *Paris, Paris Silver Skin* a pickling cultivar; well
known, fast growing; ripens early.
– *Paris Silver Skin* see 'Paris'.
– *Pearl Pickler* see 'Barletta'.
– *Polina* a spring sowing cultivar; large, solid
bulbs; a heavy cropper.
– *Presto* a mid-season cultivar for sowing *in situ*
in autumn from Switzerland.
– *The Queen* a true silver skin, good for pickling;
good quality.
– *Reliance* a good all round cultivar, particularly
for autumn sowing outside; mild flavour; keeps

well. 'Autumn Triumph' and 'Autumn Triumph
Monarch' are selections.
– *Rijinsburger* a very popular light brown
cultivar for spring sowing which stores well;
selections include: 'Bola', 'Hurst Monarch',
'Produrijn', 'Rivato', 'Robusta' and 'Wijbo'.
– *Rijinsburger – Wijbo* available as sets; grows
into a large, golden-skinned, globular bulb, which
keeps well; considered to be an advance in this
form of cultivation.
– *Senshyu Semi-Globe Yellow* an autumn sowing
cultivar; matures mid-July onwards; a good
cropper.
– *Solidity* a cultivar for sowing in autumn for
transplanting; seldom bolts and keeps well; large,
flattish bulbs.
– *Southport Red Globe* a cultivar for spring
sowing; a handsome round globe with red skin,
from which 'Mammoth Red' is a selection
particularly useful for exhibition.
– *Sturon* a set cultivar; a very attractive round
bulb with amber coloured skin, which matures
early and keeps well.
– *Stuttgart Giant* until recently the best known
cultivar for growing from sets; straw-coloured
with a flat base; keeps well. **107**
– *S.Y. 300* an Australian pickling onion of fine
quality. Hard, pungent bulbs with light brown
skins which keep crisp.
– *White Lisbon* a quick growing silver skin which
can be sown from March to September for
pulling for spring onions. **108**
– *White Lisbon Winter Hardy* see 'Winter-Over'.
– *White Portugal* larger than 'White Lisbon', and
thicker; only suitable for autumn sowing.
– *White Spanish* a spring sowing cultivar; large
flat bulbs; 'A1' is a selection with bulbs of long
keeping quality.
– *Winter-Over, White Lisbon Winter Hardy* a
distinct cultivar for salad which over-winters
better, being very hardy. Only suitable for
September sowing; very early.

Onion, Ever-Ready *Allium cepa* var. *perutile*
LILIACEAE/AMARYLLIDACEAE **109**

Onion, Tree *Allium cepa* var. *aggregatum*
LILIACEAE/AMARYLLIDACEAE **110**

Onion, Welsh *Allium fistulosum*
LILIACEAE/AMARYLLIDACEAE **111**

Parsley *Petroselinum hortense* UMBELLIFERAE
– *Bravour* a new cultivar which produces a high
yield of very curly, dark green leaves.
– *Champion Moss Curled* see 'Moss Curled'.
– *Claudia D4* recommended because of its ability
to withstand adverse weather conditions.
– *Moss Curled, Champion Moss Curled*
probably the most popular cultivar; dark green
leaves. **112**
– *Paramount* compact, closely curled; slow to run
to seed; continuous growth over a long period.
– *Plain leaved* common in France; very hardy
and of good flavour.

Parsley, Hamburg Turnip-Rooted
Petroselinum crispum 'Tuberosum'
UMBELLIFERAE **113**

Parsnip *Pastinaca sativa* UMBELLIFERAE
– *Avonresistor* a small, short-rooted cultivar,
which may be grown 8 to 10cm. (3 to 4in.) apart

in the row; very resistant to canker; uniform
size and shape. **114**
– *Evesham* an early, broad-shouldered cultivar;
short, thick roots which are easily lifted; hollow
crown type.
– *Hollow Crown* a large cultivar with a clean
white skin; a maincrop intermediate variety of
good flavour.
– *Leda* a very uniform-rooted stock with slender,
tapering roots, which show some resistance to
canker.
– *Lisbonnais* a long-rooted cultivar of excellent
quality.
– *Offenham* a short-rooted cultivar with broad
shoulders; easy to lift; favoured by market
growers.
– *Student* a good cropper with medium-sized
roots of good flavour.
– *Suttons White Gem* a white-skinned, round-
shouldered cultivar; short intermediate in length
and has some resistance to canker.
– *Tender and True* a long-rooted cultivar of good
quality with a clear white skin and considerable
resistance to canker. **115**

Pea *Pisum sativum* LEGUMINOSAE
– *Achievement* a second early and maincrop
cultivar; 1.2 to 1.5m. (4 to 5ft); produces a heavy
crop of long, narrow, dark green pods; first class
for quality and exhibition.
– *Chieftain* a second early and maincrop cultivar;
76cm. (2½ft); thin shelled; good flavour; good
freezer.
– *Dark Skinned Perfection* a second early and
maincrop cultivar; 76 to 90cms. (2½ to 3ft); a
heavy producer of medium-sized blunt pods; a
vigorous grower; suitable for freezing.
– *Douce Provence* a round-seeded cultivar; 60cm.
(2ft) high; early; heavy cropper; good flavour.
– *Dwarf Defiance* a second early and maincrop;
76cm. (2½ft) high; heavy cropper; dark green,
pointed pods; a fine variety of excellent quality.
– *Early Onward* an early wrinkled cultivar; 60cm.
(2ft) high, heavy cropper; excellent quality; 10
days earlier than 'Onward'; good for freezing.
– *Feltham First* a round-seeded cultivar; 46cm.
(18in.) high, so supports not required; a well
known early; good with or without cloches. **116**
– *Gradus* an early wrinkled cultivar; 90cm. to
1.2m. (3 to 4ft) high; still popular; good cropper;
large pods; good flavour.
– *Histon Mini* a round-seeded cultivar; 30cm.
(12in.) high; valuable for use under cloches; crops
well and has a better flavour than most round-
seeded peas.
– *Hurst Beagle* an early wrinkled cultivar; 46cm.
(18in.) high; very early; blunt pods; excellent
flavour.
– *Hurst Green Shaft* a second early and maincrop
cultivar; 60 to 76cm. (2 to 2½ft) high; a heavy
cropper, resistant to downy mildew and fusarium
wilt; sweetly flavoured.
– *Kelvedon Monarch* see 'Victory Freezer'.
– *Kelvedon Viscount* a round-seeded cultivar;
76cm. (2½ft) high; good cropper; early; good
flavour.
– *Kelvedon Wonder* an early wrinkled cultivar;
46cm. (18in.) high; very popular for early and late
crops; resists wilt and mildew; excellent for
flavour and freezing. **117**
– *Little Marvel* an early wrinkled cultivar; 46 to
50cm. (18 to 20in.) high; sometimes used as a
substitute for 'petit pois'; a useful cloche cultivar.

– *Mangetout*, 'sugar peas', a type of pea whose pod is eaten whole, see 'sugar-' cultivars, below.
– *Meteor* a round-seeded cultivar for sowing October to February; 46cm. (18in.) high; exceptionally hardy; good cloche cultivar.
– *Miracle* a second early and maincrop cultivar; 1.4m. (4½ft) high; long, dark green pods which withstand drought and keep well; excellent for exhibition and freezing.
– *Myzar* an early wrinkled cultivar; 38cm. (15in.) high; extremely early; crops heavily; good variety for cloche cultivation; blunt-ended pods.
– *Onward* a second early and maincrop; 60cm. (2ft) high; probably the best known variety; produces a heavy crop of blunt pods on a robust plant. Grows well in most conditions; ideal for successional sowings; excellent quality and freezes well. **118**
– *Pilot* a round-seeded cultivar for autumn and winter sowing; 1m. (3½ft) high; a popular, early cropping variety; crops heavily.
– *Pioneer* an early wrinkled cultivar; 60cm. (2ft) high; a good cropper of fine quality; useful for early or late crops; resists mildew.
– *Progress No. 9* an early wrinkled cultivar; 50cm. (20in.) high; a prolific cropper of good flavour.
– *Purple Podded* a second early and maincrop cultivar; 1.5m. (5ft) high; pods entirely purple; peas are green and of good flavour; suitable for drying. **119**
– *Recette* a second early and maincrop cultivar; 60cm. (2ft) high; a triple podded variety with 3 pods on most stems. Produces over a long period; peas, light green and small, like 'petit pois', sweet and tender; suitable for freezing.
– *Senator* a second early and maincrop; 90cm. (3ft) high; a distinctive pea, paler green than most varieties; produces a heavy crop of excellent flavour.
– *Shasta* a second early and maincrop cultivar; 60cm. (2ft) high; a long-podded, heavy cropping pea; suitable for freezing.
– *Show Perfection* a second early and maincrop cultivar; 1.2 to 1.5m. (4 to 5ft) high; a thin-shelled variety of fine quality; suitable for exhibition and freezing.
– *Sleaford Phoenix* a round-seeded cultivar for sowing October to February; 46cm (18in.) high; longer podded than 'Meteor'; very early and crops heavily.
– *Sleaford Three Kings* a cultivar of good flavour and good cropping value due to the triple pods on most fruiting stems; freezes well. **120**
– *Sugar Carouby de Maussane* a sugar pea; 1.5m. (5ft) high; a tall grower and well known cultivar.
– *Sugar Dwarf de Grace* a sugar pea; 76cm. (2½ft) high; may be sown from March to June for successional crops.
– *Sugar Dwarf Sweet Green* a sugar pea; 90cm. (3ft) high; a very good cropper. **121**
– *Superb* 60cm. (2ft); a round seeded, second early; very hardy; long curved pods; good cropper.
– *Victory Freezer, Kelvedon Monarch* a second early and maincrop cultivar; 76cm. (2½ft) high; an all purpose variety of good quality; a strong grower, producing a heavy crop of dark green, blunt pods consistently in pairs.
– *Vitalis* an early wrinkled cultivar; 76cm. (2½ft) high; crops more heavily than Kelvedon Wonder, but later; well-filled, curved pods; suitable for freezing.

Potato *Solanum tuberosum* SOLANACEAE
Cultivars are becoming more restricted commercially, and the amateur may have to shop around to obtain certain of the following.
– *Arran Comet* a first early; an early bulking cultivar producing numerous, pale yellow, uniform tubers; suitable for exhibition; somewhat resistant to leaf-roll but susceptible to dry rot.
– *Arran Pilot* a first early; popular for its heavy cropping capacity; kidney-shaped, white tubers; suitable for light soils; resists drought and common scab. Normally used while immature. **122**
– *Aura* a first early; a French cultivar with kidney-shaped, yellow-fleshed tubers; requires a very fertile soil; suitable for chips.
– *Catriona* a second early; kidney-shaped favoured by exhibitors for its shallow eyes and attractive, purple-splashed tubers, which are deep purple round the eyes. However, occasionally tubers lack this distinctive purple colouring. Eating quality is good and cropping ability is fair; tubers are prone to dry rot, though immune to most diseases.
– *Congo* long cylindrical tubers with deep purple skin and flesh. When cooked it is frequently used in salads as a substitute for beet as the colour does not run.
– *Craig's Royal* a second early; a quick-bulking, oval, parti-coloured, pink-tubered cultivar, popular for cooking. Suitable for chips.
– *Desirée* a maincrop bred in Holland in 1951 and marketed in the UK in 1963; very popular for its high yield of long, oval, large red tubers; 'Bonte Desirée' a tuber variant is parti-coloured red, but similar in other respects; they are of good quality and free from discoloration when cooked; suitable for boiling, roasting and for chips. **123**
– *Duke of York, Midlothian Early* a first early; oval, white tubers with yellow flesh; good quality and suitable for early forcing; a favourite in Scotland.
– *Golden Wonder* a late maincrop of highest quality when grown in cool climates, e.g. in Scotland.
– *Kerr's Pink* a maincrop favoured in Scotland and Northern Ireland; does not do well in warmer conditions.
– *King Edward VII* a maincrop cultivar; although known since the beginning of the century, it is still popular both with housewife and exhibitor, for its cooking quality and attractive appearance; oval, parti-coloured, pink tubers, which are only freely produced on highly fertile soils. Non-immune but resistant to common scab, susceptible to blight, drought-resistant. **124**
– *Kipfler* an Austrian first early, difficult to obtain in the UK; suitable for salads or frying.
– *Majestic* a maincrop cultivar; first marketed in 1911; very popular in England and noted for its keeping quality; produces a good crop of white, long, oval tubers of uniform shape. On some soils, flesh is apt to blacken after cooking, on others quality is good; susceptible to common scab and cracking but shows resistance to leaf-roll; suitable for chips and feezing.
– *Maris Peer* a second early; a high cropping variety with oval, white, uniform, medium-sized tubers; suitable for cooking and exhibition; resistant to common scab and field immune from some types of blight.
– *Maris Piper* a maincrop variety; produces heavy crop of oval, white tubers; susceptible to slugs and common scab; resistant to potato cyst

eelworm (pathotype A) and leaf-roll; cooking quality is good; suitable for chips.
– *Midlothian Early* see 'Duke of York'.
– *Pentland Crown* a maincrop cultivar; a high yielder of pale yellow, oval tubers of large or medium size which are apt to cling to the stolons. The tubers keep well when stored, are of good quality; widely produced commercially in the UK; resistant to leaf-roll and common scab; suitable for chips.
– *Pentland Dell* a maincrop cultivar; a heavy yielder of long, oval, pale yellow, medium-sized, uniform tubers; best results are obtained if seed tubers are sprouted before planting to encourage rapid establishment of the crop; keeping quality good; cooking quality fair; may be grown in a wide range of climatic conditions; suitable for exhibition.
– *Pentland Hawk* a maincrop cultivar; produces a good crop of oval, white tubers, uniform in shape and size; a multi-purpose variety which keeps and cooks quite well; resistant to leaf roll and some viruses; suitable for exhibition. **125**
– *Pentland Ivory* a maincrop cultivar; produces a good crop of oval, white tubers which keep well; moderately mealy when cooked; after cooking blackening may occur; resistant to dry rot and immune to a number of types of blight; popular for exhibition. **125**
– *Pentland Javelin* a first early; a good cropper, producing numerous oval, white tubers, uniform in shape and size and of fair quality; resistant to potato cyst eelworm (pathotype A) and some viruses; suitable for exhibition.
– *Pentland Lustre* a first early; a new cultivar of considerable promise; a large cropping cultivar, producing attractive, oval, parti-coloured pink tubers of good cooking quality; resistant to potato cyst eelworm (pathotype A); suitable for exhibition.
– *Pentland Marble* a first early; produces a large crop of small, white, round to oval tubers suitable for freezing; field immune from blight and resistant to dry rot.
– *Pink Fir Apple* if grown on very fertile soil, produces a crop of long, pink tubers, knotted and uneven in shape with yellow flesh; keeps a 'new potato' freshness for a long while and is especially appreciated in salads. **126**
– *Record* a maincrop cultivar, bred in Holland in 1925, which reached the UK in 1944; oval to round, medium-sized, uniform tubers with yellow-brown skins and yellow flesh; a moderate cropper but good where a mealy potato is favoured; used extensively for crisp manufacture and suitable for chips; susceptible to blight, although tubers are usually unaffected. **127**
– *Red Craig's Royal* a second early; a heavy cropping variant of 'Craig's Royal'; produces attractive, oval, deep pink tubers, uniform in shape and size; quality fairly good; useful for exhibition and chips, especially as early varieties are generally unsuitable for the latter purpose. **128**
– *Red King* see 'Red King Edward'.
– *Red King Edward* a maincrop cultivar; a red tuber variant from 'King Edward VII', which it resembles in other respects; attractive tubers with deep red skins; excellent cooked and for exhibition; non-immune.
– *Redskin* a maincrop cultivar; produces a heavy yield of pink, round tubers, uniform in shape but irregular in size; mealy when boiled, it is only

popular in the north of England and in Scotland; very susceptible to common scab, but, if well grown and clean, suitable for exhibition.

– *Suttons Foremost* a first early; produces oval, pale yellow tubers with shallow eyes; quality is quite good; popular for producing a very early crop under protection; unsuitable for light soils, being susceptible to common scab.

– *Ulster Chieftain* a first early; produces numerous, oval, pale yellow tubers of uniform shape which are liable to crack and become hollow at maturity; quality is fairly good; suitable for growing under cloches or frames, having a short haulm, and for exhibition. 129

– *Ulster Classic* a second early; a good cropper, producing oval, parti-coloured pink, medium-sized tubers of good cooking quality; resistant to common scab, most types of blight and some viruses; suitable for exhibition.

– *Ulster Premier* a first early; a moderate cropper; oval to kidney-shaped tubers; attractive, parti-pink in colour and useful for exhibition at early shows; shows resistance to common scab, but is susceptible to blight.

– *Ulster Prince* a first early; produces good crop of large, oval to kidney-shaped, white tubers; shows some resistance to drought; good cooking quality; suitable for exhibition.

– *Ulster Sceptre* a first early; a very early producer of a good crop of kidney-shaped, white, uniform tubers of fair cooking quality; resistant to blight, in some measure to common scab, and to the effects of drought; suitable for exhibition.

Pumpkins and Squashes *Cucurbita maxima, C. moschata* CUCURBITACEAE

– *Baby Crookneck* an F$_1$ hybrid; a heavy cropping squash; bright yellow fruits with crooked or curved necks. Cooked while young, these have a delicious flavour.

– *Caserta* a summer squash which should be used when 25cm. (10in.) in length; this size will be doubled when it is fully grown.

– *Cinderella* a pumpkin with medium-sized fruits of uniform shape, deep orange when ripe.

– *Custard White* included here rather than under marrows because its ornamental fruits are attractively shaped, with scalloped edges; these are produced on a bush type plant and have firm flesh with a delicate flavour. 130

– *Custard Yellow* as above but uniform butter-yellow in colour.

– *Gold Nugget* orange-yellow fruits of coconut size; may be used fresh; they store well if allowed to mature.

– *Hubbard's Golden* large fruits, among the best for storage when properly matured. 131

– *Hundredweight* see 'Mammoth'.

– *Mammoth* easily grown; may be used fresh or stored for winter use; usually grown for large fruits which are orange with yellow flesh. 132

– *Small Sugar* produces small fruits which are deep orange when ripe.

– *Sweet Dumpling* produces a good crop of fruits shaped like a cantaloup melon; these may be stored when mature.

Radish *Raphanus sativus* CRUCIFERAE

– *Black Spanish Long* a winter radish; a long, stumpy root with a black skin which must be removed for culinary use; white, solid flesh.

– *Black Spanish Round* a winter radish; similar to

the above except for its shape which is turnip-like. 133

– *Cherry Belle* bright scarlet; a quick grower. 134

– *China Rose* a winter radish; long red and white roots; attractive when well grown. 135

– *French Breakfast-Crimson* very quick grower; solid white flesh.

– *French Breakfast Forcing* a red and white, short-topped radish for growing under glass.

– *French Breakfast – Fusilier* stands well; good in cold glasshouse.

– *French Breakfast – Succulent* half red, half white; attractive. 136

– *Golden Yellow* yellow-skinned with white flesh; egg-shaped; medium flavour; adds extra colour to salads.

– *Inca* bright scarlet; globe-shaped; keeps well until quite large.

– *Long White Icicle* a long, attractive, white root of good flavour. 137

– *Mino Early* a Japanese cultivar for sowing from July onwards; the mild-flavoured roots grow to 38cm. (15in.) in length; may be used in salads in autumn and winter.

– *Robino* sow in October to January under glass at a temperature of 14.4°C. (58°F.) by day, 10°C. (50°F.) by night; matures in about sixty days.

– *Saxa* quick grower; short-topped; scarlet; suitable outdoors or for forcing.

– *Saxa-Red Prince* a new cultivar with a large, succulent, scarlet, globe-shaped root of good flavour.

– *Sparkler* white with scarlet tips; good quality. 138

Red Beet see Beetroot.

Rhubarb *Rheum rhaponticum* POLYGONACEAE

– *Cawood Castle* an excellent maincrop.

– *Hawke's Champagnes* excellent for forcing.

– *Macdonald* fine quality and colour. Canadian origin.

– *The Sutton* a fine maincrop; a very strong grower which seldom produces flower stems.

– *Timperley Early* the earliest cultivar; may be pulled early in March if protected with straw, or in February in warmer districts. 139

– *Victoria* well known; often offered from seed; seedlings should be carefully selected.

Sage *Salvia officinalis* LABIATAE 140

Salsify *Tragopogon porrifolius* COMPOSITAE
There is little difference between **Mammoth** and **Sandwich Island**. 142

Scorzonera *Scorzonera hispanica* COMPOSITAE
– *Giant Russian* the best variety. 141

Seakale *Crambe maritima* CRUCIFERAE
There is little choice of cultivar; the common one is apt to turn purple if exposed to light.

– *Lily White* the most easily obtained cultivar; a little better in appearance and possibly better in quality. 143

Shallot *Allium ascalonicum*
LILIACEAE/AMARYLLIDACEAE
– *True Shallot* a pear-shaped bulb, russet in colour; not commonly in cultivation.

– *Dutch, Giant Yellow* a round, somewhat flat bulb with a deep yellow skin; popular for pickling. 144

– *Giant Yellow* see 'Dutch'.

– *Hâtive de Niort* larger than the above and much favoured by exhibitors for its appearance and size; selected forms are seen, but differ little.

Sorrel, French *Rumex scutatus* POLYGONACEAE 145

Spinach *Spinacia oleracea* CHENOPODIACEAE
– *Bloomsdale* a good cropper; produces dark green, crinkled leaves.

– *Broad Leaved Prickly* a hardy cultivar; produces large, thick, dark green leaves.

– *Dominant* round-seeded; produces a heavy crop of round, dark green leaves; suitable for sowing in autumn or spring; resistant to bolting. 146

– *Greenmarket* a winter hardy cultivar; ideal for sowing in autumn or spring; resistant to bolting and mosaic; recommended for freezing.

– *King of Denmark* a well known, standard.

– *Longstanding Round* a quick growing cultivar, suitable for sowing under cloches for an early crop; should be picked continuously when it will yield heavily; sow in January under cloches, and onwards to July; suitable for freezing.

– *Medania* suitable for alkaline soils; yields heavily; highly resistant to bolting.

– *Nobel* a successful commercial cultivar; provides a heavy crop of medium green leaves.

– *Sigmaleaf* a round-seeded cultivar; may be sown in spring or autumn for over-wintering; more resistant than most cultivars to bolting.

Spinach, New Zealand
Tetragonia tetragonioides (expansa)
TETRAGONIACEAE 147

Swede *Brassica napus* var. *napobrassica*
CRUCIFERAE
– *Bronze Top* a slow growing cultivar; greenish, bronze-topped root; ideal for winter storage.

– *Chignecto* bred in Canada; a round root of good quality; resistant to club root and mildew.

– *Magnificent, Tipperary* a useful cultivar, which crops well and is of good quality. 148

– *Northern Farmer* purple-topped; a good keeper.

– *Purple Top* a quick grower, excellent for use while young but also stores well.

– *Tipperary* see 'Magnificent'.

– *Wilhelmsburger* a green-topped cultivar with a short neck; resistant to club root.

Sweetcorn *Zea mays* GRAMINAE
– *Canada Cross, John Innes Hybrid* an F$_1$ hybrid; a vigorous grower which yields well and has a good flavour; suitable for freezing.

– *Earliking* an F$_1$ hybrid; a very early variety which has cropped well in northern areas; suitable for freezing.

– *Early Xtra Sweet* an F$_1$ hybrid said to retain its flavour some time after harvesting; matures early and has done well in cold areas; isolate from other varieties as cross-pollination spoils its flavour.

– *First of All* an F$_1$ hybrid; matures early; medium-sized cobs of good quality; suitable for freezing.

– *Golden Bantam* a good yielder producing medium-sized cobs.

– *John Innes Hybrid* see 'Canada Cross'.

– *Kelvedon Glory* an F$_1$ hybrid; matures early; crops well; suitable for freezing. 149

– **Northern Belle** an F$_1$ hybrid; yields a good crop of large golden yellow cobs; excellent flavour and good for freezing.
– **North Star** an F$_1$ hybrid; has proved successful in Scotland and other cold areas.

Sweet Pepper see Chilli Pepper.

Tarragon *Artemisia dracunculus* COMPOSITAE **150**

Thyme *Thymus vulgaris* LABIATAE **151**

Tomato *Lycopersicon lycopersicum* SOLANACEAE
– **Ailsa Craig–Leader** an early selection; good for indoor and outdoor cultivation.
– **Alicante** a good cultivar for amateur growers under glass or outside; early; immune to greenback.
– **Big Boy** an F$_1$ hybrid; very large, fleshy fruits; keep to 3 trusses to ripen fruits; very fine flavour; unsuitable for outdoor cultivation.
– **Eurocross BB** an early cultivar which sets freely at low temperatures; a heated greenhouse cultivar; resistant to cladosporium.
– **Findon Cross** an early cultivar for heated glass; immune to greenback; cladosporium resistant. **152**
– **French Cross** an F$_1$ hybrid; a vigorous grower which requires 90cm. (3ft) between each plant; early; uniform fruits of superb flavour. **153**
– **Gardener's Delight** an outdoor cultivar with small fruits of exceptional flavour. **154**
– **Golden Boy** an F$_1$ hybrid; a greenhouse cultivar producing orange-yellow fruits; fleshy with good flavour; not a heavy cropper. **155**
– **Golden Sunrise** medium-sized yellow fruits, suitable for greenhouse or outdoor culture; sweet flavour.
– **Grenadier** an F$_1$ hybrid; a heavy cropping; early, large-fruited cultivar of good quality; resistant to cladosporium, fusarium and greenback.
– **Harbinger** an early cultivar; suitable for glass or outdoors; popular for its excellent quality.
– **Histon Early** a very early cultivar with potato-like leaves; produces a heavy crop of fine-flavoured, good-sized, red fruits.
– **Kirdford Cross** an F$_1$ hybrid of compact habit; shows resistance to tomato mosaic virus and cladosporium A and B; a non-greenback cultivar for mid-season cropping. **156**
– **Maascross** a vigorous grower, producing high quality fruit; very early; non-greenback and cladosporium-resistant. **157**
– **Marmande** for outdoor cultivation only; large irregular fruits of exceptional flavour. **158**
– **Peach** a yellow-fruited cultivar with a distinctive flavour and low acid content. **159**
– **Pixie** a dwarf cultivar producing a heavy crop; may be grown in window boxes, pots, or under cloches; fruits ripen fast, good flavour. **160**
– **Roma** a continental cultivar with very fleshy, straight-sided fruits; a vigorous grower; resistant to fusarium. **161**
– **Sigmabush** an F$_1$ hybrid; an outstanding bush cultivar for outdoors; a heavy cropper of good quality which ripens in adverse conditions.
– **Sleaford Abundance** an F$_1$ hybrid; a bush cultivar which ripens early and crops heavily.
– **Small Fry** an F$_1$ hybrid; a heavy cropping cultivar of excellent quality; does not require high temperatures; non-greenback; resistant to cladosporium, fusarium, tomato mosaic virus.

– **Sonata** an F$_1$ hybrid; heavy cropper of fine quality; does not require high temperatures; non-greenback; resistant to cladosporium, fusarium and tomato mosaic virus. **162**
– **Tangella** early and greenback-free; orange fruits of fine quality. **163**
– **Tigerella** early and greenback-free; fruits red with golden stripes; may be grown under glass or outdoors; flavour is good. **164**
– **Tiny Tim** only grows 38cm. (15in.) high; excellent for pots, window boxes and for growing under cloches; small, brilliant red fruits which ripen early and have excellent flavour. **165**

Turnip *Brassica rapa* var. *rapa* CRUCIFERAE
– **Golden Ball, Orange Jelly** a very hardy cultivar with outstanding keeping quality; fine, tender yellow flesh; globe-shaped, or attractive appearance and useful for exhibition; the best variety for autumn sowing.
– **Golden Perfection** a quickly maturing early cultivar; flattish golden-skinned roots. **166**
– **Green Top Stone** see 'Manchester Market'.
– **Green Top White** see 'Imperial Green Globe'.
– **Imperial Green Globe, Green Top White** a round-rooted cultivar; half green, half white; white flesh; useful for turnip tops.
– **Jersey Mavet des vertus Marteau** see 'Marteau'.
– **Manchester Market, Green Top Stone** a hardy, half green, half white globe; keeps well; good quality.
– **Marteau, Jersey Mavet des vertus Marteau** a white cylindrical root; excellent for protected cultivation for early roots or for early outside sowing.
– **Milan Purple Top Forcing, Sprinter** very early, with small, flat roots and short tops; suitable for protected cultivation or early crops in open ground.
– **Milan White** a very early flat-rooted; strap-leaved. **167**
– **Model White** see 'Snowball'.
– **Orange Jelly** see 'Golden Ball'.
– **Purple Top Milan, Red Top Milan** an early, flat-rooted cultivar; purplish red tops to roots; white underneath. **168**
– **Purple Top White Globe, Veitch's Red Globe,** round, medium-sized roots; bright red tops; white flesh; attractive appearance and good quality. **169**
– **Red Top Milan** see 'Purple Top Milan'.
– **Snowball, Model White** an early white globe; solid, white flesh; mild flavour; excellent for exhibition.
– **Sprinter** see 'Milan Purple Top Forcing'.
– **Tokyo Cross** an F$_1$ hybrid; early and uniform; white, globe-shaped roots of good quality.
– **Veitch's Red Globe** see 'Purple Top White Globe'.

Turnip-rooted Celery see Celeriac.

Watercress *Nasturtium officinale* CRUCIFERAE **170**

Winged Pea see Asparagus Pea.

FRUIT

Fruit Cultivation

Fruits and Climate

All fruits, even individual cultivars, have their own ideal climatic region in which they will grow successfully in all but the most abnormal years. As the climate departs from these best-suited conditions, their cultivation becomes increasingly difficult until limiting weather conditions are reached, beyond which the fruits cannot be grown without intensive use of gardening techniques such as heated glass or plastic cover.

These limiting conditions include the winter temperature, the length of the growing season, the summer temperature and sunshine strength, and the liability of late frosts during the spring period. Soil moisture conditions also have an effect on both yield and quality, but these can often be controlled by drainage and supplementary watering. The seasonal distribution of temperature in northern Europe is not just a simple increase from north to south. In winter the Continent to the east is cold or very cold, but the Atlantic coast to the west is relatively mild. In summer the position is reversed, with high day temperatures and long hours of sunshine to the east and southeast, and cooler, cloudier conditions in the west and northwest; south Sweden, for example can have warmer summer weather than Scotland on the same latitude, and there are higher temperatures in Burgundy than Brittany.

Damaging May frosts are most likely in the inland areas of the north and east where the soil is slow to warm up in spring, but they are not unknown in the vineyards of France. A very great deal depends on the local site and the topography of the neighbourhood. Sheltered valleys which are the warmest places in high summer, can be the coldest sites on a spring night. Gardens on a hillside or gentle slope are less liable to frost, but care must be taken not to choose land which is at too great a height, because the mean temperature decreases and the winds get stronger as the height above sea level increases. Strong winds do not favour the growth of tree fruits and they are most likely on hills and on the sea coasts. A coastal site is always the best for avoidance of late frosts, but increases the risk of wind damage, salt damage, and fungal diseases which thrive in high humidity conditions. Very little fruit is grown in Britain in areas over 250m. in height even in southern England, and little top fruit over about 150m.

Most fruits in their winter dormant state can withstand a degree of winter cold, although tree barks will split in a very severe frost and boughs will break in a heavy snowfall. Some fruits such as apples need cool temperatures in winter, otherwise they cannot develop successfully the following summer, a requirement which makes them unsuitable for the almost frost-free areas of the extreme western coasts. After fruits have begun their spring seasonal growth they become increasingly liable to frost damage, so that the date of flowering is a very important factor in the choice of site or cultivar.

The weather conditions during fertilization are a less obvious factor, but they can be equally important in regard to fruit set. The day temperatures must be favourable for pollen formation and release, and many pollinating insects such as bees cannot operate successfully in wet, cold, or windy weather, because they lose their body heat too rapidly and have to restrict their flights or die. Fruits need a good supply of soil moisture when they are swelling and increasing in size. This can be assured by skilful watering which can do much to ensure maximum yields, but the problem is not an easy one because the best taste and highest quality often require different environmental conditions to those needed for heavy cropping.

Local conditions and garden design may be the deciding factor in regard to frost incidence and shelter from the wind, but the regional climates of summer temperatures and sunshine must be some of the first considerations when selecting the fruit to grow. Each fruit needs a characteristic amount of warmth during its growth period from bud burst to maturity, and those more suitable to warmer climates need not only a long growing period but also one with adequate warm sunshine in the late maturing stage; others complete their growth cycle more swiftly and can mature at lower temperatures and with less heat from the sun.

The fruits most suited to the long warm summer climates of south and south-eastern Europe include almonds, apricots, figs, grapes, melons, nectarines and peaches. It is true that most of these have been grown in carefully selected sites of southern and south-eastern England, but it is only in outstanding summers such as 1975 and 1976 that good results can be depended upon. Such sites must be the warmest possible, on a south-facing wall or slope, to get the maximum warmth from the sun. The increasing popularity of selected cultivars of white grapes in England in recent years is a case in point. In warm summers, on a good site, rewarding results can be obtained, but in a poor rainy summer they may be very disappointing. The use of glass or plastic cover, with or without supplementary heating, obviously increases the chances of success, but these warm climate fruits must always be thought of as 'challenge' crops.

Fruits which are adapted to the cooler type of summer are mainly the smaller berries growing close to the ground or on low bushes. These include the bilberry, blackberry, boysenberry, elderberry, gooseberry (but not the Cape gooseberry which needs South African warmth), loganberry, raspberry, cloudberry, and worcesterberry. This does not imply that they cannot be grown in warmer summer conditions, but that they can be successfully cultivated in the cooler northern and north-western areas.

The fruits in the intermediate section often show a wide tolerance of climatic conditions, but they are chiefly to be found growing well in a broad geographical band from Normandy in France and the West Midlands of England northeastward to southern Scandinavia and North Germany. Much will depend on cultivar; for example, sour cherries and culinary apples are grown in cooler climates than sweet cherries or eating apples, and pears seem to need more sunshine than plums. Often soil type is a deciding factor, because most orchard fruits need a good depth of fertile, well-drained soil; quinces, on the other hand, can grow with their 'feet in the water', and so can small fruit such as the cranberry which favours bogs and marshes as its habitat. Most fruit trees and bushes will not grow well if their roots are waterlogged at any time of the year, which is why so much care is taken in the control of the water-table in the new polders of the Netherlands. Some of the slower ripening types, such as medlars, mulberries and walnuts need good sunshine in the late summer and early autumn, but earlier ripeners such as black, red and white currants can thrive in less sunny places and a degree of shade can even help to spread out the picking season in the garden.

Fruits which flower early in the season will always be difficult to grow well in a garden which is prone to night frosts; cherries, plums and cobnuts are typical examples of those which can frequently suffer frost damage, especially if the early spring has been dry, because frosts are always more likely over a dry soil. Raspberries and currants, on the other hand, tend to be late in flowering and are therefore less liable to frost losses, but it is never wise to plan extensive fruit cropping in a bad frost site. Strawberries, with their large choice of cultivars, are grown in a wide selection of climates from the south of France to the valleys north of Oslo in Norway. They are also one of the favourite fruits for growing under low glass or plastic cover. The use of cloches effectively increases the length of the growing season and helps to prevent frost, but crops under low cover are not always frost-free unless some form of soil heating is used. The British Isles, situated as they are halfway between the cold north and the warm south, and on the boundary between the temperate Atlantic and the widely varying temperatures of Europe, have a climate which varies more quickly over short distances than most other European countries. The change of climate with increase of height (usually a deterioration as far as fruits are concerned) is more rapid than on the Continent, so that greater care has to be taken in regard to type and cultivar of fruit to grow.

Although the 'warm climate' fruits are only grown with success in selected sites of southern England, many of the 'intermediate', and 'cool' climate fruits can be found growing somewhere in all lowland areas of the British Isles, with the 'cool' types predominating in the north. Some indication of the most suitable soils and climates can be deduced from the siting of commercial holdings. There is a clear preference for east and south-east England and the West Midlands. Judging by the percentage of county area (pre-1974 boundaries) devoted to fruit, the 'top ten' are as follows:

ORCHARD FRUIT Kent, Worcester, Hereford, Cambridge, Essex, Greater London, Sussex, Suffolk, Gloucester and Huntingdon.

SMALL FRUITS Kent, Hereford, Worcester, Norfolk, Lincoln, Greater London, Cambridge, Essex, Sussex and Suffolk.

Among the small fruits, Kent and Holland lead for strawberries, Suffolk and Kent for raspberries, Hereford and Worcester for black currants, and Kent and Cambridge for gooseberries. In Scotland, chiefly raspberries and strawberries are grown, mainly in the east Aberdeen and the Lothians, with smaller areas in Inverness and Lanark. Very little fruit is grown commercially in Wales, except in Monmouthshire. The eastern side of Ireland is preferable to the west, where winds are strong, sunshine limited and disease control difficult due to the high humidities. Although the commercial grower is restricted by the climate of a wide area, the amateur fruit-grower can afford to be more adventurous, and he can make the most of his garden climate to try to grow the fruits of his choice. Success to him is all the more rewarding when he has been able to cultivate a good crop in circumstances which are not completely in his favour. He does not always have to count the monetary cost

Cultural Notes
Site
Whilst it is appreciated that the amateur has very little choice as to where his fruit garden should be, ideally the site should not lie within a frost pocket. Frost at blossom time may ruin the harvest's prospects. If the garden does suffer a high incidence of frost one should consider ways and means of protecting the blossom or grow fruits which flower later and thus escape all but the latest spring frosts. It should be noted that protection may be afforded by the use of glass or plastic and even a double thickness of fruit netting will hold off a few degrees of frost. The protection should, of course, be removed during the day to enable the pollinating insects to visit the flowers. Some of the *Rubus* species flower late in the spring, for example raspberries and blackberries, and there are a few apple cultivars in the same category; one of the best known being 'Edward VII'. Some fruit cultivars are hardier than their counterparts for instance the plum 'Czar', the pear 'Conference' and the apples 'Ellison's Orange' and the 'Worcester Pearmain'.

In general the aspect of the land is not too important: suffice to say that fruit grown on a southerly slope will be early but more liable to spring frost damage. Gardens at a high altitude in the more northerly parts of Europe can be at a disadvantage in that the growing season is so much shorter and the climate cooler than those in warmer areas and at lower altitudes. This means that the fruit quality will not be as good and fruit size may also be affected.

Pollination
Pollination, and subsequent fertilization, are essential processes if good fruit crops are to be obtained. Pollination is simply the transfer of pollen grains to the stigma of the flower and is mainly the work of bees and other insects; wind is rarely an agent except for the hazelnut and the walnut. Certain kinds of tree fruits, principally apples, pears, sweet cherries and some plums and gages, require cross-pollination for successful fertilization and to set the fruit. In this context, cross-pollination means a transfer of pollen from the flower of one cultivar (variety) to that of a different cultivar, but of the same kind of fruit. Some trees are self-fertile (self-compatible) for example peaches, nectarines and certain plums and gages. No provision for pollinators is required for soft fruits.

In selecting cultivars where cross-pollination is necessary, the cultivars should be chosen from within the same flowering period, though there is usually sufficient overlap in flowering for cross-pollination to take place with the preceding or following period. Some cultivars tend to biennial bearing and cannot be relied upon to flower every year; others are triploids which cannot provide pollen and must be planted with 2 other diploid cultivars to pollinate it and cross-pollinate between themselves.

The position with sweet cherries is more complicated as cross-incompatibility also exists, as it does to a limited extent with pears and plums.

The flowering period is given for each apple

and pear listed, and where applicable for each plum and gage, both in the text and in tables. Additionally, for sweet cherries, recommended pollinators are shown. Acid cherries are self-fertile, whereas duke cherries, being a cross between the sweet and the acid, have both self-fertile and infertile cultivars.

Rootstocks
Very few tree fruits grow true from seed and, therefore, to perpetuate a good cultivar the nurseryman has to take cuttings or graft scion wood of the cultivar on to a compatible rootstock which is usually of the same species or closely related. In general most tree fruits are grafted on to rootstocks rather than taken from cuttings, as besides perpetuating the cultivar the rootstock also influences the size, vigour and fruiting capacity of the tree. The various rootstocks have been standardized and classified and the most commonly used today are as follows:
APPLES
M.9 (very dwarfing)
M.26 (dwarfing)
MM.106 and M.7 (semi-dwarfing)
M.4 (semi-vigorous)
MM.104, M.2, MM.111, MM.109 and M.1 (vigorous)
PEARS
Quince C (moderately dwarfing)
Quince A (semi-vigorous)
Pears (vigorous)
PLUMS, DAMSONS AND GAGES
St Julien A (semi-vigorous)
Damas C (moderately vigorous)
Brompton, Myrobalan Marianna (vigorous)
APRICOTS, PEACHES AND NECTARINES
St Julien A, Mussel, Damas C and Brompton
SWEET, ACID AND DUKE CHERRIES
Mazzard (Clone F.12/1), Mahaleb.

In most gardens today space is limited and, therefore, the rootstocks mainly used are those which have a dwarfing or semi-dwarfing influence on the cultivar. At present there are no really dwarfing stocks available for stone fruits though there will be in the near future.

When buying a fruit tree from a nurseryman it is important to let him know the form or shape of tree desired and the eventual size, so that he may provide one on a suitable rootstock.

Planting Fruit Trees and Bushes
Fruit trees and bushes should be planted at any time during the dormant period, November to March, unless they have been supplied in containers. Most fruit subjects represent a long term investment and, therefore, from an economic point of view at least, it is wise to ensure that they are planted in the best possible conditions. This means carrying out a thorough preparation of the planting site well beforehand so that when the fruit subjects arrive the land is fertile and weed free.

Do not plant when the soil conditions are not right, for instance when soaked with rain, but heel them in temporarily. This means taking out a trench where the soil is moist but not waterlogged and covering the roots sufficiently to keep out frost. If the ground is frozen hard keep the trees in an unheated shed or garage until the soil thaws. Under no circumstances should the roots be exposed to frost or be allowed to dry. Whilst the trees are out of the ground the roots must be kept wrapped in damp straw and hessian.

PREPARING THE SOIL
In all but the most fertile soils it will be of benefit to dig in well-rotted compost or manure thoroughly and deeply so that the roots do not come into contact with large pieces of organic material. In the final preparations, just before planting, fork in a compound fertilizer which contains all the major elements. The amounts for each subject will be found under the relevant heading. Do not apply lime to the soil, except for stone fruits, unless it is very acid, as most fruits prefer slightly acid conditions.

DRAINAGE
Remember that plants will not thrive in waterlogged soil conditions and if the water does not drain away properly after rain then some kind of drainage system should be installed. If such a system is not practicable then the trees and bushes could be planted on mounds or ridges though this method is far from ideal and should only be practised as a last resort.

STAKING
On the day of planting dig out a hole wide enough to take the roots well spread out, and deep enough to plant at the same depth as the tree or bush was in the nursery. This will be indicated by a soil mark on the stem of the plant. Ensure that the union between rootstock and scion is not buried. Fruit trees planted in the open should be staked and it is easier to drive the stake in first and then plant to the stake. Drive the stake into the soil sufficiently to give the tree a firm anchorage once it is planted. The top of the stake should just be below the crotch of the tree with no danger of the branches rubbing upon it. Fill in the hole gradually and evenly and during the process of planting gently shake the tree from time to time to settle the soil around the roots. Firm the soil by treading and finally level the surface. Tie the tree to the stake and provide a cushion between the two so that there is no risk of chafing. In districts where rabbits or hares are a nuisance protect the tree with a plastic tree guard or wire netting.

Tree Fruits: *Pome Fruits*
Apple and Pear
For cultural purposes apples and pears may be treated alike. Apples and pears in the orchard, where space is not at a premium, are usually grown in the form of open-centre bushes, half-standard or standard trees or as trees with a central stem. The half-standard and standard are grafted on to the more vigorous stocks.

Where space is limited they are grown in a restricted form on dwarfing rootstocks so that they may be closely planted, for example the cordon and the dwarf pyramid. On walls or fences they may be grown as espaliers, fans or cordons. The restricted forms are pruned in the summer so as to contain their growth and the unrestricted forms are pruned in the winter.

The gardener may either purchase a 2, 3 or 4 year old tree already partly shaped, or a one year old (maiden) tree. The partly formed tree will, of course, be quicker into cropping but also more expensive. A one-year-old tree will be cheaper and later into cropping, though the gardener will have the satisfaction of shaping the tree.
– *Open-centre bush, half-standard and standard tree*
The open-centre bush consists of a goblet-shaped tree with 3 to 5 primary branches coming off the

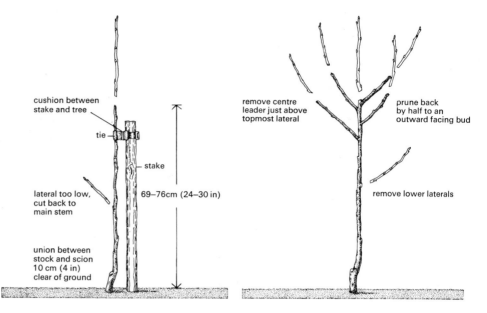

Formative pruning of an open-centre bush
1 *1 year old tree with weak laterals.*

2 *1 year old tree with good laterals.*

Labels in figure:
cushion between stake and tree
tie
lateral too low, cut back to main stem
union between stock and scion 10 cm (4 in) clear of ground
stake
69–76cm (24–30 in)
remove centre leader just above topmost lateral
prune back by half to an outward facing bud
remove lower laterals

main stem at a height of 60 and 76cm. (24 and 30in.). Half-standard and standard trees are similar in shape except that the main stem is longer, usually between 1.4 and 1.8m. (4½ and 6ft). Basically the pruning may be divided into 2 parts, the formative pruning starting with the one year old plant, and the pruning of an established tree. The half-standard and standard are pruned in the same way as the bush except for the initial pruning when they are headed back at a higher point to form the primary framework.

FORMATIVE PRUNING OF AN OPEN-CENTRE BUSH
– *One year old first winter*
After planting cut back the central stem to a bud at 69 to 76cm. (2¼ to 2½ft), ensuring that there are at least 3 good buds beneath. If the tree is on a very dwarfing rootstock then cut back to a bud at 60cm. (2ft). One year old trees which have good, strong laterals evenly spaced around the stem at the right height may be treated as for 2 year old trees, but if the laterals are weak they should be cut back short to one bud and the tree treated as above. The tree with good laterals should be headed back just above the topmost lateral chosen to constitute the highest primary branch. In the following summer, as a result of the cutting back, the upper 4 or 5 buds should break and produce sideshoots. Choose 3 to 5 to form the primary branches which should be evenly spaced around the stem and grow out at a wide angle to the stem. Rub out any unwanted shoots, for example, those too low on the stem or those forming a poor angle. Remember the objective is to obtain an open centre.
– *Two year old winter*
A 2 year old tree should consist of 3 to 5 primary branches coming off the main stem at a wide angle. Cut out unwanted shoots, for example, the

topmost shoot which is often too upright. The selected shoots to be retained, evenly spaced around the stem, should be cut back to a bud facing in the required growing direction, generally outwards. Remove between a half and two thirds of each shoot, more or less at the same height. Cut according to the vigour of the shoots, the weaker being cut harder.
– *Three year old winter*
A 3 year old tree should have 3 to 5 branches upon which will have formed some laterals or secondary branches. Possibly also on the older parts of the tree some fruit buds will have developed. As in the second winter, cut back the leaders of the previous summer's growth of each primary branch by one third to one half according to their vigour. Some of the laterals may be retained where there is room to form further branches and be cut back in the same way. The tips of each leader should be not less than 46cm. (18in.) from its neighbour. Shoots crowding the centre are best removed and other laterals cut back to 3 or 4 buds to form eventually fruiting spurs. Unwanted side shoots on the main stem should be cut back flush, preferably using a knife.

From this point onwards the basic shape of the tree has been achieved and it may be pruned as for an established tree.

FORMATIVE PRUNING OF HALF-STANDARD AND STANDARD TREES
The pruning is similar except in the first year a half-standard is cut back to a bud at 1.4 to 1.5m. (4½ to 5ft) and the standard at 1.6 to 1.8m. (5½ to 6ft). Not all fruit trees make sufficient growth in their first year to achieve the extra length of stem, and in this case are grown for another year before heading back.

PRUNING AN ESTABLISHED OPEN-CENTRE BUSH, HALF-STANDARD AND STANDARD TREES
The objectives are to build up and maintain the shape or form of the tree, to prevent overcrowding and to regulate the number and position of the fruit buds. It must be remembered that the harder the tree is pruned the more growth is obtained and the less fruit is produced. However, with no pruning at all the framework is weak, badly placed with too many fruit buds resulting in poor fruit size. The aim of pruning is to maintain a balance between vigour and fruitfulness.

Prune in the dormant period after the leaves have fallen but not during hard frosts. Complete the task before the buds begin to break in the spring. Pears are pruned in much the same way as apples and for similar reasons. They may be cut back harder if necessary without fear of rampant growth as so frequently happens with apples.

Before starting pruning it is important to understand the cropping habit of most apples and pears. Examination of the growth of a spur-bearing tree which has begun cropping will reveal that on the one year old shoots, wood or vegetative buds are carried; further back on the 2 year old wood plump fruit buds will have formed and on the 3 year old wood short shoots bearing fruit buds called spur systems are beginning to develop. On the older wood the spurs are well developed and on very old trees they are often quite complicated clusters of short, stubby growth. Many pruning systems have evolved over the years, for example, the 'established spur' and the 'renewal', but probably the simplest and that which brings the tree into bearing soonest is the 'regulated system'. Basically this entails keeping the centre of the tree open by the removal or shortening of crowding or crossing branches and

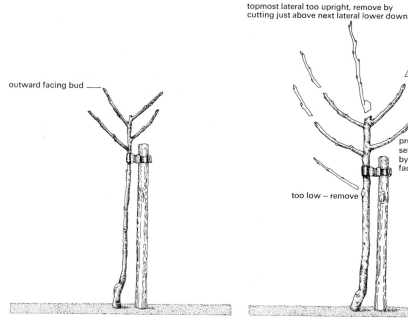

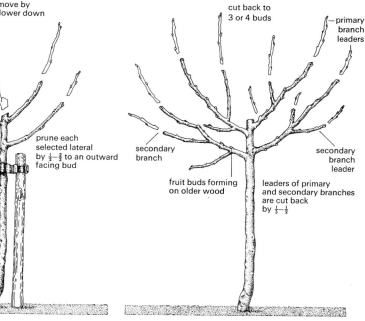

3 1 year old tree after pruning.

outward facing bud

topmost lateral too upright, remove by cutting just above next lateral lower down

prune each selected lateral by ⅓-⅔ to an outward facing bud

too low – remove

4 Winter pruning a 2-year-old tree.

cut back to 3 or 4 buds

primary branch leaders

secondary branch

fruit buds forming on older wood

secondary branch leader

leaders of primary and secondary branches are cut back by ⅓-½

5 Winter pruning a 3-year-old tree.

the cutting out of dead or diseased wood. The leaders of the previous summer's growth of the primary and secondary branches are pruned back in the early years only, removing about one quarter to one third according to their vigour. The leaders of weak growing cultivars which, if left, would make poor drooping trees are pruned harder every winter. Shoots crowding the centre are removed and those competing with the leaders are shortened back to one or 2 buds. Where there is room others may be left to develop fruit buds along their length.

In later years, as a result of this relatively light pruning, it may be found that due to over cropping, there is a reduction in the size of fruit. If this occurs, it will be necessary to prune harder, by thinning out some of the fruit carrying laterals and simplifying some of the spur systems. Where naturally formed spurs are sparse and the shoots numerous, spurs may be induced by cutting back a proportion of the one year old shoots to 6 good buds. The resultant growth in the second winter is cut back to one bud and finally in the third winter pruned back to the topmost fruit bud formed on the 3 year old wood.

Large pruning cuts should be protected with a coating of tree paint. Where it is necessary to remove a heavy branch first undercut and then complete the cut from the top so that the branch does not tear away the bark. When removing a whole branch cut it as close to the base as possible. Do not leave a stub as this may result in die-back.

INFLUENCE OF CULTIVAR ON TREATMENT

Cultivars can be classified into 2 main groups as regards their cropping habits: the spur bearers and the tip bearers.

– *Spur bearers*

These produce their fruit on short stubby growths carried on the 2 year and older, wood. Examples are the apple cultivars 'James Grieve' and 'Cox's Orange Pippin' and the pear cultivar 'Conference'.

– *Tip bearers*

These produce fruit buds at the tips of slender growth made in the previous summer and therefore should have the majority of the tips left unpruned. It is necessary though to tip the leaders of each branch to encourage the formation of more shoots to bear fruit in the following year as well as to ensure a strong framework. Examples are the apple cultivar 'Worcester Pearmain' and the pear cultivars 'Josephine de Malines' and 'Jargonelle'.

– *The cordon*

The cordon consists of a single stem and close to it, fruit-bearing laterals or spurs kept short by summer pruning. It is an ideal form for a garden where space is limited and one may expect a yield of about 2.2 to 4.5kg. (5 to 10lb.) of fruit from each tree. They are closely planted, 76 to 90cm. (2½ to 3ft) apart and thus a number of cultivars can be planted in a relatively small area. This enables the gardener more easily to choose cultivars which cover the aspect of cross-pollination as well as to obtain fruits over a longer season. The rows should be spaced 1.8 to 2.7m. (6 to 9ft) apart.

The cordon may be planted against a wall or

Newly planted oblique cordon.

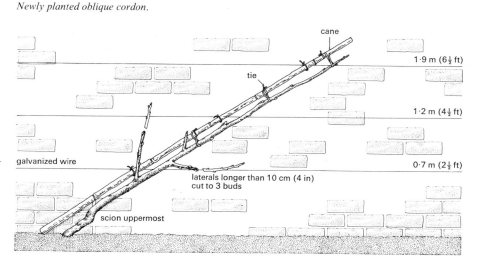

cane

tie

1·9 m (6½ ft)

1·2 m (4½ ft)

0·7 m (2½ ft)

galvanized wire

laterals longer than 10 cm (4 in) cut to 3 buds

scion uppermost

fence but wherever they are planted a permanent
system of horizontal wires is necesssary to
support the trees. The bottom wire is stretched
tightly at a height of 76cm. (2½ft) above soil level
and the others at 60cm. (2ft) intervals, the
topmost wire being 1.9m. (6½ft).

The cordon may be grown vertically or more
preferably at an angle of 45°. They are tied to
canes secured to the wires. It is best, though not
essential, that the rows run north–south with the
tops of the cordons inclined towards the north.

FORMATIVE PRUNING
– *One year old*
No pruning is necessary after planting except that
the tip-bearing cultivars should have the leader of
the previous summer's growth pruned back by
one quarter. If there are side shoots more than
10cm (4in.) long these should be shortened to 3
buds sometime in the winter. Thereafter prune in
the summer, see Summer Pruning.

– *The espalier*
The espalier consists of a tree with a central stem
upon which are borne horizontal fruit-bearing
arms or tiers spaced about 38cm. (15in.) apart.
They should be planted 3.6 to 4.5m. (12 to 15ft)
apart depending upon the rootstock.

The espalier is an excellent and most attractive
form for planting against a south, west or east
facing wall or fence and as a boundary marker
between one part of the garden and another. A
system of horizontal wires fixed to the wall or
between posts spaced 38cm. (15in.) apart is
necessary to support the arms.

Normally a 2 or 3 tier espalier is obtained from
the nurseryman and if further tiers are desired
these can be built in by the gardener. The growth
from an established espalier is pruned in the
summer, see Summer Pruning.

FORMATIVE PRUNING OF A 2- OR 3-TIER ESPALIER
After planting and securing the tiers to the wires
the leaders of the previous summer's growth of
each tier are lightly pruned, by about one quarter,
to an upward facing bud. In the following
summer, train the new leader of each arm to a
cane at 45°. If one grows faster than the other,
creating an unbalanced effect, raise the weaker
one to a more vertical position. At the end of the
summer lower the canes and shoots and tie them
to the wires. Growth from the tiers other than the
leaders is pruned in the summer, see Summer
Pruning. Once each arm has reached the desired
length it is also pruned in the summer or
shortened back in May.

PRUNING TO FORM FURTHER TIERS
If a further tier is required allow a centrally
placed shoot to grow and train it to a vertical
cane. Once it has reached the required height
choose 2 good buds, one to the left and one to the
right, nearest to the next horizontal wire, and
prune the vertical shoot back to the topmost of
the chosen buds. In the following summer 2
shoots should arise next to the wire and these will
constitute the 2 arms. Any other shoots on the
vertical stem should be pinched back to one leaf.
The 2 shoots should first be trained at an angle of
45° and eventually be tied down to the horizontal
wires at the end of the summer.

– *The fan*
The fan-shaped apple or pear tree is ideal for a
west or east facing wall, they are spaced 4.5 to
6m. (15 to 20ft) apart depending on the rootstock. The yield from an established tree may be
anything from 13 to 29kg. (30 to 60 lb.) of fruit.

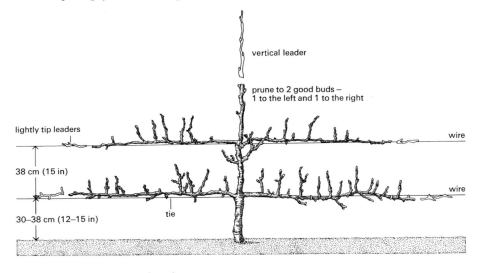

vertical leader

prune to 2 good buds –
1 to the left and 1 to the right

lightly tip leaders

38 cm (15 in)

30–38 cm (12–15 in)

tie

wire

wire

*Winter training: second tier of espalier: pruning
apple or pear to form third tier.*

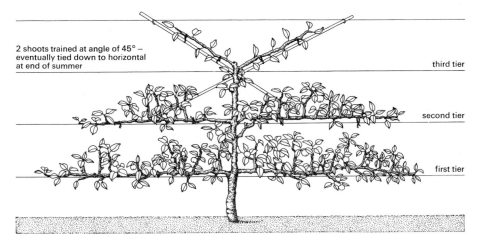

2 shoots trained at angle of 45° –
eventually tied down to horizontal
at end of summer

third tier

second tier

first tier

Summer training: third tier of espalier.

The tree is planted 15 to 23cm. (6 to 9in.) away
from the wall with the stem sloping slightly
towards it. Plant with the union between stock
and scion 10cm. (4in.) above soil level. A system
of horizontal wires should be fixed to the wall at
15cm. (6in.) or 2 brick courses apart. For details
of the formative pruning of the fan, see Peach.
Note that unlike the peach, the apple or pear is
pruned in the winter until the framework has
been achieved and thereafter in the summer, see
Summer Pruning.

– *The dwarf pyramid*
The dwarf pyramid is a tree about 2m. (7ft) high
with a central stem upon which are borne
branches spirally placed about the stem, the
longest at the base and the shortest at the top, so
that it resembles a Christmas tree in shape. The
dwarf pyramid is closely spaced, 1.4m. (4ft) apart
in a row and 2 to 3m. (7 to 10ft) apart between the
rows. It is grafted on to a dwarfing rootstock. An
established tree is pruned in the summer. The
dwarf pyramid has a crop expectancy of 1.8
to 2.2kg. (4 to 5 lb.) in the third to fifth year,
increasing to an average of 6.7kg. (15 lb.) when
mature.

FORMATIVE PRUNING
– *One year old*
Immediately after planting, the tree is headed
back in the winter to a height of 50cm. (20in.) to a
bud on the opposite side to the graft. If there are
any sideshoots over 15cm. (6in.) long these
should be shortened to 5 good buds. Sideshoots
under 15cm. (6in.) long should be left unpruned.

– *Second winter*
The centre leader of the previous summer's
growth is shortened so as to leave some 20 to
25cm. (8 to 10in.) of new growth, cutting to a bud
pointing in the opposite direction to that of the
bud chosen the previous winter; this helps to keep
the leader straight. The leader of each side branch
is cut back to 15 to 20cm. (6 to 8in.) to a downward or outward pointing bud.

– *Subsequent summers*
At the end of July in the south, or later further
north cut mature branch leaders but not central
leader to 5 or 6 leaves beyond the basal cluster.
Mature sideshoots arising directly from branches
are cut back to 3 leaves and those arising from
existing laterals or spurs to one leaf beyond the
basal cluster. In mid-August or early September

Formative pruning of pyramid

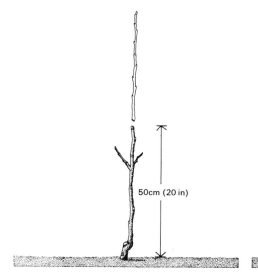

50cm (20 in)

1 year old after pruning.

1 year old – winter pruning.

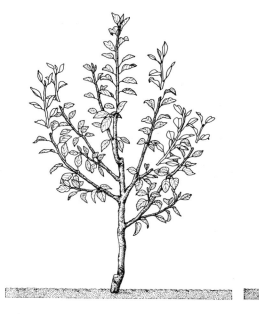

Subsequent summers – end July.

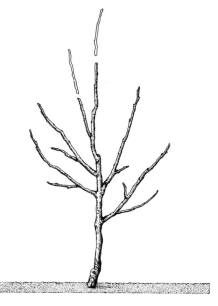

Subsequent winters.

Summer pruning (in early August) of restricted forms: cordon, espalier and fan; for apples and pears.

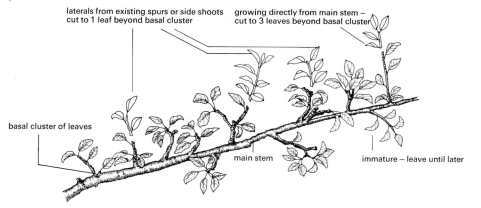

laterals from existing spurs or side shoots cut to 1 leaf beyond basal cluster

growing directly from main stem – cut to 3 leaves beyond basal cluster

basal cluster of leaves

main stem

immature – leave until later

shorten in the same manner any that were not mature in July and have since attained sufficient length.

– Subsequent winters

Shorten the central leader so as to leave 20 to 25cm. (8 to 10in.) of new growth. Also cut back to one good bud any secondary growth that may have resulted from the summer pruning.

When the trees have reached a height of about 2m. (7ft) it is best to restrict their growth by cutting back the central leader to 1.3cm. (½in.) each May. Any other shoots it is desired to restrict such as those arising from the top of the tree, or branch leaders growing into adjacent trees, can be treated in the same way.

Summer pruning

Summer pruning is normally confined to the restricted tree forms such as cordons, espaliers, dwarf pyramids and fans. The removal of leaves at the height of the summer checks the vigour of the trees, so necessary when they are growing in a confined space. If the timing is right, fruit buds should form at the base of the pruned shoots thus building up cropping laterals close to the main framework. Summer pruning may also be used to advantage on trees growing in the open which are over-vigorous and unfruitful.

About early August in the south, later further north, cut back all mature shoots of the current season's growth which are growing directly from the main stem, to 3 leaves. Those from existing sideshoots or spurs are cut to one leaf beyond the basal cluster. Mature shoots are those with a stiff woody base, dark leaves and 23cm. (9in.) or more in length. Immature shoots leave until mid-September and then treat similarly. Do not shorten the leader(s) unless the tree has become taller than is desired. It should then be cut back in May.

Harvesting and storage

The best way to test if the fruits are ready to harvest is to lift one up to the horizontal in the palm of the hand. If it is ready the fruit will part easily from the spur with the stalk remaining on the fruit. Handle gently as bruises on the fruit spoil the taste and mar the keeping qualities. The picking container should be lined with a soft material.

Early apples and pears, those ready in August or September, will not keep and are best eaten as soon as they are ready. Pears should be picked hard just before they are ripe and then allowed to mellow off the tree. The ground colour of pears changes almost imperceptibly, from green to a light greenish yellow. The fruit should part from the spur but not easily; it will require a slight tug. Early apples are picked when ripe on the tree.

Mid-season and late cultivars are picked in September or October before they are ripe and then left to ripen during storage. Store mid-season cultivars, ready for eating October to December, separately from late cultivars ready from January onwards. The season of maturity gives the months after picking that the fruit are at their best, see Dictionary.

Store apples separately from pears. Store the fruits on slotted trays or in well-ventilated fruit boxes under cool, dark and slightly humid conditions. Ideally the temperature should remain between 3°C. and 5°C. (37.4°F. and 41°F.) though this is seldom possible to achieve under amateur conditions. A garden shed, cellar, or garage will suffice so long as extremes of temperature are avoided, frost is kept out and the building is rodent proof. Ventilation is necessary but too much will cause the fruits to shrivel prematurely and too little will cause them to rot internally. Some apple cultivars, but not all, will keep longer if wrapped in oiled paper or 25cm. (10in.) squares of newspaper, provided the temperature is low. Pears should not be wrapped.

PESTS

Codling moth, apple sawfly, aphids, winter moth caterpillar.

DISEASES

Canker, scab, powdery mildew, brown rot

Medlar

The medlar, *Mespilus germanica*, is a native of northern Europe and may be found growing wild although it has been cultivated for hundreds of years. It makes a small tree of curious weeping habit, having crooked, tortuous branches. It is highly ornamental in leaf, flower and fruit, and in its autumn foliage.

The fruits vary in size with the cultivar and are nearly stalkless, russety-brown and their shape resembles the lower half of a sphere with the large, persistent calyx forming a crown round the open eye. Embedded in the flesh are 5 stone-like carpels containing the seeds which are similar to those found in the fruits of hawthorn, *Crataegus* species.

CULTIVATION

The medlar is quite hardy and is tolerant of a wide range of soils provided they are well-drained. It is grown in half-standard or standard form, allowing 4.5 to 6m. (15 to 20ft) between trees. Pruning consists of merely thinning out weak and old wood in winter.

HARVESTING

Medlars are ready for picking in late October or early November. When harvested the fruits are hard and unpalatable and have to be stored until the harshness goes and the flesh softens and turns brown, a process known as bletting. At this stage the fruits may be eaten raw, but they are not to everyones taste though they may be made into a most acceptable jelly.

PESTS

Winter moth caterpillar.

Quince

The quince, *Cydonia oblonga*, is a native of southern Europe and temperate regions of Asia, and is both ornamental and fruitful. It is a low, deciduous, thornless tree with a crooked, branching, irregular mode of growth. Once established it requires little attention and grows to a great age. In May the blooms are large, solitary, very light pink or white. The fruit is golden-yellow, has sometimes a downy skin, and is apple or pear-shaped depending on the cultivar.

SOIL AND SITUATION

The quince succeeds in most soils, but prefers one of a rich, light and moist nature and does particularly well when planted near a pond or stream. It is hardy but needs sun to ripen its fruits properly. In southern areas it may be grown in the open; elsewhere it is best planted in a sheltered position, for example against a wall with a south or south-west aspect.

POLLINATION AND HARVESTING

It is self-fertile and usually starts cropping when 5

or 6 years old. The fruits ripen in late September to late October according to locality. Being acid and sharply astringent the fruits are not normally eaten raw; however, they make a good jelly or preserve.

PRUNING

The quince may be grown as a bush, half-standard or standard. For formative pruning, see Pear. Little pruning is necessary thereafter; just sufficient to keep the tree tidy and in good shape.

PESTS

Generally trouble-free.

DISEASES

Leaf blight, brown rot.

Tree Fruits: *Stone Fruits*
Plum, Gage and Damson

For cultural purposes, gages and damsons may be treated in the same way as plums although gages prefer a warm situation and damsons will tolerate less sun and more rain.

The plum, and particularly the gage, may be grown as a fan against a warm wall or in the open as a half-standard or standard. The damson is usually grown as a half-standard. For the rootstocks used, see p.91.

SOIL AND SITUATION

Plums will succeed in a wide range of soils but prefer a deep moisture-retentive soil which is slightly alkaline. They will not thrive in light, shallow, badly drained or very acid soils. Since plums are early flowering, they will not succeed in low lying areas subject to spring frosts, and for the same reason should not be planted in exposed situations.

CULTIVATION

Plums thrive under a regime of high nitrogen and high summer moisture. The land should have plenty of well-rotted manure or compost dug in before planting and the trees should be mulched with the same materials after planting. Each

Early spring: pruning a four-year-old half-standard plum. The branch leaders have been shortened by about half.

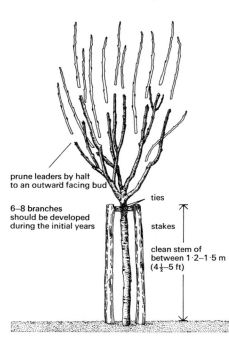

prune leaders by half
to an outward facing bud

6–8 branches
should be developed
during the initial years

ties

stakes

clean stem of
between 1·2–1·5 m
(4½–5 ft)

spring, apply a compound fertilizer at 65 to 70g. per sq. m. (2oz. per sq. yd), supplemented by sulphate of ammonia at 30 to 35g. per sq. m. (1oz. per sq. yd). Plums do best in cultivated ground rather than in grassed down areas.

POLLINATION

Some are self-fertile whereas others are self-infertile and therefore need pollinators.

FRUIT THINNING AND HARVESTING

The plum can crop very heavily in years when the spring weather has been warm and frost-free, and as the branches are brittle, they should be supported. Start thinning the crop at the beginning of June to take some of the weight off the branches and complete the thinning by the end of June. When harvesting pick the fruit by the stalk to avoid bruising. Plums cannot normally be stored but they may be kept for 10 to 14 days under cool conditions. Dessert fruits are picked when fully ripe on the trees. Fruits intended for cooking or bottling should be picked slightly under ripe.

PRUNING

Never prune plums in the winter because of the risk of silver leaf disease but prune in the spring just as the buds break, for young trees, or immediately after cropping with established trees. Very little pruning is necessary with a mature half-standard or standard plum. It will suffice to cut out any broken or diseased branches remembering to protect the wounds with a bitumen tree paint. Occasionally it may be necessary to thin the growth lightly.

– *Formative pruning of a half-standard and standard*

The formative pruning of a plum is basically the same as that for the apple and pear except that the plum will tolerate a more crowded framework and, therefore, 6 to 8 branches should be built in during the initial years. Prune in the spring just as the buds start to break.

– *Formative pruning of a fan-shaped tree*

See peach.

– *Pruning a mature fan-shaped tree*

Each spring, as soon as growth starts, rub out all buds that are growing towards or away from the wall. Starting in early July, as and when necessary, pinch back the sideshoots to 6 leaves. After cropping cut back these same laterals to 3 leaves.

PESTS

Aphids and birds.

DISEASES

Silver leaf, brown rot, bacterial canker.

Peach and Nectarine

The nectarine is a smooth-skinned form of peach and for cultural purposes it should be treated in the same way except that it is not quite so hardy.

SOIL AND SITUATION

They are tolerant of a wide range of soils and, like most other stone fruits, do best in a deep, moisture-retentive, alkaline soil. Sandy acid soils are not suitable. The peach, like the apricot and plum, flowers early and thus the flowers are always liable to be damaged by spring frosts. In more northerly areas it should be grown as a fan-trained tree against a wall with a southerly or westerly aspect. Further south the peach may be grown successfully as a bush tree in the open. It needs a sunny spring to secure adequate pollination, a hot summer to ripen the wood and the fruit, and a short cold winter to rest. The peach does not like warm wet winters when the buds

break early only to be subsequently damaged by frost. This damage to the buds may cause die-back.

POLLINATION

The peach and nectarine are self-fertile.

FORMATIVE PRUNING OF A FAN

A system of horizontal wires is necessary 15cm. (6in.) or 2 brick courses apart to secure the ribs of the fan. Peaches on St Julien A should be spaced 4.5 to 5.5m. (15 to 18ft), Mussel 5.5 to 6m. (18 to 20ft) and Brompton 6 to 7.5m. (20 to 25ft). A fan-trained peach on St Julien A is likely to cover 46 sq. m. (150 sq. ft), and correspondingly more on the vigorous stocks. Maiden, one year old trees or partly trained trees can be bought. The trees are planted 15 to 23cm. (6 to 9in.) away from the wall with the stem sloping slightly towards it.

– One year old

In the spring, as the buds break, cut back to a height of 64cm. (25in.) to a growth bud or lateral. Below this cut out all laterals back to one bud. It is useless to cut back to a flower bud as no growth will come from such buds. It is possible to cut back to triple buds, which consist of 2 flower buds and one growth bud.

– First summer

Choose 2 strong sideshoots, one to the left and one to the right at about 23 to 30cm. (9 to 12in.) above the ground. These will constitute the first ribs of the fan. Rub out all other sideshoots except the topmost. When the 2 chosen side-shoots are 46cm. (18in.) long tie them to canes at an angle of about 45°. Cut out the main stem immediately above these 2 shoots and protect the wound with a liberal application of tree paint.

– Second spring

In February cut back the 2 side branches to between 30 and 46cm. (12 and 18in.).

– Second summer

Of the resultant shoots on each of the 2 main ribs choose 2 shoots on the upper part and one on the lower to form 3 further ribs on each side. An

Pruning to form a fan-shaped peach

1 *Early spring: drawing shows a maiden tree cut to a lateral at 64cm. (25in.) just as buds break.*
2 *First summer: when 2 chosen shoots are 46cm. (18in.) long cut out vertical stem immediately above them.*
3 *Second spring.*
4 *Second summer.*

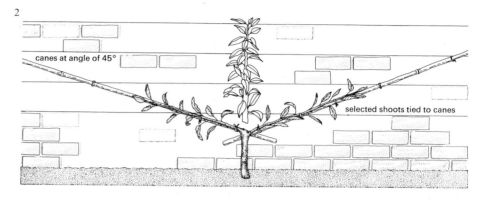

canes at angle of 45°

selected shoots tied to canes

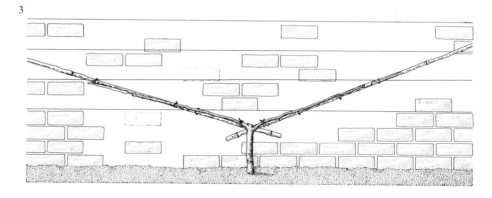

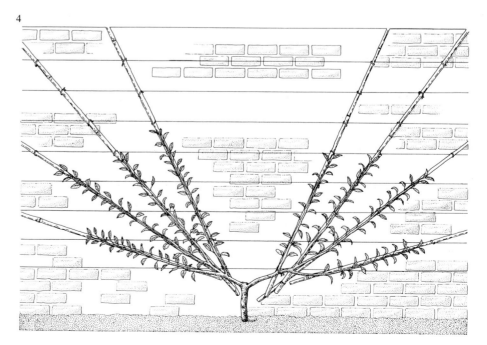

extension shoot is also allowed to grow on from the tip of each making a total of 8 in all. Unwanted shoots are pinched back to one leaf.

– Third spring

In February cut back each of the 8 branches to a triple bud so as to leave some 60 to 75cm. (24 to 30in.) of the previous summer's growth.

– Third summer

Allow the end bud on each of the 8 branches to grow on as an extension of the framework. Rub out buds going directly towards or away from the wall. From the remaining buds allow young shoots to grow out every 15cm. (6in.) or so on the upper and lower sides of each framework branch. These shoots are pinched back at 46cm. (18in.) unless required for further framework.

– Fourth and following summers

From this point onwards it must be regarded as a cropping tree though more branches can be trained in where there is space. The peach flowers on the shoots made in the previous summer and the objective must be to keep up a constant supply of young shoots to provide replacement for the fruit-bearing laterals which are cut out after cropping. Therefore, it is usual to ensure that there is always a replacement shoot at the base of the fruit-bearing laterals or nearby on the main framework.

FRUIT THINNING AND HARVESTING

Thinning the fruit down so that each one is at least 15cm. (6in.) away from the next, usually results in the tree yielding about 7 per kg. (3 per lb.). Fruit thinning is a gradual process and should be started when the fruitlets are about the size of large peas and completed when they are the size of walnuts. The test for ripeness is to hold the fruit lightly in the palm of the hand and press it gently at the stalk end. If the flesh is soft the fruit is ready and should part easily from the tree. Keep the peaches in a cool place until they are to be eaten.

– Bush peach trees

On St. Julien A or Mussel rootstock, plant 4.5 to 5.5m. (15 to 18ft) apart. On Brompton, Damas C or on peach seedling stock, plant at 5.5 to 7.3m. (18 to 24ft) apart.

PRUNING

The formative pruning is the same as for an apple except that the pruning is done in the spring. Later, when cropping has pulled down the lower branches choose some strong upright shoots nearer the centre to act as replacements for the outer shoots which have become unfruitful or badly placed. Remove crowding and crossing branches and cut any dead wood back to a healthy bud or shoot.

PESTS

Aphids, glasshouse red spider mite.

DISEASES

Peach leaf curl, bacterial canker, split stone.

Apricot

SOIL AND SITUATION

The apricot, *Prunus armeniaca*, grows best in a deep, moisture-retentive soil with a fairly high lime content. It is one of the earliest of the stone fruits to flower, generally in late February or early March. In northern areas it should be grown under glass or outside as a fan against a wall with a southerly aspect. In milder areas further south, it can be grown in the open. As there are so few pollinating insects about at its

time of flowering, pollination by hand may be necessary.

CULTIVATION

The cropping habit of the apricot is very similar to the plum, and therefore for cultural requirements, see Plum.

PRUNING

For the formative pruning of a fan-trained tree, see Peach.

PESTS

Aphid, caterpillar of winter moth.

DISEASES

Bacterial canker, silver leaf.

Almond

There are 2 types of almond, the sweet almond *Prunus dulcis* var *dulcis*, and the bitter almond *Prunus dulcis* var *amara*. In areas where almonds are grown commercially, cultivars are recognized for their fruits. In the northerly latitudes almonds are selected more for attractiveness of blossom, although in years of frost-free springs, quite useful crops may be gathered. The difficulty is that the almond, along with the apricot, is one of the earliest Prunus species to flower, and as a result is more often than not devastated by spring frosts. It may also be badly affected by the fungus, peach leaf curl. The almond is usually grown either as a bush, half-standard or standard and is grafted on to the same rootstocks as for a peach. For cultural requirements, see Peach.

PESTS

Aphids.

DISEASES

Peach leaf curl, bacterial canker.

Cherries

– Sweet cherry

There are no dwarfing stocks for the sweet cherry, *Prunus avium*, though the fruit stations are making progress: it is anticipated that in a few years there will be stocks available capable of creating small trees. In the meantime, sweet cherries are not suitable for the small garden because in no matter what form they are grown, they eventually make large trees. In gardens that have sufficient wall space, they may be grown as fans.

SOIL AND SITUATION

Sweet cherries grow and crop best under conditions of moderately light rainfall, in soils which are deep, fertile and well drained, overlying a chalk sub-soil. They will not thrive in very wet soils and will not do well in light, acid soils unless the soil is limed and irrigated. Cherries require shelter from the east winds at blossom time and protection from spring frosts.

PLANTING

For wall planting, plant 5.5 to 7.3m. (18 to 24ft) apart with a minimum wall height of 2.4m. (9ft). Plant trees in the open 9m. (30ft) apart.

POLLINATION

The sweet cherry is not self-fertile and cross-incompatibility also exists, see pp. 108, 109.

PRUNING

For details of the formative pruning of a fan, see Peach. For the pruning of the mature, fan-shaped sweet cherry, see Plum. The top growth of a fan is inclined to grow vigorously. It can be arched back, or cut back in May to one or 2 buds, to give a larger cropping area.

PESTS

Aphids.

DISEASES

Bacterial canker, silver leaf, brown rot.

– Acid cherry

The acid cherry, *P. cerasus*, is naturally a dwarf no matter what rootstock is used and is, therefore, suitable for the garden as a fan or as a bush tree. As it is self-fertile, a single specimen may be grown for fruit. The blossom is extremely attractive with clusters of white flowers in the spring and later the fruits make a delightful jam as well as being excellent for pies. It is also hardy and is one of the few subjects which may be grown against a north-facing wall.

SOIL AND SITUATION

Acid cherries may be grown in most situations including against a north-facing wall. They do best in cultivated soil and if the soil is not naturally slightly alkaline, it is a good idea to give an occasional dressing of lime in the winter.

PLANTING

Plant 4.5 to 5.5m. (15 to 18ft) apart for bush trees and 4.5m. (15ft) apart for fans.

PRUNING

For the formative pruning of a bush, see Peach; thereafter the treatment is different. Acid cherries fruit only on the previous year's wood, so pruning is aimed at obtaining an adequate and constant supply of new wood.

Once the framework of the bush and fan is formed a number of the older branches should be cut back every year to a younger lateral. This relatively hard pruning should stimulate the production of new growth.

PESTS

Generally trouble-free.

DISEASES

Brown rot.

– Duke cherry

The duke cherry is a cross between the sweet and the acid cherry, *P. avium × cerasus*, and as one might expect it is intermediate in character and flavour. It is nearly as vigorous as the sweet cherry and has the same cultural requirements. Some cultivars are self-fertile but others not.

PLANTING

Usually grown as standards planted 7.5 to 9m. (25 to 30ft) apart in the open or as fans, planted 5.5 to 7.3m. (18 to 24ft) apart.

HARVESTING

The fruit may be left on until fully ripe which will be from mid-June to late July depending on the cultivar.

Miscellaneous Tree Fruits

Fig

SOIL AND SITUATION

The fig, *Ficus carica*, must have plenty of sun and warmth if it is to fruit successfully. The best way of growing figs in the more northerly latitudes is against a south-facing wall in the fan-shaped form. In favoured areas it is possible to grow them in the open provided the site is sunny and sheltered.

PLANTING

Figs are grown on their own roots. Spacing 4.5 to 6m. (15 to 20ft) apart, as fans, and 6 to 7.5m. (20 to 25ft) when grown in the open as bushes or half-standards. The fig, given a free root run, may become very vigorous, large and unfruitful. Root restriction helps to keep the tree fruitful and of manageable size. This may be done by growing it in a concrete or brick trough, open at the base, so that the soil is free draining. The trough should be about 1.2m. (4ft) long, 90cm. (3ft) wide and about 90cm. deep. The bottom is tightly packed with broken bricks, mortar rubble or lumpy chalk to a depth of about 30cm. (1ft). The container should then be filled with a good, fertile loam.

CULTIVATION

The soil must not be allowed to become dry in the spring once the buds burst: root restriction may lead to extreme dryness and starvation resulting in fruitlet drop and poor fruit development. Each spring apply a top dressing of a compound fertilizer, 65 to 70g. per sq. m. (2oz. per sq. yd), over the rooting area, followed by a light mulch of well-rotted manure. The mulch will help to keep the soil moist throughout the summer. This is important with root-restricted figs.

WINTER PROTECTION

Without winter protection, winter damage to the young shoots and embryo figs is all too common. It is advisable to protect the tips of the shoots against frost by wrapping them loosely in bracken or a similar material. This protection is removed at the end of April.

PRUNING AND CROPPING

For the formative pruning of a fan-shaped tree, see Peach.

It is essential to understand the cropping habit of the fig in temperate areas as this factor governs the aim in pruning. The fig bears 2 crops but only one ripens outside in northern Europe. The fruits that ripen are those which were formed at the tips of the shoots in the previous August and early September. In a good year they may extend back from the tip over a space of about 30cm. (12in.) and number about 6 to 12 figs per shoot. In the winter period these embryo fruits are small, hardly discernible as figs, being only the size of pea seeds. In the spring following, provided they have survived the winter, they develop and eventually ripen about August.

The second fruits, which are unsuccessful, are those figs which form in the axils of the leaves on the young shoots in the spring of the current year. They develop throughout the summer and are quite large by the autumn, but still green. They should be removed in the autumn as the winter frosts will destroy them in any case.

It follows that pruning must be directed at keeping up a supply of young shoots for it is on their tips that the embryo figs are borne. This is best achieved by pinching out the growing points of about half the young shoots at the end of June. This pinching back will induce the remaining buds to break and form more short stubby shoots which should be mature and carrying embryo figs by the end of the summer. The remainder should be pruned in November as follows. Cut each alternative shoot back to one bud and the others train in full length parallel with the wall. Aim for a 23 to 30cm. (9 to 12in.) spacing between shoots.

PESTS

Generally trouble-free.

DISEASES

Coral spot.

Hazelnut: Cobnut and Filbert

Cobnut and filbert cultivars are derived from species of the genus *Corylus*. *Corylus avellana* is the common European hazelnut and cultivars of this species are usually known as cobnuts, the nut being roundish oval within a short husk which does not completely envelop the nut. Filbert cultivars are derived from *C. maxima* and the nut

itself is distinguished from the hazel or cobnut by the long, tapering husk which entirely envelops and protrudes well beyond the nut. The nut also is longer and proportionately narrower. The cultural treatment is the same for both.

SOIL AND SITUATION

Cobnuts and filberts are tolerant of a wide range of soils from light gravel to a heavy loam, but prefer a medium loam over limestone. Highly fertile soils induce too much growth. The flowers, which open at the end of January to early February are susceptible to damage from strong, cold or moisture-laden winds and, therefore, it is important that the planting site is sheltered. They are, in fact, woodland plants and prefer light shade though are grown quite successfully in the open.

PLANTING

The trees should be planted 4.5m. (15ft) apart at any time from late November to early March.

POLLINATION

They are monoecious, separate male and female flowers being borne on the same tree.

PRUNING

The young bushes are pruned and shaped in much the same way as young bush apples except that the one year old tree is headed back at a lower height, at about 38 to 46cm. (15 to 18in.). The objective is to achieve a goblet-shaped tree, 1.8m. (6ft) high, consisting of 6 to 8 primary branches on a stem of about 38cm. (15in.). Established bushes are pruned in late February or early March once pollination, which is by wind, has been effected. The centre of the bush must be kept open; weak, misplaced branch and sucker growth are cut out cleanly.

The female flowers are mainly borne on 2 year old twiggy side growths and these should be left unpruned. Strong laterals, unwanted to fill gaps in the framework, are pruned back to 2 or 3 buds.

SUMMER PRUNING

Summer pruning or brutting is done in August; strong young laterals are broken by hand and left hanging at a point 6 to 8 buds from the base. These same laterals are pruned in the winter back to 2 or 3 buds.

HARVESTING

The nuts should not be gathered until they are perfectly ripe and should be left until the husks are quite brown. After gathering, the nuts are laid out to dry, then dehusked and stored. Store in layers in earthenware jars, barrels or tubs covering each layer with salt.

PROPAGATION

Although cobnuts and filberts may be raised from seed and by grafting scions on to rootstocks, the most usual method is by layering or by using suckers which spring from the base.

PESTS

Nut weevil, winter moth, caterpillar.

DISEASES

Generally trouble-free.

Walnut

The walnut, *Juglans regia*, is indigenous to south-western Europe, Asia Minor, Iran, the Himalayas and China. Although not native to northern Europe, it has been successfully cultivated there for hundreds of years. The tree is commonly grown as a long-stemmed standard and eventually attains great size; up to 18 or 21m. (60 to 70ft). It is slow into bearing, named grafted cultivars being earlier, though the walnut may

take 10 to 20 years before it fruits successfully. The majority of trees are seedlings and very variable in cropping. From a cropping point of view, it is best to obtain grafted trees of named cultivars.

SOIL AND SITUATION

The walnut grows well in a wide range of soils provided the soil is deep, fertile and well drained. A moderate amount of free lime in the soil is beneficial. Freedom from spring frosts is of the utmost importance as the walnut comes into leaf quite early in the spring and the tender young growths, as well as the blossoms, are very susceptible to frost.

PLANTING

Walnut trees grown as standards should be planted in the autumn spaced 12 to 15m. (40 to 50ft) apart.

POLLINATION

The walnut is monoecious, but the flowering of the male and female flowers on the same tree is not always simultaneous. Therefore, it is best to plant more than one tree and preferably of different cultivars.

PRUNING

As little pruning as possible should be done to a walnut tree once the head of the tree has been formed, apart from the cutting out of dead or crossing branches. Pruning should be done in August. Protect the wounds with a tree paint.

HARVESTING

Walnuts should be harvested from the ground as soon as they fall. Remove the green outer husk as soon as it comes away easily from the nut and then wash the kernel by scrubbing with a soft brush to remove all traces of fibre. The washed nuts are thoroughly dried on trays in the sun or in an airing cupboard and then stored in salt. Earthenware jars make ideal containers.

PROPAGATION

The walnut may be grown from seed, but where good named cultivars are desired, selected scionwood is grafted on to seedling stocks.

PESTS

Nut weevil.

DISEASES

Bacterial blight, die-back, leaf blotch, fungus.

Sweet Chestnut, Spanish Chestnut

The sweet chestnut, *Castanea sativa*, is a native of southern Europe, north Africa and Asia Minor, and has been introduced over the centuries into virtually the whole of northern Europe. In the warmer parts of Europe it represents a valuable food and timber-producing crop, but further north, chestnuts are largely planted for effect, being excellent shade trees and suitable for screens, fence or groups or as single specimens. It makes a very large tree between 21 and 30.5m. (70 and 100ft) in height and therefore is not suitable for the ordinary garden.

There are 2 types of sweet chestnut, known as Marrons and Chataignes, but from the fruit producing aspect, the former are by far the most important. Marrons are larger, much sweeter and more aromatic than the ordinary chestnut and are the result of careful selection and cultivation over many years.

SOIL

The chestnut succeeds in sandy soils and sandy loams, indeed it is an ideal tree for dry, hot soils. Heavy clays, over clay subsoils, and alkaline soils are not suited to its growth.

PLANTING AND PRUNING

They are grown as full standards, spaced at least 15m. (50ft) apart. Very little pruning is necessary after the formative period though it may be required to thin out shoots where they cross or interfere with each other. Over-vigorous growth may be checked by root pruning which also helps to bring the tree into early fruit production.

HARVESTING

The fruits, when fully ripe, naturally detach themselves from the tree some time in the autumn. The nuts should be taken out of the outer husks and spread out for a day or two to dry. They may be stored in alternate layers with dry sand in a cool, dry place secure from frost.

PROPAGATION

Propagation is by seed, but where named cultivars are desired, selected scionwood is grafted on to seedling stocks.

Elderberry

The elder, *Sambucus nigra*, is a low-growing, deciduous tree, native to Europe and north Africa. The berries are used in conjunction with apples for making jelly, and for wine. The flowers are also used to make a champagne-type wine, and in confectionary.

SOIL AND SITUATION

It is easy to grow being tolerant of a wide range of soils and not particular as to situation: but where good fruits are required the elder should be planted in a sunny spot.

PRUNING

Pruning is simple, being merely sufficient to maintain the head in good shape. It may be grown on a single stem as a standard or as a low-growing bush with a number of branches from ground level. Unwanted suckers should be cut out. Spacing should be 4.5 to 6m. (15 to 20ft) apart.

PROPAGATION

Propagation of the herbaceous type is by division: of the shrubby type by cutting bare shoots in the autumn and planting them in open ground or by cutting half-ripe (July) shoots and growing them in a frame.

PESTS AND DISEASES

Generally trouble-free.

Mulberry

The mulberry, *Morus nigra*, is a deciduous tree, native of Iran, whence it is supposed to have been introduced into Europe by the Greeks. It was first grown more as a food plant for the silkworm than for its fruit. Silk of a better quality is obtained if the foodplant of the caterpillars is the white mulberry, *Morus alba*.

Because of its statuesque appearance, with its gnarled branches, the mulberry is usually grown as a single specimen tree in a lawn rather than in the fruit garden. It is extremely slow growing and may take 8 to 10 years before it bears fruit. The mulberry is best bought as a 4 or 5 year old tree already shaped by the nurseryman as a standard, half-standard or bush. Eventually it will require about 9m. (30ft) of space.

SOIL AND SITUATION

The mulberry should be grown in a warm, sunny situation planted in deep, fertile, moisture-retentive soil. In cold localities it may be trained against a wall with a south aspect.

PRUNING

After the formative shaping, the standard requires little pruning, merely sufficient to keep a well-balanced head. Long, coarse shoots should be shortened in the winter to within 4 buds to encourage short spurs to form along the main branches.

HARVESTING

The fruits ripen during August and September when they fall easily from the tree – hence the value of growing it in grass. A sheet of some sort should be laid on the ground under the tree to catch the fruits.

PESTS AND DISEASES

Generally trouble-free.

Bush Fruits

Black Currant

The black currant, *Ribes nigrum*, grows best in an open situation though it will tolerate a little shade. The best quality fruit and the largest proportion of the crop is borne on the one year old wood, that is the wood made in the previous summer. Cultivation is, therefore, aimed at obtaining plenty of new growth by generous feeding, and, with older bushes, by fairly hard pruning. Black currants may be affected by a serious disease called reversion which substantially reduces the yield. It is important, when purchasing new plants to obtain healthy stock.

SOIL AND SITUATION

They are tolerant of a wide range of soils provided the soil is moisture-retentive and well drained. As strong growth is wanted the more fertile the soil is the better. Generous quantities of a bulky organic manure, such as farmyard manure, should be incorporated into the soil before planting and the bushes should be heavily mulched with manure or compost each spring.

PLANTING AND PRUNING

The black currant makes a large spreading bush, depending upon the cultivar and a generous spacing should be allowed, not less than 1.8m. between the rows, by 1.5m. in the row (6ft between the rows by 5ft in the row). It is sold as a 2 year old bush by the nurseryman. Plant deeply and cut all the shoots down to within 2.5cm. (1in.) of soil level. This will mean foregoing a crop in the following summer but instead the energies of the bush will be directed into making strong growth. For the next 2 or 3 years little pruning is necessary apart from cutting out any weak shoots. Prune in the autumn.

As the bush becomes older and more established, annual pruning in the autumn consists of cutting a quarter to a third of the older wood, pruning out the least productive and most badly placed.

HARVESTING

See red and white currant.

PESTS

Black currant gall mite, aphids.

DISEASES

Reversion, American gooseberry mildew.

Red and White Currants

The method of growth and the cropping habit of the red currant, *Ribes sativum* is different from that of the black currant; in consequence the pruning also is different. The white currant is treated in the same way as the red currant. Red currants fruit on short spurs borne on the old wood and in clusters at the base of young shoots made in the previous year. They are hardy and amenable to training. Usually the red currant is grown as an open-centred bush on a short stem of about 15 to 23cm. (6 to 9in.) but it can also be grown as a standard fan, or as a single- double- or triple-stemmed cordon. The cordon is ideal against a fence or wall and as it is hardy it can be grown against a north wall.

As the fruit buds in the winter and the fruit in the summer are extremely attractive to birds, sites near woodland should be avoided if this is practicable, otherwise netting is necessary. Like the black currant it is tolerant of a wide range of soils but thrives best in a medium loam which is slightly acid.

PLANTING

Prepare the planting site well. Incorporate generous quantities of well-rotted farmyard manure as well as a compound fertilizer, at 65 to 70g. per sq. m. (2oz. per sq. yd). The red currant is prone to potash deficiency and should receive an annual dressing each spring at 30 to 35g. per sq. m. (1oz. per sq. yd). Plant at any time between October and March but the earlier the better. 2 year old bushes are spaced 1.5 to 1.8m. (5 to 6ft) apart and single cordons 36cm. (15in.) apart. Cordons should be trained up a cane for straight growth.

PRUNING

– *Two year old bush–winter*

Cut back each branch by half to an outward-facing bud. The objective is to produce an open-centred bush with about 8 evenly placed branches. Once the framework is formed, pruning is then on the spur system.

– *An established bush*

All laterals arising from the main branches should be cut back to 2 or 3 buds. Leaders should be pruned by about a third to an outward-facing bud.

HARVESTING

Red currants are ripe in July/August and should be picked on the sprig to avoid injury to the berries.

PESTS

Aphids.

Gooseberry

The gooseberry, *Grossularia uva-crispa*, is one of the easiest fruits to grow. It is long lived and like its cousin the red currant, yields well for a given area of land. It is normally grown as an open-centre bush on a short leg but may also be grown as a standard, fan or cordon. The fruiting habit is also similar to the red currant in that the fruits are borne on spurs on the older wood and at the base of the younger shoots.

SOIL AND SITUATION

The gooseberry is hardy being tolerant of a wide range of soils but it will not thrive on badly drained land. It is a useful subject for a north-facing wall or fence, and will grow in partial shade.

PLANTING

The ground should be thoroughly cleared of perennial weeds before planting as once planted, because of its thorny nature, the gooseberry may be a difficult crop to weed round. Dig in well-rotted compost or manure before planting; also fork in a compound fertilizer at 100 to 105g. per sq. m. (3oz. per sq. yd) in the final preparations.

Bushes should be planted with 1.5m. between the rows and 1.5m. in the row (5ft between and 5ft in the row). Cordons should be spaced 36cm. (15in.) apart.

PRUNING

– Formative pruning

The gooseberry is usually sold as a 2 or 3 year old bush. In winter, prune the leader of the last year's growth by half, to a bud facing in the desired direction according to whether it is upright in habit or drooping. The objective is to create a goblet-shaped bush with about 6 to 8 main branches on a single stem of about 15 to 23cm. (6 to 9in.) high. Any shoots low down on the stem or coming from below ground should be cleaned off.

– An established bush

The main objectives when pruning are the removal of diseased wood, establishing good branch formation, the promotion of new growth and keeping the centre of the bush open. A drooping or spreading habit should be corrected by cutting any low lying branches back to an upward facing bud or lateral. As older branches become too spreading or unproductive, new more upright leaders should eventually replace them.

Leaders should be tipped each year by about a quarter, usually to an inward bud, to promote the production of more laterals. The laterals of previous summer's growth should be spurred back to 8cm. (3in.). Where larger fruits are desired, particularly for dessert, the laterals should be pruned back shorter though this will mean fewer fruits.

HARVESTING

The first gooseberries of the season are picked when quite small and hard, the thinnings in fact. Nevertheless they are useful for cooking, and the remaining fruits will benefit from the thinning.

PESTS

Gooseberry sawfly, aphid, magpie moth caterpillar.

DISEASES

American gooseberry mildew, grey mould.

Cane, Drupe Fruits
Raspberry

The raspberry, *Rubus idaeus*, is the almost perfect fruit for freezing, it makes an excellent jam and is very acceptable as a dessert. It is soon into cropping and from a well grown plantation the gardener should expect a minimum yield of between 2 and 2.5kg. per m. row (1½ and 2 lb. per ft row).

The importance of starting off with clean, healthy stock cannot be over-emphasized. If the plants are virus-infected, growth will be poor and the yield light. In essence, buy your canes from a reputable nurseryman.

SOIL AND SITUATION

The raspberry grows best in the cool, moist northerly latitudes and does not thrive in the hotter climes. Nor will it thrive in alkaline soils. A slightly acid, well drained medium loam is ideal. As the raspberry flowers relatively late the importance of a frost-free site in the spring is not as great as it is with some of the other soft fruits. It will tolerate light shade provided the soil is not dry.

PLANTING

Before planting, take out a trench one spade length deep and three spade widths wide. Into the bottom of the trench dig in generous quantities of well-rotted manure or compost. Fill in the trench and then fork in a compound fertilizer at 60 to 70 g. per sq. m. (2oz. per sq. yd). Plant between November and March. Space the canes 36cm.

(15in.) apart in the row and 1.8m. (6ft) between the rows, and plant at the same depth as they were in the nursery. Be careful not to plant them too deeply as this will check growth. Once planting is complete prune the canes down to between 23 and 30cm. (9 and 12in.) from the ground. Mulch along each side of the row with well-rotted compost or manure after planting.

PRUNING

At this point it is important to understand the cropping habit of the raspberry as this dictates the pruning and training. The raspberry crops on the 2 year old canes which, after cropping, die. Each growing season new canes (suckers) are produced to replace the canes which have fruited. A system of wires is necessary to support the canes and the usual method is to have horizontal wires at 60, 110 and 150cm. (3, 3½ and 5ft) strained between posts spaced 3.6m. (12ft) apart.

After cropping, the old canes are cut down to ground level and the new canes, which are to bear next year's fruits are tied to the wires spaced 8 to 10cm. (3 to 4in.) apart.

Towards the end of the winter or in early spring the canes are tipped at about 15cm. (6in.) above the top wires. This removes winter damage and induces the canes to produce fruiting laterals along their full length.

HARVESTING

In June or July the fruits are pulled off the core (plug) leaving the stalk attached to the plant.

– Autumn-fruiting raspberry

The autumn-fruiting raspberry has the characteristic of producing the fruits at the tip of the current season's growth towards the end of summer. The fruits represent a welcome addition to the autumn harvest and strangely are not as liable to be taken by birds. The canes are not vigorous but 2 parallel wires at a height of 1.2m. (4ft), spaced 46cm. (18in.) apart will keep them upright.

CULTIVATION

The cultural treatment is basically the same as for the conventional summer-fruiting raspberry except that all canes are pruned down to the ground in February. In effect, no canes are allowed to grow older than one year.

HARVESTING

The autumn-fruiting raspberry does not crop as heavily as its summer fruiting counterpart. A reasonable crop would be between 370 and 750g. per m. row (¼ and ½lb. per ft row).

PESTS

Raspberry beetle.

DISEASES

Cane spot, spur blight, virus diseases.

Blackberry and Hybrid Berries

There are many blackberry, *Rubus* species which may be grown in the garden either for an ornamental or utilitarian purpose, or for both. Some cultivars are very vigorous with powerful thorns and should be avoided where space is at a premium. Others are not so vigorous and some are thornless and thus easy to handle.

The related hybrid berries are similar in cropping and habit. For cultural purposes they should be treated in the same way as for blackberries.

Brambles, as they are called collectively, have a rambling, sprawling habit and need some kind of support if the fruits are to remain clean and easy to pick. They may be grown in rows, against a

wall or along a fence, or over an arch or pergola.

PLANTING

Plant between October and March. Young canes or rooted tips should be planted not less than 1.8m. (6ft) apart, preferably 3m. (10ft) apart. Some of the more vigorous cultivars, 'Himalayan Giant' ('Theodor Reimers') for example, should be spaced 5.5m. (15ft) apart. Allow 1.8 to 2m. (6 to 7ft) between rows.

PRUNING

As mentioned earlier a system of horizontal wires are necessary to support the canes. The most usual is to have the wires at 90cm., 1.2, 1.5 and 1.8m. (3, 4, 5 and 6ft) strained between posts 3m. (10ft) apart. There are a number of ways of training the canes, for example, the fan, rope and weaving (see diagram overleaf).

– Young canes

Whatever method is used the basic principle is that the young canes should be kept separate from the fruiting canes to lessen the spread of diseases, and to make picking and training easier. After planting, the canes are cut down to 23cm. (9in.) from the ground, the objective being to stimulate the plant into producing plenty of strong new canes rather than fruit in the first summer.

– An established plant

Blackberry canes are pruned in the same way as raspberries. As soon as fruiting is over the old canes are cut down to ground level and the young canes tied in their place. Although blackberry canes are perennial the best quality fruits are borne on the young wood, hence the need for pruning on a replacement system.

Heathland Fruits
Bilberry, blueberries and cranberry

There are many species of the genus *Vaccinium* which are edible, indeed eminently palatable, and the number of colloquial names given to these plants is legion. The most well-known are the European, *V. myrtillus* – the bilberry, whortleberry, whinberry or blaeberry; the eastern or American, *V. corymbosum* – the swamp blueberry or high bush blueberry; the north-east American, *V. angustifolium* – the low bush blueberry; and the eastern north American, *V. macrocarpum* – the American cranberry.

– Bilberry, low bush blueberry, cranberry

All belong to the heather family Ericaceae and require much the same conditions, but some are more tolerant of shade and moisture. From a utilitarian point of view not many are suitable for the garden, and furthermore are rarely obtainable from nurseries. For example, *V. myrtillus* the bilberry is a low growing, suckering plant which bears delicious but small, bloomy, black berries. However, production from a single plant is small and the gardener would have to have a large plantation to make the yield worthwhile, assuming the garden had the necessary acid, heathland conditions. Much the same applies to the low bush blueberry. The conditions required for the American cranberry are even more demanding. It is a swamp plant requiring a moist, peaty or boggy soil in which to thrive. If these conditions are met, there are selected clones which yield a worthwhile crop. The round, red fruits ripen in September/October, but should be left on the plant until pulped by hard frosts. The berries are bottled or frozen to make the well-known cranberry sauce at Christmastide.

Three ways of training blackberries and hybrid berries

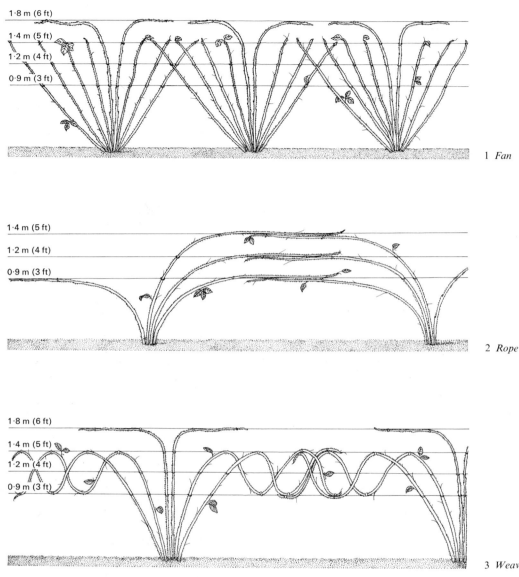

1 *Fan*

2 *Rope*

3 *Weaving*

– High bush blueberry

For most gardeners the choice narrows down to
this blueberry, *V. corymbosum*. Thanks to the
work of the American scientist, Dr Coville, there
are a number of good cultivars which give a high
yield of large-fruited, blue-black berries with a
heavy bloom. The bushes are long lived and grow
to a height and spread of about 1.5 to 1.8m.
(5 to 6ft).

SOIL AND SITUATION

Blueberries require a very acid soil, the kind that
suits heaths, *Erica*, and rhododendrons. The ideal
is an acid, sandy loam, well-drained but moisture-
retentive, pH between 4.3 and 4.8; acid soils with a
higher pH should be heavily dressed with
sawdust, peat and pine needles. It is useless to try
and grow blueberries in calcareous or badly
drained land. Gardeners on unsuitable soil
should consider growing them in containers filled
with an acid rooting medium.

PLANTING

Clear the land of perennial weeds and then
thoroughly incorporate a heavy dressing of
coarse peat plus sulphate of potash at 30 to 40g.
per sq. m. (1oz. per sq. yd). Plant at any time
between November and March, spacing 1.8m.
between the rows and 1.8m. in the rows (6ft in
and 6ft between the rows).

CULTIVATION

The blueberry is shallow-rooted and may very
quickly become affected by drought. To aid
moisture retention, to keep the soil cool and acid
as well as to feed the plant, keep the whole surface
of the plantation covered with a thick layer about
13cm. (5in.) of pine needles, sawdust, granulated
bark or peat. Water copiously in times of
drought. Feed in March with a top dressing of
sulphate of ammonia at 30 to 40g. per sq. m.
(1oz. per sq. yd) plus sulphate of potash at 15 to
20g. per sq. m. (½oz. per sq. yd).

PRUNING

Prune in the autumn as soon as the leaves are off.
Only light pruning is necessary. Tip the leaders to
induce plenty of small sideshoots and shorten
back any low lying or badly placed branches.
Later on it may be necessary to prune hard
unproductive branches to stimulate the plant into
making new growth.

HARVESTING

The berries ripen from mid-July to late September and each bush must be picked over 4 or 5
times. Wait until the berries are fully ripe before
picking. Netting is essential against birds long
before the fruits are really ripe.

PESTS AND DISEASES

Generally trouble-free apart from birds.

Miscellaneous Fruits
Strawberry

The large cultivated strawberries originated from
a cross between 2 American species, *Fragaria
chiloensis × virginiana*. A herbaceous perennial,
it is the quickest fruit subject into cropping from
planting and ideal for the small garden because it
takes up so little space. The strawberry is a short
lived plant and a system of rotation is necessary

to keep the plants free from soil-borne pests and diseases. They are therefore best grown in the vegetable garden rather than with the more permanent fruit plants. The importance of healthy stock cannot be overstressed. It is better to obtain healthy, virus-free plants from a specialist propagator than to accept runners from a dubious source.

There are 3 main types of strawberry; the summer-fruiting which is the conventional kind, fruiting from late May until July according to locality and cultivar; the perpetual-fruiting or remontant which fruits in flushes from July until checked by the autumn frosts; and the alpine strawberry. The latter is the mountain strain of *Fragaria vesca* which bears tiny fruits continually, or in flushes, from June until November. Various cultivars have been selected for garden and commercial cultivation.

– *Summer-fruiting strawberry*
SOIL AND SITUATION

The soil requirements of all 3 are similar. They prefer a slightly acid, light to medium soil which is well-drained, though they are tolerant of a wide range. Strawberries will not thrive in badly drained soils, and require a sunny situation for best results.

PLANTING

Prepare the planting site well, since the conventional strawberries will be in the ground from 3 to 5 years. The land must be made fertile as once the plants are in, there should be no further additions of organic manures. So dig in generous quantities of well-rotted manure or compost, thoroughly mixed with the soil particles so that the roots will not come into contact with large pieces of the material. In the final preparation fork in a compound fertilizer at 65 – 70g. per sq. m. (2oz. per sq. yd), and then rake off any manure or compost on the surface. The presence of organic materials on the top of the soil encourages pests and increases the incidence of grey mould, *Botrytis*, on the fruits.

It is desirable to plant early, as the earlier the planting, the better the crop in the following year. The best months to plant are July, August and the first week of September. If planted later than this, or in the spring, the plants should be deblossomed in the first summer. Plant with the crown of the strawberry just level with the soil surface. Space them 46cm. (18in.) apart in the rows and 90cm. (3ft) between the rows. On a light soil they can be as close as 36cm. (15in.) apart and 75cm. (2½ft) between the rows. Water the plants in.

SUBSEQUENT FEEDING

Strawberries are very susceptible to a deficiency of potassium, therefore, at the end of January each year apply sulphate of potash at 15 to 20g. per sq. m. (½oz. per sq. yd). Other than this no feeding is necessary assuming the initial preparation was thorough.

STRAWING DOWN

The purpose of strawing down is to keep the berries clear of the ground and, therefore, soil free. Use barley or wheat straw, black polythene or specially made strawberry mats. Straw when the fruits begin to swell and touch the earth.

NETTING

Unfortunately this is necessary against birds in most gardens. Make the height of the cage about 1.2m. (4ft) so that one can pick in reasonable comfort.

DEFOLIATION

After cropping remove the old leaves and unwanted runners. Tuck into the row, runners needed to fill in. Rake off the leaves, old straw and other debris, then burn.

HARVESTING

Pick when fully ripe and in a dry condition. For dessert pick complete with stalk. For jam the fruits are picked without calyx and stalk.

– *Perpetual-fruiting or remontant strawberry*
The cultural requirements of the perpetual-fruiting types are similar to those of the ordinary strawberry. However, as they crop at the height of the summer the soil should be highly fertile and moisture-retentive. To ensure a good, late summer crop, the blossoms should not be removed until the end of May. The yield deteriorates from the second year onwards and it is better to grow them for 2 years at the most, and then replant them.

– *Alpine strawberry*
These are selected strains of the wild strawberries growing in Europe, principally *Fragaria vesca*, and are best grown from seed sown annually. There are some cultivars which produce runners but as this kind of strawberry very quickly becomes infected with virus it is wiser to grow from seed. The seeds may either be sown in autumn and the seedlings over-wintered in a frame, to be planted out in March, or they may be sown in March and planted out in May. Plant in rows 75cm. (2½ft) apart, 30cm. (12in.) in the row. They produce a mass of tiny, white flowers and can be used to make an extremely attractive edging to a flower garden. They will tolerate light shade.

HARVESTING

The fruits are small and it takes a long time to gather a reasonable amount. Nevertheless the effort is well worthwhile, for if crushed, sprinkled with sugar and a very sweet, white wine and allowed to stand overnight, alpine strawberries make a most delectable dish.

PESTS

Aphids, slugs.

DISEASES

Virus diseases, *Botrytis*.

Melon
The melon is the fruit of *Cucumis melo*, an annual and native of some parts of tropical Asia and Africa. It has been cultivated over many centuries and in consequence developed a multitude of forms or varieties in the shape, size and colour of the fruits and also in the thickness, colour and flavour of the flesh. The flesh may be white, green or scarlet.

Being tropical it needs some form of protection if it is to be grown successfully in northern Europe. In essence all types of melon can be grown in a heated house or frame but only the more hardy cultivars may be grown in a cold frame or cloche. The melon is monoecious, that is it bears male and female flowers on the same plant.

– *Heated and unheated greenhouse*
Melons take 3 to 5 months from sowing to harvesting depending upon temperature, light and the cultivar used. Seeds sown in March should provide fruit in July and seeds sown in May should be ready about September.

SOWING

The seeds need a minimum temperature of 18°C for germination and to maintain growth. The month of May is the earliest the melon may be sown under glass without heat, earlier than this some form of artificial heat is essential.

Sow one seed per 8cm. (3in.) pot containing a good quality potting compost. Sow the seed edgeways for optimum germination 1.3cm. (½in.) deep, and stand the pots in the warmest part of the greenhouse, windowsill or in a propagating case.

PLANTING

The soil is usually placed in the beds in the form of a ridge 60cm. (2ft) wide at the base and 46cm. (18in.) high down each side of the house assuming the house to be between 3 and 4.5m. (10 and 15ft) wide. Soil made up from good quality grass turves, stacked four months prior to use is ideal. Do not add manure as this leads to over luxuriant growth. Plant singly 36cm. (15in.) apart, if grown as single vertical cordons, or 75cm. (30in.) apart if they are to be grown with 2 vertical shoots. Plant on top of the mound with the surface of the root ball just showing; avoid over-deep planting. Do not firm the soil and gently water the plants in.

TRAINING

It is usual to grow the melons at the sides of, and up to the ridge of the house for maximum light and heat. A system of horizontal wires is necessary spaced 30cm. (12in.) apart and 36cm. (15in.) away from the glass to support the growth. The stem or cordon is trained up a cane secured to the wires.

Train the stem vertically and stop the leader at about 1.8m. (6ft) to induce the production of laterals which are tied horizontally to the wires. Pinch back each lateral at 5 leaves to encourage the growth of sideshoots which will bear the male and female flowers. Ideally each single cordon should bear 4 fruits and it is essential for even development that there are enough female flowers open at the same time to obtain a set of 4 good fruits. In this connection hand pollination is necessary to transfer pollen from the male to the female flowers. Pollinate for 2 or 3 days in succession more female flowers than are required. Remove any flowers that grow on the main stem and, once the fertilization of the 4 selected flowers has been achieved, remove all others. Do not grow more than one fruit on a sideshoot.

WATERING AND VENTILATION

Keep the soil evenly moist, too much will result in split fruits. Avoid watering the base of the stem as this might cause stem rot. Maintain a humid atmosphere by spraying the leaves with a fine mist and damp the borders and paths. However, during pollination a drier atmosphere is needed. It should be noted that melons delight in heat, the minimum at night should be at least 21°C (65.2°F) in the early spring months and 24°C (75.2°F) later on with the day temperature initially at 24°C to 30°C (75.2°F to 86°F) as daylight increases. Ventilate during the day when the temperature exceeds the recommended figure but close the vents at night except during very hot weather. Provide temporary shade on very hot sunny days.

FEEDING

Start feeding when the melons are about the size of walnuts. Feed with liquid feed diluted according to instructions. Give 4 or 5 pints of liquid feed per plant every 7 to 10 days and stop feeding and gradually reduce watering once the fruits start to ripen. Avoid wetting the stem.

SUPPORTING THE FRUITS.

Once the melons have reached the size of a tennis ball it is necessary to give them some kind of support otherwise, as they develop further, they are liable to break the stem with their weight or snap off altogether. Support each one in a net secured by a sling to the roof rafters or wires.

HARVESTING

As the melon nears the ripened stage it gives off a characteristic scent and starts to crack around the stalk. The fruit is ready for gathering when the melon yields slightly to finger pressure at the end opposite to the stalk. Harvest with about 5cm. (2in.) of lateral on either side of the fruit stalk.

– Cold frames and cloches

The hardier cultivars may be grown in a cold frame, under cloches or in a polythene tunnel.

The plants are started in heat in early April and planted out mid- to late May according to locality. The colder the area the later they are planted out. In the warmer areas the seed may be sown direct into the frames in early May.

PLANTING OUT

The glass should be put into position about a week before the young plants are set out, to warm up the soil. The preparation of the soil is the same as for greenhouse melons. Assuming a Dutch light frame 148cm. × 77cm. (4ft 11in × 2ft 6¾in.) is used, one plant planted in the centre is all that is necessary. If the melons are to be grown under cloches, in line, plant them 90cm. (3ft) apart. The plants should be planted with the ball of soil protruding about 1in. above ground level to help keep the base of the stem dry and to reduce the danger of collar (stem) rot.

TRAINING, VENTILATION AND POLLINATION

The plant should be stopped at the fifth leaf to induce production of sideshoots. Select the 4 strongest and pinch off the others and any others that may develop. In a cold frame, train the 4 shoots each to a corner. With cloches train 2 shoots in each direction along the line of cloches.

Little ventilation should be given for the first 2 weeks after planting, hot sun being counteracted by shading; thereafter ventilate freely. In warm weather leave the glass off to allow free access to insects for pollination purposes, though the only certain way to obtain a good fruit set is to pollinate by hand. As in the case of greenhouse melons 3 or 4 fruits must be set at the same time on the sub-laterals and once these have been obtained the growth can be trimmed up, leaving at least 2 leaves beyond the fruits. Grow only one melon on each shoot.

Feed in the same way as for greenhouse melons. Stop feeding and gradually reduce watering once the fruits start to ripen. Keep the fruits clear of the soil by placing a slate or tile under each melon.

PESTS

Aphids, eelworms, glasshouse red spider, woodlice.

DISEASES

Foot rot, downy mildew.

Cape Gooseberry, Golden Berry

The cape gooseberry or golden berry, *Physalis peruviana edulis*, is a native of South America where it has been cultivated by the Indians over many centuries, and from there has been introduced by travellers and sailors to all tropical and sub-tropical parts of the world. It will grow in the warmer, temperate regions but requires

protection against the winter frosts. Hence it is best grown as an annual. Besides the edible form, there are many ornamental species all of which are noted for their lantern-like calyx, which is papery at maturity.

CULTIVATION

Cape gooseberries will succeed on quite poor soils while too much compost will encourage excessive vigour and delay fruiting. The plants are grown from seed or cuttings. Sow in a sunny position, in early March, 0.5cm. (¼in.) deep and cover the seed with glass to assist germination. Once large enough, prick the seedlings into 12cm. (4½in.) pots. Protection from spring frosts under glass, by cloches or frames, is essential until the end of May, when they can be planted outside. Space the plants 75cm. (2½ft) in the row with the rows 105cm. (3½ft) apart. Alternatively, pot again into 23cm. (9in.) pots and allow to fruit in the greenhouse or outdoors. In the greenhouse, tap the flowers to release the pollen, and give adequate ventilation. Plants should be watered frequently in dry weather.

PRUNING

If the plant has not branched out naturally by a height of 30cm. (1ft), pinch out the growing points. Cape gooseberries will grow to around 100cm. (3½ft). Each plant should be tied to a cane for support. By pinching out the lateral shoots when they first appear, the plant can be kept to the required size. Long, straggling stems may be cut out when re-potting to ease handling. New growth will follow.

HARVESTING

The fruits are ready by late summer when the calyx changes from green to golden brown and has a papery texture. The fruits inside should be a deep yellow to orange. Store with the calyx intact under dry, mild conditions when they may be kept up to 3 months (i.e. until Christmas). A 1m. (3ft) plant yields 1 to 2kg. (2 to 4lb.) of fruit. The fruit may be eaten raw though they are best served stewed or in pies. Apart from freezing well, they make an excellent jam or may be dried and used in place of raisins in cakes.

PESTS AND DISEASES

Generally trouble-free.

Chinese Gooseberry, Kiwi Fruit

The Chinese gooseberry, *Actinidia chinensis*, as its name implies, is a plant native to China. It was first brought to Europe in the early part of this century from New Zealand, hence its alternative name. Whilst the plant has been grown for some time as an ornamental in botanic and large private gardens, its value as a fruit crop has only recently been realized. The fruit contains 3 to 5 times the vitamin C found in a lemon.

The Chinese gooseberry is a vigorous climber, entwining around whatever support is available. The leaves are large, heart-shaped, and the female flowers creamy white. It may look most attractive climbing over a pergola, trellis or wall.

SOIL AND SITUATION

It is tolerant of a wide range of soils, but from a fruiting aspect must have a warm, moist situation and does best on a south or west facing wall. For ornamental purposes it may be grown in full sun or shade, but whatever the situation ample space should be provided as growth is rampant. In the colder areas of northern Europe the fruiting forms are best under glass, as young growth is very susceptible to spring frosts.

PLANTING

A strong fence system is necessary to support the entwining growth; such as is recommended for the vigorous blackberries would suffice. The plants should be spaced 4.5 to 6m. (15 to 20ft) apart with one male to 6 or 7 females.

POLLINATION

The plant is dioecious; the female-fruiting plants require a flowering male plant close by, for fertilization. Planting is usually in the proportion of one male to 6 or 7 females, as mentioned above. There is a hermaphrodite, self-fertile clone but this does not crop as heavily as the female plants.

PRUNING

In the early years the massive growths may be shortened and tied in to fill the framework or wall. Once the plant is established it may be treated in much the same way as wall-trained grape; the previous summer's growth should be cut back short to allow fruiting spurs to develop on the older wood. This pruning should be done in winter.

HARVESTING

The fruit is ripe for picking in November. It is usually served fresh, in thin slices as an addition to a fruit salad.

PROPAGATION

The best fruiting forms are perpetuated by cuttings though Chinese gooseberries may be grown quite easily from seed.

PESTS AND DISEASES

Generally trouble-free.

Grape

Grapes, *Vitis* species and hybrids, may be grown under glass, on walls or out in the open depending upon the locality. In the more northerly latitudes grapes are grown under glass and on walls with a southerly aspect.

– Grapes under glass

In view of the cost of the structure, the cost of fuel if heat is used, and the amount of detailed work necessary this form of culture is reserved for only the best dessert cultivars. Grapes may also be grown in plastic structures. The cultural treatment then is the same except that as the humidity is usually very much higher more attention has to be paid to ventilation.

The vine is usually grown as a vertical rod (cordon) either in single or multiple form, each rod being spaced 1.2m. (4ft) apart. The soil must be fertile and well drained and it is usual when planting to restrict the width of the border until the root system of the vine has fully utilized that soil space before the roots are allowed to grow out further. A very generous feeding policy throughout each growing season is also needed for satisfactory results.

NOVEMBER/DECEMBER

Prune as soon as the leaves begin to fall. The laterals, the previous summer's side-shoots, are pruned back to one bud. Certain cultivars are apt to produce barren shoots with the first bud and with others the bud fails to break; the sideshoots of these are pruned longer – anything between 2 and 6 buds according to the cultivar. After pruning is completed the rods should be gently scrubbed with a tar oil winter wash, to get rid of mealy bugs and scale insects, and the glass and superstructure cleaned.

JANUARY/FEBRUARY/MARCH

The vines are rested. The ventilators are left open.

The double Guyot system

January: winter pruning completed. Replacement shoots tied on lower wire and immature wood removed, leaving 60 to 75cm. (2 to 2½ft.) each side. Third shoot cut to 3 buds.

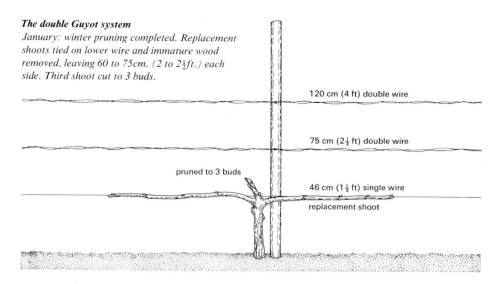

120 cm (4 ft) double wire

75 cm (2½ ft) double wire

pruned to 3 buds

46 cm (1½ ft) single wire
replacement shoot

August: fruiting laterals trained through double wires. Cut tops to 2 or 3 leaves above top wires using secateurs. Remove sub-laterals completely. Replacement shoots (3) grown on to 180cm. (6ft.) their sub-laterals pinched to one leaf. In first year (3 years old) allow 4 bunches per vine and in second fruiting year allow 6 bunches. Full cropping thereafter.

replacement shoots

fruiting lateral

November: prune as soon as possible after leaf fall, but no later than end December. Old wood cut out and 2 replacement shoots tied in – one to left and one to right. The other cut to 3 buds (see top diagram).

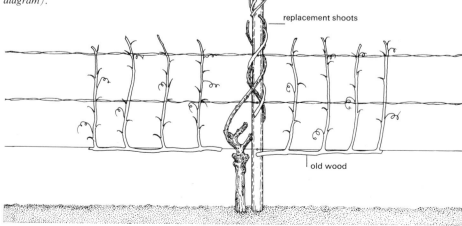

replacement shoots

old wood

APRIL

The soil surface is raked over lightly and given a dressing of well rotted stable manure followed by a good watering. The glasshouse is closed to increase the temperature and so induce the buds to break. The rods are sprayed with water twice daily and the border soil and paths damped down. Where heat is used the temperature is increased gradually from 7°C to 20°C (46°F to 68°F) by the end of May. Under these conditions the buds swell very quickly and soon it is possible to select those shoots which are to be retained. Select the strongest, one from each spur, the others are rubbed out over a period, finally keeping those with the best and longest flower trusses. The laterals carrying trusses are stopped at 2 leaves beyond the bunch, others at the fourth or fifth leaf and sub-laterals at the first. Ventilation is progressively increased as the danger of frost recedes.

MAY

Shading on the roof is necessary. When the laterals begin to lengthen to over 23cm. (9in.) they are gradually and carefully tied down to the supporting wires. Once the flowers are open a slightly drier and warmer but buoyant atmosphere is maintained to improve pollination. Hand pollination is also carried out. After the flowers have set, the temperature is lowered a little and regular damping down of the border and patch begins.

JUNE/JULY/AUGUST

The berries swell quickly and thinning must be completed over a period of 7 to 10 days whilst the stalks on the grapes are easily accessible. After thinning gradually admit more air according to weather conditions. Full ventilation should be started when the grapes are nearing the end of the 'stoning' period with the ventilators left open a little at night. When the grapes begin to show colour watering is reduced, the border only being damped sufficiently to prevent a dry atmosphere. By the end of August most of the bunches should be fully coloured depending upon the cultivar but the grapes should hang for at least another 3 to 4 weeks to ensure complete ripening.

SEPTEMBER/OCTOBER

A close watch is kept on the temperature by the judicious use of heat and careful ventilation until the last bunches have been cut. The temperature is then allowed to fall gradually.

PESTS

Wasps.

DISEASES

Powdery mildew.

– Grapes on walls

The grape on a wall must be in full sun so as to ripen the wood, to ensure the flowers set and to ripen the fruits. A wall or fence with a south, south-east or south-westerly aspect is used.

The wall affords plants shelter, radiated warmth and a better climate than an open site, thus vines may be grown in areas which would otherwise be too cold for outdoor viticulture. Even in the more favoured areas grapes grown on a wall are sweeter and better flavoured than those grown in the open.

The grape is amenable to many forms of training, for example, as an espalier or fan, but in general it is grown as a cordon and ideally in similar fashion to those under glass though attention to detail is not as critical. It may be grown as a single or multiple cordon spaced 1.2m.

(4ft) apart. The soil requirements are also similar and it should be noted that the soil against a south wall may become very dry, therefore heavy mulching and irrigation are necessary.

Whatever form is used a system of wires is necessary to support the vine. The wires spaced 2 brick courses apart are held 15cm. (6in.) away from the wall by vine eyes (nails).

– Grapes in the open

If the vines are to succeed in the more northerly latitudes the cultivars should be of the early kinds ripening not later than early October. The cultivars grown may be the true *V. vinifera* kinds or hybrids derived from crossing *V. vinifera* with North American species. There are good and poor hybrids, the better ones crop well and are resistant to mildew but in general the fruit quality is not as good as the true *V. vinifera*.

The vine may be propagated on its own roots or on to various rootstocks according to the type of soil. Where the pest *Phylloxera* is a problem grafted rootstocks must be used. Plant at any time during the dormant period though in very cold areas spring planting is to be preferred. Vines are winter hardy but the blossom and the young shoots in the spring are very susceptible to frost, and, therefore, frost pockets should be avoided. The site ideally is a south or south-west facing slope and at a fairly low altitude in the north. They are tolerant of a wide range of soils except the very acid. The plants are extremely deep rooted and will not thrive in poorly drained land.

PRUNING

Many systems of training have evolved in the wine producing countries and of these probably the easiest from the amateur's point of view is the Guyot cane replacement method, either in single or double form. The double Guyot system is illustrated on the previous page. This is a system of pruning and training established outdoor vines.

PESTS

Aphid, mealy bugs, red spider mite, scale insect, wasps, birds. *Phylloxera* (not in UK).

DISEASES

Powdery mildew.

To save repetition only the starting month is given for such jobs as watering, which may spread over several months.

January
Continue to look over stored apples and pears and pick out diseased ones. Apples should be used as they ripen. As they come into season, pears need ripening in a warm room (16°C to 60°F) for 2 to 3 days before they develop their full flavour, aroma and juiciness. Guard against mice. Prune established trees except during hard frosts. Collect and burn prunings and apply this ash – which contains potassium – while still warm and dry, to other fruit plants. Apply tar-oil winter wash to fruit trees, canes and bushes once in 2 to 3 years to clean up algae and control eggs of pests laid in cracks in the bark etc. Towards the end of the month apply nitrogen as sulphate of ammonia at the rate of 35 to 90g. per sq. m. (1 to 3oz. per sq. yd) over the rooting area of trees grown in grass. Apply potassium every other year and phosphate once in 3 years. Check tree stakes and ties and the framework supporting raspberry and cane fruits.

February
Apply sprays against peach leaf curl to peach and cherry and repeat after 14 days. In preparation for spring grafting, select bundles of scionwood and bury them with only the tips of the shoots showing in a shady part of the garden. Prune fruit trees and bushes planted in the previous autumn. Prune autumn-fruiting raspberries right to the ground. Firm newly-planted trees and bushes after soil has been loosened by frost. Apply nitrogen as sulphate of ammonia to trees and bushes growing in clean cultivated soil towards the end of the month. Protect the blossoms of early flowering fruits, like apricot, using hessian or double-thickness netting. For cropping under protection place glass cloches, or erect polythene tunnels over strawberries planted in the previous autumn. At the bud-swelling stage, spray fruit trees and bushes with DNOC-petroleum, especially where there are fruit tree red spider mite eggs. Prepare for planting the spring deliveries of trees and bushes.

March
Complete the pruning of established trees and bushes before bud burst. Plant newly delivered trees and bushes: if there is a delay, untie the bundles and cover the roots with moist soil, firming it with the heel ('heeling-in'). Prune newly planted fruit, gooseberries and red currants. Plant strawberry runners on cold soils (on which over wintering losses would have been heavy). Remove winter protection from the shoots of cane fruits and figs and tie shoots on to framework wires. Hand pollinate the flowers of wall-trained trees and bushes at bud burst and spray as necessary. Spray black currants with lime sulphur when the first flowers are open.

April
Complete all planting. Mulch newly planted fruit trees and bushes to conserve moisture later in the season. Check on tree ties to prevent wind rocking before trees have established their new roots. Protect flowering trees and bushes against spring frosts. Ventilate strawberries, under protection, by day, to reduce temperatures and to allow access by pollinating insects. Graft fruit trees when the root stocks have started in to growth with fully dormant scions taken in the winter. Tie grafts securely and seal all cut surfaces with grafting wax. Inspect trees and bushes for blossoms, numbers and overlap of flowering periods, as a first indication of cropping performance. Watch for pest or disease attacks and spray as necessary, but avoid spraying fully opened flowers with persistent insecticides because of the risk of damage to bees and other pollinating insects. Apply a second spray to black currants, about 3 weeks after the first.

May
In northern areas continue to guard against late spring frosts. After the risk of frosts and where the crop 'set' seems good, give a further application of nitrogen at 30 to 40g. per sq. m. (1oz. per sq. yd) to assist fruit swelling. Check that tree ties are not cutting into growing stems and branches. Water newly planted trees and replenish mulches: give a good watering rather than several smaller applications. Water strawberries under tunnels or cloches if rainfall is short or the plants look dry. Put down straw or a suitable alternative between strawberries to protect the fruit from soil splashing. De-blossom spring- and autumn-planted strawberries which should not be allowed to crop until they have become established. De-blossom autumn-fruiting strawberries to prevent them fruiting in the summer. Put down pellets against slugs and strawberry beetles, also net against birds. Bark-ring over-vigorous trees, quickly covering over the strip to prevent it drying out. Tie up new growth on blackberry and loganberry to keep it away from the old canes and remove unwanted suckers of raspberry. Attend to wall-trained peaches, rubbing out unwanted shoots and removing any branches growing directly towards or away from the wall. Control weeds growing round trees and bushes by shallow cultivation. Watch for outbreaks of pests and diseases and treat accordingly: particular problems may be aphids and gooseberry sawfly.

June
Pick strawberries for cooking, red and white currants, cherries and raspberries. Continue watering, spraying and training. Disbud wall-trained peaches and nectarines and tie-in selected shoots to fruit in the following season. Protect cherries, plums and peaches against birds. Where crops are heavy, start thinning, but do not complete this until the end of the natural drop. Remove protection from strawberry beds at the end of fruiting. Where the beds are to be kept on for later cropping, clean them up by cutting off old leaves and burning them along with the straw. New growth will be produced quite quickly from the crowns. Watch for outbreaks of red spider mite, gooseberry sawfly and aphids and spray if necessary. Spray against raspberry beetle.

July
Harvest strawberries, gooseberries, raspberries, black currants, cherries, peaches and blackberries. To increase the stock of strawberries, root the runners from plants which were certified and have been planted in the garden no more than 12 months, so that they are reasonably sure to be disease-free. Cultivate the soil around plants shallowly and peg down runners into this soil.

If plants are to be forced, root runners into pots filled with compost so that they may be removed later with minimum root disturbance. On newly planted strawberries remove runners if the aim is to keep rows to isolated plants and to have larger fruit. Where the maximum crop is required and berry size is less important adopt the matted row system: train runners along the rows and allow them to root. After summer-fruiting raspberries have finished cropping, cut out old wood that has fruited and reduce the new canes to 8 to 10 per plant. Tie these to the supporting framework. Black currants can be pruned either after harvesting or in the early winter after leaf fall. Protect cherries, plums and peaches against attacks by birds and prune them immediately after picking; apply bituminous wound-protective paint to large cuts. Small cuts will heal rapidly against attacks by silver leaf. Tie down vigorous, upright growing shoots of apple and pear on young trees. If they are held near horizontal they will be inclined to form fruit buds along their length which will crop in the following season. Prop or tie up branches of trees carrying heavy weights of fruit. Look over early cultivars of apple towards the end of the month for fruit ready to pick.

August
Pick strawberries, raspberries, loganberries, blackberries, red currants, gooseberries, figs, plums, damsons, peaches, cherries, apples and pears. Harvest early cultivars of apple and pear when slightly under ripe as they mature fast outside in warm conditions and most cultivars quickly go past their best. Prune loganberries when fruit picking is over and in sheltered sites train young canes on to framework wires. Where there is a risk of winter losses in exposed positions, keep the young canes bundled up over winter. Summer prune first the pears and then the apples growing in restricted forms. Continue pruning into September as the current season's shoots become woody at the base. Cut back to 12cm. (5in.) where the trees are growing well, otherwise do not summer prune. Cut out fruited shoots of wall-trained peaches and tie-in replacement branches on to framework wires. Watch supports to heavily laden branches (e.g. plum). After picking, prune shoots especially split ones which are particularly prone to silver leaf. Protect autumn-fruiting raspberries and remontant strawberries against birds. Plant pot-grown runners of strawberry in the first half of the month for maximum yields in their first season of cropping, and in the second half of the month for protecting in the spring. Also plant into larger pots for forcing under glass: these plants should not be taken indoors until the New Year so that they get an adequate period of cold to cause flower initiation. Spray apples against storage rots.

September
Gather strawberries, autumn-fruiting raspberries, blackberries, plums and damsons, peaches, figs, apples and pears. When picking from fruit trees work from the top, then the sides and finally the centre making sure that the fruits part readily from the spur. For long-term storage pick under ripe fruit, and handle gently. Put aside over or under sized fruit and those with non-progressive blemishes and without stalks for early use. Continue planting strawberries. Cover autumn-

fruiting strawberries like 'Redgauntlet' to assist
fruit ripening. After blackberries have finished
cropping, prune out old shoots and tie-in new
wood. Cover outdoor grapes with polythene to
assist ripening. Order new fruit trees and bushes,
preferably for autumn delivery. Ask for certified
stock or virus-tested material. Order cross-
pollinating cultivars.

October

Pick strawberries, raspberries, blackberries,
plums, apples and pears. Take cuttings of
gooseberry. Prune black currants and take
cuttings from bushes certified within the last 12
months as free from big bud mite infestations and
reversion. Prune gooseberry and red currant at
leaf fall. If they are liable to bird attack delay
pruning until near bud swelling in the spring.
Prepare the ground for tree planting by breaking
up the sub-soil and incorporating fertilizers. Take
out planting holes immediately before planting
otherwise they may fill with water which can have
an adverse effect on newly planted trees. Plant
newly delivered trees immediately so that new
roots may be formed in warm soil. Complete the
planting of strawberry runners.

November/December

Finish harvesting apples and pears before the risk
of hard frost or winter gales. Plant trees and
bushes unless the soil is very wet when newly
delivered material should be heeled in (see
March) in a dryer part of the garden. A light frost
on the surface of the soil is no deterrent to
planting as long as this surface crust is removed
before planting is done. Put stakes into position
before planting to avoid damaging roots. Root
prune over-vigorous trees. Move trees that are
not doing well in one position to another and
prune them hard to encourage growth in the
spring. Prune apples and pears except in periods
of hard frost. Cut out and burn dead, damaged
and diseased branches as well as carrying out the
pruning appropriate to the type of fruit.

COLOUR PLATES

1

2

3

4

5

Apple
Malus sylvestris
3 Annie Elizabeth
4 Ashmead's Kernel
5 Blenheim Orange

6 △

8 △

7 △

9

10 △

11 △

12

13

Apple (continued)

6 Bramley's Seedling
7 Claygate Pearmain
8 Cox's Orange Pippin
9 Crawley Beauty
10 Crispin
11 D'Arcy Spice
12 Discovery
13 Egremont Russet

 14 △

 15 △

 16 △

 17

 18 △

 19

 20

Apple (continued)
14 Golden Delicious
15 Golden Noble
16 Granny Smith
17 Grenadier
18 Holstein
19 Idared
20 Jonathan

21 △

22 △

23

24

Apple (continued)
21 Kidd's Orange Red
22 Lane's Prince Albert
23 Laxton's Fortune
24 Laxton's Superb

25 △

26 △

27

28

29 △

30

31

32 △

33

34 △

35 △

36

37

38

39 △

40 △

41 △

42

43

44 △

45 △

46

47 △

Apricot
Prunus armeniaca
44 Breda
45 Moorpark

Blackberry
Rubus fruticosus
46 Himalaya
47 Parsley Leaved

48, 49 **Cape Gooseberry**
Physalis peruviana edulis

48

49

50 △

51 △

52

53 △

54

Cherry
Prunus avium and *P. cerasus*
50 Bigarreau Napoleon
51 Early Rivers
52 Merton Bigarreau
53 Merton Glory
54 Morello
55 Stella

55

56 △

57 △

58

59

56 **Chinese Gooseberry**
Actinidia chinensis

57 **Cloudberry**
Rubus chamaemorus

Crab Apple
Malus pumila
58 Golden Hornet
59 Malus × Robusta

Currant, Black
Ribes nigrum
60 Baldwin
61 Boskoop Giant
62 Jet

60 △

61

62

63 △

64 △

65

66

Currant, Red
Ribes sativum
63 Jonkheer van Tets
64 Laxton's No. 1
65 Red Lake

Currant, White
Ribes sativum
66 Dutch
67 White Grape

67

68 △

69

70

71 △

72

Damson
Prunus domestica and *P. insititia*
68 Farleigh Damson
69 Merryweather
70 Shropshire Prune

71 **Elderberry**
Sambucus nigra

72 **Fig**
Ficus carica

73 △

74 △

75 △

76

77

78

Gooseberry

Ribes grossularia

73 Careless
74 Early Sulphur
75 Green Gem
76 Langley Gage
77 Whinham's Industry
78 Whitesmith

Grape
Vitis vinifera
79 Alicante
80 Black Hamburgh
81 Cascade
82 Chasselas Doré de Fontainbleu

79 △

80 △

81

82

83△

84

85

86 △

87

88

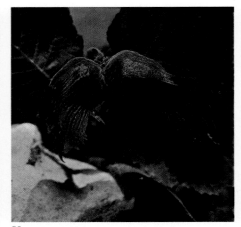

89

90

91 △

92 △

93 △

94

95

96

Hazelnut and Filbert
Corylus arellana and *C. maxima*
88 Nottingham Cob
89 Purple Filbert
90 White Filbert

Hybrid Berries
Rubus spp.
91 Boysenberry
92 Loganberry – Thorned LY59
93 Loganberry – Thornless L654
94 Nectarberry
95 Veitchberry

96 **Japanese Wineberry**
Rubus phoenicolasius

97

98 △

99 △

100

101

102

97 **Medlar**
Mespilus germanica

Melon
Cucumis melo
98 Charentais
99 Ogen
100 Ringleader

101 **Mulberry, Black**
Morus nigra

Nectarine
Prunus persica
102 Lord Napier

103 △

104 △

105

106

107

Peach
Prunus persica
103 Bellegarde
104 Hale's Early
105 Peregrine
106 Redhaven
107 Rochester

Pear
Pyrus communis
108 Beurré Alexandre Lucas
109 Beurré Clairgeau
110 Beurré Diel
111 Beurré Hardy
112 Beurré Superfin
113 Bristol Cross

108

109 △

110 △

111 △

112

113

114 △

115 △

116 △

117

118 △

Pear (continued)

114 Catillac
115 Conference
116 Doyenné du Comice
117 Durondeau
118 Emile d'Heyst
119 Fertility
120 Glou Morceau

119

120

121 △

122

123 △

124

125

126

Pear (continued)
121 Gorham
122 Louise Bonne of Jersey
123 Roosevelt
124 Seckle
125 Williams' Bon Chrétien
126 Winter Nelis

127 △

128

129

130 △

131

132

Plum
Prunus domestica
127 Anna Späth
128 Ariel
129 Belle de Louvain
130 Cambridge Gage
131 Count Althann's Gage
132 Early Laxton

133 △

134

135 △

136

137

138

Plum (continued)
133 Early Rivers
134 Early Transparent Gage
135 Golden Transparent
136 Greengage
137 Kirke's Blue
138 Laxton's Cropper

139 △

140 △

141

142

Plum (continued)
139 Laxton's Delight
140 Marjorie's Seedling
141 Merton Gem
142 Mirabelle Grosse
143 Monarch

143

144 △

145 △

146 △

147

148

149

Plum (continued)

144 Myrobalan
145 Pershore
146 Pond's Seedling
147 Quetsche
148 Victoria
149 Warwickshire Drooper

150

151

152

Quince
Cydonia oblonga
150 Portugal
151 Vranja

Raspberry
Rubus idaeus
152 Delight
153 Malling Exploit
154 Malling Jewel
155 Malling Promise
156 Zeva

153 △

154 △

155

156

157 △

158 △

159

160 △

162 △

161

Strawberry

Fragaria spp.

157 Cambridge Favourite
158 Cambridge Rival
159 Cambridge Vigour
160 Grandee
161 Redgauntlet
162 St Claude
163 Talisman
164 Tamella

163

164

165 △

166

167

168 △

169 △

170

171

Sweet Chestnut
Castanea sativa
165. 166 Doré du Lyons

167 **Bilberry**
Vaccinium myrtillus

High Bush Blueberry
Vaccinium corymbosum
168 Berkeley
169 Coville
170 Elizabeth
171 Jersey

172 △

173

174

172 **Cranberry, Small**
Vaccinium oxycoccus

Walnut
Juglans regia
173 Mayette

174 **Worcesterberry**
Ribes divaricatum

Dictionary of Fruit Cultivars

Explanatory Notes

The cultivar descriptions refer to typical examples grown with a good level of nutrition and management. Old or under-nourished trees or bushes will produce smaller fruits than are described; similarly, a lack of nitrogen for example, will make the fruit more highly coloured than is typical. Before an attempt is made to name a specific cultivar, several specimens should be examined for the characteristics of the cultivar: shape, size, colour, the features of the stalk and so on. Fruit from a seedling tree or bush will not have been given a cultivar name and although it may be possible to make a guess at the parentage, the characteristics of fruit on such a tree or bush may be quite dissimilar to either parent. Anyone who thinks that they have a seedling which represents an improvement on existing cultivars, may perhaps take heart from the fact that most of those described arose initially as seedlings. The procedure, however, for establishing the improved nature of a seedling over existing cultivars is long and tedious and it is probably better, when promoting a new one, to seek the help of a local nurseryman.

The following notes may be useful in connection with the cultivar descriptions:

Name
The most commonly used name is listed first, with synonyms or names by which the cultivar is commonly known in other northern European countries following it. The names and synonyms are cross-referenced throughout.

Use
The main use is given – whether it is a culinary or dessert cultivar.

Season of maturity
This refers to the south of Britain so appropriate adjustments should be made for distance from this area.

General comment
This is a concise summary of the characteristics of the cultivar.

Origin and approximate date of introduction
This gives the parentage of the cultivar, its place of origin and its age. Details of parentage may give an indication of how a new cultivar is likely to perform, whereas the place of origin will suggest the likely value of the fruit in other parts of northern Europe. The age helps in deciding whether it has been well tried and therefore likely to give satisfaction in garden use, or whether it is still under trial when it might be prudent to plant an old-established cultivar.

Distribution
This information read in conjunction with the previous item will help to explain how acceptable and popular a cultivar is. If it is widely planted commercially, this may be because its financial viability depends on such characteristics as its ability to travel, rather than on its superior flavour, a feature which would recommend it to the home grower.

Pollination
Detailed information on the pollination requirements of individual cultivars of such fruits as apples, pears, plums and cherries may be found in specialist literature. If cultivars are to cross-pollinate, they must have similar or overlapping flowering periods. Tables have here been included to guide the choice of cultivars. Where pollination requirements are complex, as they are for sweet cherries where incompatibility groups occur, suitable pollinators are named. This is not to say that other cultivars may not be suitable, and so detailed lists need consulting. Where cultivars are unsuitable as pollen donors this is stated. See also Pollination p.93.

Fruit characteristics
Fruit size, shape and colour are described in that order. These are the characteristics most used in the identification of cultivars. The terms small, medium, large, refer to the size of normally-grown fruit and will depend on tree age and overall crop. Fruit size generally declines as trees get older. If the crop is very heavy then individual fruits are often small. The next feature is the shape of the fruit: first as seen from the side and then as seen from above or below when terms like 'regular' are used in description, (see illustration overleaf). Any special features of the stalk or calyx end ('eye') are mentioned. The colour of a fruit, especially the presence or absence of a flush depends on whether or not it is grown in full sun. Fruit grown in shade tends to have only the ground colour of green or yellow. Here again, in choosing a typical fruit it is important to select one which is not grown in extremes of either light or shade.

Flesh characteristics
These include colour, texture and flavour.

Vigour and cropping
This information is for average soil conditions and a reasonable site.

Other characteristics
Here, points of horticultural interest, such as resistance or susceptibility to a particular pest or disease are included, together with a summing-up of the suitability of a cultivar for garden use.

Flowering Periods – Apples

For pollination, select cultivars with the same or adjoining flowering periods. Some cultivars tend to biennial bearing and cannot be relied upon to flower every year; others are triploids, see descriptions of cultivars.

1: very early
Gravenstein

2: early
Egremont Russet
George Neal
Idared
Lord Lambourne
Margil
Rev. W. Wilks
Ribston Pippin
St Edmund's Pippin
Transparente de Croncels
Warner's King
White Transparent

3: early mid-season/mid-season
Belle de Boskoop
Belle de Pontoise
Blenheim Orange
Bramley's Seedling
Cox's Orange Pippin
Crispin
D'Arcy Spice
Discovery
Emneth Early (Early Victoria)
Granny Smith
Grenadier
Holstein
James Grieve
Jonathan
Kidd's Orange Red
Laxton's Fortune
Merton Worcester
Ontario
Owen Thomas
Peasgood's Nonsuch
Reinette du Canada
Rosemary Russet
Spartan
Sturmer Pippin

Sunset
Tydeman's Early
Wagener
Worcester Pearmain

4: late mid-season
Annie Elizabeth
Ashmead's Kernel
Calville Blanc d'Hiver
Claygate Pearmain
Duke of Devonshire
Dumelow's Seedling (Wellington)
Ellison's Orange
Encore
Golden Delicious
Golden Noble
Howgate Wonder
Ingrid Marie
Lane's Prince Albert
Laxton's Delight
Laxton's Superb
Merton Charm
Monarch
Orleans Reinette
Starking
Starkcrimson
Suntan
Tydeman's Late Orange
Woolbrook Russet

5: late
Merton Beauty
Mother (American Mother)
Newton Wonder

6: late
Edward VII

7: very late
Crawley Beauty

Apple shapes.

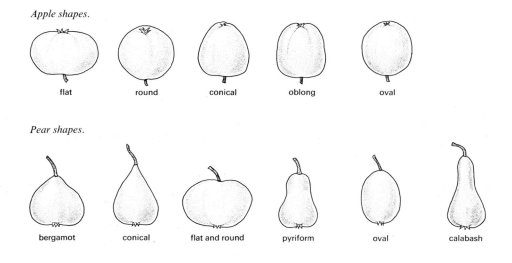

flat   round   conical   oblong   oval

Pear shapes.

bergamot   conical   flat and round   pyriform   oval   calabash

Flowering Periods – Cherries

The pollination requirements of cherries are complex. Most cultivars are neither self-fertile nor will they be cross-pollinated satisfactorily by cultivars in the same incompatibility group. They will set fruit when pollinated by a cultivar in another incompatibility group, provided they flower at or about the same time i.e. they are in the same or adjacent flowering periods.

INCOMPATIBILITY GROUPS	FL. PERIOD 1: VERY EARLY	FL. PERIOD 2: EARLY	FL. PERIOD 3: MID-SEASON	FL. PERIOD 4: LATE-MID-SEASON	FL. PERIOD 5: LATE	FL. PERIOD 6:
0		Merton Glory			Bigarreau Gaucher	
1	Early Rivers		Roundel			
2		Bigarreau de Schrecken Merton Favourite Waterloo	Merton Bigarreau Merton Bounty	Merton Crane		
3				Bigarreau Napoleon		
4				Kent Bigarreau		
5	(No cultivars described here)					
6			Elton Governor Wood			
7						Bradbourne Black Geante d'Hedelfinger
Self-fertile			Stella			

Flowering Periods – Pears

For pollination, select cultivars with the same or adjacent flowering period. Choice is also subject to the incompatibility between certain pear cultivars regardless of their flowering periods.

1: very early
No cultivars described here

2: early mid-season
Beurré Alexandre Lucas
Beurré Clairgeau
Beurré d'Amanlis
Beurré Diel
Emile d'Heyst
Louise Bonne of Jersey
Packham's Triumph
Passe Crasanne
Président Drouard
Seckle

3: late mid-season
Beurré Hardy
Beurré Superfin
Conference
Dr Jules Guyot
Durondeau
Fertility
Fondante d'Automne
Jargonelle
Joséphine de Malines
Merton Pride
Roosevelt

Thompson's
Triomphe de Vienne
Williams' Bon Chrétien

4: late
Bristol Cross
Catillac
Clapp's Favourite
Comte de Lamy
Doyenné du Comice
Glou Morceau
Gorham
Marie Louise
Nouveau Poiteau
Onward
Pitmaston Duchess
Winter Nelis

INCOMPATIBILITY GROUPS
Group 1
Fondante d'Automne
Louise Bonne of Jersey
Seckle
Williams' Bon Chrétien
Group 2
Beurré d'Amanlis
Conference

Flowering Periods – Plums

With self-fertile cultivars there is no problem over pollination. For cultivars in Groups A or B, select a cultivar with the same or adjacent flowering period from any of the groups (A, B or C) but observing the notes on cross-incompatibility of plums at the foot of the table.

FLOWERING PERIOD	SELF-INFERTILE GROUP A	PARTLY SELF-FERTILE GROUP B	SELF-FERTILE GROUP C
1: very early	Jefferson		Monarch Myrobalan
2: early	Coe's Golden Drop	Ariel	Denniston's Superb Reine-Claude Bavay Warwickshire Drooper
3: mid-season		Early Laxton Early Rivers Goldfinch Merton Gem	Anna Späth Czar Golden Transparent Laxton's Cropper Merryweather Pershore Severn Cross Victoria
4: late mid-season	Count Althann's Gage Kirke's Blue Laxton's Delight Mirabelle Petite	Cambridge Gage Farleigh Damson	Bradley's King Early Transparent Gage Oullin's Golden Gage
5: late	Mirabelle Grosse Greengage		Belle de Louvain Marjorie's Seedling Shropshire Prune

INCOMPATIBILITY GROUPS

Group 1	*Group 2*
Jefferson	Greengage
Coe's Golden Drop	Cambridge Gage

Almond *Prunus dulcis* ROSACEAE
- *Ferraduel* Introduced by the Institut National de Recherche d'Agriculture, France, and fairly extensively grown there. Very late flowering and capable of being pollinated by 'Ferragnes'. Produces a branched tree and is very productive.
- *Ferragnes* A new French cultivar first listed in 1973. Very late flowering and can be pollinated by 'Ferraduel'. Makes a moderately spreading tree and crops well.
- *Marcona* Late. A very productive, Spanish cultivar generally recommended in France. Introduced in 1961. Flowers mid-season. **1, 2**

Apple *Malus sylvestris* ROSACEAE
- *American Mother* see 'Mother'.
- *Annie Elizabeth, Carter's Seedling* Culinary. December/June. Long-established, large showy and long-keeping cooker. Believed to be a seedling from 'Blenheim Orange', originating at Knighton, Leicester, UK, and introduced about 1890. Widely planted. Flowering period 4. Fruit large/very large, conical, irregular, with ribs towards the eye end. Greasy, pale yellow skin with red flush and stripes; short stalk. Flesh white, firm and acid. Makes an upright, compact tree. Self-fertile and reliable cropper, also fairly resistant to scab. Suited to northern areas. **3**
- *Ashmead's Kernel* Dessert. December/March. An old russet, now recommended for its flavour. Raised about 1700 by Dr Ashmead of Gloucester. Not widely planted in Britain. Flowering period 4, suitable pollinator for 'Cox's Orange Pippin'. Fruit medium, round with somewhat flattened sides; skin green-yellow with a brown flush and covered with russet. Firm yellowish flesh, sweet aromatic flavour, much liked by tasting panels. Trees of moderate vigour, tendency to light cropping. A cultivar worth looking for. **4**
- *Belle de Boskoop* Dessert and culinary. December/March. An old variety tending to give large apples. Possibly a bud sport of 'Reinette de Montfort' discovered about 1860 and widely planted on the Continent. Flowering period 3 but a triploid cultivar and not, therefore, capable of producing viable pollen. Medium/large, round/flat. Skin yellow, flushed with red and much thin russet. Flesh firm, yellow, tending to be acid and with aromatic flavour. Both growth and cropping are only moderate. Although a useful dual-purpose cultivar, its restricted cropping has led to a decline in popularity.
- *Belle de Pontoise* Culinary. December/February. A cultivar of late season and attractive appearance. Raised about 1870 by M. Remy at Pontoise, France with one parent 'Emperor Alexander'. Grown on the Continent, not listed by British nurseries. Flowering period 3 but tending to irregular flowering and so not reliable as a pollinator. Fruit large, flat, slightly ribbed, stalk very long. Skin pale yellow, with red flush and broken red stripes, also some russet. Flesh white, tender and crisp, sub-acid. Vigorous, and a heavy cropper, but often only in alternate years. A culinary cultivar of limited value because of its unreliability over cropping.
- *Blenheim Orange* Dessert and culinary. November/January. A good old cultivar esteemed for its flavour. Originated at Woodstock near Blenheim, Oxfordshire, UK, by a Mr Kempster and distributed from about 1820. Widely grown. Flowering period 3, a triploid cultivar reputed to be self-sterile and also can be

irregular in flowering. Fruit large, flattened and rectangular with slight ribbing. Eye large and open. Skin yellow with flush and stripes of dull red, also fine russeting. Flesh yellow, crisp, sweet, sub-acid with a nutty flavour. Growth vigorous and spreading, making a striking tree. Resistant to mildew. One of the few cultivars which comes fairly true from seed, so there are a lot of seedlings resembling 'Blenheim Orange' in cultivation. An excellent dual-purpose garden cultivar. **5**
- *Bramley's Seedling* Culinary. November/March. The best known, and probably the best of the cooking apples but making a large tree under most conditions. From an original tree at Southwell, Nottinghamshire, UK, around 1810, and widely distributed in Britain but little grown on the Continent. Flowering period 3; notorious for susceptibility to frost damage which can even kill unopened flowers. A triploid cultivar. Fruit large, round, flattened characteristic angular shape. Eye closed in a broad basin, stalk short. Green skin, ripening to yellow-green, sometimes flushed and striped red. Flesh white, firm and acid. Not suitable for growing in restricted tree forms (cordon) on account of its vigour and tends to produce a large tree, although stays small when grown on very dwarfing root stocks. **6**
- *Calville Blanc D'Hiver, Winter White Calville* Dessert. January/February. Very old cultivar requiring warm growing conditions to succeed. Originated in France or Germany about 1600 and widely grown on the Continent; not listed by British nurseries. Flowering period 4. Fruit medium/large, flat, with prominent ribs. Stalk rather long. Skin yellow, possibly with slight red flush. Flesh yellow, soft, juicy; flavour sweet and aromatic.
- *Carter's Seedling* see 'Annie Elizabeth'.
- *Claygate Pearmain* Dessert. December/March. Not well known but a good late dessert cultivar of quality. Discovered in a hedge near Claygate, Surrey, UK, by John Braddick and exhibited in 1821. Flowering period 4. Fruit medium, conical, with a thick stalk of medium length. Dull green, with faint orange/red flush and some russet. Flesh greenish white, crisp, juicy and sweet with a good flavour. Of moderate vigour and fair cropping ability. Deserves to be better known. **7**
- *Cox's Orange Pippin* Dessert and culinary. Late October/January. The best known dessert cultivar, renowned for its flavour, but needing good conditions for success as a garden cultivar. Widely distributed throughout northern Europe, Australia and New Zealand. The most widely planted commercial apple in Britain. Said to be a seedling from 'Ribston Pippin', raised at Colnbrook, Slough, UK, by Richard Cox, a retired brewer, and introduced about 1850. Flowering period 3 and 'Worcester Pearmain' has been widely recommended as a pollinator but has been superseded by preferred cultivars (e.g. 'Egremont Russet'), fruit medium, round, eye half open in a shallow basin; shortish stalk. Skin yellowish green changing to golden yellow when ripe with brownish red flush, faint stripes and patches of russet. Flesh yellow, crisp and juicy; sharp flavour when under-ripe, becoming sweet with characteristic rich, aromatic flavour when ripe. Moderately vigorous in growth, producing an upright, dense tree of medium size and cropping regularly but generally not heavily.

Needs good soil conditions and does not thrive

in wet or cold areas. Susceptible to apple scab and mildew and so more difficult to grow in gardens. Alternative cultivars while lacking the flavour of 'Cox's Orange Pippin' will give greater satisfaction under a wide range of garden conditions. Understandably, a good number of sports, such as 'Queen Cox', have arisen from this cultivar. **8**
- *Crawley Beauty* Dessert and culinary. December/February. The special merit of this cultivar is its habit of flowering later than any other, giving the best chance of avoiding spring frost damage to flowers in low-lying, frost-prone situations. Otherwise its appeal is limited, so it is not widely planted. Found in a cottage garden in Crawley, Sussex and introduced in 1906. Flowering period 7, but self-fertile to a limited extent. Fruit medium/large, flattish round, with an open eye. Green/pale yellow with orange-red flush and stripes. Flesh green-white, sub-acid, slightly sweet. Tree growth of moderate vigour. **9**
- *Crimson Bramley* A sport of 'Bramley's Seedling'.
- *Crimson Gravenstein* see 'Gravenstein'.
- *Crispin, Mutsu* Dessert. Late October/February. A new cultivar, the product of controlled breeding in Japan, noted for large fruit size and green colour, although it is in fact a sweet dessert apple. Cross between 'Golden Delicious' and 'Indo' from Japan. Recently introduced and so not widely planted yet. Flowering period 3 but a triploid cultivar so no good as a pollinator for other varieties. Fruit large, oblong, narrowing towards the calyx, with ribbing at that end. Stalk long, slender. Skin bright green, turning to golden yellow when ripe. Flesh white, juicy and of pleasant flavour similar to 'Golden Delicious'. Vigorous grower, tip and spur bearer. Open, spreading tree habit, cropping regularly and heavily. Harvested 2 to 3 weeks after 'Cox's Orange Pippin' and a cultivar noted for its flavour and crispness. **10**
- *D'Arcy Spice* Dessert. December/April. A connoisseur's cultivar, late-keeping and of good flavour but shy and often irregular in cropping. Not widely grown. Originated at Tolleshunt D'Arcy, Essex, UK, introduced about 1850 and seems particularly successful in Essex. Flowering period 3. Fruit medium, round, prominently ribbed, greenish yellow unattractive looking fruit with a covering of russet and occasionally also a dull flush. Flesh greenish white, firm, crisp, acid and aromatic. Growth tends to be weak and this cultivar is prone to biennial bearing, but, nevertheless, cannot be dismissed on account of its notable flavour. **11**
- *Delicious* 'Golden Delicious' and 'Red Delicious' are sports; see 'Golden Delicious'.
- *Discovery* Dessert. August/September. A newly introduced, attractive and promising cultivar for the early part of the season and capable of keeping longer than many other early cultivars. A seedling, reputed to have 'Worcester Pearmain' as one parent, discovered in a garden at Langham, Essex, UK, introduced early 1960s as 'Thurston August'. Renamed 'Discovery' in 1962 and planted commercially in place of older-established cultivars for maturing early in the season. Flowering period 3. Fruit medium, flat/round with a medium long stalk. Skin pale greenish yellow, flushed with bright red and often russeted. Flesh white, crisp, juicy, sub-acid with a pleasant flavour. A tip and spur bearer, sometimes slow to start cropping unless grafted on to

the framework of a tree of another cultivar and also prone to heavy fruit drop during the growing season. **12**

– *Duke of Devonshire* Dessert. February/March. A well-flavoured, late-keeping, russet-covered variety. Raised at Holker Hall, Lancashire, UK by the Duke of Devonshire's gardener in 1835 and introduced about 40 years later but not widely planted. Flowering period 4. Fruit medium, rectangular/round, almost no cavity at the eye end, stalk short and stout. Dull golden yellow with russet often almost covering the fruit. Flesh pale greenish yellow and rather dry, but crisp and of good flavour. Growth moderate and a regular cropper inclined to variegation in both leaf and fruit. Another late-keeping apple, now being recommended again on account of its flavour.

– *Dumelow's Seedling, Wellington* Culinary. November/March. A late-keeping cooker and parent of several other listed varieties. Possibly a seedling of 'Northern Greening' raised at Shakerstone, Leicestershire, UK, about 1800 and called 'Dumelow's Crab'. Renamed 'Wellington' about 1820 and later 'Dumelow's Seedling'. Flowering period 4. Fruit medium, flat, even; stalk on the surface almost without any cavity. Skin greasy, yellow with red flush and russet spots. Flesh white, crisp, firm, sharply acid. Vigorous grower with a slight biennial bearing tendency. Hardy, suitable for northern areas.

– *Early Victoria* see 'Emneth Early'.

– *Edward VII* Culinary. December/April. A later keeper than 'Bramley's Seedling'. Flowering period 6, so less susceptible to frost damage than 'Bramley's' and useful in sites where spring frosts are a hazard. Product of a 'Blenheim Orange' × 'Golden Noble' cross, introduced by Messrs Rowe of Worcester about 1910 and widely planted in Britain. A difficult cultivar for which to plan cross-pollination because most other cultivars flower before it. However, 'Mother' and 'Crawley Beauty' have earlier and later flowering respectively, but are of roughly overlapping flowering times. Fruit medium, oblong/conical, regular. Open eye in a shallow basin; short stalk. Yellowish green, smooth, waxy skin with occasional red flush. Flesh firm, yellow, juicy, acid and translucent when cooked; an excellent cooker. Tree growth vigorous and fertility moderate. A recommended cultivar, although susceptible to mildew.

– *Egremont Russet* Dessert. October/November. An old-established cultivar, increasing in popularity on account of its flavour and as a pollinator for 'Cox's Orange Pippin'. Of unknown English origin, widely planted commercially in recent years. Flowering period 2. Fruit medium, round and regular. Eye open, stalk very short. Green-yellow, usually completely covered with russet. Flesh creamy yellow, dry with sweet aromatic flavour. Growth moderate/vigorous, upright and a good cropper. A good mid-season garden cultivar with distinctive flavour and resistant to scab. **13**

– *Ellison's Orange* Dessert. October. An old-established cultivar introduced in 1911, distinctive aniseed flavour. A seedling of 'Cox's Orange Pippin' × 'Calville Blanc' parentage raised at Bracebridge, Lincoln, and like 'Cox's Orange Pippin' in appearance. Widely grown in Britain. Flowering period 4 and resistant to spring frost damage. Fruit medium, round/conical and regular; stalk fairly long, often protruding. Golden yellow skin with crimson stripes and often an orange-red flush. Flesh creamy white, crisp and juicy, sweet, with distinctive flavour. Moderately vigorous growth, making a fairly upright tree. Tends to biennial bearing. Hardy, suitable for northern area.

Coloured sports of this variety exist, for example, 'Red Ellison'.

– *Emneth Early, Early Victoria* Culinary. July/August. The first culinary apple of the season but with correspondingly short useful life which restricts its value where garden space is limited. Thought to be the result of a 'Lord Grosvenor' × 'Keswick Codlin' cross. Raised by William Lynn of Emneth, Cambridgeshire, UK, about 1900 and widely planted commercially in Britain. Flowering period 3 and can be irregular in blossoming. Fruit medium, conical, irregular, with a short stalk in a deep basin. Skin greenish yellow with greenish white, rather soft flesh, cooking frothily. Growth fairly weak, trees compact and upright. Tends to biennial bearing. In cropping years, some of the fruits may have to be thinned otherwise they will all be too small. The best early cooker and surplus fruit may be kept after suitable treatment, for example, deep frozen. Fairly hardy.

– *Encore* Culinary. November/June. A very late-keeping and good culinary cultivar to follow 'Bramley's Seedling'. Raised by Charles Ross from a cross of 'Warner's King' × 'Northern Greening'. Introduced about 1910 by Messrs Cheal's of Crawley, Sussex, UK, but not widely grown. Flowering period 4, large, round, flattened, with a short stalk in a deep, narrow cavity. Skin green, yellow at ripening, greasy, occasionally with red-brown streaks and flush. Flesh greenish white, soft and slightly acid with a fair flavour. Looks like a 'Bramley's Seedling' and could replace that cultivar in garden planning where long-keeping qualities are required.

– *Fortune* see 'Laxton's Fortune'.

– *George Neal* Culinary and dessert. September/October. Usually regarded as a culinary cultivar but of reasonable flavour for dessert use. Of unknown origin, raised by Mrs Reeves of Otford, Kent, introduced by R. Neal & Sons, Wandsworth, London, UK, in the early 1920s. Flowering period 2. Fruit medium/large, round, with ribs on the body and at the eye end. Open eye in a deep basin, long stalk. Skin white-yellow with orange-scarlet flush and stripes, also spots of russet. Flesh greenish white, crisp, firm, slightly acid. Growth vigorous and a free and regular cropper.

– *Golden Delicious* Dessert. December/February. The most universally planted variety for commercial production throughout the world. Chance seedling from West Virginia, USA, introduced in 1914 and now extensively planted in France, Holland and northern Europe generally, including Britain. Flowering period 4. Fruit small/medium, round/oblong, slightly ribbed. Stalk long and thin. Greenish yellow/golden yellow with prominent pores, and sometimes a slight orange flush. Flesh yellowish white, crisp with a pleasant flavour. Growth moderately vigorous in Britain but may be very vigorous in southern parts of northern Europe when it both grows strongly and also is capable of forming fruit buds on one year old wood. This gives it a potential for producing heavy yields quickly after planting, and it is a cultivar which responds well to close planting and intensive methods of cultivation. Requires favoured situations in Britain and northwards to give good skin finish and in many gardens is unlikely to produce quality comparable to that of imported fruit, although an easy apple to grow. **14**

– *Golden Noble* Culinary. September/January. An excellent cooker for garden cultivation. An introduction dating from about 1820 by the gardener to Sir Thomas Hare of Stowe Hall, Downham, Norfolk, UK. Flowering period 4. Fruit medium, conical, ribbed at eye end. Stalk very short in a wide cavity. Skin golden yellow, sometimes flushed slightly with orange and occasional russet. Flesh yellow, soft, crisp, acid. Growth vigorous and fertile in cropping. Cooks frothily and with a golden colour. **15**

– *Granny Smith* Dessert. December/May. Late-keeping cultivar requiring warm conditions to finish well. A seedling originating from New South Wales, Australia, and reported fruiting in 1868. Widely planted in some parts of the world but listed by very few British nurseries. Flowering period 3. Fruit medium, conical, with short, deep set stalk. Skin green-yellow with brown flush in the sun. Flesh greenish yellow, hard, crisp, moderately sweet, sub-acid. Moderate vigour and fruitfulness, especially in warm positions. **16**

– *Gravenstein* Dessert. September/October. An old-established continental cultivar widely planted in Germany. Its country of origin is uncertain but it was believed to have been first reported in Denmark in 1670. Flowering period 1, but it is a triploid and so not suitable as a pollinator for other cultivars. Fruit medium/large, round irregular, eye closed and stalk short. Skin orange-yellow with orange-red flush and markings, greasy. Flesh yellowish white, crisp, sweet and with a distinctive perfumed flavour. Moderately vigorous grower and cropper. A number of coloured sports of this variety have been found, for example, 'Crimson Gravenstein', 'Red Gravenstein'. Although quite popular on the Continent, it is listed by only one or two nurserymen in the UK.

– *Grenadier* Culinary. August/September. A popular commercial cultivar. Of unrecorded origin, introduced about 1875 and widely grown. Flowering period 3. Fruit medium/large, flat/conical, irregular with prominent ribs at the eye end. Stout stalk, knobbed at the end. Skin greenish yellow, smooth and sometimes greasy with slight flush of brown. Flesh white, crisp, juicy and acid, cooking to a froth. Moderately vigorous, giving a spreading tree and a good cropper. Follows 'Emneth Early' in season and will pollinate 'Bramley's Seedling'. 'Grenadier' needs another cultivar to cross-pollinate with it because 'Bramley's' itself does not produce viable pollen. **17**

– *Holstein* Dessert. November/December. A German bred variety with a flavour similar to 'Cox's Orange Pippin', one of its parents. A seedling introduced from Schleswig-Holstein about 1920 and planted widely in northern Europe. Flowering period 3 but a triploid. Fruit large, conical/round, open eye in a shallow basin. Skin yellow with orange flush. Flesh firm, pale yellow, juicy and sub-acid. Very vigorous in growth producing a spreading tree. **18**

– *Howgate Wonder* Culinary. December/February. A giant among apples, more shapely than 'Bramley's Seedling', but not a rival in cooking quality. Product of a 'Blenheim Orange' × 'Newton Wonder' cross made at Bembridge, Isle of Wight, UK, introduced in 1932, but not widely planted. Flowering period 4. Fruit large/very large, round, flattened with a short, thick stalk in a deep cavity. Skin green, ripening to yellowish green with pale red flush and streaks. Flesh creamy white, slightly acid, juicy. Growth very vigorous making an upright and spreading tree. A heavy, regular cropper when established. Only a replacement for 'Bramley's Seedling' in special situations, for example, on sites subject to early spring frosts. Suited to northern conditions.

– *Idared* Dessert. November/April. A highly coloured, late-cropping American variety, product of a cross between 'Jonathan' and 'Wagener' made in Idaho and introduced in the early 1940s but not so far widely planted in Europe. Flowering period 2. Fruit large, flat, rectangular with ribs; stalk short/medium. Skin yellow with red flush on the sunny side of the fruit. Flesh white, somewhat juicy and with a fair flavour: can also be cooked. Growth moderately vigorous, cropping regular. Another late and good keeping apple. **19**

– *Ingrid Marie* Dessert. November/February. A late-keeping variety of Danish origin thought to be a seedling with 'Cox's Orange Pippin' as one parent, propagated on the island of Fyn, Denmark, and first fruiting about 1915. Fairly widely planted. Flowering period 4. Fruit medium/large, flat/convex with slight ribbing at the eye and on the body of the apple. Skin almost entirely flushed with deep crimson over a ground colour of greenish yellow. Flesh greenish, tinged yellow, firm, sub-acid and sweet. Fruit tends to crack around the stalk cavity. There are coloured sports such as 'Red Ingrid Marie'. Fairly hardy and suited to northern conditions.

– *James Grieve* Dessert. September/October. A good garden cultivar best eaten straight from the tree to sample the flavour at its best. Raised by James Grieve and introduced by his employers, Messrs Dickson of Edinburgh, UK, about 1890. Variously reported as having as one parent 'Pott's Seedling' or 'Cox's Orange Pippin'. Widely grown in Europe. Flowering period 3 and resistant to frost. Fruit medium/large, round/conical, fairly regular, stalk rather long, knobbed and deep set. Skin pale yellow with orange-red flush and stripes. Flesh creamy white, very juicy, slightly acid and with a pleasant flavour. Growth moderately vigorous, initially upright then spreading. A good cropper. A good cultivar for the north, tending to drop its fruit just before maturity in warmer areas. Susceptible to brown rot and canker. Fruit bruises easily, and so less favoured as a market variety, but of great garden merit. Has given rise to sports such as 'Red James Grieve', said to bruise less easily.

– *Jonathan* Dessert. November/February. An American cultivar also grown in northern Europe. Said to have 'Esopus Spitzenberg' as one parent and found on a farm at Woodstock, Ulster County, New York, USA, and named in 1826. Flowering period 3. Fruit medium, round/slightly conical, ribbed at the eye end. Skin with bright red flush over yellow ground colour with some stripes. Waxy with a slight bloom. Flesh white,

firm, sub-acid. Tree fairly vigorous and spreading, fertile with grey foliage. A brightly coloured, late-keeping cultivar. **20**

– *Kidd's Orange Red* Dessert. November/February. A better flavoured, late-keeping apple of New Zealand origin. Product of a cross between 'Cox's Orange Pippin' and 'Golden Delicious', introduced into Europe in the early 1930s but not widely planted. Flowering period 3. Fruit medium, conical with ribs towards the calyx end. Skin lemon yellow with large areas of scarlet flush and stripes and variable amounts of grey russet. Flesh light cream, firm, sweet and crisp with a pleasant aromatic flavour. Tree of moderate vigour and regular cropping. A fine keeper with good flavour. **21**

– *King Edward VII* see 'Edward VII'.

– *Lane's Prince Albert* Culinary. November/March. An old-established and late-keeping cooker of fair quality. Raised at Berkhamsted, Hertfordshire, UK, and first described about 1880. Flowering period 4; showy. Fruit large, round/conical, eye closed in a wide basin. Skin yellow-green, striped with red. Flesh greenish white, soft and acid. Compact in growth and regular in cropping and a suitable variety for growing in the north of Britain. Sensitive to sulphur sprays applied post blossom. **22**

– *Laxton's Fortune, Fortune* Dessert. September/October. Noted for its flavour and cropping ability, it is also a seedling resulting from a cross between 'Cox's Orange Pippin' and 'Wealthy'. Bred by Messrs Laxton Brothers Ltd of Bedford, UK, introduced in 1931 and it has been widely grown in Britain. Flowering period 3 and resistant to frost; sometimes tends to biennial bearing. Fruit medium, round/conical, regular, with a small eye. Skin pale greenish yellow covered with red flush and streaks. Flesh creamy white, crisp and juicy, sweet with an aromatic flavour. Growth fairly vigorous, cropping usually regular but performance less satisfactory in some areas. Where this cultivar is reliable in cropping its flavour is unsurpassed in its season. Fairly resistant to scab. **23**

– *Laxton's Superb, Superb* Dessert. November/March. Probably the most widely planted of the Laxton varieties and a good flavoured late apple with a pronounced tendency to biennial bearing. Parentage 'Wyken Pippin' × 'Cox's Orange Pippin' from Messrs Laxton Brothers Ltd of Bedford, UK, introduced about 1920 and widely grown in Britain. Flowering period 4. Unreliable as a pollinator because of its tendency to biennial bearing. Flowers frost resistant. Fruit medium, shape variable: normally round/conical. Stalk fairly long. Skin yellow-green, covered with a dark red flush and streaks. Flesh white, firm and juicy with a pleasant aromatic flavour. Growth moderately vigorous giving an upright tree. A cultivar with a disadvantage which may, to some extent, be overcome by blossom thinning. Its compensations are: flavour, long season and suitability for northern conditions. **24**

– *Lord Lambourne* Dessert. October/November. Not quite a replacement for 'Cox's Orange Pippin' where this cultivar does not succeed because of its earlier season, but of notable flavour. Raised by Messrs Laxton Brothers Ltd of Bedford, UK, from 'James Grieve' × 'Worcester Pearmain', introduced in the early 1920s and widely grown. Flowering period 2, but resistant to frost. Fruit medium/large, round/conical, with

an open eye in a wide basin. Skin yellow-green with red flush and darker stripes. Flesh creamy white, firm, crisp and juicy with a good flavour. Makes moderately vigorous growth and trees have an upright compact habit. Recently, trees of this cultivar have been affected by virus diseases causing reduced fruit size and shoots which lack the normal rigidity. These have now, generally, been eliminated and the cultivar can be recommended with confidence. **25**

– *Margil* Dessert. October/January. An old-established, long-keeping cultivar with a good flavour. Origins unknown, but recorded in England from about 1750, although not extensively planted. Flowering period 2. Fruit medium, flat, with prominent ribs, very small eye and slender stalk. Skin yellow with red-brown flush and russeting. Flesh yellow, firm, of rich, sweet, aromatic flavour. Vigour medium and only a fair cropper, but compensating for this with fruit of good quality. **26**

– *Merton Beauty* Dessert. September/October. A new cultivar bred by the staff at the John Innes Horticultural Institute, from 'Ellison's Orange' × 'Cox's Orange Pippin', raised while the Institute was at Merton, London, UK, in 1932 and released in 1962. Not widely planted on account of its recent origin. Late flowering and hence of value in frost-prone situations. Fruit medium, flat/conical. Skin pale yellow but almost completely covered with bright scarlet flush and stripes. Flesh creamy, firm, crisp, sweet and strongly aromatic. Fertile and bears regularly. Needs to be test-grown under a wide range of conditions to confirm its promise as a garden cultivar. **27**

– *Merton Charm* Dessert. Late September/November. Another new cultivar of promise which may replace present ones because of its good flavour. Bred at the John Innes Horticultural Institute in London in 1933 from a 'McIntosh' × 'Cox's Orange Pippin' cross and released in 1962, but not widely planted because of its recent introduction. Flowering period 4. Fruit medium, flat, rectangular, with closed eye in a shallow basin. Skin greenish at first, turning yellow with occasional brownish flush. Flesh white, crisp, tender, sweet, sub-acid of good quality and flavour. Tree vigour only moderate; good cropping ability. Being recommended for garden use. **28**

– *Merton Worcester* Dessert. September/October. A modern cultivar with its season following 'Worcester Pearmain', one of its parents. Raised at the John Innes Horticultural Institute, Merton, London, with 'Cox's Orange Pippin' the other parent; named in 1947, and has been planted on a fair scale in spite of its recent introduction. Flowering period 3. Fruit medium, round/conical; less conical than 'Worcester Pearmain'. Skin pale yellowish green with attractive crimson and scarlet flush. Flesh white, firm, sweet, juicier than 'Worcester' and of good flavour. Tree of moderate vigour and rather spreading growth habit; crop tends to be heavier in alternate years and the fruit tends to be affected by bitter pit. **29**

– *Monarch* Culinary. November/February. An old-established cultivar, possibly not more widely grown because its season is so like 'Bramley's Seedling'. Product of 'Peasgood's Nonsuch' × 'Dumelow's Seedling' raised and introduced by Messrs Seabrook's, Chelmsford, Essex, UK, about 1920 and quite widely planted. Flowering period 4 and tends to be biennial. Fruit large, round, oblong without ribs; open eye in a shallow basin. Skin yellow with pinkish red flush and stripes, also a tendency to greasiness. Flesh white, soft, juicy and acid, bruising readily but of good cooking quality. A vigorous spreading cultivar and good, if sometimes irregular, cropper suited for northern conditions. Trees have rather brittle branches.

– **Mother, American Mother** Dessert. October/November. A well-flavoured, mid season cultivar with the advantage of flowering late. Of unknown origin, from Massachussetts, USA, about 1850 but not widely planted. Flowering period 5. Fruit medium, conical with a short, stout stalk. Turns yellow when ripe, with carmine streaks and flush which may cover the fruit. Flesh yellow, tender, sweet, juicy with aromatic flavour. Moderate cropper.

– **Mutsu** see 'Crispin'.

– **Newton Wonder** Dessert and culinary. November/March. A dual-purpose cultivar but inclined to biennial bearing. Believed to originate from 'Dumelow's Seedling' × 'Blenheim Orange', raised at King's Newton near Melbourne, Derbyshire, UK, and introduced about 1890. Widely planted in Britain. Flowering period 5. Fruit large, round, yellow with scarlet flush and stripes. Often a fleshy swelling at the base of the very short stalk due to the high proportion of 'king' fruits that are retained on the tree. Flesh yellow, firm, crisp, juicy, sweet, sub-acid. Vigorous grower and produces a spreading tree with moderate cropping potential, but especially useful in northern areas. Its biennial bearing habit is not easy to overcome once established, since blossom thinning is difficult on a large tree. **30**

– **Ontario** Culinary. December/May. Known for its very long season. Raised from a 'Wagener' × 'Northern Spy' cross at Paris, Ontario, Canada, about 1820. Flowering period 3. Fruit medium/large, flat, rectangular, with prominent ribs on the body. Small eye and long, slender stalk. Skin greenish yellow flushed and striped brownish red. Flesh pale yellow, crisp, juicy, sub-acid. Growth vigorous but tends to biennial bearing. Not generally listed by nurseries in Britain. **31**

– **Orleans Reinette** Dessert. December/February. A cultivar of notable flavour, probably of French origin and known since about 1780. Widely planted under a variety of names. Flowering period 4. Fruit medium, flat, rectangular, ribbed at the eye end; stalk short and stout. Golden yellow with limited red flush and patches of russet. Flesh yellow, crisp, juicy, sweet and perfumed. Upright, vigorous cultivar of fair cropping ability. May shrivel in the New Year.

– **Owen Thomas** Dessert. Mid-August. Short-seasoned and of good flavour. Raised by Messrs Laxton Brothers Ltd of Bedford, UK, and introduced 1920, but not widely grown. Flowering period 3. Fruit medium, flat rectangular, ribbed with a very short stalk. Skin yellowish green with crimson streaks and somewhat greasy. Flesh white, soft, crisp, juicy and of good flavour, but in peak conditions for only a short period. Growth only moderate and tending to bear biennially. Like most early cultivars it has a limited season which is a disadvantage to many gardens.

– **Peasgood's Nonsuch** Dessert and culinary. October/November. Dual-purpose, of good cooking quality and fair flavour. Reputed to be a cross of 'Catshead' raised by Mrs Peasgood at Stamford, Lincolnshire, UK, about 1860 and widely grown. Flowering period 3. Fruit large, flat, rectangular, with a short stalk in a large cavity. Skin greenish yellow with faint carmine flush and stripes. Flesh yellowish, white, crisp, soft, very juicy. Forms a vigorous spreading tree and a fair cropper. A useful garden cultivar.

– **Queen Cox** A sport of 'Cox's Orange Pippin'.

– **Red Delicious** A sport of 'Delicious'.

– **Red Ellison's** A sport of 'Ellison's Orange'.

– **Red Gravenstein** A sport of 'Gravenstein'.

– **Red James Grieve** A sport of 'James Grieve'.

– **Reinette du Canada** Dessert and culinary. November/April. A very old-established cultivar of moderate cropping potential. Probably originated in Normandy, France, and first reported about 1770; widely grown on the Continent but not in Britain. Triploid, flowering period 3 but not producing viable pollen. Fruit medium/large, flat, with rather indistinct ribs on the body. Open eye and short, thick stalk. Skin pale yellow-green with orange flush and irregular russet. Flesh pale yellow, firm, flavour good, sub-acid. Makes a spreading tree but of restricted cropping potential in Britain and rarely listed by nurseries.

– **Rev. W. Wilks** Culinary. September/November. A well known large and excellent cooker, unfortunately inclined to biennial bearing. The product of a cross between 'Peasgood's Nonsuch' and 'Ribston Pippin', raised by Veitch's of Chelsea, London and introduced about 1910. Flowering period 2 but unreliable as a pollinator. Fruit large, flat/conical, slightly ribbed on the body and towards the eye. Stalk slender, short. Fruit creamy white with pink flush and striping. Flesh white, soft, acid. Makes a small tree. Heavy cropper, usually in alternate years, but nevertheless, recommended for garden use. **32**

– **Ribston Pippin** Dessert. November/December. A good, old-established apple which has been grown world-wide. A seedling reputedly of French origin, first grown at Ribston Hall, Yorkshire, UK, in the early 1700s, since which it has been widely planted. Flowering period 2 and a triploid. Fruit medium, oval and angular with a long stalk. Skin greasy, yellow with orange-red flush and some russet; flesh yellow, firm, crisp, aromatic and highly flavoured. Of good vigour and regular cropping habit. Recommended for its flavour. **33**

– **Rosemary Russet** Dessert. December/February. Old-established, now of greater interest on account of its flavour and as a contrast to the colour of other late apples. Veteran English cultivar of unknown origin, first reported in 1831 and not widely grown. Flowering period 3. Fruit medium, flat, ribbed at the eye and with an unusually long stalk. Skin yellow-green, flushed red-brown, very lightly covered with brown russet. Flesh yellowish green, firm, fine, aromatic flavour. Medium vigorous and a good cropper. Of interest in the search for apples of improved flavour. **34**

– **St Edmund's Pippin, St Edmund's Russet** Dessert. September/October. Old-established, finding favour for garden use as an early golden russet. Raised at Bury St Edmund's, Suffolk, UK,

by R. Harvey around 1875, but not widely grown. Flowering period 2. Fruit medium/small, round, even, with a long, slender stalk. Skin greenish yellow with orange russet usually completely covering the fruit. Also a red-brown flush. A rough looking apple. Flesh creamy white, crisp, firm, juicy and of sweet aromatic russet flavour. Makes a compact tree, cropping heavily. Probably the best early russet apple. **35**

– **Spartan** Dessert. November/January. A typical American (actually Canadian) apple, dark red in colour and with crisp flesh. A 'McIntosh' × 'Newton Pippin' cross from British Columbia, introduced in 1936. Widely planted in North America and familiar to British consumers because of imports. Now being recommended for commercial planting in northern Europe as a cultivar of different colour from those available during its season. Flowering period 3. Fruit medium/large, flat/oblong. Skin yellow, normally completely covered with deep purplish red and a distinct bloom. Flesh notably white, firm, crisp and of a pleasant vinous flavour. Moderately vigorous, upright growing then spreading, with crops which are generally heavy and regularly produced. Hardy and suitable for northern conditions. **36**

– **Starking** Dessert. January/March. A sport of 'Delicious' with a long-keeping season. Discovered by Louis Mood at Monroeville, New Jersey, USA about 1920, introduced in 1924 and being planted commercially in North America. Flowering period 4. Fruit medium/large, oblong, with prominent ribs at the eye end and on the body. Dark red stripes and flush over yellow skin. Flesh yellow, fine and firm, sweet. **37**

– **Starkrimson** December/February. A tree variation of 'Starking', discovered by Roy Bisbee, Hood River, Oregon, USA, about 1953, patented 1957 by Stark Brothers Nurseries in USA. Commercially planted in North America. Flowering period 4. Fruit like 'Starking' but taller. Red colour covers more of the fruit.

– **Sturmer Pippin** Dessert. January/April. A very late cultivar noted for its flavour. Possibly from 'Ribston Pippin' × 'Nonpareil', raised at Sturmer, Essex, UK, distributed from about 1830 and now widely planted mainly in other parts of the world whence it has been exported back to Britain. Flowering period 3. Fruit medium, round/flat, fairly long stalk; skin greenish yellow, flushed with brown. Best left on the tree as late as possible before picking. Flesh yellow-green, crisp and firm with a good flavour. Growth compact and a regular cropper. One of the best of the late apples, but needing a light soil and warm situation to develop its full flavour. **38**

– **Sunset** Dessert. November/December. A seedling of 'Cox's Orange Pippin', less demanding over soil than its parent. Raised at Ightham, Kent, UK, and named in 1933. Has been quite widely planted. Showy flowers, flowering period 3. Fruit small/medium, round and flattened, regular. Golden yellow with red flush and russet in the eye like 'Cox's Orange Pippin'. Flesh creamy yellow, crisp, juicy, aromatic and of excellent flavour. Forms a compact tree and crops regularly. Fruit size can be disappointing as the tree gets older but the cultivar can be considered as an alternative to 'Cox's Orange Pippin' on many soils, is very reliable and recommended for the garden. **39**

– **Superb** see 'Laxton's Superb'.

– *Transparente de Croncels* Dessert.
September/October. A northern European
variety of short season. Originated in France by
M. Baltet, introduced about 1870 by Baltet
Frères, Croncels, Troyes and widely planted in
France. Fruit large, flat/intermediate, rectangular, with ribs at the eye end and on the
body. Pale yellow with dull, red flush and rather
greasy skin. Flesh white, soft, dry, sweet and
slightly aromatic. Quickly goes past its best and
not generally available in Britain.
– *Tydeman's Early, Tydeman's Early Worcester*
Dessert. End August/early September. A seedling
of 'Worcester Pearmain', ripening 10 days earlier.
'McIntosh' × 'Worcester Pearmain', developed
at East Malling Research Station, Maidstone,
Kent, UK, by H. M. Tydeman in 1929 and quite
widely planted commercially to meet the demand
for early, highly coloured apples. Flowering
period 3. Fruit medium, round/conical, stalk
long, slender and protruding. Skin greasy, usually
covered with bright red flush and streaks. Flesh
white, crisp and flavour good for a short season.
Growth vigorous and a tip-bearer like 'Worcester
Pearmain'. Like most early maturing cultivars,
has a limited life in peak condition and, therefore,
does not appeal as much as later cultivars that
can keep for longer without losing quality. **40**
– *Tydeman's Late Orange* Dessert. January/
March. Later maturing than 'Cox's Orange
Pippin' with a slight tendency to biennial bearing.
Raised from 'Laxton's Superb' × 'Cox's Orange
Pippin' at East Malling Research Station,
Maidstone, Kent, UK, introduced in 1949 and
not yet widely grown. Flowering period 4. Fruit
small/medium, oval/round, stalk of moderate
length. Skin golden yellow with orange-red flush
and russet patches. Flesh cream, firm, crisp, not
juicy and of good flavour. Growth vigorous but
due to 'Laxton's Superb' parentage can become
biennial bearing, if, for instance, frost prevents
cropping in one year, and starts the habit.
A worthwhile cultivar given good storage
conditions and recommended for growing in
northern areas. **41**
– *Wagener* Culinary and dessert. January/April.
An old American cultivar noted for its reliability
and resistance to problems rather than its flavour.
Originated in New York State, USA, around
1800. Flowering period 3, not always regularly.
Fruit medium, flat/round, small eye and long,
slender stalk. Skin green-yellow, greasy with
carmine red flush. Flesh yellow, juicy with a
pleasant flavour. Growth compact and can
become biennial in bearing. Resistant to canker,
scab and frost and, therefore, suitable for
northern conditions. **42**
– *Warner's King* Culinary. October/December.
Vigorous and large fruited. Probably originated
in Kent and called 'King' apple. Sent by Warner
to Messrs Rivers of Sawbridgeworth, Hertfordshire, UK, who re-named it and has been known
under the present name since the early 1800s.
Widely grown. Flowering period 2 and a triploid,
not producing viable pollen. Fruit very large,
roundish, flattened; closed eye, stalk long in a
deep, uneven cavity. Skin pale yellow with
orange-red flush and sometimes stripes. Flesh
white, tender, crisp and sub-acid. Strong growing
cultivar and a good cropper but susceptible to
scab.
– *Wellington* see 'Dumelow's Seedling'.
– *White Transparent* Dessert and culinary.

August. An old cultivar, possibly originating in
Russia, giving dual purpose early fruit. Of
uncertain origin, one authority quoting Russia,
or originating in the Baltic States, arriving in
Europe in the middle 1800s and widely grown on
the Continent. Flowering period 2. Fruit
medium, tall and conical, with ribs and a knobbed basin at the eye end; long, thin stalk. Skin
white or pale yellow with lighter dots and slight
greasiness. Flesh greenish white, crisp, and sub-
acid. Vigorous and fertile cultivar, of note
because there are not many other August apples
which are suitable for both dessert and culinary
use. Not available from British nurseries.
– *Winter White Calville* see 'Calville Blanc
D'Hiver'.
– *Woolbrook Russet* Culinary. November/April.
A long-keeping cooker, unusual also in being a
russet apple. From 'Bramley's Seedling' ×
'King's Acre Pippin' and fruiting first in 1912.
Introduced by J. H. Stevens & Son, Woolbrook
Nursery, Sidmouth, Devon, UK, but not widely
planted. Flowering period 4. Fruit large, flat,
rectangular. Faint ribs give it an uneven appearance. Open eye and short stalk. Skin green-
yellow with faint brown flush and occasional red
streaks, covered usually completely with fine
russet. Flesh white, firm and crisp, sweet, sub-
acid. Crops regularly and cooks well, and not
subject to scab.
– *Worcester Pearmain* Dessert.
August/September. Widely grown in commerce
as a pollinator for 'Cox's Orange Pippin';
commercial growers also keep this cultivar in cold
storage so that it can be sold over a longer season
than quoted. Not generally highly regarded but of
admirable flavour if left to ripen on the tree and
eaten soon after picking. Reputed to have
'Devonshire Quarrenden' as one parent and
originated with Mr Hale at Swan Pool, near
Worcester, UK. Introduced by Smith of Worcester about 1875 and extensively planted although
other pollinators for 'Cox's Orange Pippin' are
now being commercially planted in preference to
'Worcester'. Flowering period 3. A tip-bearer.
Fruit medium, round, conical, eye closed and
short stalk. Bright red flush and streaks over
golden yellow skin. Flesh white, firm, very juicy
and crisp, sweet, perfumed. Growth moderate but
a regular cropper. Inclined to be susceptible to
scab, but resistant to mildew. Although the fruit
is readily available, it is often difficult to find this
cultivar at its best and appreciate its flavour. The
flowers are frost-resistant and it is a useful
cultivar in areas subject to spring frosts; does well
in northern areas. **43**

Apricot *Prunus armeniaca* ROSACEAE

– *Alfred* Late July/early August. A new introduction from America with less predisposition to
die-back of the shoots but not widely grown. The
apricot is self-fertile so there is no need to plant
several cultivars to ensure cross-pollination, or to
take account of flowering periods. Fruit
medium/large, round and flattened. Orange with
a pinkish flush. Flesh orange, juicy with a good
flavour; suitable for bottling. Very vigorous,
forming a spreading tree. Tends to biennial
bearing, easily started since the flowers are very
early and exposed to frost or wind damage. Once
a crop has been missed, the habit is then established. Protection of the flower is needed.
– *Bergeron* Late July/early August. One of the

principal French apricots. A chance seedling
originated by M. Bergeron, Saint-Cyr-au-Mont
d'Or (Rhone) which first fruited in 1926. Now
well established as one of the principal commercial cultivars. Fruit large, long and rounded
with the halves not of equal size. Skin deep yellow
with red flush and dots. Flesh orange, very fine
and firm, sweet and perfumed, of moderate
flavour. Makes a vigorous tree, cropping well;
resistant to pest and disease but blossoms are
susceptible to blossom wilt. Clones of this variety
are now available which are free from all known
virus diseases.
– *Breda* Mid-August on walls in Britain or
September in the open in sheltered conditions.
May have originated in Africa but came to
Britain from Breda, Holland and has been known
for at least 100 years. It is not widely grown in
Britain but is planted in other northern European
countries. Flowers mid-early to late and susceptible to cold, wet weather. Fruit medium/large,
squarish; skin orange, flushed on the exposed side
with reddish orange and dotted with brown and
red. The skin is fairly thick and difficult to peel.
Flesh yellow-orange, tender/medium firm, very
juicy, sub-acid, aromatic and of good flavour.
The tree is of moderate vigour, precocious and
can be heavy cropping but tends to be short-lived,
exhausting itself early. Needs a favoured situation
with warm soil, also adequate and constant
moisture if it is going to give of its best. **44**
– *Canino* Early August. A large-fruited cultivar
grown on the Continent and known as 'Canino
Grosso' by some authorities. Makes a vigorous
tree.
– *Early Moorpark* Late July. Resembles 'Moorpark' but ripens about 3 weeks earlier. Fruit
round/oval with a deep line from base to apex.
Skin yellow with crimson flush and dots on the
sunny side. Flesh deep orange, very juicy with a
rich flavour. Tends to make vigorous growth in
its early years which should be checked if the tree
is to crop satisfactorily.
– *Gros Pêche* see 'Peach'.
– *Hemskerk* Early August. Believed to be a
cultivar of 'Moorpark' but hardier. An old-
established variety but not widely planted. Fruit
large, conical, flattened at either end with a deep
line joining them. Skin yellow with red blotches.
Flesh orange, sweet and of good flavour for
which it is recommended. Of moderate vigour
and crops well.
– *Luizet* End of July. Another old-established
French cultivar. Raised by M. Luizet, nurseryman, at Ecully, near Lyons, France, introduced
in 1853. Flowers mid-season, self-fertile. Fruit
large, oval with the two halves unequal. Skin
orange-yellow with carmine flush and darker
dots, sometimes marbled with grey or russet; the
skin is fairly thick. Flesh orange-yellow, firm,
moderately juicy, sweet and perfumed. The tree is
vigorous but not a good cropper. It is resistant to
pest and disease and hardy in Britain, neither is it
too demanding either regarding climate or soil.
– *Moorpark* Late August. The most commonly
grown apricot in Britain. Introduced from the
Continent and first called by its present name in
1788. No doubt planted at Moorpark, near
Watford, Hertfordshire, UK, but the credit for its
introduction has been ascribed to a number of
different people. Fruit large, round, with a
pronounced line from base to apex separating
halves of unequal size. Skin pale yellow with red-

brown flush and darker spots on the sunny side. Flesh orange, juicy, sweet and of fine flavour. Grows strongly in the early years after planting and may have to be checked by root pruning in early August in order to reduce the vigour. Crops regularly. Rather prone to dieback. Can be grown as a standard tree in sunny situations, otherwise better against a wall. A south-easterly aspect avoids the fruit being directly exposed to full sun which can lead to uneven ripening of the fruit. **45**

– *New Large Earl* Mid-July. The earliest apricot, raised from 'Augoumois' by Messrs Rivers of Sawbridgeworth, Hertfordshire, UK, first cropping in 1873 but not widely planted. Fruit large, round/oval, pale orange, deeper colour on the sunny side. Flesh orange, sweet, melting and juicy, of good flavour. Growth and cropping good, possibly a cultivar to grow indoors although it makes a large tree.

– *Orange de Provence* see 'Polonais'.

– *Peach, Pêche de Nancy, Gros Pêche* A similar cultivar to 'Moorpark', possibly brought to Britain from the Continent by the Duke of Northumberland about 1765. Widely grown in France. Fruit large, round, flattened, with a deep line from base to apex. Pale orange with a deep red flush on the sunny side. Flesh reddish yellow, firm, juicy and of excellent, rather musky, flavour. Growth vigorous and tolerant of pruning, unlike some apricots. Can be grown in a restricted form.

– *Polonais, Orange de Provence* Late July. An important French cultivar adapted to parts of the lower and middle Rhone area particularly. Flowers late, self-fertile, fairly resistant to frost with a short flowering season. Fruit large, round with prominent line from base to apex. Skin yellow-light orange, flushed red. Flesh yellow-orange, fairly firm, sweet and perfumed, of quite good flavour. Particularly useful for canning. Tree growth vigorous and a good cropping cultivar, although the flower buds are liable to drop. Good resistance to pest and disease. Clones free from all known viruses are available.

– *Rouge du Roussillon* Mid-July in France. A widely grown French variety, particularly suited to the south of France. Flowers early mid-season, self fertile. Fruit medium/medium large, round/oval, flattened laterally, with a well-marked line from base to apex separating unequal halves. Golden yellow, flushed red. Flesh orange-yellow, juicy, sweet, perfumed and of very good flavour, although the quality tends to vary from year to year. Tree vigorous, cropping regularly, resistant to disease and drought although may get blossom wilt. Frost resistant. The young fruit is inclined to drop prematurely and may rot after rain. Clones which are resistant to all known viruses are available.

Bilberry see *Vaccinium*.

Blackberry *Rubus fruticosus* ROSACEAE

– *Bedford Giant* End July/early August. Very early cropping and sweet fruit. Raised from a selfed seeding of Veitchberry in 1937 by Messrs Laxton Brothers Ltd of Bedford, UK, and widely grown in commerce. Fruit large/very large, shiny black, sweet and juicy, but without a strong blackberry flavour. Vigorous grower making 3 to 4m. (10 to 12ft) of growth in a season. A heavy and consistent cropper.

– *Cutleaf* see 'Parsley Leaved'.

– *Himalaya, Himalayan Giant, Theodor Reimers* Mid-August. A vigorous, almost rampant growing cultivar, cropping heavily. Said to be a selection of *Rubus procerus*, a species indigenous to western Europe and widely grown. Fruit large with medium sized druplets, jet black, round, carried in large trusses. Flavour moderate when ripe. A very vigorous cultivar, very heavily thorned. Good reliable cropper. Needs adequate space and strong supports. **46**

– *John Innes* Late August until severe frost. The best late cultivar and of good flavour. Raised from a *Rubus rusticanus inermis* × *Rubus thyrsiger* cross at the John Innes Horticultural Institute, Merton, London, but not widely planted because its season clashes with the wild blackberry. Fruit medium on medium-sized trusses, very sweet and juicy without many seeds and of true blackberry flavour. Moderately vigorous and a heavy cropping cultivar.

– *Parsley Leaved, Cutleaf, Oregon Thornless* Late August/September. A selection from the wild British species, *Rubus laciniatus* with deeply lobed, evergreen leaves. Fruit large, round, shiny black in trusses of good size; sweet and of good flavour. Makes quite strong growth and needs good growing conditions; crops well. A thornless form 'Oregon Thornless', is thought to have originated from 'Parsley Leaved' and has been introduced to Britain from the USA. **47**

– *Theodor Reimers* see Himalaya

Black Currant see Currant.
Blaeberry see Bilberry.
Boysenberry see Hybrid Berries.
Brambles see Blackberry.

Cape Gooseberry, Golden Berry
Physalis peruviana edulis SOLANACEAE
Dessert and culinary. September/October. Native of South America. Flower yellow with black centre; calyx green ripening to brown, papery texture. Fruit deep gold when ripe, up to 1cm. ($\frac{3}{4}$in.) across. Sweet, unusual flavour. **48, 49**

Cherry *Prunus avium* and *P. cerasus* ROSACEAE

– *Amber Heart* see 'Kent Bigarreau'.

– *Bigarreau* see 'Kent Bigarreau'.

– *Bigarreau de Schrecken* Dessert. Mid-June. Large-fruited, good flavoured early cherry. May have originated in Germany but quite widely grown in Britain. Flowering period 2, can be pollinated by 'Early Rivers'. Fruit large, heart-shaped, with a long stalk; shiny black. Flesh reddish-black, firm, juicy and of good flavour. Does not hang well on the tree once ripe. Growth vigorous, heavy cropping.

– *Bigarreau Gaucher* Dessert. Mid-late July. A relatively new variety of promise. Listed in German references about 1905 but not widely grown. Flowering period 5 and can be pollinated by 'Bigarreau Napoleon'. Fruit large, round with a stout stalk. Skin dark red almost black when ripe. Flesh dark red, fairly firm and juicy, of good quality. Hangs well. Tree very vigorous when young, with branches radiating upwards.

– *Bigarreau Napoleon* Dessert. Late July. A variety widely grown in commerce, of unknown origin, first referred to under another name about 1790. Flowering period 4, can be pollinated by 'Elton' or 'Bigarreau Gaucher'. Fruit very large, long, heart-shaped; skin white or yellow with dark red mottling. Flesh white/pale yellow, very

juicy and of good flavour. Tree weak growing, upright at first, then becoming spreading; regular cropper. Tree susceptible to bacterial canker and silver leaf and fruit very inclined to split, especially if wet weather occurs at fruit ripening. **50**

– *Bradbourne Black* Dessert. Late July. Recommended for flavour and does not make a big tree. Flowering period 6, possibly avoiding spring frosts. Can be pollinated by 'Bigarreau Napoleon'. Fruit large, round; skin very dark red. Flesh dark red, juicy, susceptible to splitting. To avoid this problem fruit can be picked when coloured but before it is fully ripe if a wet period can be anticipated. Tree vigorous with long branches reaching to the ground, a distinction from the similar 'Géante d' Hedelfingen', which also ripens later.

– *Early Rivers* Dessert. Mid-June. Usually the earliest cherry on the market in quantity. A seedling from 'Early Purple Gean', raised by Messrs Rivers of Sawbridgeworth, Hertfordshire, UK, about 1865 and widely planted. Flowering period 1, can be pollinated by 'Merton Glory'. Fruit very large, round, uneven, with a slender stalk. Skin red, darkening to black when fully ripe. Flesh red-black, tender and of good flavour when ripened on the tree; fairly resistant to splitting. Tree vigorous, tall with drooping lateral branches, and cropping well. More tolerant than many cherries of imperfect soil conditions and recommended also for its flavour. **51**

– *Elton, Elton Heart* Dessert. Early July. A high quality cultivar for garden use, being rather too uncertain in cropping for commercial cultivation. Raised about 1800 by T. A. Knight and widely planted. Has performed better in Worcestershire than, for instance, in Kent. Flowers large and flowering period 3; can be pollinated by 'Merton Bigarreau'. Fruit medium, long, heart-shaped with a long stalk. Pale yellow skin flushed with red, with dots and streaks of the same colour. Flesh pale yellow, juicy, sweet and judged by some to set the standard for flavour in cherries. Vigour moderate making a small upright tree with drooping lateral branches. Not a heavy, or reliable, cropper. Susceptible to bacterial canker and fruit liable to splitting.

– *Géante d'Hedelfingen* Dessert. Late July. Large, rich-flavoured, similar to 'Bradbourne Black' in many respects. Flowers very prominent, flowering period 6, and can be pollinated by 'Bigarreau Napoleon'. Fruit large, round/oval, heart-shaped with a rather long stalk. Deep red skin becoming almost black when fully ripe. Flesh dark red, juicy and of good quality; makes a large tree, cropping well. Fruit rather prone to splitting.

– *Governor Wood* Dessert. Early July. A reliable cropping variety but the ripening fruit is very subject to cracking in wet weather. Of American origin, raised in Cleveland, Ohio, about 1840 and used to be widely grown until cultivars without its drawbacks became available. Flowering period 3, can be pollinated by 'Kent Bigarreau'. Fruit medium/large, round. Skin dark red and pink flush over yellow ground colour. Flesh pale yellow, soft, juicy, generally of good flavour but subject to splitting. Moderately vigorous, making a small tree and cropping heavily. Both flowers and fruit subject to brown rot even when the fruit is only a little split.

– *Kent Bigarreau, Amber Heart, Bigarreau* Dessert. Mid-July. The commonest mid-season cherry, extensively grown in Kent, UK. Flowering period 4, large, can be pollinated by 'Elton' or 'Bigarreau Gaucher'. Fruit medium, round, flattened at top and bottom with a long, slender stalk. Skin white or yellow with red flush and dots. Flesh white with a pink tinge, crisp. Vigorous grower and fertile.

– *May Duke* Culinary and dessert. Mid-June. An acid cherry, early, but not as early as its name implies. An old-established cultivar, especially grown in the Netherlands. Flowering period 3 of sweet cherries and is partly self-fertile while being capable of pollinating sweet cherries flowering at or about the same time. Flowers large. Fruit medium/large, flattened and long-stalked. Skin dark red. Flesh of a similar colour, soft, juicy, sub-acid and sweeter than any other acid cherry. Resistant to splitting. Growth vigorous, cropping reliable and heavy. A good cultivar to grow on a wall.

– *Merton Bigarreau* Dessert. Mid/late July. A late mid-season black cherry recommended for its flavour. A cross between 'Knight's Early Black' and 'Napoleon', raised by the John Innes Horticultural Institute while at Merton, London, and released in the late 1940s. Quite widely planted. Flowering period 3, cannot be pollinated by 'Bigarreau de Schrecken', 'Merton Bounty', 'Merton Favourite' or 'Waterloo'. Fruit large, flattened at base and sides and with a short stalk. Deep purple becoming almost black when full ripe. Flesh light crimson, firm, juicy, excellent flavour. Makes a vigorous and very spreading tree and crops heavily. 52

– *Merton Crane* Dessert. July. Recommended for flavour. A product of the John Innes Horticultural Institute, not yet widely grown. Flowering period 4, can be pollinated by 'Bigarreau Napoleon'. Fruit medium, round/conical with flattened sides. Skin dark red ripening to near black. Flesh similarly coloured, firm and of excellent flavour ripening over a period and, therefore, desirable from the garden point of view. Tree vigorous and upright. A cultivar to note.

– *Merton Favourite* Dessert. Late July. Has been given the Royal Horticultural Society's Award of Merit. Another variety bred by the John Innes Horticultural Institute from 'Knight's Early Black' and 'Bigarreau de Schrecken' and more widely planted than 'Merton Crane'. Flowering period 2, can be pollinated by 'Waterloo'. Fruit large, round with a fairly long stalk. Skin black, juicy, sweet and of excellent flavour. The fruit is scattered over the tree rather than carried in clusters. Grows vigorously, making an upright, spreading tree which crops well.

– *Merton Glory* Dessert. Mid-July. A large-fruited, yellow cherry of good flavour. Another cultivar bred by the John Innes Horticultural Institute, from 'Ursula Rivers' × 'Noble', introduced in 1947 but not widely planted. Flowering period 2, pollinated by 'Merton Favourite'. Fruit very large, round, with shoulders. Pale yellow with red flush. Flesh yellow, very juicy and of good flavour. Vigorous growing cultivar making a spreading tree and cropping heavily. 53

– *Morello* Culinary. August/September. Often regarded as synonymous with acid cherry, but there are a number of cultivars of acid cherry of which this is easily the best known. Self-fertile and can be planted with confidence where a sweet cherry would not succeed because of soil conditions. Good as a fan-trained tree on a wall, even

a north-facing one. Satisfactory as a standard tree, although more difficult to net against birds than a wall-trained specimen. A very old-established cultivar, mentioned in 1629 and widely planted in limited quantities. Flowers late, and although capable of pollinating sweet cherries, is too late for many cultivars. Fruit large, round, with a long, thin stalk; crimson, ripening to near black. Flesh deep crimson, juicy and slightly astringent, having a bittersweet flavour when fully ripe. Comes larger and later on a north-facing wall. Moderately vigorous, making a pendulous tree and a heavy and regular cropper under a wide range of conditions. The best acid cherry. There are some selections like 'Wye Morello', especially grown for making cherry brandy. 54

– *Reine Hortense* Culinary. Mid-end July. A large-fruited, continental cultivar. Raised at Neuilly near Paris, first fruited about 1840. Fruit very large, flattened on the sides with a long, slender stalk. Skin pale red, darkening as it ripens. Flesh yellow, tender, juicy, sub-acid. Vigorous grower and an excellent cropper but not commonly grown in Britain.

– *Roundel, Roundel Heart* Dessert. Early July. A notably large-fruited cherry. An old-established cultivar of unknown origin found in Hertfordshire, UK, and widely grown commercially. Flowering period 3 and will not cross-pollinate with 'Early Rivers'. Fruit very large, round, short, heart-shaped with a long stalk in a deep cavity. Skin dark red and shiny. Flesh of similar colour, soft, juicy, sweet and recommended for flavour. Growth upright, giving a vigorous tree, cropping regularly and heavily. Fruit not usually subject to splitting.

– *Royal Duke* Culinary and dessert. Mid-July. Another duke cherry of rather unreliable cropping ability. An old-established cultivar of uncertain origin but commented on in old French reports. Not widely grown. Flowering period 3 of sweet cherries, is capable of pollinating them as well as being able to set a light crop when self-pollinated; results are better if they are planted with other acid cherries - 'May Duke' would be an ideal partner. Fruit large, rather rectangular, with a long, slender stalk. Skin deep red. Flesh yellow with red streaks, juicy, sub-acid and with a delicious flavour. Growth vigorous and very upright but not a consistent cropper. The fruit is quite resistant to splitting.

– *Stella* Dessert. Late July. Represents a step forward in being self-fertile and a pollinator for other sweet cherries as well. Originated at Summerland Agricultural Research Station, British Columbia, Canada, from 'Lambert' × 'John Innes Seedling 2420', introduced in 1968 and still undergoing testing in Europe. Flowering period 4 and reported to be fairly susceptible to frost. Fruit large, heart-shaped, red ripening to black and rather susceptible to splitting. Flesh black, medium, firm, relatively coarse. Tree vigorous, upright, spreading and crops well in Canada. If not found after further testing to be ideal for northern European conditions it is still likely to be heard of increasingly in connection with breeding of other self-fertile cultivars. 55

– *Waterloo* Dessert. Late June/early July. Possibly the best-flavoured black cherry but is rather erratic in cropping. Raised by T. A. Knight from a cross between 'Bigarreau' and 'May Duke' about 1815, named after the famous battle which

took place shortly before it produced its first fruit. Widely grown in Britain and, to a lesser extent, on the Continent and North America. Flowering period 2, flowers small, and cannot be cross-pollinated by 'Bigarreau de Schrecken', 'Merton Bigarreau' or 'Merton Favourite'. Fruit medium, flattened, with a long and rather slender stalk. Skin very deep reddish black, shiny. Flesh very dark red, tender, sweet and of excellent flavour with a small stone. Fairly resistant to splitting. Vigour moderate, making a round-headed tree.

– *Wye Morello* see 'Morello'.

Chinese Gooseberry, Kiwi Fruit
Actinidia chinensis ACTINIDIACEAE
Dessert. November. Native of China, introduced to Europe early 20th century. Female flowers creamy-white, in May/June. Dioecious, female-fruiting plants need flowering male for fertilization. Fruit 4cm. (1½in.) across and 7.5 to 10cm. (3 to 4in.) long. Skin furry brown when ripe. Flesh brilliant green, of subtle, refreshing flavour. 56

Cloudberry *Rubus chamaemorus* ROSACEAE
A dwarf shrubby plant which grows wild in northern Europe, particularly in boggy, mountainous areas of Scandinavia. It is not usually cultivated in gardens. The plant grows up to 25cm. (10in.) high with slender, thornless shoots. The flowers are 3cm. (1in.) in diameter, pure white and appear in June. The fruits are few in number up to 2.5cm. long, pale orange and have a distinctive flavour. 57

Cobnut see Hazelnut.

Crab Apple *Malus pumila* ROSACEAE
These trees are known for their ornamental flowers and foliage (depending on species and cultivar) as well as their ornamental, edible fruit. This list is restricted to those which are best known for their fruit. Culture is like that of half-standard or standard apple but since the overall garden effect is usually the sought after feature, pruning is usually limited and spraying is not usually done.

– *Golden Hornet* Dessert and culinary. October/November. The best of the yellow-fruited varieties, of unknown origin but generally available from nurserymen in Britain and quite widely planted. Flowers white, mid-season (first 2 weeks of May) and a generous source of pollen for the pollination of dessert apples. Has been planted as a pollinator in commercial orchards as an alternative to established pollinator cultivars with fruit of doubtful market value. Fruit large for a crab apple, about the size of a large cherry, tapering. Long retained on the tree, usually well after leaf fall. Skin bright yellow. Flesh pale yellow, acid. Makes a small spreading tree. 58

– *John Downie* Culinary. September/October. One of the best fruiting crab apples. Of unknown origin, widely grown as an ornamental tree. Flowers white with pink on the outside, produced late. Fruit conical, 3cm (1¼in.) long, skin bright orange-scarlet on a yellow ground. Flesh yellow, flavour sharp, but good for making jelly. Makes a small, erect tree up to 4.5m. (15ft) high when established. Susceptible to apple scab.

– *Malus* × *Robusta, Siberian Crab* Culinary. October. An ornamental tree for flower and fruit.

Flowers in May; white with pink outside. Fruit the size of large cherries, round; skin bright scarlet and hanging well on the tree. Flesh yellow, acid; mainly of value for making jelly. Tree of medium vigour and cropping well, reaching up to 6m. (20ft) high, with spreading branches. **59**

Cranberry see *Vaccinium*.

Currant, Black *Ribes nigrum* GROSSULARIACEAE
– *Amos Black* August. The latest of the established cultivars to ripen but tending to light cropping. Raised at East Malling Research Station, near Maidstone, Kent, UK, from 'Goliath' × 'Baldwin' in 1926, named in tribute to Jesse Amos, a plant breeder at the Station. Flowers latest of all and could miss spring frosts on this account. Fruit medium/large, fairly firm with a tough skin carried in fairly short bunches. Flavour fair, tending to acid. Makes a small, compact bush with stiff, erect shoots. Variable in cropping with a tendency to fruit fall. A cultivar to consider for extending the season, but see 'Jet'.
– *Baldwin* July/August. The most widely grown cultivar; fruit will stay in good condition on the bush when ripe over a long period. Old-established, and of unknown origin. Flowers early. Fruit medium/large, even, in bunches of medium length. Tough skin, acid flavour, rich in vitamin C and freezes well. Hangs well without splitting over a relatively long period. Bush of medium vigour, compact and cropping reliably especially on the western side of Britain. Susceptible to leaf spot. Responds to generous manuring and is known to be reliable. **60**
– *Blackdown* July/August. A new promising cultivar. Raised at Long Ashton Research Station, Bristol, UK, in 1960 from 'Baldwin' × 'Brödtorp', a Continental cultivar and granted plant breeders rights in 1971. Being multiplied for larger scale trials and commercial evaluation. Flowers early mid-season. Medium sized bunches of 4 to 5 berries; one or two bunches together. Medium/large, firm, of good, sweet flavour and easy to pick. Bush large and spreading but fairly dense. Cropping in trials has been heavy on young bushes and more consistent than standard cultivars. Resistant to mildew (American gooseberry mildew) which can attack blackcurrants.
– *Blacksmith* July/August. A late flowering, large-fruited cultivar which is easy to pick. Raised by Messrs Laxton Brothers Ltd of Bedford, UK, introduced by them in 1916, but not widely grown. Flowers relatively late so may avoid late spring frosts. Fruit large, in bunches of one or two together each having 7 to 10 berries; easy to pick, sub-acid and of fair flavour. Hanging fairly well when ripe. Makes vigorous growth giving a large, slightly spreading bush, cropping regularly and heavily.
– *Boskoop Giant* July. Probably the favourite garden cultivar because it is early. Raised by Messrs Hoogendijk in the Netherlands about 1885, introduced to Britain about 1895, but not extensively grown in commerce because of its short season. Flowers mid-season. Fruit usually in a single bunch of 8 to 10 large, even, juicy and moderately sweet berries which do not hang well once ripe. Thin skin. Makes a large, vigorous bush, slightly spreading which crops well. Winch's selection of the variety appears heavier yielding. **61**
– *Cotswold Cross* August. Originating in the

West of England this cultivar seems most successful there. Raised at the Long Ashton Research Station, Bristol, UK, in 1920 from a 'Baldwin' × 'Victoria' cross and not widely planted. Flowers early but not quite as frost susceptible as this would suggest, probably due to the compact habit of the bush. Fruit medium, usually trusses in pairs with 7 to 9 berries on each. Tough-skinned, sub-acid and of good flavour, hanging fairly well, but not easy to pick. A good cultivar for canning or quick freezing. Makes a vigorous, tall, rather spreading bush, cropping well in western areas.
– *Hilltop Baldwin* A selection from the original cultivar and is more vigorous.
– *Laxton's Giant* July. A competitor with 'Boskoop Giant', producing berries of show size. Raised by Messrs Laxton Brothers Ltd of Bedford, UK, and introduced in 1946. Flowers mid-season/late. Fruit large/very large, usually 2 bunches together, with berries juicy, acid and with a thicker skin than 'Boskoop Giant'; easy to pick. A vigorous, spreading bush with rather brittle, easily damaged branches. Cropping no better than 'Boskoop Giant'.
– *Jet, Malling Jet* August. A new, late, heavy yielding cultivar, of particular interest because of its ease of picking. Raised at East Malling Research Station, Maidstone, Kent, UK, from a backcross *Ribes 'fuscescens'* × 'Brödtorp', granted Plant Variety Rights in 1974 and only planted on a trial scale. Flowers late, thereby possibly avoiding late spring frost damage. Fruit medium, firm, on a very long stalk with up to 20 berries on each. These hang in good condition for several weeks and are easy to pick. Satisfactory for jam making and canning, ripening about ten days later than 'Amos Black'. Bush vigorous, stiff with stout, slightly spreading branches; cropping better than many comparable varieties in trials. **62**
– *Malling Jet* see 'Jet'.
– *Mendip Cross* July. A competitor for 'Boskoop Giant', quite widely grown and especially likely to succeed in the west of England. Bred from 'Baldwin' × 'Boskoop Giant' at Long Ashton Research Station, Bristol, UK, introduced in 1933. Flowers mid-season. Fruit medium size, thin-skinned in long bunches of 8 to 9 berries each bunch. Slightly acid. Quickly becomes over-ripe and falls off. Bushes of moderate vigour, stronger in high rainfall areas, cup-shaped and compact. Heaviest cropping of the early cultivars in a favourable situation.
– *Raven* July/August. An easily-picked cultivar with large fruit. Raised by Messrs Laxton Brothers Ltd of Bedford, UK, from 'Baldwin' × 'Boskoop Giant' and introduced in 1935. Not widely planted. Flowers mid-season. Fruit medium large, usually carried singly on long bunches making picking easy, and does not hang well. Thin skin. Good, sweet flavour. Vigorous, making a large, upright bush, cropping well. For succession, follows 'Boskoop Giant'.
– *Seabrook's Black* July/August. A commercially grown cultivar, but cropping sometimes variable. Re-introduced by Messrs Seabrook's of Chelmsford, Essex, UK, an old-established cultivar, possibly a good strain of 'French Black', which has been grown widely. Flowers mid-season. Fruit in trusses, carried singly or up to 3 together, each with 7 or 8 berries. Medium/large, oval, rather acid with a thick, tough skin. Grows vigorously, making a compact upright bush.

Crops regularly, but not heavily in some areas. The coarse foliage makes it especially difficult to distinguish shoots affected by black currant reversion virus.
– *Silvergieters Zwarte* July/August. A Dutch cultivar being evaluated in Britain. Introduced in 1936 and planted on a trial scale. Flowers late. Fruit on long trusses, large with fairly tough skin, easy to pick. Terminal fruits tend to fall off, reducing overall cropping compared with established cultivars of similar season. Makes a large, very tall, vigorous bush, but has not lived up to the good reports from its country of origin in UK trials.
– *Wellington XXX* July. An old-established cultivar that has been grown successfully in many areas. Raised by R. Wellington at East Malling Research Station, Maidstone, Kent, UK, from 'Boskoop' × 'Baldwin' in 1913, introduced about 1927 and very widely grown. Flowers early. Fruit in bunches of 2 or 3 together, 7 or 8 berries rather crowded on a medium stalk. Medium/large with a tough skin, sweet, of good flavour, but not hanging well when ripe. Growth vigorous, making a notably spreading bush requiring more space than other cultivars. A heavy and regular cropper. Rather sensitive to lime sulphur.
– *Westwick Choice* August. A substitute for 'Baldwin' on heavy soils. Raised by G. D. Davison, Westwick Fruit Farm, Norfolk, and introduced in the 1920s; quite widely grown. Flowers mid-season. Fruit medium/large in short bunches of 2 to 3 together with 6 to 8 berries on each bunch. Fairly tough skin, sweet, sub-acid, of good flavour, but rather difficult to pick. Fairly vigorous, making a compact bush which could be planted more closely than many cultivars. Crops well, better than 'Baldwin', where the conditions do not suit 'Baldwin'.

Currant, Red *Ribes sativum* GROSSULARIACEAE
– *Jonkheer van Tets* July. Dessert and culinary. A relatively new, promising, Dutch cultivar. Raised by J. Maarse, Schellinkhout, Netherlands, from a cross between 'Fay's Prolific' and an unknown cultivar, introduced in 1941; quite widely planted. Flowers early. Fruit on very long trusses. Large berries. Fairly tender, juicy, very acid with moderate aroma and flavour. Ripens very early and picks easily. Bushes grow vigorously with very strong erect stems and long fruiting shoots. Crops well. **63**
– *Laxton's No.1* July. Regular and prolific. Raised by Messrs Laxton Brothers Ltd of Bedford, UK, around 1918 and released about 1925; fairly widely planted. Fruit medium/large in moderate sized bunches. Firm and of bright red colour with small seeds. Fruit of good quality. Bushes vigorous, upright/slightly spreading and very heavy cropping. Recommended for performance and flavour. **64**
– *Minnesota* July/August. Introduction from America of good cropping potential. Produced by the University of Minnesota Fruit Breeding Farm, Excelsior, Minnesota, USA, which has released a number of cultivars under numbers; this description refers to 'Minnesota No. 71'. Bunches fairly large, 11 to 14 berries each. Berries medium/large, rather uneven in shape. Flesh red; soft and juicy, sub-acid. Still on trial in northern Europe.
– *Red Lake* August. An American cultivar which is proving to be heavy bearing in Britain. Of

unknown parentage, originating at the University of Minnesota Fruit Breeding Farm, Excelsior, Minnesota, USA, introduced in 1933 and grown widely. Long, loose bunches, many berries which are large/very large, on long stems and easily picked. Bright red with darker red veins, juicy. Bush upright and moderately vigorous and heavy cropping. The fruit is excellent for jelly and has a good flavour. **65**
– *Rondom* August. A heavy yielding, promising new cultivar. Raised by Dr. I. Rietsema, Breda, Netherlands, from a cross of *Ribes multiflorum*. 'Red Versailles' and an old, sweet, Dutch cultivar. Introduced in 1949 and already being planted on a limited scale. Flowers mid-season. Fruit on moderately long trusses. Berries of medium size, glossy, densely clustered and therefore rather difficult to pick. Flesh red, acid with a rather tough skin. Growth very vigorous and cropping heavy. A useful cultivar which also appears resistant to wind damage.

Currant, White *Ribes sativum* GROSSULARIACEAE
– *Dutch, White Dutch, White Holland* Dessert. July. An old-established cultivar producing currants of good flavour. Of unknown parentage, believed to date back to the early 1800s. Bunches moderately long; berries large, flattened, creamy yellow of good flavour. Bushes grow moderately vigorously, giving rather a spreading bush, cropping freely. **66**
– *White Dutch* see 'Dutch'.
– *White Grape* July. This produces both large clusters and large berries. This is a very old cultivar of European origin which has also been grown in North America since about 1850. Fruit in long bunches of 8 to 16 berries. Berries medium/large, round/oval, clear yellowish white. Flesh firm, juicy and pleasantly sub-acid. Bushes of medium size, tending to spread. Crops well. **67**
– *White Holland* see 'Dutch'.
– *White Versailles* Dessert. July. Probably the best garden cultivar. Raised by Bertin of Versailles, France, about 1843, of unknown parentage and introduced a few years later. Widely grown. Bunches very long. Berries large, round, pale yellow, sweet and of good flavour. Growth moderately vigorous, producing an upright bush cropping heavily.

Damson *Prunus domestica* and *P. insititia*
ROSACEAE
– *Bradley's King* Mid-September. A large-fruited damson. Of unknown parentage, probably originated in Kent, UK, and first recorded in 1880. Fairly widely grown. Flowering period 4 and is self-fertile – see table 4. Fruit large, round/oval, narrowing to the stalk end. Dark reddish/purple with thick bloom. Flesh greenish yellow, sub-acid, not notably of damson flavour. Grows vigorously, making a medium sized tree with a round head, cropping heavily.
– *Crittenden's Damson* see 'Farleigh Damson'.
– *Farleigh Damson* Mid-September. Claimed to be the best cultivar. Raised by Mr Crittenden of East Farleigh, Kent, UK, in the early 1800s, sometimes known as 'Crittenden's Damson'. Recommended as a wind-break tree. Flowering period 4 and is partially self-fertile, see table 4. Fruit small, oval, tapering to either end, black with blue bloom. Flesh greenish yellow, firm, of good flavour. A pyramidal tree, crops heavily. **68**

– *Merryweather* September. Recommended for bottling and jam making. Parentage and origin not recorded but quite widely grown. Flowering period 3 and is self-fertile, see table 4. Fruit large, oval and black with thin bloom. Skin thick. Flesh green-yellow, but not of pronounced damson flavour. Growth vigorous and a heavy cropper. **69**
– *Shropshire Prune* Late September. Recommended for bottling and jam making. Of unrecorded origin but widely grown. Flowering period 5, hence avoiding spring frost damage and is self-fertile, see table 4. Fruit small, oval, tapering to the stalk end. Skin blue-black. Flesh yellowish green, of good flavour. Growth moderate, making a small tree. Crops regularly, but not heavily. **70**

Elderberry *Sambucus nigra* CAPRIFOLIACEAE
Culinary. September/October. Flowers creamy white, June/July. Fruit clusters of black berries. Usually found in hedges and waste places. **71**

Fig *Ficus carica* MORACEAE
– *Angélique* see 'Madeleine'.
– *Bourjassotte Grise, Grizzly Bourjassotte* End September. A rich-flavoured cultivar suitable for pot culture. Fruit medium/large, round, flattened with a short neck. Skin dark brown, ripening to black with a thin bloom. Flesh red with a thick juice of excellent flavour. Heavy cropping under suitable conditions.
– *Brown Turkey* August/September. A reliable cultivar under a range of conditions; old-established, one of the most widely grown figs. Known by a number of names. Fruit large, pear-shaped, with a thick stalk. Brownish red with blue bloom. Flesh red, rich and sweet. Tree hardy and prolific, one of the best for outdoor culture against a wall. **72**
– *Brunswick* Mid-August. A hardy cultivar but not cropping quite as well as 'Brown Turkey'. Fruit very large, pear-shaped with a short, thick stalk. Greenish yellow skin with pale brown flush on the sunny side. Flesh yellow near the surface, reddening towards the centre, sweet and of rich flavour, hardy and of fair cropping ability. Not a variety for forcing, but a good one to grow fan-trained on a wall.
– *Castle Kennedy* Late July/early August. An early but good-sized fig. Fruit very large, greenish/yellow around the stalk end, pale brown towards the eye. Flesh white with some red round the seeds near the eye end of the fruit. Not richly flavoured. Heavy cropping.
– *Grizzly Bourjassotte* see 'Bourjassotte Grise'.
– *Madeleine, Angélique* August. A small fig of good quality. Fruit about 5cm. (2in.) long, round, flattened. Skin yellow with greenish white streaks. Flesh white, but pink towards the centre. Should be well ripened on the tree and is then of good quality and perfumed. Forces well or can be grown against a wall outside.
– *Negro Largo* A large-fruited, black fig of rich flavour. Fruit up to 10cm. (4in.) long, elongated, pear-shaped. Skin jet black with ribs running from the short stalk to the open eye. Flesh pale red, tender, juicy, melting when full ripe and of excellent flavour. Benefits from the root restriction of a pot.
– *White Marseilles* August/September. One of the best figs, hardy, but can also be grown under glass or against a wall. Fruit large, round, with ridges running from the short, stout neck to the

open eye. Pale green skin, ripening to near white. Flesh practically transparent, sweet and of rich flavour.

Filbert see Hazelnut.
Golden Berry see Cape Gooseberry.

Gooseberry *Ribes grossularia* GROSSULARIACEAE
– *Careless* Culinary. June/July. Probably the most important commercial cultivar. Raised by a Mr Crompton before about 1860 and widely grown. Fruit large, oval and tapering to the stalk end. Skin green, ripening to white; smooth, transparent skin. Good flavour and much used for jam making, also suitable for freezing. Bush spreading, moderately vigorous, but weak on poor soils. Reliable and good cropper. The fruit can be picked when under-ripe and used for culinary purposes when they will still be of good size. **73**
– *Early Sulphur* Dessert. May/June. Noted for its earliness and flavour. Known for at least 100 years, but not widely cultivated. Fruit medium size, round, golden yellow, hairy and of excellent flavour. Makes a moderately vigorous, erect bush, cropping well. Susceptible to damage by lime sulphur, although this fungicide has been superseded by dinocap for the control of American gooseberry mildew. **74**
– *Golden Drop* Dessert. June. Another yellow gooseberry of good flavour. There are several cultivars of this name including one raised by Thompson about 1842 and now being sought again because of its flavour, but rarely grown. Fruit small, round, yellow and hairy with a rich flavour. Of moderate vigour, making an upright bush. Susceptible to mildew.
– *Green Gem* Dessert and culinary. June/July. A useful cultivar for picking green or left until ripe as a dessert fruit. Distributed by Messrs Laxton Brothers Ltd, of Bedford, UK, in 1922 and quite widely planted. Medium/large fruit, round, oval, deep green with pale green veins. Flesh green, of good flavour. Bush moderately vigorous, spreading a little and cropping freely. For the largest fruit of dessert quality, can be thinned with advantage and should be grown on good soil. **75**
– *Keepsake* Dessert and culinary. June/July. A green gooseberry, one of the earliest to give a good size culinary berry. Old-established, of unknown parentage, raised by Banks of Acton, Northwich, Cheshire, UK, and recorded in 1841; widely planted in commerce. Flowers susceptible to spring frost injury. Fruit medium/large, oval, hairy, green ripening to off-white. Good flavoured, suitable for deep-freezing. Bush vigorous, spreading and cropping well. Susceptible to mildew.
– *Langley Gage* Dessert. June/July. A choice garden cultivar. Raised by Messrs Veitch, UK, from 'Pitmaston Green Gage' × 'Telegraph' and introduced about 1897. Fruit small/medium, round/oval, smooth, greenish white and with a transparent skin. Flavour excellent. Grows vigorously, makes an upright bush. Not generally available since it is only now in demand for its flavour. **76**
– *Leveller* Dessert and culinary. June/July. A popular dessert gooseberry. Raised by J. Greenhalgh of Ashton-under-Lyne, Lancashire, UK, and introduced in 1885, since when it has been widely grown with success especially in good soil

conditions and drainage. Fruit very large, oblong/oval, yellowish green and smooth skinned. Good flavour and, if picked green, suitable for freezing. Bushes moderately vigorous except on poor soils. Produces a spreading bush, cropping regularly and heavily. One of the best yellow gooseberries.

– *Whinham's Industry* Dessert and culinary. June/July. Good all-round cultivar, hardy and more suited to heavy soils than many gooseberries. Raised by R. Whinham, Morpeth, Northumberland, UK, and widely grown. Fruit large, oval, hairy, dark red and of good flavour; also well-suited to bottling and preserving. Growth fairly vigorous, making a spreading bush with pendulous branches. Crops heavily. Susceptible to mildew. **77**

– *Whitesmith* Dessert and culinary. June/July. A good all-round green gooseberry. Of uncertain origin, but known in the early 1800s and quite widely planted. Fruit medium/large, oval, covered with down; pale green with a yellow tinge. Of good flavour. Grows vigorously and crops well. **78**

Grape *Vitis vinifera* and hybrids VITACEAE

– *Alicante* Late. One of the best of the late, black, greenhouse grapes. Has many synonyms, suggesting that it is an old cultivar, probably originating in Spain. Widely grown. Fruit in large often long bunches, usually well supplied with berries. These are large, oval, jet black with a thin, blue bloom. Flesh tender, juicy, of good flavour. Growth vigorous and this cultivar is free setting. In the south of Britain there is no need for artificial heat for ripening, although it is best grown with heat. **79**

– *Appley Towers* Late. An improvement on 'Alicante', especially in requiring less heat. Raised by T. Myles of Appley Towers, Ryde, Isle of Wight, UK, from 'Gros Colmar' × 'Alicante'. Has been widely grown. Bunches medium, berries large, oblong/oval, dark blue-black, heavy blue bloom. Skin leathery, flesh firm and crisp, of very good flavour. Growth vigorous and free setting. This is one of the best late grapes under glass.

– *Black Hamburgh, Frankenthal* Late. Probably the most reliable cultivar for cultivation under glass, well known and widely grown. Reputed to have been imported from Hamburg by a merchant of Rotherhithe, London, in the early 1700s. Widely grown in eastern Europe at that time and since. Known better in France by its alternative name. Bunches large, conical. Berries round, oval, deep blue-black and with a blue bloom. Flesh firm but very juicy, sugary and highly flavoured especially when fully ripe. A free-bearing cultivar and if only one can be grown in the greenhouse, this should probably be chosen. **80**

– *Black Muscat of Alexandria* see 'Muscat Hamburgh'.

– *Brant* Early. A Canadian cultivar producing small black grapes outdoors. Raised by Charles Arnold of Paris, Canada and has been fairly widely grown outside, particularly against walls. Bunches small; berries small, round/oblong, fairly tender and of fairly good flavour. Vigour moderate to good. Fairly free cropping. This cultivar is notable for the good autumn colour which the leaves develop.

– *Buckland Sweetwater* Early. A popular white grape. This cultivar was known at least 100 years ago and has been grown quite widely under glass since then. Bunches large, heart-shaped and usually well set with berries. These are large, round/oval with thin transparent pale green skin ripening to amber. Flesh tender, very juicy, sweet and well-flavoured. Hardy and prolific.

– *Cascade, Seibel 13053* Very early. Has been described as the best, black, wine grape, originating in France and now being grown in Britain. Bred by M. Albert Seibel in Aubanas Ardeche, France, from a cross between 2 of his earlier seedlings. Bunches small. It gives a Beaujolais style of wine which is rather pale in colour but is suitable for blending with better coloured samples or keeps well on its own. Vigorous and productive and ripening fruit in most seasons but susceptible to downy mildew. Adapted to high rainfall areas with short growing seasons. The range of 'Seibel' seedlings were identified by numbers. Recently named 'Cascade', this one seems particularly suited to British conditions. **81**

– *Chasselas Doré de Fontainbleau, Royal Muscadine* Early. A small fruited old-established cultivar recommended for walls in the open. The synonym is better known in Britain and listed under this name by nurseries. Not widely grown. Bunches long and loose, sometimes compact and cylindrical, according to the conditions under which it is grown. Berries large, round with thin transparent skin, greenish yellow ripening to pale amber, sometimes with spots of russet; covered with white bloom. Flesh tender, juicy, sweet and richly flavoured. A cultivar to grow in a cool greenhouse as well as against a wall. **82**

– *Chasselas Rose Royale* Late. A cultivar for indoor cultivation in Britain. Presumed to be of Italian origin. Bunches medium/long, berries round of a rose colour when ripe. Flesh sweet perfumed and agreeable, of good quality. Vigorous and fertile.

– *Dusty Miller* see 'Miller's Burgundy'.

– *Early Saumur Frontignan* see 'Muscat Précoce de Saumur'.

– *Foster's Seedling* Early. Once one of the popular white grapes. An old-established cultivar raised by Mr Foster, gardener to Lord Downe of Beningborough Hall, York, UK, about 1835, not widely grown although still listed by British nurseries. Bunches large and well set with berries which are large, round/oval. Skin green/yellow, ripening to amber. Flesh tender, melting, very juicy, sweet and of fair flavour. Vigorous growing and reliable in cropping. Best for early forcing or sets freely in an unheated house.

– *Frankenthal* see 'Black Hamburgh'.

– *Madeleine Angevine (7972)* A grape for wine-making and recommended for British conditions to produce a white wine. Introduced into commerce by M. Moreau-Robert of Angers, France, in 1863. Vigorous and reliable in cropping.

– *Madeleine Royale* Early. A cultivar for wine-making, recommended for outdoor cultivation in Britain. Originated by M. Moreau-Robert of Angers, France and introduced in 1851. Bunches quite large, conical; berries medium/large, round, pale yellow. Flesh white, juicy, sweet. A vigorous and fertile cultivar.

– *Madeleine Sylvaner 28/51* Early. A new German hybrid giving regular crops of well-flavoured white grapes. Makes excellent wine and should be tried in Britain even under cold conditions.

– *Madresfield Court* Early. One of the better known black grapes, recommended for quality and cultivation indoors. Raised by Earl Beauchamp's gardener at Madresfield Court, Worcestershire, UK, from 'Muscat of Alexandria' and 'Morocco' around 1855. Quite extensively grown. Bunches large, long and tapering with a short, stout stalk. Berries large, oval, even in size, black with greenish flesh. Tender, juicy and with a 'Muscat' flavour although not so pronounced as in some cultivars. Can be grown with or without heat.

– *Miller's Burgundy, Pinot Meunier, Dusty Miller, Wrotham Pilot* A good, outdoor grape, easily distinguished by its downy leaves, the down being maintained for most of the season hence the alternative name 'Dusty Miller'. Bunches short, cylindrical, compact on long stalks. Berries small, round/oval, black with blue bloom. Flesh red, sweet, juicy and highly flavoured. Will do better against a wall, away from the south of Britain or where the garden is exposed.

– *Mrs Pince, Mrs Pince's Black Muscat* Late Possibly the best late for the greenhouse. Named after the owner of an Exeter nursery. First fruited in 1863, since grown by connoisseurs and still listed by specialists. Bunches large, tapering, shouldered on a stout stalk. Berries of a medium size, oval and set on short stalks. Purple/black with thin bloom. Flesh rather firm, sweet with a fine 'Muscat' flavour. Hardy, sets freely and hangs as late as any cultivar. Can be ripened without artificial heat in Britain. **83**

– *Müller Thurgau, Riesling × Sylvaner* Late September/October. An early ripening German cultivar suited for wine production. Raised in 1882 by Professor H. Müller at Hesse, German Democratic Republic from 'Riesling' and 'Sylvaner' the name by which it is known in Britain. Bunches medium/large, often shouldered. Berries of medium size, oval, yellowish green with a 'Muscat' flavour. Grows strongly, crops heavily and ripens the earliest of the German cultivars. Susceptible to several diseases including grey mould. Early harvesting is recommended to avoid this.

– *Muscat of Alexandria* A choice cultivar requiring heat at both flowering and fruit ripening to give best results. An old-established variety, with many synonyms, which was widely grown in the heyday of the large private garden in Britain and abroad. Bunches long, large and loose with a long stalk. Berries large, oval, unequal in size with long, slender stalks. Skin greenish yellow ripening to amber and covered with a white bloom. Flesh firm, not very juicy but sweet and rich with a fine 'Muscat' flavour. Bunches are abundant but they set badly unless the hand is passed over the flowering bunches to assist pollination. **84**

– *Muscat Hamburgh, Black Muscat of Alexandria* Late. Probably the finest black eating grape, preferring hot-house conditions but ripening in cool-houses, even under cloches. Re-introduced by Lady Cowper's gardener, Wrest Park, Silsoe, Bedford, UK. Rarely grown now. Bunches large, loose; berries large, round and oval, dark reddish purple with thin blue bloom. Flesh very juicy, rich, sugary and of excellent 'Muscat' flavour. Rivals the white 'Muscat of Alexandria' but with slightly smaller berries and not needing such high temperatures.

– *Muscat de St Vallier* A good grape for cloche

growing, giving a crop of large, white berries.
– *Muscat Précoce de Saumur, Early Saumur Frontignan* Very early. A quality grape which can be grown outdoors in Britain and certainly on a sheltered wall, also under glass. Raised in 1842 by M. Coutiller of Saumur, France, a seedling of 'Ischia', little grown in Britain and not available from nurseries in the UK. Bunches compact, berries medium, often flattened, with a transparent skin, white ripening to amber with thin russet. Flesh firm, sugary, sweet with 'Muscat' aroma. A hardy cultivar which bears well.
– *Noir Hatif de Marseilles* Very early. An old-established black, French cultivar, introduced in 1871 by M. A. Besson of Marseilles. Grown in the Midi area of France. Bunches medium; berries medium, round/oval. Black and quite firm, of 'Muscat' flavour and good quality. Average vigour but crops heavily. A fine, black grape, safest under cloches in the UK and given rich soil.
– *Perle de Csaba* A cultivar from the Baltic states which is being recommended for growing under cloches in the UK. Produces white fruit of good size and flavour.
– *Pinot Meunier* see 'Miller's Burgundy'.
– *Pirovano 14* Very early. Essentially a cultivar for wine-making which can be grown outdoors in Britain. It can produce fruit of dessert quality if it is ripened under cloches or grown against a wall. Early flowering. Berries medium, red/black, of excellent flavour. Can be relied on to ripen in the UK in most seasons. **85**
– *Précoce de Malingre, Early Malingre* Very early. One of the earliest grapes but inclined to uneven setting and small berries. Produced about 1845 by M. Malingre, a gardener near Paris, France and grown mainly in the country of its origin. Bunches of good size, loose and tending to be badly set. Berries very small, round/oval, white. Flesh juicy, sweet and richly flavoured. Can be grown under a range of conditions and ripens early, even against a wall.
– *Royal Muscadine* see 'Chasselas Doré de Fontainbleau'.
– *Riesling × Sylvaner* see 'Müller Thurgau'.
– *Seibel 13053* see 'Cascade'.
– *Seyve-Villard 5–276, Seyval* Early mid-season. Another recommended wine grape, one of a considerable and increasing series identified by numbers and recommended for growing in the UK. Originated in St Vallier, Drome, France, by Seyve-Villard from a cross between 2 'Seibel' seedlings, introduced about 1930 and widely cultivated in France. Bunches small, cylindrical; berries small, round, golden yellow. Of medium vigour. Hardy, the fruit ripening in most seasons in the UK. Fairly resistant to downy mildew. Cropping heavy but can be variable. Wine light yellow and aromatic, of Loire type and suitable for blending with 'Riesling' × 'Sylvaner'. **86**
– *Siegerrebe* Very early. A wine grape grown fairly extensively in the UK. Bred in Germany. Berries fairly large, golden yellow, sweet. Good for wine and in a good season produces fruit of dessert quality.
– *Tereshkova* Very early. A new Russian hybrid with medium berries of purple-red and delicate 'Muscat' flavour. **87**
– *Wrotham Pinot* see 'Miller's Burgundy'.

Hazelnut, Cobnut *Corylus avellana,*
Filbert, *C. maxima* CORYLACEAE
– *Bergers* October. A fine French cultivar.

Introduced by J. Mackoy of Liege, Belgium, about 1865. Large, square-shouldered with a medium-thin shell. The kernel long, tapering and fluted, of good flavour. Growth and cropping moderate.
– *Cosford* September/October. One of the well-known British nuts. Originating from Cosford, Suffolk, UK, about 1816. Catkins produced freely and a good pollinator variety. Nut large, oblong, smooth with small husk; thin-shelled. Kernel large, well-flavoured. Produces a vigorous bush and bears abundantly.
– *Kent Cob Nut, Lambert's Filbert* October. A good all-round filbert. Originated from Lambert of Goudhurst, Kent, UK, about 1830 and widely planted. Catkins rather sparingly produced, rather short and thick, but with good pollinators like 'Cosford' will crop abundantly. Nuts very large, long, of good flavour. Shell fairly thick. A heavy cropper.
– *Merveille de Bollwiller* October. An old-established, good-flavoured cultivar. Raised by an amateur in Silesia and introduced by Messrs Baumann of Bollwiller about 1820. The nut is short, square and of good flavour. Growth is rather vigorous and upright and recognizable in winter by the red pointed buds. A heavy cropper.
– *Nottingham Cob, Pearson's Prolific* October. An old cultivar originating in Labrador. Introduced by Messrs Pearson & Company of Chilwell, Nottinghamshire, UK. Catkins very freely produced, usually fairly thick and long. Produces round, rather short, flattened nuts of good flavour. Growth short but cropping abundant even on small trees. **88**
– *Purple Filbert* October. This cultivar produces excellent filberts and the deep purple of the leaves make it an ornamental shrub too. The fruit is similar to 'Red Filbert' but a deep purple colour. **89**
– *Red Filbert* October. An ornamental cultivar of excellent flavour. Only a small number of catkins so planting should be with a pollinator flowering more freely. Nuts small, medium, long and narrow, red-skinned. Flavour excellent. Growth vigorous with characteristic long, slender shoots.
– *White Filbert* October. Like the 'Red Filbert' but with a white skin over the nut and pale green foliage. Like 'Red Filbert' is restricted in its production of pollen and should be planted with a cultivar which produces catkins more freely. Grows strongly and crops regularly, given adequate pollination. The nuts are of excellent flavour. **90**

Hybrid Berries *Rubus* species ROSACEAE

Boysenberry Culinary. July/August. Possibly a hybrid between loganberry, blackberry and raspberry; giving large black fruit. Originated in Napa, California, USA, by Rudolph Boysen and introduced in 1935. 'Himalaya' may have been one parent. Fruit very large, red, ripening to purplish black, covered with a dusty bloom. Rather soft with a distinct aroma and cropping over a period. Makes a trailing bush growing vigorously. A thornless Boysenberry is available. **91**

Loganberry The original loganberry is thought to have been raised by Judge J. H. Logan in California, USA about 1881. There is some dispute about its precise parentage, but probably a

number of seedlings arose from an open-pollinated (i.e. only the female was known) plant of the wild dewberry of California, *Rubus ursinus*. Subsequently, it was found that the other parent was a raspberry and in the USA the new hybrid was called *Rubus × loganobaccus*.
Plants were imported into Northern Europe and the first fruits were exhibited in the UK about 1897. The loganberry is now widely grown. Since its introduction, further seedlings have arisen or there may have been mutations from the original from which the following clonal selections have been made.
– *Thorned LY59* Culinary and dessert. Late July/early August. An established, thorn-bearing cultivar which will probably be superseded by the L654 clone which is more productive. A virus-tested clone built up from the original selection made in the early 1950s. Fruit medium/large, pointed, similar in appearance to L654. Still the most commonly available cultivar. Of fair vigour and cropping well. **92**
– *Thornless* Culinary and dessert. Late July/early August. The smooth stem is an obvious advantage but its reduced vigour, when compared with LY59, has not increased its popularity. Probably the American Bauer Thornless selection, introduced to Britain in 1938, but not extensively planted. The colour and quality of the fruit is similar to other loganberries. Growth only moderately vigorous but a good cropper.
– *Thornless L654* Culinary and dessert. Late July/early August. A fairly recently selected clone from 'Thornless' and in trials found more vigorous and productive. A sport from the original loganberry, Bauer Thornless, was distributed in the USA during 1934/5. L654, also imported from California, is regarded as an improvement on the original 'Thornless' loganberry. Not yet widely planted because of its recent introduction. The fruit are large, oblong/pointed, deep maroon, darkening when full ripe. Heaviest yielding and of good vigour. Virus-tested canes are available from specialist nurseries. **92**

Lowberry August. The fruit is large, 2.5 to 5cm. (1 to 2in.) long, jet black. Borne in clusters and in appearance like a loganberry. Flavour like a blackberry. Grows vigorously.

Nectarberry Mid-July. A very similar fruit to boysenberry produced on a trailing bush of very similar habit. Originated by H. G. Benedict in El Monte, California, USA. Introduced in 1937, and possibly a chimera of boysenberry. Fruit resembling boysenberry but with larger individual drupelets and fruit size, and a sweeter flavour. **94**

Veitchberry July/August. A hybrid of a blackberry and 'November Abundance' raspberry. The flowers are self-fertile. The fruit is large, round, mulberry-red but otherwise resembles a blackberry. A distinct, sweet flavour. Growth is vigorous and erect. Crops heavily. Cultivation as for blackberry. **95**

Japanese Wineberry *Rubus phoenicolasius* ROSACEAE
August. A decorative plant resembling a raspberry and also called a Chinese blackberry. The species originated in the Far East and is widely grown in Japan and north China, as well as in other parts of the world, for its attractive berries.

These are golden yellow turning wine-red with soft red hairs. They are sweet, juicy and refreshing. The canes produced annually often reach 3m. (9ft) in length and are covered with soft, red bristles. **96**

Kiwi Fruit see Chinese Gooseberry.
Loganberry see Hybrid Berries.
Lowberry see Hybrid Berries.

Medlar *Mespilus germanica* ROSACEAE
– *Dutch* November. The largest and commonest cultivar. Of unknown origin. Fruit large, flattened. Eye wide open. Flavour fair. Makes a spreading tree with crooked branches. **97**
– *Nottingham* November. Smaller fruited but better flavoured than 'Dutch'. A smaller, more upright tree.

Melon *Cucumis melo* CUCURBITACEAE
– *Charentais* Early. A French cultivar of excellent flavour. The fruit is globe-shaped with a slightly ribbed skin. The flesh is orange. Although generally regarded as half-hardy it can be grown under glass, under frames or plastic, or even outdoors. **98**
– *Hero of Lockinge* A cultivar suitable for growing under glass and under frames. Fruit large, oval with a lightly netted, yellow skin. The flesh is white and good-flavoured.
– *Ogen* Early. The fruit is small, round with pale green, smooth, thin skin. The flesh is green and juicy. It can be grown either under glass or frames. **99**
– *Ringleader* A green-fleshed cultivar suitable for growing under glass. **100**
– *Superlative* An indoor cultivar with scarlet flesh.
– *Sweetheart* This is an F₁ of Charentais type, which has been bred for northern climates. Small and with orange flesh.

Mulberry, Black *Morus nigra* MORACEAE
Dessert and culinary. August/September. Native of Iran. Flowers small, unisexual, pendulous, green catkins. Fruit raspberry-red ripening to dark red, juicy with a sub-acid flavour. **101**

Mulberry, White *Morus alba* MORACEAE
Dessert and culinary. September. Native of China. Introduced into Europe as food plant of the silkworm. Fruit white or pinkish, flavour sweet and insipid.

Nectarberry see Hybrid Berries.

Nectarine *Prunus persica* ROSACEAE
A variety of *Prunus persica*, the peach, but having a smooth skin and being sufficiently distinct from the peach to warrant separate description.
– *Early Rivers* Mid/late July. One of the best nectarines. Bred by Messrs Rivers of Sawbridgeworth, Hertfordshire, UK, from 'Early Silver' peach and introduced about 1870. Fairly widely grown. Fruit large, yellow with scarlet flush and streaks. Flesh pale yellow, juicy and rich. A cultivar which can be grown outdoors on a wall in Britain and under glass.
– *Elruge* August/September. A late, hardy cultivar. The name is an anagram of the breeder, a nurseryman of Hoxton, London, who raised it from unknown parents. Not widely grown. Fruit medium, round/oval, pale green with dark red

flush. Flesh greenish white but becoming red near the stone. Perfumed. Recommended for flavour.
– *Humboldt* Mid-August. Recommended for flavour. Raised by Messrs Rivers of Sawbridgeworth, Hertfordshire, UK, as a seedling of 'Pine Apple'. Not widely grown. Fruit medium/large, yellowish orange with crimson flush and streaks on the sunny side. Flesh golden, tender and juicy with a rich flavour, hanging well. Grows well on a wall. Crops heavily. Large showy flowers produced late, thereby reducing the risk of damage from late spring frosts.
– *Lord Napier* Early August. A cultivar for greenhouse cultivation in Britain, recommended for its flavour. Raised by Messrs Rivers of Sawbridgeworth, Hertfordshire, UK, from 'Early Albert' peach. Flowers large. Fruit large, yellow-green with red flush on the sunny side. Flesh very white, melting, juicy with a rich flavour. Skin inclined to be thin and subject to sun-scorch unless shaded. **102**
– *Nectarose* July. An American cultivar which may be of value in northern Europe. Originated by M. A. Blake at the Agricultural Experimental Station, Brunswick, New Jersey, USA, with 'Garden State', 'Goldmine' and 'Belle' in its parentage. Introduced in 1947. Flowers showy. Fruit large, yellow with dark red flush almost completely covering it. Flesh white of good quality. Tree vigorous and productive.
– *Pine Apple* Early September. Possibly the best-flavoured nectarine, needing warm conditions, not less than a warm wall outside and preferably under glass. Bred from 'Pitmaston Orange' and introduced by Messrs Rivers of Sawbridgeworth, Hertfordshire, UK. Fruit medium/large, yellow with crimson streaks. Flesh yellow, juicy, of rich flavour, reminiscent of pineapple. A tender cultivar.
– *Précoce de Croncels* July. Of French origin, raised by M. E. Baltet of Troyes, France, in 1887. Supposed to be a seedling from 'Amsden' peach and widely grown in France. Fruit medium, round, greenish yellow. Flesh pale cream, tender, juicy and sweet. Inclined to split. Listed by British nurseries.

Peach *Prunus persica* ROSACEAE
– *Alexander* Mid/end July. Good for cultivation outdoors. Raised by O. A. Alexander, Mount Pulaski, Illinois, USA, and introduced about 1870 but not widely grown in northern Europe. Flowers large. Fruit medium/small, creamy white with red flush and mottle. Flesh creamy white, juicy and of fair flavour.
– *Amsden June* Mid-July. Popular in France. Raised by L. C. Amsden of Carthage, Missouri, USA, in 1863 and for many years the earliest peach. Medium, round, greenish white with a red flush, sometimes purplish black. Flesh creamy white, melting and of good flavour. Hardy. For forcing quality, 'Duke of York' is superior.
– *Bellegarde* Early/mid-September. Hardy, giving good crops. Known since 1732. Flowers small. Fruit large, striking deep red in colour. Flesh yellow, juicy, rich. Recommended for its good flavour. **103**
– *Duke of York* Mid-July. An early cultivar for growing under glass or fan-trained against a wall. Raised by Messrs Rivers of Sawbridgeworth, Hertfordshire, UK, from 'Early Rivers' nectarine × 'Alexander' in 1902. Fruit large, rich crimson. Flesh pale yellow, tender and good flavoured.

– *Grosse Mignonne* Late August/early September. An old-established cultivar, first recorded in 1667. Like most peaches it comes fairly true from seed and a number of seedlings have come from this cultivar. Flowers large. Fruit large, round, slightly flattened with a deep line from top to bottom; mottled red over yellow skin, deeper red on the sunny side. Flesh pale yellow, rich and well flavoured. Not hardy and subject to mildew. Not listed by British nurseries.
– *Hale's Early* Mid/end July. An early ripening, good flavoured, American cultivar. Introduced about 1860 by Hale of Summit County, USA, and very widely grown. Flowers large but not self-fertile. Fruit medium, yellow with red mottling and flush. Flesh pale yellow, soft and of good flavour; free stone. Hardy and has been grown for markets, and forces well. **104**
– *Peregrine* Early/mid-August. The first cultivar recommended for outdoor cultivation in tree form in the UK. Raised by Messrs Rivers of Sawbridgeworth, Hertfordshire, UK, from 'Spenser' nectarine and introduced in 1906. Has been quite widely grown outdoors but the results have sometimes been disappointing due to frost and wind damage to the flowers. Fruit large, round, crimson. Flesh greenish white, firm, juicy and good flavoured. **105**
– *Redhaven* Mid-August. An American cultivar promising in northern European conditions. Originated at the Agricultural Experimental Station, Southhaven, Michigan, USA, by S. Johnston from 'Halehaven' × 'Kalhaven', and introduced in 1940. Flowers red, medium sized, self-fertile. Fruit medium, round, with a distinct line from stalk to base; deep red over yellow skin. Flesh yellow, reddening near the stone, very firm, melting, of good flavour. Tree growth vigorous, spreading. Under good conditions the fruit size may be small unless the crop is thinned. **106**
– *Rochester* Mid-August. Now regarded by some as the best outdoor peach but like all peaches, flowers very early and is subject to damage by wind and spring frost unless grown in a sheltered position. A seedling raised by Mr Wallen of Rochester, New York, USA, about 1900, and widely grown. Fruit medium, yellow with deep crimson flush. Flesh yellow, juicy and of fair flavour. Recommended for growing as a bush tree in sheltered situations in south of England. **107**
– *Royal George* Late August/early September. Recommended for flavour. An old-established cultivar, probably introduced in the reign of George I by Millet, a nurseryman of Fulham, London, but probably replaced by another cultivar easier to propagate. Still available from specialist nurseries in the UK. Flowers small. Fruit large, round, yellow, speckled red on the shady side, marbled red in the sun. Flesh pale yellow, very red at the stone. Juicy, rich and highly flavoured. Forces well and equally good outdoors, particularly in a sheltered situation.

Pear *Pyrus communis* ROSACEAE
– *Aldermaston Pear* see 'Williams' Bon Chrétien'.
– *Bartlett* see 'Williams' Bon Chrétien'.
– *Beurré Alexandre Lucas* Dessert. November/January. An exhibition cultivar, scented at maturity. Found as a seedling in the Department of Loire et Cher, France, and imported from France into the UK about 1890. Flowering period 2 but a triploid cultivar which therefore does not produce viable pollen. Fruit

large, conical, even; stalk medium/long and stout. Pale green turning to gold with russet spots, occasionally flushed with red. Flesh white, melting, juicy and aromatic. Growth vigorous and makes an upright, arching tree. A moderate cropper. Like all late maturing pears needs to be ripened off in a warm room to develop its full flavour which, in this case, is very good. **108**

– *Beurré Clairgeau* Culinary. November. A heavy cropper but probably not a cultivar to be recommended for planting in a limited space. Raised by Pierre Clairgeau, a gardener of Nantes, France, about 1850. Flowering period 2. Fruit long, large and oval. Skin rough, golden brown often with red flush. Large, open eye, stalk short and fleshy. Flesh white with a musky flavour. An upright tree which grows vigorously and crops heavily. **109**

– *Beurré Curtet* see 'Comte de Lamy'.

– *Beurré D'Amanlis* Dessert. Early/mid-September. A good-flavoured early pear. Raised at Amanlis near Rennes, France and generally distributed about 1830. Widely grown. Flowering period 2. A triploid cultivar which will not produce viable pollen and is incompatible with 'Conference'. See table 2. Fruit medium/large, pyriform. Open eye in a shallow basin, slender stalk. Yellow/green, flushed with reddish brown. Flesh creamy white, very sweet and juicy. Like other early cultivars, it should be picked while still green so that the fruit can be watched as it ripens. Grows vigorously but gives a rather untidy tree. A useful and hardy pear with a short season.

– *Beurré Diel* Dessert. October/November. Popular in France but requires a warm season to finish well. Found near Vilvorde, France, about 1800, and widely planted on the Continent. Flowering period 2 and another triploid. Very large conical fruit with flattened sides and tapering towards the stem, which is stout and generally curved; open eye. Skin yellow with brown/red flush and spots of russet. Flesh white, tender and melting when well-ripened and after a good season. A vigorous growing cultivar which crops heavily, but is dependent on the season for best results. **110**

– *Beurré Hardy* Dessert. Mid-/late October. A good quality pear requiring a sheltered position. Raised by M. Bonnet at Boulogne, France, in the early 1800s and named after the then director of the Luxembourg Gardens. Widely grown. Flowering period 3 but rather erratic as a pollinator. Fruit medium/large, conical and uneven; stalk medium/long and stout. Greenish yellow with patches of russet and occasional faint red flush. Flesh white, juicy, sweet, and of good flavour. For best results pick before it parts easily from the spur and ripen off the tree. A vigorous growing, heavy cropping variety but often slow to start bearing. **111**

– *Beurré Superfin* Dessert. October. A high quality, good-flavoured cultivar. Raised near Angers, France, about 1850 and widely planted. Flowering period 3. Fruit medium, conical, with a small eye in a deep basin. Golden yellow with scarlet flush and fine, brown russet. Flesh white, melting, juicy, sweet and perfumed. Of moderate vigour and cropping potential. **112**

– *Bristol Cross* Dessert. End September/end October. A new cultivar of moderate flavour and, although not a triploid, does not produce viable pollen. Introduced 1931 by Long Ashton Re-

search Station, Bristol, UK, from a 'Williams Bon Chrétien' × 'Conference' cross. Not widely planted because of its recent introduction and limited value as a pollinator. Flowering period 4; male component of flower sterile. Fruit medium, tapering to stalk which is short and stout. Green turning golden yellow with fine russet and occasional red striping on the sunny side. Flesh white, tender and juicy, sweet and of moderately good flavour. Tree quite vigorous, upright becoming spreading. Earlier than 'Conference' and of better quality but with only a short season. **113**

– *Catillac* Culinary. December/April. One of the best pears for stewing. Found near Cadillac in the Gironde Department of France, and described under this name in 1665. Flowering period 4, and a triploid. Fruit large and round, stalk large and stout. For best results the pears should be left on the tree as late as possible. The fruit has a brown-red flush over dull green ripening to yellow. Flesh white, firm and acid. Growth vigorous, spreading and a heavy cropper. A good choice for anyone wanting a cooking pear. **114**

– *Choix de l'Amateur* see 'Nouveau Poiteau'.

– *Clapp's Favourite* Dessert. August. An early pear with a correspondingly short season. Raised by Thaddeus Clapp of Dorchester, Massachusetts, USA, and widely grown commercially for early sale. Flowering period 4. Fruit medium, pyriform with an open eye. Stalk long and stout. Pale yellow with scarlet flush and stripes. Flesh pale yellow, crisp, juicy and sweet. Upright, vigorous growing cultivar and cropping heavily. The fruit should be picked before it matures.

– *Comte de Lamy, Buerré Curtet* Dessert. October/November. Raised by M. Bouvier of Joidoigne, France about 1830 and originally named 'Beurré Curtet'. Flowering period 4. Fruit small, bergamot and usually lopsided. Yellow/green, flushed red-brown and with some covering and dots of russet. Flesh white, melting, of delicious flavour. Growth moderate, making a low-spreading, fertile tree.

– *Conference* Dessert. Mid-October/late November. A widely planted commercial cultivar which can be stored under refrigeration to extend its season considerably. A regular and heavy cropper of fair flavour. Introduced in 1894 from a cross of 'Leon le Clare de Laval' with the other parent unknown by Messrs Rivers of Sawbridgeworth, Hertfordshire, UK. Extensively planted. Flowering period 3 and often thought to be self-fertile: can produce parthenocarpic fruit (without pollination or the formation of seed). Fruit medium, banana-shaped, seedless, with longish stalk. Skin dark olive-green with brown russet. Flesh pale yellow, juicy and sweet. Moderately vigorous tree and heavy cropper. Reliable and hardy but since it is a well-known commercial variety it is probably wiser to plant better flavoured cultivars in the garden. **115**

– *Dr Jules Guyot* Dessert. Late August/early September. Another commercial cultivar with a short season. Raised by M. Baltet of Troyes, France in 1870 and widely grown. Flowering period 3. Fruit pyriform and an open eye in a shallow basin. Pale yellow, covered with golden dots of russet and pinky flush on the sunny side. Should be ripened off the tree. Flesh yellow, juicy, slightly musky and of moderate flavour. Growth moderate and a heavy cropper but its short season limits its appeal.

– *Doyenné du Comice* Dessert. Late October/late November. The 'Cox's Orange Pippin' of pears which needs good growing conditions to crop regularly. Raised by the Horticultural Society of Maine et Loire at Angers, France, and introduced to Britain in 1858. Widely planted throughout northern Europe. Flowering period 4. Fruit medium/large, pyriform; stem medium, stout. Greenish yellow with a brownish red flush. Flesh white, melting, juicy and of excellent flavour. Vigorous, fairly upright tree. It fruits best in sheltered sites or while still on the tree the individual fruits can be inserted into polythene bags. With suitable pollinators like 'Glou Morceau' it can be a regular cropper. **116**

– *Durondeau* Dessert. October/November. Raised by M. Durondeau of Tongre near Tournai, Belgium about 1810, it has been widely grown commercially although it is now replaced by others with more suitable market qualities. Flowering period 3. Large, calabash, uneven with a short stalk. Golden-yellow when ripe, with red flush and covered with brown russet. Flesh white, sweet, juicy and tender if given generous manuring and water as needed. Growth is compact and it crops heavily so it is a good garden cultivar. **117**

– *Emile d'Heyst* Dessert. October/November. A hardy and reliable cultivar which succeeds under most conditions. Raised about 1850 by Major Esperen of Malmet, France and called after its namesake of Heyst-op-den-Berg. Flowering period 2. Fruit medium, oval, with a slender stalk. Pale yellow with russet patches particularly at the stalk end. Flesh yellow/green, melting, juicy and perfumed. A compact tree which crops heavily. Recommended for reliability as much as for flavour. **118**

– *Fertility* Dessert. October. A heavy cropper of only fair flavour. Raised from a seedling of 'Beurré Goubalt' by Messrs Rivers of Sawbridgeworth, Hertfordshire, UK, about 1875 and grown widely in commerce. Flowering period 3. Fruit small if not thinned, conical, with short, stout stalk and an open eye. Brown russet over a yellow skin. Flesh white, juicy, crisp of only fair flavour. Growth upright, moderate vigour, cropping heavily and susceptible to pear canker. **119**

– *Fondante d'Automne* Dessert. September/October. A reliable cultivar with a good flavour. Raised about 1820 by M. Fievée at Maubeuge, France, and widely grown. Flowering period 3. Incompatible with cultivars in Group 1. Fruit medium bergamot, with an open eye and short, stout stalk. Greenish yellow with russet patches. Flesh tender, juicy and sweet.

– *Glou Morceau* Dessert. December/January. A fine late pear which does best if grown in a warm situation. Raised by the Abbé Hardenpont, a pioneer raiser of new pear cultivars in the 18th century. Flowering period 4. Fruit medium/large, oval and uneven with a long, stout stalk often set at an angle. Bright green at first changing to greenish yellow when ripe. Flesh white, tender and of delicious flavour. Growth moderate, giving a spreading tree, cropping regularly and well in a warm site. Pears should be left on the tree as late as possible. **120**

– *Gorham* Dessert. Mid-/late September. An American cultivar with a reasonably long season and fairly good flavour. A product of 'Williams Bon Chrétien' × 'Joséphine de Malines' cross made at the New York State Agricultural Experimental Station, Geneva, New York, USA, introduced in 1923 and planted widely in commerce. Flowering period 4. Fruit small/medium, conical with a short, thick stalk. Pale yellow with light brown russet. Flesh white, tender, juicy, with a musky flavour. The fruit is best picked early so that it does not ripen on the tree. Moderately vigorous, upright tree and a fair cropper. **121**

– *Jargonelle* Dessert. August. A very old and hardy cultivar, suited to northerly situations. Of French origin, known before 1600 and widely grown. Flowering period 3. A triploid not able to pollinate other varieties although they can pollinate it. Fruit medium, calebash with a long, slender stalk. Greenish yellow with red flush on the sunny side. Flesh pale yellow, tender and juicy. The pear has a short season and must be picked early to prevent it going past its best while still on the tree. Grows vigorously, making a large, spreading tree which crops well, although the season is short.

– *Joséphine de Malines* Dessert. December/January. A well-flavoured, late pear, requiring careful ripening if it is to develop its full and delicious flavour. Raised by Major Esperen in 1830, named after his wife, and widely planted. Flowering period 3. Fruit small, short, with an open eye. Greenish yellow with russet round the stalk. Flesh pinkish white, tender, juicy and of delicious flavour. A weak grower, although it is fertile and a reliable cropper. Inclined to produce a weeping tree when grown as a standard.

– *Louise Bonne of Jersey, Louise Bonne d'Avranches* October. One of the best pears. Raised by M. Longueval of Avranches in France about 1780 and widely grown. Flowers showy, flowering period 2. See tables for incompatibility in Group 1. Fruit medium, pyriform; long, woody stalk. Colour yellowish green with red flush and prominent red dots. Flesh white, melting and sweet, of excellent flavour. Strong, upright tree which crops regularly. **122**

– *Marie Louise* Dessert. October/November. Another mid-season cultivar which is recommended for its flavour. Raised by the Abbé Duquesne of Mons in France about 1810 and named after Napoleon's second wife. Widely planted. Flowering period 4. Fruit medium, oval, with a large open eye. Pale green, yellow when ripe, with fine russet especially round the eye. Flesh white, sweet, juicy and of excellent flavour. Of medium vigour making a spreading tree. Cropping moderate.

– *Merton Pride* Dessert. Mid-/late September. A new cultivar which has large, good quality fruit and a regular but not heavy crop. Product of a 'Glou Morceau' × 'Williams' Bon Chrétien' cross made at the John Innes Horticultural Institute, UK, in 1941, but not yet widely planted due to its recent introduction and limited cropping from the commercial viewpoint. Flowering period 3 and is a triploid. Fruit medium/large, conical. Pale green with brown russet round the eye. Flesh creamy white, firm, juicy, of excellent flavour. Moderate vigour.

– *Michaelmas Nelis* see 'Winter Nelis'.

– *Nouveau Poiteau* Dessert. November. The French synonym 'Choix de l'Amateur' speaks for itself. Raised by Van Mons about 1845 and dedicated to a pomologist of the day, M. Poiteau. Flowering period 4. Fruit large, oval and irregular, stalk long, stout, often set in the fruit at an oblique angle. Red russet and flush over greenish

yellow. Flesh greenish white, not very juicy, sweet and of good flavour. Growth upright but spreading and a moderate cropper.

– *Onward* Dessert. Mid-September/early October. A new cultivar still under trial, but which crops regularly and heavily. Raised in 1948 at the National Fruit Trial Ground at Wisley, Surrey, UK, from 'Laxton's Superb' × 'Doyenné du Comice', but not yet widely planted to date. Flowering period 4. Fruit medium, sometimes large, tapering to the stalk which is medium stout. Green/yellow-green when ripe, with pinkish flush and brown russet in patches. Flesh creamy white, melting and juicy, recommended for its flavour. A vigorous growing and free cropping cultivar. Like many cultivars of its season, it is only at its best for a limited time. This variety has to prove itself under a wide range of conditions before it can be generally recommended.

– *Packham's Triumph* Dessert. November/December. An Australian cultivar of merit. Raised by C. H. Packham about 1895 at Molong, New South Wales, Australia and thought to be of 'Uvedale's St Germain' × 'Williams' Bon Chrétien' origin. Widely planted commercially. Flowering period 2. Fruit medium, conical and irregular due to ribbing on the surface. Stalk long, curved and often attached obliquely to the fruit. Green, ripening to clear yellow with orange flush and fine russeting. Flesh white, melting, sweet and very juicy. Growth may be weak, but it is a good cropper and well-flavoured.

– *Passe Crassanne* Dessert. March/April. A late cultivar familiar in the UK because of spring imports from the Continent. Raised by M. Boisbunel of Rouen, France, about 1850, and widely grown, mainly on the Continent. Flowering period 2. Fruit large, round, oval and uneven due to ribs on the surface. Large closed eye. Dull yellow with a russet covering. Flesh pale yellowy white, very sweet, juicy and of good flavour. Makes a dense tree and crops well. Needs a warm situation in the UK to finish to perfection and then attention when ripening out of store.

– *Pitmaston Duchess* Dessert or culinary. October/November. An old, dual-purpose cultivar, now being superseded by single-purpose ones with better flavours. Raised by Mr Williams of Pitmaston about 1865 from 'Duchess d'Angoulême' × 'Glou Morceau' and widely planted. Flowering period 4 and is a triploid. Fruit large, pyriform with an open eye and a long, woody stalk. Golden yellow with red russet. Pale yellow flesh, tender, very juicy, but of only moderate flavour. A vigorous growing and good cropping cultivar which is therefore not suited for growth in a restricted form.

– *President Drouard* Dessert. January/March. An old cultivar grown mainly in France. A seedling of 'Beurré Napoleon' raised by M. Olivier-Perroquet about 1885 and grown commercially. Flowering period 2. Fruit medium, oblong, with an open eye in a rather deep basin. Pale yellow with a covering of russet dots. Flesh white, very melting, sweet and perfumed. Needs careful handling for best results: leaving late on the tree before harvesting and storing in cool, humid conditions before allowing to ripen for several days in a warm room. Vigorous, upright tree, fertile. Rather prone to scab.

– *Roosevelt* Dessert. October/November. A large-fruited, good-flavoured cultivar. Introduced

about 1905 by Messrs Balet of Troyes, France. Flowering period 3. Fruit large, oval and regular. Green with red flush, prominently spotted. Flesh white, juicy, of good flavour. Vigour moderate, making a compact, upright and fertile tree. Blossoms are attractive early in the year. **123**

– *Seckle* Dessert. October/November. A choice cultivar, reputed to have been found as a seedling near Philadelphia, USA, by a trapper called Jacob and named by him after the man who later cultivated the site. Introduced to Britain about 1820. Quite widely grown. Flowering period 2 and, although preceding the flowering season of 'Williams' Bon Chrétien', will not cross-pollinate with it and is not self-fertile. Fruit small, bergamot, with an open eye on the surface. Red-brown with prominent white dots. Flesh yellow/white, tender, sweet and juicy. Weak growth making an upright tree and cropping only moderately. Recommended for flavour. **124**

– *Thompson's* Dessert. October/November. Another good-flavoured cultivar. Raised by Van Mons and sent nameless to Britain about 1820. Named by the secretary of the Royal Horticultural Society, UK, after the fruit foreman at Chiswick. Flowering period 3. Fruit medium/large, pyriform and ribbed with an open eye in a shallow basin. Golden yellow with red flush and russet marking. Flesh white, melting, juicy and of delicious flavour. A moderately vigorous, upright growing tree with moderate cropping potential.

– *Triomphe de Vienne* Dessert. September. A delicately flavoured, early pear. Raised about 1865 by M. Collaud and introduced by M. Blanchet of Vienne, France. Flowering period 3. Fruit medium, conical and irregular. Yellow with red flush and russet patches, especially round the attachment of the long stem to the fruit. Flesh almost white, juicy and melting, of delicate flavour which is at its best if the fruit is picked before it is fully mature and ripened off the tree. A vigorous growing, heavy cropping cultivar. The leaves are strikingly coloured in the autumn.

– *Williams' Bon Chrétien, Bartlett, Aldermaston Pear* Dessert. Mid-September/early October. Probably the best early pear, certainly the most well-known September cultivar and imported in quantity after canning on the Continent. Raised by Mr Stair of Aldermaston, Berkshire, UK, about 1770. Its local name 'Stair's Pear' did not persist after Mr Williams, nurseryman of Turnham Green introduced it. Later Mr Bartlett took the cultivar to America and it has been widely planted throughout the world. Flowering period 3, not self-fertile, nor compatible with 'Seckle', see table 2. Fruit medium/large, pyriform with a short, stout stalk generally set at an oblique angle. Pale green changing to golden yellow with red streaks on the sunny side and patches and dots of russet. Flesh white, melting, juicy with a strong, musky flavour. As good for bottling as for eating fresh. Grows strongly and crops heavily. Rather susceptible to scab. Like most early maturing cultivars, it should be harvested while still green and ripened off the tree. Has a relatively short season. **125**

– *Winter Nelis, Michaelmas Nelis* Dessert. November/January. A useful winter pear. Raised by M. Nelis at Malines, France and introduced to the UK about 1820. Flowering period 4. Fruit small/medium, bergamotte. Dull green with dark brown russet, mainly around the eye which is open in a deep basin. As it ripens, the fruit becomes yellow with blackish dots but once its season has been reached, it should be eaten before it has changed much from its earlier green colour. Flesh pale yellow, very juicy, sweet and with a rich flavour. Should be left on the tree as late as possible before picking. Grows moderately vigorously and crops heavily. One of the best cultivars in its season. **126**

Plum *Prunus domestica* ROSACEAE
– *Anna Späth* Dessert. Mid/late September. A late, dark plum from the Continent. A seedling found in Hungary at Kadoszbeg in 1870. Introduced by Späth, a Berlin nurseryman in 1874 and sent to Britain from France in 1947. Still under trial in Britain and not yet grown to any extent, although planted in France, Belgium and Germany. Flowering period 3 and is self-compatible. Fruit medium/large, oval, dark purple with bloom. Flesh green/yellow, firm, sweet and juicy. Growth fairly vigorous, giving an upright tree, but not cropping heavily in trials to date. Can be kept in a refrigerator for a short time after harvesting. **127**
– *Ariel* Dessert and culinary. Mid-September. A new Swedish cultivar on trial in the UK. Raised at the Horticultural Research Station, Alnarp, Sweden from 'Autumn Compôte' × 'Reine Claude d'Althann'; introduced in 1960. Flowering period 2. Fruit large, oval/oblong, red. Flesh golden, juicy, sweet, sub-acid. A dual-purpose cultivar. **128**
– *Belle de Louvain* Culinary. Late August. A widely grown, multi-purpose cultivar. Found in the Van Mons collection in 1845, widely grown in commerce. Flowering period 5 and is self-fertile. Fruit large, long and flattened with a prominent line. Long stalk and skin red, ripening to purple. Flesh yellow, juicy, of fair flavour. Rather large for bottling and canning, but good for jam and passable for dessert. Growth vigorous, free cropping but susceptible to brown rot. **129**
– *Cambridge Gage* Dessert and culinary. End August. An excellent cultivar indistinguishable from 'Greengage'. Grown extensively in the county after which it is named. Flowering period 4 and is partly self-fertile. Fruit small, round, green with bloom, ripening to yellow green with occasional flush. Flesh yellow green, firm, juicy, of good flavour. Tree vigorous, compact, regular, often a heavy cropper. Fruit inclined to crack. Can be grown from suckers. **130**
– *Cherry Plum* see 'Myrobalan'.
– *Coe's Golden Drop* Dessert. End September/October. A well-flavoured late plum, giving its best in favoured situations. Probably from 'Greengage' × 'White Magnum Bonum', raised by Mr Coe of Bury St Edmund's and introduced about 1800, since when it has been grown widely. Flowering period 2, self-infertile and incompatible with 'Jefferson'. Fruit medium/large, oval, tapering to stem and with no prominent line. Skin straw yellow with red spots on the sunny side. Flesh yellow, sweet, juicy and of good flavour. Will keep a short while after harvesting if in a dry place. A spreading tree whose cropping is variable unless planted against a wall or in a warm place.
– *Count Althann's Gage, Comte d'Althann's Gage* Dessert. Mid-September. A good cultivar of Belgian origin, imported to the UK about 1860 after being produced by the Count's gardener at

Swoyschitz, Belgium. Fairly extensively grown in gardens. Flowering in period 4 and is self-infertile. Fruit medium/large, flattened at both ends. Dark crimson on a yellow ground with yellow dots, some russet and prominent bloom. Flesh golden yellow, sweet, moderately juicy and of excellent flavour; good for dessert or bottling. Growth vigorous, cropping well, particularly when grown against a wall. **131**
– *Czar* Culinary. Early August. Probably the best known early plum, of only moderate flavour. Product of a 'Prince Engelbert' × 'Early Prolific' cross, raised by Messrs Rivers of Sawbridge-worth, Hertfordshire, UK, about 1870 and named in honour of a visit to Britain by the Czar of Russia. Widely grown because of its hardiness and reliability. Flowering period 3, is self-fertile and reported to be frost-resistant. Fruit small/medium, oval, flattened at calyx and stalk ends, with a wide, shallow line between the ends. Purple with bloom covering the fruit. Flesh yellow, inclined to be mealy. Cooking well and of acceptable dessert quality when fully ripe. Growth moderately vigorous and a good, reliable cropper. Will succeed on a north wall. Susceptible to silver leaf.
– *Denniston's Superb* Dessert. Mid-August. A good garden plum. Reputedly of American origin, raised by Mr Denniston of Albany, New York, USA, about 1840, and widely grown. Flowering period 2 and is self-fertile. Fruit medium, round and reminiscent of 'Greengage' with a broad, shallow line from the stem to the calyx end. Green with red flush and some bloom. Flesh greenish yellow, juicy and with a gage-like flavour. Growth moderately vigorous, cropping well and regularly under a wide range of conditions.
– *Early Laxton* Dessert and culinary. Mid-July. The earliest plum of good flavour, but only short seasoned. Probably of 'Jaune Hâtive' × 'Early Orleans' parentage and raised by Messrs Laxton Brothers Ltd of Bedford, UK, released in 1916 and quite widely planted considering its fairly recent introduction. Flowering period 3 and partially self-fertile. Fruit medium, round/oblong, yellow with red flush and pale blue bloom. Flesh firm, juicy, sweet and of pleasant flavour. Makes a medium-sized tree with tendency to weep. Branches brittle. Susceptible to bacterial canker but with some resistance to frost. Pick early, otherwise the fruit may drop as it ripens. Good for canning and bottling. **132**
– *Early Rivers, Rivers Early Prolific* Culinary. Late July. Follows 'Early Laxton' in season, pleasant as a dessert plum when fully ripe. Raised by Messrs Rivers of Sawbridgeworth, Hertfordshire, UK, about 1830 from 'Précoce de Tours' and introduced as 'Rivers Early Prolific'. A commonly grown commercial cultivar. Flowering period 3 and is partially self-fertile. Fruit small, round, with a short stalk. Skin purple and covered with bloom. Flesh greenish yellow, juicy, sweet, and acceptable for dessert. Vigour moderate, making rather a weeping tree with brittle branches. Moderate cropper, reliable in most districts. **133**
– *Early Transparent Gage, Reine–Claude Diaphane* Dessert. Mid-/late August. A choice cultivar, another product of Messrs Rivers of Sawbridgeworth, Hertfordshire, UK, and reputed to be a seedling from 'Old Transparent Gage.' Flowering period 4 and is self-fertile. Fruit

small, round, with a slender stalk. Yellow green with red dots and flush, also pale yellow bloom. Flesh yellow, transparent, sweet with a rich flavour. Makes a compact tree, heavy cropping. The fruit is inclined to split just before ripening. Can be used as a cooker although one of the best early dessert plums. **134**
– *Golden Transparent* Dessert. Early/mid-September. Recommended for flavour, a seedling from 'Transparent' listed by Messrs Rivers of Sawbridgeworth, Hertfordshire, UK, from 1894. Not widely grown. Flowering period 3 and is self-fertile. Fruit large, round, flattened at both ends with a very short stalk. Clear golden yellow with red dots. Flesh firm, very sweet, of delicious Gage flavour. Grows vigorously, although best as a fan against a wall or in a pot. Not a heavy cropper but of distinctive flavour. **135**
– *Goldfinch* Dessert. End August. Another Gage of delicious flavour raised by Messrs Laxton Brothers Ltd of Bedford, UK, in 1935 from 'Early Transparent Gage' × 'Jefferson', introduced as 'Laxton's Goldfinch' and fairly widely planted. Flowering period 3 and is partially self-fertile. Fruit medium, round, frequently having a deep line from top to bottom. Golden yellow, veined with green, red flush and spots. Flesh golden, juicy, of good flavour and fairly tough skin. Growth is strong, and it is a good cropping cultivar. The fruit has a fairly long season, hanging well on the tree when ripe.
– *Greengage, Old Greengage, Reine–Claude Vert* Dessert. Late August/early September. A small, but choice plum inclined to light and uncertain cropping. Supposedly from Greece, reaching the UK via France where it was named 'Reine Claude' about 1500. Sir William Gage of Hengrave Hall, Bury St Edmunds, Suffolk, UK is credited with importing the cultivar into the UK around 1725, although it may have been introduced up to a century earlier. Flowering period 5 and is self-infertile. Fruit small, round, flattened at either end, with a conspicuous line from calyx to the stout stalk. Olive green, ripening to yellow green with slight flush and dots of red, with some bloom. Flesh greenish yellow, very juicy, sweet and of delicious flavour. Grows vigorously but can be rather irregular in cropping. **136**
– *Jefferson, Jefferson's Gage* Dessert. Early September. Recommended for flavour and a reliable cropper. Originated in Albany, New York, USA about 1825, reputedly raised by Judge Buel from 'Washington' × 'Coe's Golden Drop'. Widely grown. Flowering period 1, is self-infertile and incompatible with 'Coe's Golden Drop'. Fruit medium/large, round/oblong, sometimes lopsided with the long stalk attached at the surface. There is a broad, but shallow, line from calyx to stalk. Golden yellow with red flush and dots, also spots of russet and sometimes a light bloom. Flesh golden yellow, very juicy, sweet and of delicious flavour. Grows vigorously, crops well and the fruit has quite a long season. A good garden cultivar.
– *Kirke's Blue* Dessert. Mid-September. A choice cultivar which needs a sheltered situation to encourage regular cropping. Of unknown parentage but distributed about 1830 by Joseph Kirke, a nurseryman of Brompton, London. Not widely grown because of its uncertain cropping. Flowering period 4 and is self-infertile. Fruit medium/large, round, dark purple with a thick

covering of blue bloom. Flesh greenish yellow, juicy, sweet and of excellent flavour. Moderately vigorous growing, producing a rather spreading tree. Has been called the 'Cox's Orange Pippin' of plums. **137**

– *Laxton's Cropper* Culinary. Mid-/late September. A prolific and self-fertile cultivar with a long season. Reputed to be from 'Victoria' × 'Aylesbury Prune', introduced by Messrs Laxton Brothers Ltd of Bedford, UK, about 1930. Not widely grown. Flowering period 3 and is self-fertile. Fruit medium/large, slightly smaller than 'Victoria', oval, purple red, ripening to blue black and covered with bloom. Flesh golden yellow, a good culinary plum. Moderately vigorous, crops well and will hang on the tree into November. **138**

– *Laxton's Delight* Dessert. Early September. A promising cultivar raised by Messrs Laxton Brothers Ltd and introduced in 1945 but not widely planted. Flowering period 4 and is self-infertile. Fruit large, oval, golden yellow with green streaks and thin bloom. Flesh golden yellow, soft, very juicy, of good flavour. Tree vigorous, upright then spreading with rather brittle branches. Cropping good. Susceptible to bacterial canker. **139**

– *Marjorie's Seedling* Dessert and culinary. Late September. One of the best of the late culinary cultivars which will hang into October if required Of fair dessert quality when fully ripe. Of unknown origin, found at Hillfoot Farm, Beenham, Berkshire, UK, in 1912, introduced in 1928 and distributed by Burleydam Nurseries, Oaken, Staffordshire, UK in 1943. Widely grown commercially. Flowering period 5 and is self-fertile. Fruit large, oval, dark purple with blue bloom. Flesh yellow, firm, juicy, fairly sweet. Vigorous grower, producing a fairly upright tree which crops heavily. **140**

– *Merton Gem* Dessert and culinary. Early September. A new, promising cultivar, recommended for its flavour. Raised at the John Innes Horticultural Institute, UK, in 1923 from 'Coe's Violet' × 'Victoria'. Named in 1965. Not widely planted. Flowering period 3, and is partly self-fertile. Fruit medium/large, oblong, yellow with red flush, darkening to purple when fully ripe; with a heavy bloom. Flesh yellow, very juicy and of good flavour. Growth fairly vigorous, making a rather spreading tree. Cropping moderate in trials so far. **141**

– *Mirabelle Grosse, Mirabelle de Nancy* Culinary. Mid-August. In the UK a shy cropping cultivar. Probably of Eastern origin and brought to France in the 1400s and widely grown on the Continent. Flowering period 5 and is self-fertile. Fruit very small, round, yellow. Flesh golden, rather dry and sweet. **142**

– *Mirabelle Petite, Mirabelle de Metz* Culinary. Late August. An old European cultivar. Said to be of Eastern origin, first described in France in 1675 and grown also in Morocco. Flowering period 4 and is self-infertile. Fruit very small, round, yellow. Flesh golden, moderately juicy with a sweet, rather insipid, flavour.

– *Monarch* Culinary. End September. A widely planted, commercial, late plum. Raised from open-pollinated 'Autumn Compôte' by Messrs Rivers of Sawbridgeworth, Hertfordshire, UK, introduced about 1885 and widely grown. Flowering period 1 and is self-fertile. Fruit large, flattened at the stem which is short and fairly thick. Reddish purple, becoming blue black with

a blue bloom, sometimes russet spots. Flesh greenish yellow, juice of only average flavour but a good cooker. Growth vigorous and makes a spreading tree which crops irregularly. **143**

– *Myrobalan, Cherry Plum* Culinary. Early August. Small ornamental fruit carried on trees of *Prunus cerasifera*. There are many cultivars bearing fruit of different colours. Some are grown as plum rootstocks, others as ornamental hedging, where the fruit is insignificant. Originated in western Asia and a common ornamental tree in gardens. The flowers, in period 1, are white, showy and self-fertile. The fruit of the red cherry plum is small, heart-shaped with a slender, short stalk. The skin is scarlet, the flesh yellow and moderately juicy. It makes a large, round-headed tree which grows vigorously. The fruit is mainly for cooking or canning. **144**

– *Old Greengage* see 'Greengage'.

– *Oullins' Golden Gage.* Dessert and culinary. Mid-August. A regular cropping and especially good culinary cultivar. Of unknown origin, first brought to notice by a nurseryman, M. Massot of Oullins, near Lyons, France, about 1860; widely grown. Flowering period 4, self-fertile. Fruit large for a Gage, round, golden yellow when ripe with greenish dots and grey bloom. Flesh pale yellow, transparent, sweet, fair for dessert, but not of the finest Gage flavour. Vigorous, upright growing tree, a fair cropper, but slow to come into bearing. Recommended for bottling.

– *Pershore, Yellow Egg* Culinary. Late August. Although hardy, heavy-cropping and commercially good, there are superior culinary plums for garden use. A chance seedling, thought to have originated in Worcestershire, UK, and widely grown. Flowering period 3; self-fertile. Fruit medium, oval, tapering to the long stem. Skin and flesh yellow, firm, of only moderate flavour. Probably the most widely grown plum for processing, usually picked green and under-ripe. Makes a fairly large, but compact, tree which crops regularly and heavily. Resistant to silver leaf and can be propagated from suckers. **145**

– *Pond's Seedling* Culinary. Mid-September. Its size makes it distinctive, but otherwise it is of only limited use as a garden cultivar. Of unrecorded origin, grown in the Royal Horticultural Society's trials at Chiswick, UK, about 1830 and since then widely planted commercially. Flowering period 5 and is self-infertile. Fruit very large, round/oval, often lopsided and with a long stalk. Dark red, covered with small dots and thin bloom. Flesh yellow, firm, flavour poor. Good for cooking but not for canning. Growth moderately vigorous, branches inclined to be brittle, and susceptible to silver leaf. A heavy cropper although the fruit is inclined to crack in a wet season. **146**

– *Quetsche, Zwetsche* Culinary. Late September. A cultivar grown for drying as prunes in eastern Europe or for canning in Germany. Probably originated in Russia and now widely grown on the Continent. Flowers self-fertile. Fruit medium, oval, narrowing to the long stalk. Dark purple with spots of grey and russet and a blue bloom. Flesh golden yellow, firm, juicy and sweet. Makes a tree of moderate size which crops moderately well. **147**

– *Reine–Claude Diaphane* see 'Early Transparent Gage'.

– *Reine–Claude de Bavay* Dessert. Late September. A Continental cultivar of rich gage flavour. Named in honour of the director of the Horticul-

tural Station at Vilvorde, Belgium and introduced about 1845. Not widely grown in Britain. Flowering period 2, self-fertile. Fruit medium/large, round/oval, with a short stalk. Pale yellow with many white and red spots. Flesh yellow, juicy, with a delicious, sweet flavour. Moderately vigorous growth, crops regularly and well. The fruit hangs late on the tree, giving a relatively long season of use.

– *Reine–Claude Vert* see 'Greengage'.

– *Rivers Early Prolific* see 'Early Rivers'.

– *Severn Cross* Dessert. Mid-/late September. A promising new, large-fruited cultivar. Raised at Long Ashton Research Station, Bristol, UK, from a 'Coe's Golden Drop' × 'Giant Prune' cross, introduced in 1932 and not sufficiently established to be grown widely. Flowering period 3, self-fertile. Fruit large/very large, oval, slightly lopsided. Golden yellow when ripe, sometimes speckled with red and with a pink flush. Flesh pale yellow, juicy and of fair dessert quality. Growth moderately vigorous, upright. Crops well and the fruit hangs well on the tree to extend the season. Fruit size is maintained even with heavy crops. Obtained the Royal Horticultural Society's Award of Merit in 1951.

– *Victoria* Dessert and culinary. Mid-/late August. The best-known plum. A hardy, reliable and heavy cropper giving a culinary fruit which is also well-known as a dessert cultivar. Its precise origins are uncertain: it was found in a garden at Alderton, Sussex, UK, introduced as 'Sharp's Emperor' and then as 'Denyer's Victoria' when sold by a nurseryman, Denyer, of Brixton, London, about 1840. Very widely grown. Flowering period 3 and sufficiently reliably self-fertile to be planted on its own without any other varieties to provide cross-pollination. Fruit oval with flattened sides. Red speckled with dots of dark red and bloom. Flesh golden yellow, quite juicy and of good flavour if picked when almost full ripe. Medium-sized, fairly vigorous, spreading tree. Usually a heavy and regular cropper even on a north wall. Branches brittle and readily break under a heavy crop unless supported. These wounds frequently attacked by silver leaf and damaged shoots should be cut off the tree immediately after fruit picking to reduce the risk of this disease getting established. **148**

– *Yellow Cherry* A yellow-fruited sport of 'Myrobalan'.

– *Yellow Egg* see 'Pershore'.

– *Warwickshire Drooper* Dessert and culinary. Mid-September. A commercial cultivar of characteristic tree shape, the best fruits of which are of dessert quality. Most probably originating in Warwickshire, and widely planted. Flowering in period 2, self-fertile. Fruit medium, round/oval, yellow speckled with red. Flesh yellow, fairly soft, of poor flavour except when fully ripe, but cooking well. Trees vigorous, very drooping, cropping well. Can be propagated from suckers. **149**

– *Zwetsche* see 'Quetsche'.

Quince *Cydonia oblonga* ROSACEAE

– *Champion* Culinary. October. Fruit medium/large, round, uneven and golden yellow. Flesh yellow of mild flavour. Growth vigorous and crops well.

– *Portugal* October. A vigorous cultivar but not free bearing. Imported by Tradescant, gardener to Charles I, for Lord Burleigh in 1611. Fruit large, pear-shaped, uneven. Green ripening to pale orange which turns red when cooked. A mild flavoured quince. **150**

– *Vranja* October. Probably the handsomest cultivar. Grown in Vranja, Yugoslavia. A very similar cultivar was named in commemmoration of the Hungarian pomologist, Bereczki. A large fruit, pear-shaped and pale golden yellow. Fragrant flesh of good quality and flavour. Probably the best quince and can make a showy tree fan-shaped on a south-facing wall. **151**

Raspberry *Rubus idaeus* ROSACEAE

– *Delight* July. A new cultivar cropping very heavily in early trials. Raised at the Scottish Horticultural Research Institute, Dundee, with complex parentage including 'Preussen', 'Burnetholm', 'Malling Promise', 'Lloyd George', 'Baumforth A' and 'Pyne's Royal', selected for trial in 1969 and granted plant breeders' rights 1974. Becoming available but has been planted only on a trial scale. Fruit large/very large, pale red, sub-acid of good flavour, easy to pick. Jam tends to be rather pale. Canes fairly thick, moderate in number. The long, robust fruiting laterals are rather susceptible to grey mould. It is resistant to aphids, so tending to avoid aphid-borne virus diseases. **152**

– *Glen Clova* July. A heavy cropping, new cultivar, good for eating. Originated at the Scottish Horticultural Research Institute, Dundee, as a seedling of complex origin. Introduced in 1969 and with plant patents held by the National Seed Development Organization Ltd. Widely available and is already becoming one of the main commercial cultivars. Fruit medium, short, conical, of medium red colour. Flesh firm and good for jam-making, canning or freezing. Canes tall, erect, very vigorous, hardy and cropping the heaviest of all cultivars in some trials. Susceptible to some virus diseases and mildew but tolerant of cane spot. Medium-sized berries and fair flavour are limitations as a garden, dessert cultivar.

– *Lloyd George* July and September. Good-flavoured and can be treated as an autumn-fruiting cultivar by varying the pruning time. Originated as a chance seedling in a wood in Dorset and introduced by Mr Kettle, Corfe Castle, Dorset, UK. Grown worldwide in commerce at one time, reintroduced 'virus-free' to the UK from New Zealand in the early post-war years and the health of such selections is superior to that of ordinary stocks. The New Zealand strain should be specified and is the selection grown by good nurserymen. Fruit large, long, conical, dark red and of good flavour. Canes tall, growing vigorously even on light soils. May need thinning to reduce the amount of cane. Crops well if free from virus diseases. As a summer-fruiting cultivar it crops mid-season, otherwise if completely cut to the ground in February it will carry an autumn crop. Cultivars such as 'September' and 'Zeva' are more usually recommended for autumn cropping.

– *Malling Admiral* August. A new, good-flavoured and late-maturing cultivar to extend the season of harvesting. Was developed at East Malling Research Station, Maidstone, Kent, UK, from a cross including 'Burnetholm', 'Preussen' (two old varieties not now planted), 'Norfolk Giant' and 'Malling Promise', selected in 1964. Received a grant of plant breeders' rights in 1974.

Not widely planted but of commercial value because of its processing qualities. Fruit large, long, very firm, dark red; fairly easy to pick and of good colour. Canes tall, vigorous, fairly thick with long fruiting laterals which can be damaged by wind in exposed situations. Appears moderately resistant to cane diseases and virus attacks.

– *Malling Exploit* July. A Malling cultivar, introduced fairly recently, which has not been widely planted. Originated from a cross between 'Preussen' and an earlier Malling seedling at the East Malling Research Station, Maidstone, Kent, UK; introduced in 1950. Fruit large, conical, firm, bright red, of fair flavour. Produces less attractive jam than other Malling cultivars because the seeds lose their whiteness. Canes numerous, strong, upright with good cropping potential. **153**

– *Malling Jewel* July. A most widely grown commercial cultivar. Bred at the East Malling Research Station, Maidstone, Kent, UK, with a parentage of 'Preussen', 'Pyne's Royal' and 'Lloyd George'. Introduced in 1950 and extensively planted. Fuit large, conical, firm and juicy, bright red, darkening when full ripe. Flavour good and sweet. Fruit not hidden by foliage. Canes vigorous, moderate in number, cropping heavily and consistently. Somewhat susceptible to cane blight but tolerant of virus diseases. **154**

– *Malling Orion* July/August. A new, promising cultivar raised at East Malling Research Station, Maidstone, Kent, UK, of complex parentage and granted plant breeders' rights. Selected for testing in 1964, it has only been planted on a trial scale. Fruit medium large/large, round, compact, and firm. Medium dark red, easy to pick and of good flavour, suitable for canning and quick freezing. It is less satisfactory for jam-making because of the darkening of the seeds making them inconspicuous in the jam. Canes numerous and vigorous with the new growth tending to obscure the raspberries on the lower part of the fruiting canes. Resistant to aphids but susceptible to grey mould and spur blight.

– *Malling Promise* July. The first of the Malling cultivars to be introduced, probably the most widely grown, its main disadvantage being the over-abundant production of new canes. It crops heavily and regularly and is fairly good flavoured. Produced at East Malling Research Station, Maidstone, Kent, UK, from a cross of 'Newburgh' and a Malling seedling, introduced in 1944 and very widely planted. Fruit medium/large, conical, firm, dull red and easy to pick except under dry conditions. Growth vigorous with too many suckers especially in the first few years after planting. Fairly tolerant of virus diseases but susceptible in wet weather to grey mould. **155**

– *Norfolk Giant* July/August. An old cultivar, reputed to have been found in a garden in Norfolk, introduced in 1926 but still a good all-rounder for the garden. It has been widely grown. Fruit medium/large, blunt, conical, bright red, easy to pick, sub-acid, of fair flavour but tending to crumble. Growth vigorous, canes abundant, erect and cropping heavily and regularly. The latest in season of the summer-bearing cultivars. Resistant to virus diseases.

– *September* August/September. Introduced especially for autumn cropping which depends on cutting the canes to the ground in February: the fruit is then carried on the current season's wood.

Originated at the Agricultural Experimental Station, Geneva, New York, USA, from 'Marcy' × 'Ranere', introduced in 1947 and fairly widely planted. Fruit medium, round, bright red, of fair flavour. Difficult to pick but the berries are firm with no tendency to crumble. Fruits over a long season. Vigour not great and this reduces the total weight of the crop. The canes should be planted fairly close together to offset this.

– *Zeva* Remontant. A new Swiss cultivar fruiting from July until November but heaviest in autumn. Parentage includes 'Romy' and 'Indian Summer'. Fruit large, long conical, dark red, fairly firm and of good flavour. The calyx is rather large and curved back so that picking is sometimes difficult; the first fruits are often double ones. Canes are moderately vigorous with free production of new shoots. There are few spines and cropping is heavy. A promising cultivar particularly because of its long fruiting season, although the heaviest cropping is in the autumn. **156**

Strawberry *Fragaria* spp. ROSACEAE

– *Baron Solemacher* June/October. The alpine strawberries approach the wild one in flavour and are produced over an extended season starting in the summer. 'Baron Solemacher' is the best known red-fruited cultivar, berries being small, conical, dark red, of characteristic sub-acid flavour; at its best when full ripe. It is runnerless and has to be propagated from seed sown in spring or autumn. Plants are fairly vigorous and cropping is light but continuous throughout the summer.

– *Cambridge Favourite, Cambridge 422* Late June/mid-July. The most widely grown of the Cambridge cultivars, heavy cropping and giving fruit of fair flavour when full ripe. Raised by D. Boyes, at the Horticultural Research Station, School of Agriculture, University of Cambridge, UK, from a cross of a seedling from a selection of *Fragaria chiloensis* × 'Blakemore', selected in 1944 and very widely grown since then. Fruit medium/large, round, blunt, short, conical with a large calyx. Pale scarlet becoming pinkish red with flesh pale scarlet. Fairly juicy, sub-acid and of fairly good flavour. Plant large, vigorous, with large flowers held clear of the plant. Crops heavily and regularly, fruit susceptible in wet weather to grey mould but tolerant of virus diseases. Can be grown under cloches. A reliable cultivar and the main commercial strawberry, the fruit being readily available in most areas. **157**

– *Cambridge Late Pine* Late. A dark-fruited, pine flavoured cultivar. Of similar parentage to the other Cambridge cultivars with 'Fairfax', an American cultivar, one parent. Introduced in 1947 and planted on a small scale in gardens. Fruit medium/large, round/conical, dark red and appearing over ripe when it is not. Of good flavour. Vigour good, crops well. Resistant to frost and mildew. Recommended for its unusual flavour.

– *Cambridge Prizewinner, Cambridge 134, Prizewinner* Mid-June. A cultivar with attractive fruit, not produced in great quantity, which can also be grown under protection for earlier production. Bred at Cambridge from 'Early Cambridge' × an American cultivar, introduced in 1947 and commonly grown under cloches. Fruit large, conical, bright red and shiny. Flesh scarlet, firm and juicy, of good flavour. Plant medium/large, cropping not heavy; fruit size decreasing as cropping proceeds. Susceptible to poor soil conditions but otherwise a good early cultivar.

– **Cambridge Rival** Mid-/late June. Possibly the best of the Cambridge cultivars and a replacement for 'Royal Sovereign'. Bred at Cambridge from 'Dorsett' × 'Early Cambridge', introduced in 1948, grown commercially on a limited scale because the dark colour of the fruit suggests it is over-ripe. Fruit large, the size maintained throughout its short season. Conical, red with a green tip, turning to dark red when ripe; shiny. Flesh pale red, fairly firm, juicy, rich, sub-acid, of good flavour. Vigour moderately good, foliage erect, yellow/green flowers well hidden. Fairly good cropping but with some variation from year to year. Resistant to red core and least susceptible to grey mould. However, susceptible to virus diseases. Suitable for growing under protection. **158**

– **Cambridge Vigour, Cambridge I** Late June/early July. A good-flavoured cultivar, ripening earlier in its maiden year (when it can be protected to advance the season) than in subsequent years. Raised at Cambridge from 'Aberdeen', 'Fairfax' and 'Early Cambridge', introduced in 1946 and widely planted as an early cultivar. Fruit large, its size decreasing to the end of the picking season, and orange-red, turning to scarlet. Flesh red, juicy, moderately sweet, of good flavour. Plants very vigorous, medium/large flowers, protected by the leaves. Fruit soft when over-ripe and rather subject to grey mould. The cultivar is particularly sensitive to drought. **159**

– **Elista** Early July. One of the recent introductions to Britain from the Continent. It is good flavoured with a heavy cropping potential. Raised by Dr H. Kronenberg at the Plant Breeding Institute, Wageningen, Holland, from a cross of 'Jucunda' and an American seedling, introduced in 1964. Fruit medium, declining in size with successive crops, round/conical. Orange-red becoming intense scarlet when ripe. Flesh red, of reasonable flavour, a little acid. Vigorous with an open habit, flowers within the leaf spread but readily visible because the plant is open. Capable of heavy cropping, especially in a wet season. Appears resistant to grey mould and mildew.

– **Gento, Hummi Gehro, Hummi Gento** Remontant, June/October. A German cultivar of similar character to 'Sans Rivale' and 'St Claude'. Bred by Herr R. Hummel of Stuttgart, German Federal Republic and quite widely planted; it is a protected cultivar. Fruit medium size, conical, regular. Red and shiny, orange-red flesh, perfumed, sweet, sub-acid and of slightly musky flavour. Plant quite vigorous.

– **Gorella** Late June. Its large, early and glossy fruit attract attention. Raised by Dr H. Kronenberg at Wageningen, Holland, from 'Juspa' × an American seedling and introduced in 1960. Now planted on a limited scale in Britain. Fruit very large, round/conical, crimson-red, sometimes with a green tip. Flesh crimson, firm, juicy, of fair flavour. Moderate growth, upright with sparse leaves. Suitable for growing under protection. Susceptible to mildew but not grey mould.

– **Grandee, Hummi Grundi, Grossa di Verona** Mid/late June. A very large-fruited, vigorous cultivar. Bred by Herr R. Hummel in Stuttgart, German Federal Republic, of unknown origin, available in Britain from about 1968 and quite widely grown in gardens. It is a protected cultivar. Fruit exceptional in size, irregular, often wider than high. Colour irregular, shiny dark red with clear, tender, red flesh. Slightly sweet and acid, rather soft-fleshed, easily damaged. **160**

– **Grossa di Verona** see 'Grandee'
– **Hummi Gehro, Hummi Gento** see 'Gento'.
– **Hummi Grundi** see 'Grandee'
– **King George V** see 'Royal Sovereign'
– **La Souveraine** see 'Royal Sovereign'
– **Litessa** Mid-July. A heavy-cropping cultivar from the German Federal Republic, being tested in Britain. It is a protected cultivar. Fruit medium, uniform, round/conical. Orange-red/intense red. Flesh pale orange, fir, sub-acid, sweet and of good flavour. Plants moderately vigorous, spreading. The flowers are protected by the foliage but the fruit is quite visible.

– **Montrose** Early/mid-July. A new high-yielding cultivar which can be grown under protection. Raised at the Scottish Horticultural Research Institute, Auchincruive, Ayr, Scotland, from 'Crusader' × 'Redgauntlet', introduced in 1964 and received a grant of plant breeders rights in 1974. Now undergoing trials. Fruit large, medium sized by the third crop. Round-conical/round, orange-red/scarlet. Flesh pale orange and soft, a little acid, of good flavour. Plant moderately vigorous, upright and spreading. Fruit at the edge of the leaf canopy. Has given good results under cloches.

– **Ostara** Remontant. June/October. A cultivar from the Netherlands, slow to produce runners. Produced by the Plant Breeding Institute, Wageningen, Netherlands, from 'Red Gauntlet' × a German cultivar; not widely grown in Britain. Fruit medium, irregular in shape, shiny red. Flesh moderately firm, juicy, sweet, sub-acid, perfumed and of good flavour. Plant vigorous.

– **Prizewinner** see 'Cambridge Prizewinner'.
– **Redgauntlet** Mid/late July. A large-fruited cultivar of only fair flavour but which may give a second crop in the autumn. Bred by R. D. Reid at Auchincruive, Ayr, Scotland, from an American seedling × 'Auchincruive Climax', introduced in 1957 and widely grown commercially. Fruit large, conical/wedge-shaped, crimson/bright scarlet when fully ripe. Flesh scarlet, firm, juicy and of fair flavour. Plant growth is vigorous, leaves partly protecting the flowers. In early areas a second crop is likely, especially if the spring crop was protected (i.e. under cloches). Flowers in August/September, produces fruit from mid-September to the frost; these generally need covering with cloches in order to ripen. This second crop does not seem to detract from the following spring's crop. Not susceptible to grey mould or mildew. Responds well to warm sites and sheltered situations; of limited garden value unless flavour is less important. **161**

– **Royal Sovereign, King George V, La Souveraine** Late June/early July. The 'Cox's Orange Pippin' of strawberries, an old cultivar introduced by Messrs Laxton Brothers of Bedford, UK, in 1892 and widely grown in gardens up to the 1940s and '50s. Fruit large, conical or wedge-shaped, shiny scarlet, soft, easily bruised and subject to grey mould. Regarded as the best-flavoured cultivar but can be sharp. Growth vigorous when healthy, leaves produced early with flowers well exposed.

Cropping good. Very susceptible to virus diseases and should be planted well away from virus-carrying varieties which are tolerant of these diseases and hence show no symptoms. Its susceptibility to diseases has led to its replacement by more robust cultivars.

– **St Claude** June/October. Remontant. French origin. Fruit medium/large, conical, shiny, dark red. Of good flavour in summer and during the early part of the autumn. Growth vigorous. **162**

– **Sans Rivale** Remontant. June/October. Of French origin, grown on a limited scale in the UK. Fruit medium, long and conical. Deep red, of fair flavour and produced in 'flushes'. Growth moderately vigorous, crops heavily and probably the most popular remontant strawberry.

– **Souvenir de Charles Machiroux** Late June/mid-July. A Belgian cultivar which has been tested in the UK. Found as a seedling by M. C. Machiroux at Amey, Belgium, in 1943. Fruit large/very large, irregular, conical. Bright red, very juicy, sub-acid, very perfumed. Plant compact. Flowers large and slightly protected by the foliage. Does not appear to be a significant improvement on any British cultivars.

– **Surprise des Halles, Surprise Pointue** Remontant. Late June. A French cultivar known for its heavy cropping although in the UK the fruit is small. Of unknown parentage, raised by M. Guyot at Dijon, France and introduced in 1964. Widely grown in France. Fruit small/medium, round/conical, orange-red, turning scarlet. Flesh orange, sub-acid, of moderate flavour. Vigorous plants with flowers and fruit just clear of the leaves. Resistant to grey mould and mildew.

– **Talisman** Mid-/late July. A good-flavoured, late and hardy cultivar. Originated at Auchincruive, Ayr, Scotland, by R. D. Reid, from an American seedling × 'Auchincruive Climax', introduced in 1955 and widely grown commercially. Fruit medium at first, becoming smaller as the season advances, conical/wedge-shaped. Bright scarlet, deep red when full ripe. Flesh pale red, sweet, juicy, of good flavour. Plant moderately vigorous, slow to grow in the spring; flowers protected by the foliage. Crops heavily. **163**

– **Tamella** Mid-July. A winter-hardy cultivar from the Netherlands, now being tested in the UK. Produced by the Plant Breeding Institute, Wageningen, Holland, from 'Gorella' × 'Talisman'. Fruit medium/large, elongated. Deep red, tender, juicy, a little acid, sweet, slightly perfumed. Rather easily damaged. Plants vigorous, flowers just protected by the foliage. Further testing is needed before recommending it for gardens. **164**

Sweet Chestnut, Spanish Chestnut
Castanea sativa FRAGACEAE
– **Doré du Lyons** October. A superior French cultivar. The nuts are large, round, light-coloured and of superior flavour. **165, 166**

Vaccinium Species ERICACEAE

Bilberry, Blaeberry, Whinberry, Whortleberry
Vaccinium myrtillus ERICACEAE
Dessert and culinary. September/October. A low-growing shrub. Flowers May, pink. Berries 1 cm. ($\frac{1}{4}$in.) across; black with bloom. A wild plant of northern heathland areas. **167**

High Bush Blueberry *Vaccinium corymbosum*
ERICACEAE
– *Berkeley* August. A large-fruited cultivar. Originated at the New Jersey Agricultural Experimental Station, Weymouth, New Jersey, USA, from a cross made in 1932 with parentage of 'Stanley', 'Jersey' and 'Pioneer'. Introduced in 1949 and one of the few cultivars grown in the UK. Fruit a loose cluster with individual berries very large, round, flattened at either end. Skin light blue. Flesh firm with a slight aroma, of medium quality, slightly sub-acid and not prone to cracking. Will keep a little time in cool conditions after harvesting. Cropping good, easy to propagate. **168**
– *Bluecrop* Dessert. July/August. A reliable cultivar. Bred at the New Jersey Agricultural Experimental Station, Weymouth, New Jersey, USA, with parentage of 'Jersey', 'Pioneer', 'Stanley' and 'June', introduced in 1952. Fruit in a large, fairly loose cluster, berries round, flattened at either end, with a very light blue skin. Flesh firm, sub-acid, of good flavour, moderately aromatic and resistant to cracking. Bush vigorous, upright, crops consistently in the USA. Hardy and drought resistant.
– *Coville* August/September. A good quality cultivar. A product of the New Jersey Agricultural Experimental Station, Weymouth, New Jersey, USA, from a cross of 'Jersey', 'Pioneer' and 'Stanley', introduced in 1949. Fruit in a loose cluster, berries very large, firm and tart until ripe; aromatic, of good quality and resistant to cracking. Bush vigorous and crops well. **169**
– *Earliblue* July. The earliest to ripen of those described. Produced at the New Jersey Agricultural Experimental Station, Weymouth, New Jersey, USA, from 'Stanley' × 'Weymouth', introduced in 1952. Fruit in a loose cluster of medium size, berries large, light blue. Flesh very firm and sub-acid, of good flavour, moderately aromatic and resistant to cracking. Bush hardy, vigorous, upright, but cropping disappointing in Eire.
– *Elizabeth* August/September. A cultivar with a number of characteristics good for garden use. Of unknown parentage, originated in Whitesbog, New Jersey, USA, by Mrs Elizabeth White, introduced in 1966. Fruit in a loose cluster, but individual berries very large. Excellent flavour and ripens over a long season. Bush upright, spreading. **170**
– *Goldtraube* September. A new German cultivar. Raised by Dr W. Heermann, Grethem uber Schwarmsted, German Federal Republic. Presumably a cross between *Vaccinium corymbosum* and *V. pennsylvanicum*. Fruit medium size, blue/black with attractive grey-blue bloom. Grows vigorously, producing a rounded bush with good autumn colour. Heavy cropping.
– *Herbert* August. A late-blooming, large-fruited cultivar. Originated at the New Jersey Agricultural Experimental Station, Weymouth, New Jersey, USA, from 'Stanley' × 'Pioneer' and introduced in 1952. Flowers late. Fruit in loose clusters. Berries very large and hang well on the bush when ripe. Cropping consistently good.
– *Ivanhoe* July/August. A good-flavoured cultivar. Originated at the New Jersey Agricultural Experimental Station, USA, from a cross between 'Rancocas', 'Carter' and 'Stanley', introduced in 1952. Fruit in a medium sized, loose cluster, berries large, round, flattened at

either end. Skin light blue. Flesh firm, aromatic flavour. Bush vigorous, erect and crops well.
– *Jersey* September. A relatively old-established cultivar widely grown in the USA and possibly the best known in northern Europe Originated in Whitesbog, New Jersey, USA, by F. V. Coville of the United States Department of Agriculture from 'Rubel' × 'Grover', introduced in 1928. Fruit in a long, very loose cluster. Berries medium blue, firm, keep well but lack aroma and only of fair quality. Bush vigorous, erect, hardy and cropping well. **171**

Cranberry, American *Vaccinium macrocarpum*
ERICACEAE
– *Early Black* Culinary. September/October. Selected for its heavy crop. A low-growing shrub. Flowers June/August, white tinted with pink, unusual shape with petals rolled back revealing stamens. Fruit round, red, 1.2 to 2cm. ($\frac{1}{2}$ to $\frac{3}{4}$ in.) across.

Cranberry, Small *Vaccinium oxycoccus*
ERICACEAE
Culinary. September/October. Evergreen, creeping shrub. Flowers May/July, pink with petals rolled back revealing stamens. Fruit round, red, 1cm. ($\frac{1}{3}$in.) across. Flavour very acid. **172**

Walnut *Juglans regia* JUGLANDACEAE
– *Bijou* October/November. Distinctive for its large size of nut; the shells are used for jewel boxes. A French cultivar with nuts of diameter 4 to 5cm. (1$\frac{1}{2}$ to 2in.). The skin is rough and the shell is often thin. The flesh is good when eaten direct from the tree but does not keep well. Tends to produce a very tall tree.
– *Cornet du Perigord* October/November. Popular in the Dordogne and Lotie departments of France. Originated in the Dordogne department. Fairly late in flowering. Nuts medium/large with a hard shell. Round/oval and of good quality, fairly late in ripening.
– *Franquette* October/November. A popular French cultivar. A seedling found in Notre Dame de l'Osier, Isère, France, by M. Franquette. Nuts large, elliptical with a medium-thick shell, well-filled and of good flavour. Tree vigorous and very spreading; late leafing and flowering.
– *Mayette* November. Another French cultivar which also leafs and flowers late and therefore tends to avoid spring frost damage in Britain. Known for over a century in the department of Isère, France, named after M. Mayet. Nuts fairly large, round and tapering, well-filled with a flavour reminiscent of hazelnut. Tree vigorous and spreading. **173**

Whinberry see *Vaccinium*.
White Currant see Currant.
Whortleberry see *Vaccinium*.
Wineberry see Japanese Wineberry.

Worcesterberry *Ribes divaricatum*
GROSSULARIACEAE
Mid-July. A hybrid with gooseberry and black currant in its parentage. Like gooseberry, forms a low-growing bush with large spines on the shoots. The fruit is the size of a large currant, round/oval, purplish black, with a slight currant flavour. Berries in bunches like grapes. Hardy, and a prolific cropper which should be cultivated and pruned like gooseberry. **174**

PESTS & DISEASES

	ROOTS, BULBS, AND TUBERS	BRANCHES, STEMS AND SHOOTS	FOLIAGE	FLOWERS, BUDS, SEEDS AND FRUITS	GENERAL
Pests	Cabbage root fly	Aphid, woolly	Aphid, black bean	Apple sawfly	Birds
	Carrot fly	Cabbage root fly	Aphid, cabbage	Bean seed fly	Mushroom flies
	Cutworm		Aphid, lettuce	Black currant gall mite	Slugs
	Onion eelworm		Apple and pear sucker	Capsid bugs	
	Onion fly		Asparagus beetle	Codling moth	
	Potato cyst eelworm		Black currant leaf curling midge	Glasshouse whitefly	
	Wireworm		Cabbage white butterfly	Plum sawfly	
	Woodlice		Cabbage moth	Strawberry beetle	
			Capsid bugs		
			Celery fly		
			Colorado beetle		
			Flea beetle		
			Fruit tree red spider mite		
			Glasshouse red spider mite		
			Glasshouse whitefly		
			Gooseberry sawfly		
			Leaf mining fly		
			Leafhopper		
			Pea and bean weevil		
			Pea thrip		
			Strawberry mite		
Diseases	Club root	Apple and pear canker	Apple and pear scab	Apple and pear canker	Frost damage
	Damping off	Bacterial canker	Bacterial canker	Apple and pear scab	Grey mould
	Foot and root rots	Cane spot	Black currant leaf spot	Bitter pit	Mineral deficiencies
	Honey fungus	Celery heart rot	Blight	Blight	Potato virus diseases
	Parsnip canker	Fireblight	Celery leaf spot	Blossom end rot	Powdery mildews
	Potato virus diseases	Spur blight	Chocolate spot	Blotchy ripening	Replant disease
	Scab diseases		Downy mildews	Brown rot	STORAGE:
	Splitting		Onion mildew	Dry set	Apple and pear canker
	Violet root rot		Parsnip canker	Russeting	Tomato virus diseases
	Wart disease		Peach leaf curl	Splitting	Virus diseases of fruit
			Rusts	Tomato greenback	Virus diseases of vegetables
			Silverleaf		

Pests

Aphid, Black Bean, Black Fly, Bean Aphid, Dolphin Fly *Aphis fabae*
Very common on broad beans and heavy infestations can cause considerable damage to the crop. Also attacks beetroot, spinach, French and runner beans. Over-winters in the egg stage on *Euonymus europæus*, the spindle tree. Nicotine is still an effective insecticide when temperatures of 18.3°C. (65°F.) or over are prevalent. Under this malathion is to be preferred. Derris is also effective, as are dimethoate and formothion. Where less hazardous materials are preferred pyrethrum may be used.

Aphid, cabbage *Brevicoryne brassicae*
This is a mealy, grey aphid which causes severe damage to Brussels sprouts, cabbage, cauliflower, kales and swedes, especially on the underside of the leaves. As the aphids are waxy a spreader is usually necessary to ensure wetting of the insects and foliage. Nicotine can be effective at temperatures over 18.3°C. (65°F.), malathion at lower temperatures and good results have been obtained from spraying with dimethoate.

Aphids, Lettuce *Nasanovia ribisnigri*
If allowed to get inside the heart this aphid is difficult to control. When seen, spray with malathion or, if within a week of cutting, use derris or pyrethrum. The systemic insecticides, dimethoate or formothion are also effective controls.

Aphid, Woolly *Eriosoma lanigerum*
Colonies of this aphid occur on apple and sometimes pear in the early summer, producing white, protective wool. If uncontrolled they can over a period of years cause woody galls to form on shoots and branches. The whole life cycle is spent on the tree, but in winter the young aphids hide in cracks in the bark, etc and are without wool so that they are inconspicuous. Control by painting colonies with spray strength gamma-BHC or malathion in early summer, before the protective wool has been produced in quantities. Otherwise give a drenching spray with malathion or menazon or dimethoate between petal-fall and early July.

Woolly aphids on apple.

Control by natural enemies often occurs in unsprayed orchards and a specific parasite, *Aphelinus mali*, has been introduced in some areas of Britain. 'Malling-Merton' rootstocks are resistant to woolly aphis but do not confer resistance on scion varieties.

Apple Sawfly *Hoplocampa testudinea*
A common problem affecting young fruit into which the caterpillars of this pest bore after eggs have been laid in open flowers by the inconspicuous adults. The pest may be identified by shallow tunnels on the surface of immature fruit, which have a brown 'frass' at the mouth. Attacked fruits often fall and others are marked by tunnels. The caterpillars leave after about 4 weeks, i.e. late June to early July, and pupate in the soil until the following spring. Sawfly should not be confused with codling moth which attacks apples from mid-June to harvest.

Culinary apples are rarely attacked, however 'Worcester Pearmain', 'James Grieve', 'Ellison's Orange' are especially susceptible. Control by hand-picking affected fruit in early June before caterpillars leave. Spray within seven days of 80% petal fall with gamma-BHC or dimethoate.

Asparagus Beetle *Cricoceris asparagi*
The adults are rather attractive yellow and black beetles with greyish black larvae, both of which feed on asparagus foliage until the plants are defoliated. As soon as damage is noticed, dust or spray with gamma-BHC unless cutting is still taking place, when derris should be used.

Bean Aphid see Aphid, Black Bean.

Bean Seed Fly *Delia platura*
The larvae attack the germinating seeds of French and runner beans by tunnelling into the seeds and young stems, killing or stunting the plants. The worst damage occurs in early sown crops, especially where soil is wet and cold and germination is slow. A seed dressing based on gamma-BHC is effective or bromophos granules can be used.

Big Bud Mite see Black Currant Gall Mite.

Birds
These cause damage to brassicas, seedlings, buds and fruit. Protection with netting is the best remedy. Scaring devices may have a temporary effect, but require site changes to prevent familiarity breeding contempt. Repellants may be used, if scaring devices or netting are insufficient.

Black Currant Gall Mite *Cedidophyopsis ribis*
The mite itself is microscopic but large numbers may build up inside buds causing them to swell, hence the alternative name, big bud mite. These buds often fail to open properly in the spring. Around flowering time the mites begin to migrate. This continues during April, May and June and other buds become affected. It is the most serious pest of black currants, being responsible for carrying the disease black currant reversion (*q.v.*). Once affected by this disease there is no cure and bushes should be grubbed up and burnt. Plant new certified bushes as far away as possible from old and infected bushes. Spray with ½/1% lime sulphur when the flowers open, repeating 3 weeks later.

Black Currant Leaf Curling Midge *Dasyneura tetensi*
Leaves in the growing point of black currants

Black currant damaged by aphids.

become twisted and distorted due to small, white maggots feeding inside them. First signs of attack usually appear towards the end of June and damage is apparent by mid-July. Where the attacks are not serious hand-picking will give control, otherwise spray with dimethoate at the first sign of attack.

Black Fly see Aphid, Black Bean.

Cabbage Root Fly *Erioischia brassicae*
Little white maggots up to 1.3cm. (½in.) long eat the roots and tunnel in the stems especially in early summer and soon after transplanting. Cabbage and cauliflower are chiefly attacked. Poor growth and considerable wilting of plants results. Attacked plants should be dug up and burned, as should the soil immediately around the roots. Seedlings can be protected by adding bromophos or diazinon granules to the soil. A spray strength solution of trichlorphon watered into the soil around transplants on one or two occasions after planting provides adequate protection.

Cabbage root fly maggots.

Cabbage White Butterflies *Pieris brassicae; P. rapae*
Cabbage Moth *Mamestra brassicae*
The small and large cabbage white, their caterpillars and cabbage moth all cause extensive damage, eating holes in leaves and also tunnelling into the heart. Two attacks often occur of which

the late summer one is most damaging. Crushing the egg clusters and hand picking the caterpillars will control small numbers. Dust the plants with gamma-BHC or derris or, where picking is only 2 weeks away, spray with derris or trichlorphon.

Capsid Bugs:
Apple Capsid *Plesiocoris rugicollis*
Common Green Capsid *Lygocoris pabulinus*
The adults are green and easily visible on leaves. The adults and nymphs feed on soft growing tissues of apple and other soft fruits, bush and cane fruits, the damage showing first as brown spots at feeding sites leading to distortion of leaves and fruit. On fruit the damage often appears as irregular, light brown corky areas. The damage caused by different species is similar and is most likely seen in May and June in the UK. Attacks on apple and pear should be anticipated by spraying at petal-fall with dimethoate, fenitrothion or malathion. The number of capsids may be determined by tapping the shoots or branches over a tray during the blossom period to dislodge adults feeding on the foliage. Spray currants or gooseberries at the end of flowering and raspberry or loganberry before flowering. The pest over-winters as eggs on trees and bushes and can also be controlled by winter washes.

Carrot fly maggots.

Carrot Fly *Psila rosae*
This is a most destructive pest, especially on light soils. The small, yellow maggots attack the roots, leave rusty brown tunnels and spoil them for culinary use. Sowing thinly in open positions, so that the odour of bruised foliage does not attract the adult flies, is a useful precaution. Bromophos or diazinon, being granular, are easily applied along the seed rows. Diazinon or trichlorphon can be applied as a soil drench in May and June on early carrots and in July and August on maincrops. This pest also attacks parsley, parsnip and occasionally celery.

Celery Fly, Leaf-miner *Phylophylla heraclei*
This is the chief pest of celery. The grubs, after hatching, work their way through the tissues of the plant, leaving the well-known, brown blisters from May/June. Blistered leaves can be removed in the early stages or the maggots crushed between the fingers. To control, spray with malathion or trichlorphon and the systemic dimethoate may also be used. A light dressing of nitrogenous fertilizer of 20 to 25g. per sq. m. (½oz. per sq. yd) will stimulate growth.

Codling Moth *Cydia pomonella*
Damage is normally confined to fruit of the apple

Apples damaged by codling moth caterpillars.

but pears are sometimes attacked. Damage occurs from mid-June to harvest – it is the codling moth grub that is found in apples in the second half of the season, as opposed that of the Apple Sawfly which is present from the fruitlet stage through to late June. Grubs leave the fruit in late summer and over-winter in cocoons under loose bark or tree ties. They can also be attracted to bands of sacking tied round tree trunks from mid-July on. These should be removed and burnt in early autumn. Otherwise control by spraying with fenitrothion or malathion in mid-June repeating 3 weeks later. The time of adult moth emergence and egg-laying depends on weather, and chemical control involves both a good cover of trees with spray and timing the application between egg-laying and before the fruit has been attacked (about two weeks).

Colorado Beetle *Leptinotarsa decemlineata*
This is more familiar on posters outside police stations in the UK than on the potato crop. This North American pest has crossed the Atlantic to Europe and the orange and black striped beetles and their red grubs destroy the foliage, killing the plants. This is such a serious pest that it is notifiable in the UK, so its suspected presence should be passed on immediately to the Ministry of Agriculture or the local police station.

Cutworm *Agrotis* spp., *Noctua pronuba*
This pest frequently attacks lettuce, severing the roots just under soil level, in June and July and is especially prevalent in dry seasons. Dig around the severed plant and a soil-coloured caterpillar will be found just over 2.5cm. (1in.) long; usually a few more can be destroyed by following along

Cutworms.

the row. The addition of bromophos or diazinon granules to the soil before planting or sowing will provide some control.

Dolphin Fly see Aphid, Black Bean.

Flea Beetle, Turnip Fly *Phyllotreta* spp.
This pest seriously damages and sometimes eliminates newly germinated seedlings of brassica crops by eating holes in the leaves. Damage is usually worst in dry springs during late April and early May. Seedlings can be protected with a seed dressing based on gamma-BHC. This should not be used on radishes or turnips which may be tainted. BHC dust applied as leaves emerge above the ground is effective, especially if repeated at weekly intervals until the rough leaf stage is reached. Spraying with water in the evening will encourage growth and discourage the pest. Spray or dust weekly with BHC.

Flea beetles.

Fruit Tree Red Spider Mite *Panonychus ulmi*
Damage usually becomes obvious in hot, dry weather when attacked leaves of apple, plum, damson and sometimes pear, turn brown and may even die and fall prematurely. High temperatures cause a rapid increase in numbers of these tiny mites which feed on the undersides of leaves between the veins. They are too small to be seen readily with the naked eye, but under a hand lens can be seen moving about; they are more typically pale yellow orange rather than red. Eggs are laid between May and September and the pest over-winters as clusters of shiny red eggs on the barks of trees or in crevices. This pest is often controlled naturally on unsprayed trees by predatory insects and persistent insecticides sprayed on to them, especially post-blossom, will kill beneficial insects, and may encourage this pest. DNOC petroleum winter wash effectively controls over-wintering eggs when applied to dormant trees up to early February. Summer sprays should alternate between malathion, dimethoate and formothion; this variation will reduce the chance of a population of spider mite building up resistance to any one insecticide. Some fungicides like dinocap, used to control powdery mildew of apple, will also give some control of this pest.

Glasshouse Red Spider Mite *Tetranychus urticae*
This pest of plants under glass can also attack outdoor crops such as wall-trained fruit trees, currants, raspberries and strawberries, which are not attacked by fruit tree red spider mite; aubergine, capsicum, beans and cucurbits. Attacks are worse in hot, dry weather and the first signs are small, white spots on the upper surfaces of leaves corresponding with feeding punctures made by mites on the undersides. Severe attacks cause loss of leaf and may involve crop reduction. The adults over-winter hidden among débris on the ground and are deterred by garden hygiene. Where attacks are severe, spray with dimethoate, malathion or formothion, varying the chemical to avoid the build-up of resistant strains of mite. The hot, dry, atmospheric conditions required, for instance, by peaches under glass, favour attacks, and such trees should be syringed over frequently with water as a deterrent. Old strawberry plants are more generally attacked than young ones. If you want an early crop of strawberries then there is this danger of mite attack as the atmosphere under a cloche tends to be drier. Therefore try to keep the atmosphere damp by watering.

Glasshouse Whitefly *Trialeurodes vaporariorum*
This is a different species to the cabbage whitefly but is similar in appearance. The adults and larvae suck the sap of the plants, which become sticky from the excreted honeydew and the resultant sooty mould. The fruits are also affected. A very persistent pest in glasshouses, which requires frequent fumigation with gamma-BHC smokes, or sprayings with BHC, malathion or pyrethrum as the eggs and pupae seem immune to insecticides. The parasitic wasp *Encarsia formosa* which is available to amateur gardeners is effective in a warm temperature 21°C. (70°F.) where it will breed faster than the pest and eradicate it.

Gooseberry sawfly caterpillar.

Gooseberry Sawfly *Nematus ribesii*
There are a number of closely related sawflies which attack gooseberry and also currant causing severe defoliation. The yellow, black-spotted caterpillars of one species hatch in May and can be active until September. They then fall to the

ground to pupate in the soil over winter. At the first signs of attack, usually in mid-May, hand-pick caterpillars or dust or spray with derris, fenitrothion or malathion. Control measures are important because the severe loss of leaf may result in smaller fruit.

Leafhopper *Zygina pallidifrons*
This is a yellow insect which jumps when disturbed. Leafhoppers sometimes attack young tomato plants growing in a glasshouse with other plants that are infected. Spots about 1mm. in diameter can be seen on the leaves. Spraying with malathion or diazinon is effective on established plants and BHC dust or smokes for young plants.

Leaf-miner see Celery Fly.

Leaf Mining Fly *Pegomya betae*
This pest damages the leaves of beetroot and spinach. Control as recommended for celery fly.

Mushroom Flies *Sciarid* spp.
These may be controlled to some extent by pyrethrum dust or malathion, or drenching with the former 24 hours before cutting.

Onion Eelworm *Ditylenchus dipsaci*
A microscopic pest which causes young plants to become swollen and distorted; these symptoms are usually referred to as 'onion bloat'. The pest lives inside the stem and bulbs and causes infested onions to go soft and rot when stored. No suitable chemical treatment is known and as it can be carried in the seed, seeds and sets should only be obtained from reputable suppliers of treated seeds. No onions should be grown on sites for 2 years after infestation.

Onion Fly *Delia antiqua*
A major pest of onions, especially on dry soils. If plants are attacked they should be dug up and burned, as should any larvae found in the soil around the roots. The white maggots up to 1.3cm. (½in.) long attack the roots and also tunnel inside the bulb. An application of diazinon granules to the soil before sowing should control and this can be supplemented by a 10cm. (4in.) band after sowing. Transplanted onions from an autumn sowing or onions from sets seem less liable to attack.

Pea and Bean Weevil *Sitona* spp.
This pest frequently attacks broad beans in the early stages of growth, eating semi-circles out of the leaf edges, giving a scalloped effect. To prevent the plants being severely checked dust with derris.

Pea Moth *Laspeyresia nigricana*
This produces caterpillars, which feed on the peas inside the pod, by laying eggs in the flowers between June and mid-August. Peas sown early or late in the season, thereby avoiding the moth's flight period, usually escape attack. Control can be obtained by spraying with fenitrothion or gamma-BHC, 10 days after flowering in the above mentioned period.

Pea Thrips *Kakothrips robusta*
These are very tiny insects which suck the sap from leaves and pods, causing distortion of the

pods and a silvery discoloration. Control by spraying with fenitrothion as advocated for pea moth, especially around mid-June when damage is most likely to be seen.

Plum Sawfly *Hoplocampa flava*
Young plum fruits are attacked, the caterpillars boring into them making holes which exude a black, sticky substance. Attacked fruit may fall prematurely. If a severe attack is likely, spray with dimethoate 7 to 10 days after petal-fall.

Potato Cyst Eelworm *Heterodera rostochiensis*
A microscopic and serious pest which is widespread in gardens and allotments where it builds up when potatoes are grown too frequently in the same area. Affected plants are stunted in growth and turn yellow prematurely from the lower leaves upwards, causing the plants to die early and only produce tiny tubers.

Two species are common, distinguishable by the colour of the developing cysts, one golden, the other white. Breeders have developed cultivars of potato which are resistant to the golden type but these are still susceptible to the white type. Resistant cultivars which are available are, 'Maris Piper', 'Pentland Javelin', 'Pentland Lustre' and 'Pentland Meteor'. Self-set potatoes can carry on an infestation and should be cleared before eelworms can complete their development. As eelworm eggs sometimes survive for ten years, a very long rotation may be necessary to ensure the pest is completely starved out. Plants grown in soil known to be infested should not be transferred to cyst-free areas, nor should their roots be conveyed to the compost heap.

None of the pesticides available to amateur gardeners are effective against this pest but it is now thought that sterilizing the soil with dazomet (Basamid) might be worth trying.

Tomatoes are also affected and show similar symptoms. As no tomato cultivars are known to have resistance, some precautions are essential, particularly to prevent glasshouse infestation. Soil which has been used for growing potatoes should never be taken into the glasshouse for tomato culture. If soil in the glasshouse becomes infested, complete resoiling will be necessary unless ring-culture methods are employed.

Rain Beetle see Strawberry Beetle.

Raspberry Beetle *Byturus tomentosus*
The yellowish-white maggot is found in fruits of raspberry, also loganberry and blackberry. The adult beetles, after over-wintering in the soil, lay eggs in the flowers of raspberry and loganberry in June, or later than this on blackberry. Spray loganberry when most of the blossoms are open and again as the first fruits colour. Raspberries should be sprayed once, as the first fruits colour, and blackberry once as the first flowers open. Suitable chemicals include derris and malathion which should be applied in the evening to minimize damage to pollinating insects.

Slugs *Arion* spp; *Milax* spp; *Limax* spp.
These cause damage to many crops and this can be serious in heavier soils in warm, wet seasons. Preplanting applications of metaldehyde or methiocarb can be followed up by applications of pellets of the same materials.

Strawberry Beetle, Rain Beetle *Harpalus rufipes*
The beetle is black and shiny up to about 8mm. (⅓in.) long and a common soil inhabitant, which hides under rubbish and clods of soil. The ripening fruit is attacked, holes being dry and narrower at the neck. Another related species removes and eats the seeds. They are difficult to control once the plants have been strawed to protect ripening berries against soil splashing, because this gives shelter to the beetles. Attend to garden hygiene and remove hiding places. Broadcast methiocarb pellets over the beds about a week before starting fruit-picking.

Strawberry Mite *Tarsonemus pallidus*
A microscopic mite which attacks young strawberry tissues causing roughening and wrinkling of the leaves and down-curling of the leaf margins in certain cultivars, such as 'Cambridge Favourite'. This damage takes place in the centres of plants when leaves are very young and small and badly attacked plants are stunted from about July onwards, especially under high temperature conditions. Certified runners of strawberries should be bought as they will be free of this mite. Lime sulphur sprays are some deterrent.

Turnip Fly see Flea Beetle.

Wireworms *Agriotes* spp.
The larvae of click beetles, often attack the potato crop, especially where a new garden has been brought into cultivation. The thin rusty brown larvae, up to 2.5cm. (1in.) in length make small holes in the tubers. The application of bromophos or diazinon granules to the soil when planting establishes some control. Some can be picked up during preliminary cultivation and robins will also take some. After a few years of cultivation the larvae become less numerous.

Wireworms.

Woodlice *Oniscus* spp; *Porcellio* spp; *Armadillidium* spp.
These sometimes destroy young cucumber and tomato plants in the seedling stage. Attention to hygiene and dusting or spraying the soil with gamma-BHC should control these pests.

Apple and Pear Canker *Nectria galligena*
This appears as sunken, brown areas on shoots and branches. The central parts die and flake off, but the surrounding tissue becomes swollen, thus forming cankers. These often eventually girdle branches which then die back beyond the canker.

Apple canker.

A rot around the eye may also develop in fruit on the tree or in store, or affected fruit may shrivel and hang on the tree in a mummified condition throughout the winter. Infection takes place through small wounds including scars caused by apple scab and thus control of scab helps prevent canker especially on heavy soils, which pre-dispose trees to the disease. Some apples are particularly susceptible such as 'Cox's Orange Pippin', 'James Grieve', 'Worcester Pearmain' and a few pears such as 'Fertility'. In serious attacks affected branches should be cut out and burnt. On large branches, pare down the loose bark to healthy green tissue and paint with a specific canker paint and spray with Bordeaux mixture just before the start of leaf-fall, again at 50% leaf-fall, and finally at bud break. Old and badly diseased trees should be cut down and burnt.

Apple Scab *Venturia inaequalis*
Pear Scab *V. pirina*
These diseases appear as dull, olive green patches on the leaves in the spring, usually following periods of warm, damp weather. In bad attacks, premature leaf-fall may be heavy. Subsequently, infection spreads to the fruit and, if this happens early in the season, severe spotting may occur, and the surface of the fruit may crack. Later infection produces small spots which, though unsightly, may easily be removed by peeling. The diseases over-winter either on the young shoots thus forming entry points for canker or on fallen leaves. Infection in the following spring may take place from either of these places. Prune out affected young shoots in winter; these shoots are those produced during the previous season's growth which have enlarged scabs on them. In spring, spray at 10-day intervals from bud burst to mid-May with either captan, benomyl or thiophanate-methyl. A reduced programme of spraying with benomyl a short time before the end of an infection period in the bud burst to

mid-May time, i.e, a period of warm, moist weather, can be almost as effective. Some of the choicest cultivars are susceptible to this disease but most gardeners put up with slight attacks without attempting control measures.

Bacterial Canker *Pseudomonas mors-prunorum*
A common disease of cherries, plums and peaches causing the formation of large flattened cankers on branches which exude gum, and a 'shothole' appearance of the leaves, which look as if they have been fired at with a shotgun. The bacteria re-infect shoots in the autumn and trees should be sprayed with Bordeaux mixture in mid-August, repeating at monthly intervals until October. Prune stone fruits in summer so that wounds heal quickly; large cuts should be covered with wound-protective paint. Many cherries are worked on F12/1 rootstock which is resistant to canker but scion cultivars are still affected. If the attack is severe it may be possible to cut out and burn badly cankered branches but this may seriously affect tree shape and eventually the whole tree will have to be cut down and burnt. This disease is one of the main reasons for the decline of cherry growing in many countries.

Bitter Pit
This disorder affects apples, especially in hot, dry seasons where crops are light and individual fruits large. Light brown, irregular corky spots appear in the flesh of the apple just beneath the skin, sometimes associated with sunken areas on the surface. The trouble is due to a deficiency of calcium within the fruits, but its incidence is influenced by various factors; thus it is most common on young vigorous trees especially those fed excessively with nitrogen, and it also appears to be connected with a shortage of water at critical times so trees should be mulched and watered in dry periods. Trees should also be sprayed with calcium nitrate, 200g. in 20 l. (8oz. in

Apple scab.

Bitter pit on apples.

5 gal.) of water in mid-June, repeating 3 times at intervals of 3 weeks.

Black Currant Leaf Spot *Pseudopeziza ribis*
This disease first appears as irregular spots on the leaves of black currant. Outbreaks which start before fruit-picking lead to premature defoliation which may reduce cropping in the year of attack and may produce effects carrying over to subsequent seasons. The same fungus also attacks gooseberry where the symptoms are similar.

Spray with benomyl, thiophanate-methyl or zineb at the first sign of infection and repeat if necessary.

Black Currant Reversion
This disease is specific to black currants and leads to a severe reduction in cropping. The leaves become coarser in appearance and the leaf

margins have fewer serrations, so that the bush appears to have 'reverted' to a wild, (unfruitful) type. Reverted bushes generally grow strongly because they do not devote any energy to fruit production. Flowers are noticeably pinker in the spring, due to reduction in hairs. The black currant gall mite is the carrier of this disease and control measures should aim at preventing the mite spreading on to healthy bushes. Certified black currant bushes are available, which are free from reversion. These should be planted as far away as possible from diseased bushes. Badly diseased bushes should be dug up and burnt: it is not possible to prevent the spread of the disease within the bush by cutting out affected branches since it will have already spread throughout the bush even though it may take some time for the symptoms to appear.

Blight *Phytophthora infestans*
Dark spots on potato leaves and stems become brown, with a whitish mould underneath the leaf. The disease develops rapidly in humid weather and tubers become affected. Bordeaux or Burgundy mixtures have long been used as controls, as have other copper compounds. Maneb and zineb also control blight, and destruction of haulm reduces the risk of tuber infection. In wet seasons spraying in June, repeating every fortnight, is a useful precautionary measure.

This disease also affects tomatoes grown outdoors and can be severe in wet seasons, affecting the fruits, which become unusable. If potato blight is in the vicinity precautionary spraying as advised above should be carried out from the end of July.

Blossom End Rot
This physiological disorder results in the withdrawal of water from the furthest fruit tips. It shows at the blossom end of the fruit as a dark green patch, which becomes blackish brown and shrunken. It occurs in tomatoes.

Blotchy Ripening
This physiological disorder affects tomatoes and is caused by variability of temperature, especially in small glasshouses where high day time temperatures are followed by low temperatures at

Brown rot on apple.

night. This results in the patchy ripening of the fruit which will be part red and part green. A deficiency of potash may be an associated factor, so better temperature control and sulphate of potash 65 to 70g. per sq. m. (1 to 2oz. per sq. yd) should remedy the condition.

Bootlace Fungus see Honey Fungus.

Brown Rot *Sclerotinia fructigena; S. laxa*
These two species of fungus cause brown rot on apple, pear, plum, peach, nectarine, apricot, cherry, quince and medlar fruits. Brown rot starts as soft, brown spots which gradually increase in size until the whole fruit becomes covered with yellowish cushion-like growths often arranged in concentric circles. Control starts with the removal and burning of dead flower trusses and related spurs which are cankered. Later in the season, destroy mummified and shrivelled fruits which otherwise would remain attached to the shoots all winter and could be a source of infection in spring. Pick off fruit if affected by brown rot before harvest, and remove and burn affected fruit in store.

Spraying is not usually necessary if the recommended hygiene measures are followed. The fruit should be protected as far as possible against damage by birds or insects and the trees from pests and disease to minimize the points of invasion for the fungus. Benomyl sprays used to control other diseases may reduce brown rot on the tree, and spraying with thiophanate-methyl before picking will check rotting of stored fruit.

Cane Spot *Elsinoe veneta*
This disease of raspberry, loganberry and hybrid berries produces small, purplish circular spots on the canes, visible in May and June. The spots become elongated as the canes grow and the centres turn greyish-white with a purple border. If many such spots occur they will reduce cane vigour and those that are badly affected should be

Black Currant reversion. The leaves on the left are diseased, those on the right are healthy.

removed. Spray with benomyl, dichlofluanid, thiophanate-methyl or thiram when the buds are 1.3cm. (½in.) long and repeat every 14 days until the end of flowering.

Celery Heart Rot *Erwinia carotorra*
A wet brownish rot develops at the centre of the plant where nitrogen is used to excess, and damage has been caused to the plants by slugs, celery fly larvae or when earthing up. To prevent the trouble, control slugs, include potash in the trench before planting and earth up carefully.

Celery Leaf Spot *Septoria apiicola*
This is now uncommon because gardeners can buy treated seed. As it is a seed-borne disease clean seed should be obtained from a reliable source, benomyl, Bordeaux mixture or maneb should keep control if the trouble appears.

Chocolate Spot *Botrytis fabae*
This is quite a common disease in broad beans when they are autumn sown, though it is not so common in those sown in spring. Chocolate-coloured spots occur on the leaves, stems and pods; these sometimes appear as streaks on the stems. The spots coalesce in very wet weather and often kill waterlogged plants. Growing the crop on well drained soil which has adequate nutrients should result in disease-free plants, while spraying in the early stages with Bordeaux mixture gives good control.

Club Root *Plasmodiophora brassicae*
Also known as 'finger and toe' this is a fungus disease which thrives in acid soils and can only be remedied in severe cases by dressing the ground with ground chalk or limestone. 13kg. will be sufficient for 30sq. m. (28 lb. for 30sq. yd). If hydrated lime is used a lighter dressing 8 to 10kg. (15 to 20 lb.) will suffice for the same area, reducing it by half in succeeding years. Cultivate thoroughly by deep digging thereby providing good drainage. 2 or 3 years may elapse before satisfactory control becomes possible so take the added precaution of dipping the roots in a thick cream made with 4% calomel dust, water and a little clay, before planting or drench planting holes with a solution of benomyl (1ml. in 1 l. in

water). This disease is very troublesome in many gardens and where this is so, sterilizing the soil with dazomet ('Basamid'), is very effective.

Damping-off *Pythium* spp. *Phytophthora* spp.
Several fungi can affect germinating seedlings causing them to collapse at ground level, especially when germination is hindered by cold soil conditions early in the season. Treating seed with a captan seed dressing, watering the soil with captan, zineb or Cheshunt compound are effective measures which can be taken. In such important crops as lettuce or tomatoes the use of sterilized soil is recommended.

Die-back
The death of shoot-tips or branches can be due to unfavourable growing conditions or to attacks by specific diseases like apple canker. If possible, the cause should be established by close examination so that appropriate control measures can be taken. Remove affected shoots, cutting back to healthy buds or branches and treating large wounds with proprietary protective paint. This pruning should be done at the appropriate time of year, viz. fruits subject to silver leaf and bacterial canker (plum, cherry, etc) in summer after fruit picking; otherwise (apple, pear) as soon as the problem is seen or during winter pruning. With peaches it is normal to prune young trees in spring as soon as healthy buds become obvious.

Downy Mildews
These affect lettuce (*Bremia lactucae*), brassicas (*Peronospora parasitica*), and spinach (*P. effusa*). White tufts or downy patches of fungal growth develop on the undersides of the leaves which have discoloured areas on the upper surfaces. Downy mildews are most troublesome on overcrowded seedlings on wet soils, so sow thinly in well-drained soil and use a different site each year for the seed bed. Spray with zineb on all crops or use Bordeaux mixture on brassicas and thiram on lettuces. In frames, sterilize the soil with formalin or dazomet.

Dry Set
This is indicated by embryo fruits which fail to swell. If these do not drop off they ripen into

Dry set of tomatoes.

small seedless tomatoes. Generally due to unsuitable atmospheric conditions dry set can be overcome by a light spraying with water and a fairly moist atmosphere, kept buoyant by careful use of the ventilators. Shaking or tapping the plants on sunny days also helps.

Fireblight *Erwinia amylovora*
A bacterial disease of apple, pear and related ornamental plants which enters stems often through flowers, sometimes carried by bees, and can cause rapid death, especially in high temperature conditions. Shoots or branches may suddenly appear to have been scorched as if by fire – hence the name – and the disease is widespread in northern Europe. Provided cutting out is started as soon as the disease is noticed it may be possible to prevent spread and while in some conditions the disease can die out, progressive attacks, encouraged by wet weather and warm conditions, may kill trees. Cut out 30 to 60cm. (1 to 2ft) behind where any staining can be seen in the wood and burn diseased shoots. Disinfect cutting tools with 3% lysol between treatments. Also treat hawthorn, whitebeam, mountain ash, cotoneaster, pyracantha and stranvaesia if affected. The problem has been particularly serious on pear, especially 'Laxton's Superb' which is now no longer propagated for sale. It is now fairly widespread on apple, and also affects hawthorn hedges which are very common round gardens. Suspected outbreaks should be notified to the nearest office of the Ministry of Agriculture, Fisheries and Food.

Foot and Root Rots *Pythium* spp., *Phytophthora* spp., *Rhizoctonia solani*, *Thielaviopsis basicola*; also *Fusarium* spp. and *Verticillium* sp. wilts
Numerous soil-borne organisms cause rotting of plants either at the base (foot rot) or of the roots, so that the top growth wilts or collapses. Peas, beans, tomatoes and cucumbers are most susceptible to infection particularly where the

Club root of cabbages. The plant on the left is healthy, that on the right diseased.

same type of plant is grown in the same soil year after year, so rotate crops to prevent attack. Pot-bound plants are also liable to infection so tease out roots and strip off paper pots before planting out. Place fresh compost around the base or stems of affected tomatoes and spray with a foliar feed to help get a reasonable crop. Use sterilized soil for raising seedlings and for greenhouse plants. Seed dressings of captan help to prevent infection. Watering with a solution of captan, Cheshunt compound or zineb may check these diseases on slightly affected plants. Burn severely diseased plants.

Frost Damage

In areas subject to very low winter temperatures, trees can be severely damaged and may even be killed. This problem is generally confined to the continent of Europe. Spring frost damage is more widespread, causing scorching of young leaves, and more important, flowers, leading to loss of crop. Obvious symptoms include blackening of flowers, as in 'black eyes' in strawberry. On more mature fruit, cracking may occur. Less severe frost may not produce noticeable symptoms such as lack of fruit set and the dropping of young fruitlets (e.g. 'running (dropping) off' of black currants) for several weeks afterwards.

On frost-prone sites, remove obstructions to air movement on to lower ground, by, for example making gaps in hedges running across the slope. Select late-flowering cultivars, e.g. 'Crawley Beauty' apple or avoid spring flowering fruits altogether, and plant instead blackberries or raspberries. On frosty nights cover early flowering fruits, e.g. apricot or peach with fine netting, and plants lower to the ground, like strawberry, with newspaper. Keep soil free of weeds and water well before frost where possible. This will encourage the soil to retain daytime sun heat which will be re-radiated overnight and may just save flowers from being damaged. Apply water through sprinklers (application rate 0.3cm. ($\frac{1}{8}$in. per hr)) to flowers at temperatures below freezing point, so that as the water freezes the latent heat is given up to the plant to prevent the plant from freezing. This demands available water, special nozzles not likely to freeze up and well-drained soil able to withstand this rate of water application. Plants receiving this treatment will have ice form on them. The only disadvantage of this protective measure is that trees may be damaged by branch splitting.

Grey Mould *Botrytis cinerea*

Attacking all vegetables, this is particularly destructive to lettuces out of doors and under glass, the stem being attacked at soil level by the fungus which causes the plant to wilt quickly. It is encouraged by cold, damp conditions when growth is slow. Good soil conditions are very important to encourage well-rooted plants and careful planting is essential.

Quintozene raked into the soil before sowing or planting, helps to prevent this fungus. Plants which are being over-wintered can be sprayed at 3 or 4 week intervals with thiram. Benomyl has also been found useful.

Grey mould also affects tomatoes under glass when humidity is high and there is insufficient ventilation. All debris from previous crops should be cleared and the structure and soil surface treated with formalin as for lettuce. Tomatoes

should have all affected leaves and fruits removed cleanly and burned. When trimming do not leave broken stalks and improve air circulation by ventilation. Dust with captan, or spray with maneb every 7 days after defoliation. Fumigation of greenhouses with tecnazene also gives a good control.

On fruit grey mould is a common, rotting disease of both leaves and fruits. It shows as a soft rot followed by a characteristic grey mould that produces clouds of spores which are responsible for further spreading, if affected fruit is not removed and destroyed. The disease normally affects dead tissues but can then spread to adjoining living material. It enters by wounds which should be avoided where-ever possible, for instance, by netting trees against birds. The same disease also causes die-back in gooseberries and where this is a common problem bushes have to be grown from below ground, not with a bare stem or 'leg' below the branches. Preventive spraying with benomyl has led to resistant strains of the fungus being produced and the frequent

Grey mould on strawberry.

change of spray chemicals is recommended using dichlofluanid, benomyl, thiophanate-methyl, thiram and captan. On strawberries, especially vulnerable in wet seasons, start spraying as the first flowers open and repeat at 10-day intervals, up to 4 times in severe cases.

Honey Fungus, Bootlace Fungus
Armillariella mellea

A common fungus attacking roots which causes trees to die. Fruit crops may be affected as can some vegetables such as potatoes; ornamental woodland trees and shrubs may also be affected. Where any trees or canes appear unhealthy with premature shrivelling and dropping of leaves followed by death without apparent cause, the bark should be examined at about soil level to see if the fungus can be found. The bark in that region on affected trees is loose and can be removed to show fan-like growths of fungus growing up into the tree. These have a pronounced mushroom smell. Below ground, black strands (hence bootlace fungus) can sometimes be seen following the roots and attached to them. In the autumn, honey-coloured toadstools may appear at the bases of badly affected trees until the first frosts. Where any tree dies and the roots are left in the ground, the fungus is estimated to be capable of spreading at a rate of about 1m. per

year, from the affected root system in search of other trees through the soil. These are often only attacked after they have suffered a check, for example, waterlogging. Affected trees usually die and the disease is difficult to eradicate even if the root systems are dug up and burnt to remove the source of food from the fungus. Control may be possible by soaking the ground in which affected trees are growing with a product containing cresylic acid ('Armillatox'). Careful removal and burning of affected trees, particularly their roots will help to prevent spread. Otherwise the only means of control is by putting a physical barrier into the soil, such as a continuous polythene sheet down to the impervious sub-soil, well in advance of the known position of the bootlaces of the fungus.

Mineral Deficiencies

A plant will not remain healthy if it does not receive sufficient quantities of a number of nutrient elements. All plants should be given the correct fertilizer treatment to provide the food materials they require, and deficiencies of nitrogen, phosphorus and potassium should not then arise. Some soils, however, lack certain minerals or contain them in a form unavailable to plants and specific deficiency symptoms then arise; these are described under Bitter Pit, Blotchy Ripening, Brown Heart and Magnesium Deficiency. In addition, some crops particularly raspberries and peaches may show severe yellowing or whitening of leaves when grown in very alkaline soil. Then apply a chelated compound (e.g. 'Sequestrene') or fritted trace elements to restore the green colour to the foliage and dig in acidic materials to make the soil less alkaline.

Magnesium deficiency

Magnesium deficiency in tomatoes shows up as orange bands between leaf veins and is caused by high potash content in the soil. Spray at 10-day intervals with magnesium sulphate, $\frac{1}{2}$lb. in $2\frac{1}{2}$ gal. water (20g. in 1 l.) with a few drops of washing-up liquid as a spreader.

Onion Mildew *Peronospora destructor*

This appears as purplish or grey streaks or spots on the leaves, which should be sprayed with zineb as soon as seen or the plants dusted when moist with copper dust (Bordeaux powder).

Parsnip Canker *Itersonilia pastinaceae*

This is the most serious disease of parsnips. The tissues at the shoulder of the root, rot during autumn and winter and may also attack leaves. There is no effective cure, though cultivars of parsnip are available which have varying degrees of resistance. Crop rotation should be practised as a preventive measure.

Peach Leaf Curl *Taphrina deformans*

A common problem on peach which can also affect almond, apricot and nectarine, also other species of *Prunus*. The leaves become distorted, blistered, curled and red although as the disease progresses this colour changes due to the production of a white covering of spores. With new outbreaks it may be possible to arrest spread by picking off and burning affected leaves. Where the disease is well-established, this would involve too great a loss of leaf area and a preventive spray

Peach leaf curl.

programme should be followed. Apply Bordeaux mixture in late January and again 14 days later, repeating in the autumn just before leaf fall. Once the disease is established, it is unlikely to disappear spontaneously.

Potato Virus Diseases

Potatoes are subject to certain virus diseases. Leaf Roll and Mosaic, the symptom of which is curled leaves, produce stunted plants. These diseases should not appear if certified seed is purchased. Aphids are often responsible for their spread and should be controlled. A more serious disease is spraing particularly in 'Pentland Dell'. Reddish brown wavy lesions develop in affected tubers. This disease is spread by eelworms in the soil, so potatoes should be grown on a fresh site the following year. Cultivars are now available which are immune to certain virus diseases.

Powdery Mildews

Podosphaera leucotricha attacks apple and occasionally pear, quince and medlar. Another powdery mildew (*Sphaerotheca mors-uvae*) attacks gooseberry (American gooseberry mildew) and black currant producing white mould on leaf surfaces. Strawberry mildew (*Sphaerotheca macularis*) produces thin, white felting on leaves and fruit, also reddening of foliage.

Slight attacks of apple mildew can often be controlled by winter pruning of infected shoots which have silvery looking withered tips and thin buds. Those shoots which have not been removed in winter can be hand-picked in spring when they grow out from infected buds producing white shoots with a mealy appearance. The alternative is to spray against severe attacks using benomyl, dinocap, or thiophanate-methyl at 7 to 14-day intervals from bud-burst to the fruitlet stage.

American gooseberry mildew produces a white powdery covering on leaves and a brown felt-like mould on leaves and fruit. Black currants can also be affected usually at the tips of rapidly growing shoots which show characteristic white mould; the fruit is less commonly affected. Spray with dinocap or benomyl before flowering, after fruit set and again three weeks later, and cut out infected shoots.

Spray strawberries with dinocap or benomyl before flowering and again, if necessary, at intervals of 10 to 14 days.

With peach mildew spray with sulphur, starting with the first signs of disease. Dryness at the roots encourages mildew – it is especially difficult to maintain uniform soil moisture conditions either under glass or on trees planted against walls.

Replant Disease

Where trees of closely related species are re-planted on the same site they are inclined to grow slowly compared with those planted on a fresh site. These symptoms occur where apple is planted after apple or pear but not after plum and vice versa. The precise cause of the disease is not known and in some cases it is probably a complex including eelworm and fungus diseases.

It is unwise to replant with the same or a similar fruit on the same site without a break, although the intensity of the problem varies. Changing the soil completely will prevent the trouble to some extent if replanting a tree of the same type cannot be avoided. Cherries are particularly susceptible.

Russeting

This occurs on tree fruits and may be natural as in some cultivars which are usually covered in russet ('Egremont Russet') or may have only a small amount of russet on them ('Cox's Orange Pippin'). In some circumstances, cultivars which are not normally russeted ('Golden Delicious') may have russet on them or those which normally have a small amount of russet may have the quantity increased by, for instance, weather or spray damage. It may be possible to reduce the amount of russeting which occurs due to cold weather round about blossom time by protecting the flowers with windbreaks or covering the trees with netting.

Rusts *Puccinia* spp.

These affect various vegetables. On asparagus the stems and needles appear brown and powdery. Spraying with Bordeaux mixture has given good results, and should be repeated if necessary.

Leek rust has become more troublesome recently. In the past it occurred mainly in wet areas, especially in nitrogen rich soils deficient in potassium. If diseased parts are cut away, the remains will be edible. The infected debris should be burned and a fresh site used for next season.

Rust is prevalent on mint in some areas. The disease may be checked by packing dry straw all over the bed in September or October and burning it off. This disease can also be controlled by hot water when plants are badly affected. Lift the roots, clear away soil, and immerse in hot water for 10 minutes; the water temperature should be 40 to 46°C (105 to 115°F). Wash in cold water and replant.

While a number of fruits – apricot, blackberry, black currant, gooseberry, peach and raspberry can be affected, rusts are normally rare except on plum. On upper leaf surfaces small bright yellow spots appear; on lower surfaces there are brown spots on which the spores are produced and by means of which the disease spreads. In severe attacks, leaves yellow and fall prematurely. Most rusts have complex life histories and part of the cycle of plum rust, *Tranzschelia pruni-spinosae*, is spent on anemone, both cultivated and wild.

Infected anemones near to plum should be destroyed. In severe attacks on plum, spray with zineb or thiram, but it is usually sufficient to encourage vigour by good cultivation as weak trees are more susceptible to infection.

Scab Diseases:
Common Scab *Streptomyces scabies*
Powdery Scab *Spongospora subterranea*
These potato diseases do not normally worry the amateur unless he wants to exhibit tubers. However, a bad attack will lead to considerable wastage through rotting in store and deep peeling will be necessary to remove scarred skin.

The two forms are somewhat difficult for the average gardener to distinguish between. Common scab is generally found on tubers grown on poor, gravelly or very light soils which are very short of organic matter. The addition of organic matter such as leaf-mould, compost, peat or well rotted farmyard manure will not only benefit the crop but be helpful to the production of clean tubers. Another useful method is to grow a green

Common scab of potato.

manure crop such as mustard or rye grass and dig in before planting. I have found lawn-mowings useful not only around the tubers when planting but also as a dressing previous to earthing up, provided the grass had not been treated with a selective weed-killer.

Powdery scab is prevalent on potatoes grown in badly drained soil, and naturally is worse in wet seasons. Some cultivars show some resistance.

Silver Leaf *Stereum purpureum*

A common disease of plum which rarely affects apple, cherry or pear, causing silvering of the leaves. Usually only one or two branches are affected, but if these are not cut out promptly the whole tree may become affected in time, although given good nutrition spontaneous recoveries have been claimed. When removing affected branches, cut sufficiently back into healthy wood until there is no visible brown stain left in the centre of the branch. Burn affected shoots and do not leave prunings lying about because they can develop fruiting bodies which produce spores causing further spread. The leaves appear silvered because of an air layer beneath the surface and they are not themselves a cause of spread of the disease. The fruiting bodies can also be produced on dead or dying wood left in neglected trees and such branches should be cut out and burnt. Avoid injuring trees in any way as this may well let the fungus in. Prune established plum trees in summer, usually immediately after harvest, so that the cut heals quickly. Cover large cuts with proprietary wound-protecting paint. 'Victoria' plum is especially susceptible to silver leaf; it is a brittle-branched cultivar, prone to splitting of shoots which should be supported when carrying heavy crops. 'Yellow Egg' is more resistant to attack and more likely to recover from one.

Splitting

This disorder affects root crops, tomatoes and top fruits when a dry period is followed by heavy rain. The use of nitrogenous fertilizers may be a contributory factor. It can be prevented by mulching and watering before the soil dries out completely.

Spur Blight *Didymella applanata*

This disease of raspberry and loganberry causes purple spots near the buds, usually visible towards the end of the summer. These spots turn silver, the buds die and cropping potential of canes is reduced. Badly affected ones should be cut out. Keep plants open to let in light and air by removing old fruited canes immediately after picking and thinning out superfluous new canes. Spray with the same chemicals as recommended for the control of cane spot, starting when the new canes are only a few inches high and repeat 3 or 4 times at fortnightly intervals. Where the attack is slight reduce spraying to one application of thiram., Bordeaux mixture or liquid copper at bud-burst and another just before blossom, directed mainly at the young canes.

Stem Rot *Didymella lycopersici*

This sometimes attacks tomatoes 3 weeks or so after planting. Dark brown sunken lesions appear and can sometimes be eradicated if painted with captan in the early stages.

Tomato Greenback

This is a condition in which the area of the tomato fruit around the calyx remains green and refuses to ripen, spoiling the palatability. This need no longer be a cause of concern as several cultivars are immune.

Tomato Virus Diseases

A number of viruses can affect tomatoes causing such symptoms as stunting of plants, distortion of foliage, yellowish or dark green mottling or spotting of leaves, dark streaks on leaf stalks and stems, bronzing of leaves and fruit and brown pock-marks on fruit. Destroy any plant showing any of these symptoms and do not leave any root debris in the soil. Keep down all insect pests, which spread some of these viruses, by suitable spraying. Some viruses are extremely infectious so take care when handling and trimming plants.

Violet Root Rot *Rhizoctonia crocorum* syn. *Helicobasidium purpureum*

This fungus affects many vegetables, particularly asparagus. Infected roots become covered with reddish violet strands, foliage turns yellow and

the plants eventually die. The trouble spreads outwards until a large gap is formed. Infected plants should be lifted and burned and, if the attack has been severe, the bed should be cleared and a fresh start made on a new site. If the bed is to be retained it can be isolated from the infected area by sinking a sheet of thick polythene 30cm. (12in.) deep in the soil. Neither asparagus, red beet, carrots, potatoes, nor seakale should be planted on the diseased plot, which should also be kept clear of weeds, particularly bindweed, docks and dandelion.

Virus Diseases of Fruit

Strawberries and raspberries are very susceptible to infection by a number of viruses which cause severe stunting of plants, yellow mottling or blotching of leaves which are often distorted or crinkled and a reduction or complete loss of crop.

Raspberry Virus disease.

Blackberries are occasionally affected but gooseberries rarely show symptoms. Do not propagate from any plant showing these symptoms but dig up and burn it. Buy new stock certified to be free of virus infection and plant on a fresh site or in new soil as some viruses are transmitted by eelworms in the soil. Other viruses are spread by aphids so control them by suitable spraying. Top fruits are not affected so severely by viruses but, when available, buy trees certified as being virus free. See also Black currant Reversion.

Virus Diseases of Vegetables

Numerous viruses can affect vegetables causing different symptoms such as colour changes in leaves, stems and tubers, distortion of organs, killing of tissues, wilting and withering and stunting of growth. One of the most troublesome viruses is cucumber mosaic which has a wide host range and is readily transmitted by aphids and on tools and even hands if diseased plants are handled. Crops most severely affected by viruses are marrows (including courgettes) which become stunted and have distorted and blotched leaves and fruits and lettuces which become dwarfed and bear crinkled and mottled leaves and fail to

heart up. Destroy all plants showing these symptoms. See also Potato Virus Diseases and Tomato Virus Diseases.

Wart Disease *Synchytrium endobioticum*

This is almost unknown in the UK now that most cultivars of potato grown are immune to this disease. It is still a notifiable disease, so that if it appears the occurrence has to be reported to the Ministry of Agriculture under the Order of 1958. Most likely to occur in a wet season or in wet areas, the disease appears as warts which enlarge into cauliflower-like swellings which can be larger than the tuber.

White Rot *Sclerotium cepivorum*

Sometimes known as 'mouldy nose', this fungus causes losses in salad onions, particularly of the 'White Lisbon' cultivar, and can affect maincrop onions, leeks, shallots and garlic. The roots and base of the bulb are affected, causing the leaves to turn yellow and fall over, when it will be seen the bulbs are covered with the white fungus. Affected plants should be burned and the ground not used for onions, if possible, for 8 years. Some control can be obtained by dusting the drills at sowing time with 4% calomel dust at the rate of $\frac{1}{2}$kg. per 25m. (1 lb. per 25 yd) of drill. Better still use a different site each year where possible.

HOME PRESERVATION

Preserves

When fruits and vegetables reach peak eating condition, deterioration follows, either quickly for soft produce like strawberries and salad plants, or more slowly for firmer apples and root vegetables. To prevent loss some means of preservation is essential.

Ancient man noticed the extended eating period of foods dried by the sun and wind and soon developed simple racks to hasten the process although he was entirely unaware of the underlying principles. Similarly, it is thought that curing in brine developed from observation of the preservative effect of salt sea water. In 1807, Sir John Sinclair in his *Code of Health and Longevity* lists 8 methods of food preservation: sun drying, the use of artificial heat, pickling, salting, covering with melted butter, adding sugar, keeping cold with ice, and by the use of charcoal. All except the last of these are still in use and have nowadays the backing of sound principles which have developed from the work of Louis Pasteur (1822–95). Preservation was formerly the province of the country housewife. Increasing scientific knowledge led to the development of sophisticated methods and the thriving food processing industry which today plays an important part in feeding our increasingly urbanized population. However, it is still possible to produce first class preserves at home and these have the added advantage of being made to please the family palate.

Safety is the first and most important requirement for any food and, in this respect, fruits of temperate climates have a natural acidity (below pH 4.5) which makes their safe preservation a relatively simple matter. They are subject to decay and other spoilage but the micro-organisms present are rarely pathogenic. The situation differs with vegetables which are less acid and therefore provide a base for the growth of food poisoning micro-organisms. This does not preclude their preservation at home but it is essential to use sound methods and to follow them exactly. Apart from safety, preserved produce should retain as much of its original quality as possible and this is usually considered under the headings of colour, texture, aroma and, above all, flavour. Home gardeners have the opportunity to pick and preserve their crops in first class condition. Not only does this ensure good palatability but it has been established that nutrients are well retained in these circumstances. This is particularly the case with vitamin C (ascorbic acid) and the vitamin B group. Where some delay between picking and use is unavoidable, the produce should be kept cool in shallow containers, lightly covered, but speed from plot to pot is the rule for quality retention.

Both metric and imperial measures are given in the text. Use one or the other for any particular operation, as the quantities do not convert exactly.

Fruit Bottling

This method of preservation depends on heating the fruit in the bottling jar, which should then be sealed. The initial heating must be sufficient to destroy most of the micro-organisms present, leaving only heat-resistant types, which are unable to grow in the acid conditions of the final product. The heating also prevents colour and other changes from developing in the fruit during subsequent storage. It is essential for the heat to penetrate to the centre of the pack of fruit and to ensure this, extra time must be allowed for large bottles and very tight packs.

Vegetable Bottling

Home bottling of vegetables is not advised. They are potentially more dangerous than bottled fruit and the only safe process is by the use of a pressure pan. Vegetables have to be blanched before packing, then processed under pressure for a much longer period than fruit, and the final product tends to be rather over-cooked. Freezing is recommended.

Jars

Bottling jars are made of glass and have tight fitting metal or glass lids with inbuilt or separate gaskets, rubber bands, screw bands or clips which are used to apply pressure on the lid during cooling so that the jar is made airtight. As cooling proceeds, air pressure in the jar drops below atmospheric pressure and thus a seal is made which will hold when the screwband or clip is removed. Fruit acid corrodes unprotected metal and lids, which should therefore have a lacquer coating. Straight-sided bottles are easiest to pack. Twist-top jam jars, although not made for bottling, have been found satisfactory for small quantities of fruit. The lid must be undamaged, rested on the jar during processing and twisted down securely for the cooling period. It should not be loosened until the fruit is required for use.

4 types of bottling jar. From left to right a screw-top, a clip-top, a kilner and a converted coffee jar, with metal lid and rubber band in foreground.

Metal lids and rubber bands are available for converting some types of instant coffee jars for fruit bottling. The original lid of the coffee jar provides the necessary pressure during cooling. Rolls of a synthetic skin material from which appropriate size squares can be cut and tied (with the special string supplied), make a cover for any suitable jar. This material balloons during the heating of the bottle and cools to form a concave seal. An American method of sealing is to melt paraffin wax and pour this into the neck of the bottle after the heating process. It is essential to dry the inside of the neck of the bottle before adding the wax. A more pliable seal is obtained if 1 part of liquid medicinal paraffin is added to 3 parts melted wax. Clarified mutton fat can be used as a cheap substitute for paraffin wax but bottles with this seal must be stored out of reach of mice. Whatever type of bottle is chosen, it must be inspected to make sure that it is sound and free from chips at the neck as these prevent a firm seal. Wash the jars thoroughly, rinse and invert. A slightly damp interior surface helps when packing the fruit. Check lids, clips or screw bands to make sure they are the right size for the jars. Test rubber bands for resilience and discard any that have stretched. Soak bands in warm water for 10 to 15 min. before use.

Fruit can be bottled in water but, unless this is necessary for dietary reasons, a sugar and water syrup is recommended for appearance and flavour.

Syrup is usually made with granulated sugar but honey, unrefined brown sugar, golden syrup or treacle can be used to replace all or part of the white sugar. Each of these gives its own characteristic flavour to the syrup and should be used according to tate. Sweeteners such as saccharin are best added when the bottle is opened for use.

Covering Liquid

The strength of the syrup is a matter of family taste. As a guide 400g. to 800g. of sugar to 1 litre water (½lb. to 1 lb. sugar to 1pt water) covers the usual home preferences from a weak to a fairly heavy syrup, although some commercially canned fruits are in very much heavier syrups. To make syrup, heat the water in a clean saucepan, add the sugar and stir until it dissolves. Bring the syrup to the boil for 1 min, then cover and remove from the heat. Syrup quickly boils away if left on the stove. If syrup is required cold and it has not been made in advance, it can be prepared with half the quantity of water and the remainder added cold, providing that good drinking water is used.

The addition of sugar to water increases the volume but this can easily be lost with overboiling.

Fruit

Fruit for bottling must be clean and should not be washed unless necessary, in which case it should be washed carefully and quickly. It should be in prime dessert condition, slightly under ripe rather than over ripe.

– *Gooseberries* are the exception to this rule. They should be bottled while firm and green. When topping and tailing gooseberries for bottling in syrup, a tiny slice should be cut from each end of the berry. This enables the syrup to penetrate, otherwise the fruit is likely to shrivel on storage. The less handling given to soft fruit the better.

– *Raspberries* and *loganberries* are spread out on a large dish and left for an hour in a cool place. Any maggots present will crawl out and can be easily removed.

– *Plums* should be wiped to remove their bloom which, if left on, gives a waxy appearance.

– *Apples* and *pears* are liable to discolour and need careful, quick handling. Have ready a bowl holding about 2 l. (4pts) cold water with 25g. (1oz.) salt and, if available, 10g. (½oz.) citric acid. Peel the fruit with a stainless knife. Apples are usually cored and sliced, pears are cut in halves or quarters. The core and fibres of a ripe pear can be easily and neatly removed with a pointed teaspoon. Hard pears are not recommended for bottling, as, although they can be stewed and then bottled, they lack the quality of ripe dessert pears. As soon as each piece of apple or pear is prepared it should be dropped into the bowl of water and kept submerged under a plate until ready to pack. A quick rinse in clean water is necessary before packing to wash off the salt.

– *Rhubarb* Spring rhubarb is usually preferred for bottling, and does not require peeling. Summer rhubarb is better used for jam-making.

– *Strawberries* are rather unsatisfactory as they lose colour, shrink and develop a somewhat slimy texture. Artificial colour added to the syrup improves them.

Strawberries and rhubarb can be soaked overnight in hot syrup; this shrinks the fruit and enables more to be packed into each bottle.

– *Mixed fruits* Mixed soft fruit make a palatable variation. Black currants should be used with discretion in a mixed pack because of their dark colour. Rhubarb is very useful for filling up as it takes the flavour of the other fruit.

Apart from special preparation given above, fruit is generally prepared as for normal cooking, stalks, leaves, hulls removed, etc. Large plums and apricots are usually halved and stoned, peaches are blanched for ½ to 1 min. in boiling water, then cooled and skinned. Free stone cultivars are halved and the stones removed, cling stone cultivars are better sliced. Tomatoes, if small, can be bottled whole, with or without their skins, but it is more usual to preserve them peeled and halved. The tomatoes, which should be firm and evenly red, are dipped into fast boiling water for a maximum of ½ min., then cooled in cold water and peeled. The skin should come off thinly. If veining shows on the fruit, allow less time for blanching subsequent batches. Prepared tomatoes soon become watery so the whole process should be completed as quickly as possible. If whole fruit are being bottled, the jar is filled up with salted water using about 25g. (½oz.) salt to 1 l. (1pt) of water. To halve the fruit, cut from the stem downwards. A red line can be seen on the surface of many peeled tomatoes, and if this is followed the seeds will not be exposed. Pack the halves cut side downwards and sprinkle with a mixture of salt and sugar 5ml. (1tsp.) of each to 450g. (1 lb.) of tomatoes. Add 1 to 2 tbsp. of water and the juice from the tomatoes will provide enough liquid to make a good pack.

Packing the Bottles

For economical use of jars and a well balanced proportion of fruit and syrup, the packing of the fruit should be firm, taking care not to bruise or crush it. If the quantity available is sufficient, it is worthwhile grading the fruit to size. To prevent light coloured fruits from darkening, put a little syrup into the jars first and then add the fruit so that it is covered all the time. When packing is complete, top up with syrup and put on the rubber band, if used, and the lid and screw band or clip. In some methods of bottling, the syrup is added later but these are not suitable for light coloured fruits.

Choice of Bottling Methods

The heating of the fruit in the bottles can be:
in a deep saucepan on the hob
in the oven
in a pressure pan.

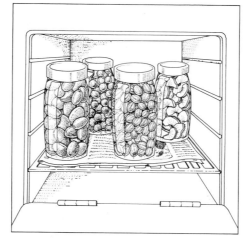

Two heating methods: in a saucepan with a false bottom (top) and in an oven, where bottles are placed on newspaper.

– *In a deep saucepan*

In former years a large fish kettle or false-bottomed boiler could be found in most homes. These were ideal for bottling, but any saucepan deeper than the bottles can be used. A false bottom can be made from a little piece of trellis or several layers of newspaper. If the bottles are in direct contact with the base of the saucepan there will be considerable risk of cracking and loss of contents.

– *Slow method of bottling* This method starts with cold water in the saucepan and cold liquid in the bottles and uses gentle heat to reach the required temperature in 1½ to 2 hours.

– *Quick water bath method* This is the preferred method nowadays. Place the false bottom in the saucepan and add water to half the height of the jars. Warm the water to blood heat. Fill up the packed bottling jars with syrup at 60°C (140°F), fit lid and seal loosely. Stand the bottles in the pan and adjust the water level to come to the top of the bottles. Put the lid on the pan and heat up to simmering 88°C (190°F) in 25 to 30 min. Simmer for the period given in Table 1, then remove the bottles, tighten seals if necessary and leave until the next day. Take care to stand the hot bottles on a dry surface, preferably of wood or layers of paper.

Although a thermometer is useful, it is not essential as the syrup can be heated until it stings the finger and simmering is indicated by the rising of small bubbles over the whole surface of the water.

– *In the oven*

Many housewives prefer to use the oven for bottling. There is a choice of methods here, as the liquid can be added either before or after processing. Good results can be obtained when the syrup is added after heating but it is not suitable for all fruits because of discoloration in the dry oven heat. Also there is a risk of scalds and of bursting

1 Time-table for bottling by quick water bath

FRUIT	MAINTAIN AT SIMMERING (TIME IN MINUTES)		
	½–1kg. jars (1–2 lb.)	1½–2kg. jars (3–4 lb.)	2½–3kg. jars (5–6 lb.)
SOFT FRUITS normal packs			
gooseberries *for pies* rhubarb *for pies* sliced apple	2	7	12
SOFT FRUITS tight packs			
gooseberries *for dessert* rhubarb *for dessert* cherries plums *whole*	10	15	20
plums *halved* peaches *halved or sliced* nectarines *halved* strawberries *soaked*	20	25	30
tomatoes *whole* pears	40	45	50
tomatoes *solid pack*	50	60	70

2 Time-table for bottling by pressure pan and in a moderate oven

FRUIT	PROCESSING TIME (MIN.)		
	Pressure pan ½–1kg. jars (1–2 lb.)	Moderate oven ½–1½kg. (1–4 lb.) load	2–4kg. (5–10 lb.) load
SOFT FRUITS normal packs			
gooseberries *for pies* rhubarb *for pies* sliced apple	1	30–40	45–60
SOFT FRUITS tight packs			
gooseberries *for dessert* rhubarb *for dessert* cherries plums *whole*	1	40–50	55–70
plums *halved* peaches *halved or sliced* nectarines *halved* strawberries *soaked*	3–4	50–60	65–80
tomatoes *whole* pears	5	60–70	75–90
tomatoes *solid pack*	15	70–80	85–100

bottles when filling them up with boiling syrup after processing. For these reasons the alternative oven method is given here.

Clear the oven except for one rack, which should be placed so that the bottles will occupy the centre of the oven. Set the oven control to give a temperature of 150°C (300°F): Gas 2. Have ready a shallow baking tray lined with several layers of newspaper. Stand the packed bottles on the tray and pour in boiling syrup. Put on bands, lids, and the screw bands loosely, put the tray in the oven and close the oven door. The newspaper will protect the bottom of the bottles and also absorb any syrup which boils out, thus preventing a patch of burnt syrup on the oven floor. There should be 5cm. (2in.) between the bottles and 5cm. (2in.) space along the oven walls. Processing times are given in Table 2. It will be seen that a full oven load of bottles will require longer than 1 or 2 bottles. At the end of the processing time, take out the bottles, stand them on a dry surface, complete the seals and leave until the next day.

– In a pressure pan

A pressure pan provides a quick method of bottling fruit but directions must be followed exactly to avoid overcooking. The pan must have sufficient depth to hold the jars comfortably when they stand on the shallow rack provided with the pan. Before packing the jars, it is important to check them carefully for flaws or cracks as the pressure will reveal any weaknesses. Also check how many jars can be put into the pan without touching and whether the pan lid fits comfortably over the jars. There must be room for some expansion as the jars heat. Pour water into the pan to 3cm. (1in.) depth and then add the shallow rack. A teaspoonful of vinegar added to the water helps to preserve the surface of the pan and in no way affects the fruit. Heat the water and pour boiling syrup into the jars to within 3cm. (1in.) of the top. Complete the seal, leaving screw bands loose. Stand the jars on the rack, and secure the

lid of the pan leaving the vent open. Increase the heat gently and as soon as steam appears close the vent to give a temperature of 107°C (228°F) within 5–10 min. Many pressure pans use weights to give the required temperature and one marked '5' or 5lb. pressure is used for fruit bottling. It is important that timing to reach pressure should be between 5 and 10 min. to avoid under- or over-processing. Pressure is maintained according to the table. A steady pressure is essential for a good result. At the end of processing time, gently remove the pan from the heat and leave for 10 min. before removing the lid and taking out the bottles. Stand them on a dry surface, complete the seals and leave until the next day.

Testing the seals

The next day, clips and screw bands should be removed and the seal tested by lifting the jar gently by the lid. This is not possible when using twist-top jam jars and care must be taken not to loosen them absent-mindedly. There is no need to replace screw bands or clips. Gently wash the jars with a cloth to remove any stickiness and dry them. Stick on the label giving cultivar and kind of fruit, strength of syrup and date, and store jars in a cool dark place. Clips and screw bands should be washed, dried and lightly greased before storing.

If any bottle has not sealed it is pointless to reprocess it without trying to find the fault, e.g. a chip at the neck, a raspberry seed under the rubber band, a wrong size clip, a screw band that does not grip, etc. Where one jar has not sealed, it is best to use up the contents quickly. It is most unlikely that several will fail but in this event the whole process must be repeated. No short cut is effective once the lid has been removed.

Bottled fruit keeps its quality from one season to the next. If a few jars can be bottled as each fruit comes into season, a good store is soon built up for winter use.

Fruit Pulp or Purée

This is a quick way to bottle fruit and is particularly suitable for uneven samples and windfall apples. Look the fruit over and remove any leaves, stalks or blemished portions; peel, core and cut up apples; stone plums. Put the fruit into a saucepan with a little water and cook until tender and well broken down; some soft fruits do not need the addition of any water. Sweeten to taste and pour at once into warmed bottling jars and cover. For purée, the softened fruit must be sieved, sweetened to taste, reheated, poured into warmed jars and covered.

Have ready a saucepan of hot water with a false bottom or layers of newspaper. Put in the bottles of pulp, releasing seals if necessary and put the lid on the saucepan. Bring the water to the boil and boil steadily for 5 min. Take out the bottles, complete the seals and leave to cool. The next day test the seals, label and store as for bottled fruit. Pulping is particularly useful for apples: if boiling unsweetened apple pulp is poured into hot bottling jars and sealed immediately, the pulp will keep without further processing. To ensure that it will keep the apple must be thoroughly cooked down in the saucepan and very quickly bottled and sealed.

Tomato Purée

This is a useful preserve. Work quickly as tomatoes lose their texture if the process is delayed. Cut up sound tomatoes and cook them in a covered saucepan with a very little water until they are soft. Rub them through a sieve, return the purée to the saucepan and adjust the seasoning to taste. The addition of a little sugar and pepper as well as salt may add flavour. Reboil the purée; pour at once into warm bottling jars and cover loosely. Stand the bottles in a pan of hot water, as for fruit pulps, bring to the boil and boil for 10 min. Remove the bottles, complete the seals and leave to cool. The next day test the seals, label and store.

Preserving Fruit with Chemicals

Campden tablets are inexpensive and easily obtainable from chemists and other shops dealing with home wine-making equipment. In use, the tablets release sulphur dioxide, a widely used preservative. Sulphur bleaches the colour from fruits and this can be a definite advantage with apples. The method is simple but there are a few rules that must be observed. The proportion of preservative must be in accordance with the weight of the fruit, contact with metal must be avoided, and, before use, the fruit must be boiled until the smell of sulphur is driven off. This method is *not* suitable for less acid fruits such as pears, blackberries, strawberries, cherries or tomatoes and certainly not for vegetables. It is particularly good for dealing with gluts of plums, damsons or apples. The fruit should be in firm, ripe condition; plums can be left whole or halved and stoned, apples are peeled, cored and sliced or quartered.

Large stone jars or glass sweet jars can be used for quantities of fruit but usually ordinary bottling jars suffice. The prepared fruit is packed – not too tightly – into the clean jars and the weight of fruit in each jar should be noted. The easiest way to do this is to weigh the empty jar and re-weigh when it is packed. To make up the solution, put the required number of tablets into a bowl, crush them with a wooden spoon and add a little (1 or 2 tablespoonsful) tepid water. Stir until they are dissolved and then at once add 250ml. ($\frac{1}{2}$pt.) cold water per tablet. Fill up the jars with the solution which should cover the fruit entirely. Seal the jars at once. If a jar has no suitable lid, a fitting cork can be used and sealed by running melted paraffin wax over the top. Metal lids should have a protective coating inside to prevent interaction between the metal and sulphur. A square of synthetic skin material or calico dipped in melted wax makes a satisfactory cover if tied on securely.

To use, turn the contents of the bottle (fruit and liquid) into a saucepan, preferably enamel, and boil until there is no smell of sulphur (about 5 to 10 min.), then sweeten the fruit and use as required. The colour largely returns to the fruit during boiling and as the sulphiting process tends to harden fruit, the boiling does not break it down as much as would be expected with fresh fruit.

Pickles, Chutneys and Sauces

The keeping quality of these preserves depends mainly on first reducing the water content of the ingredients by brining or cooking them and then adding vinegar to correct the acidity. A wide variety of fruits and vegetables can be used with the addition of spices, salt and usually sugar as well. In a pickle the fruit or vegetable used is in recognizable pieces, whereas in a chutney the ingredients are cooked down to a fairly firm and even texture, while a sauce is a sieved chutney thinned to give a pouring consistency.

Fruits and vegetables should be in good condition, especially those for pickling, but they need not be perfect in shape. The good parts of windfall apples and bruised pears or plums can be used but old runner beans, over ripe marrows, etc. will give poor results.

VINEGAR

This is an essential ingredient and must be of good quality with a minimum acetic acid content of 5%. Many pickle manufacturers use a 6% acetic acid vinegar and this strength can be obtained for home use if ordered in advance. Brown malt vinegar has a robust flavour which blends well with vegetable pickles; cider vinegar is pleasant in fruit chutneys and pickles; white distilled vinegar enhances bright colour in tomato chutney or pickled silverskin onions. The delicate flavour of wine vinegar is largely lost in pickling.

SPICED VINEGAR

To add interest to the flavour, vinegar for pickles is usually spiced. Spiced vinegar can be bought but it is simple to prepare at home and the spices can be varied to suit family taste. A useful general purpose mixture is made by weighing 10g. ($\frac{1}{4}$oz.) each of whole cloves, cinnamon bark, mace and allspice, and adding a few peppercorns to 2 l. (3pt) vinegar. Whole spices are used in preference to ground spices to ensure a clear result. Immediately before use the spices are folded in a clean cloth and beaten with a rolling pin to bruise them and release their essential flavours.

There are two methods of spicing vinegar. The truest flavour is obtained by putting the bruised spices into a bottle of vinegar, sealing securely, and shaking daily for 2 weeks. It is then left for one month after which the vinegar is strained off the spices. It is convenient to use half quantity of vinegar and add the remainder after straining.

This method takes time and for a quicker result the bruised spices and vinegar are placed in a basin over a saucepan of water. A lid or plate is used to cover the basin, the water is brought to the boil and the saucepan is then removed from the heat and left for two hours before straining the vinegar.

The spiced vinegar is added hot for soft pickles, such as pickled pears, and cold for crisp pickles, such as red cabbage, but this rule can be varied to suit home preferences.

Chutneys and sauces may be made with spiced vinegar but it is more usual to add ground spices unless these dull the colour as in ripe tomato sauce.

HERB VINEGARS

In a few chutney recipes herb vinegar is recommended but its more common use is in mayonnaise and salad dressings. Basil, borage, chives, tarragon and thyme are popular herbs to use, either singly or mixed. Pick the leaves just before flowering, bruise them lightly and half fill a wide mouth jar. Fill up the jar with vinegar, preferably distilled, and stopper tightly. Give the jar an occasional shake and leave for 14 days before straining off the vinegar for use.

Pickles

There are 3 types which may be made from produce grown in temperate climates:
- vegetable pickle, with either a single vegetable or a mixture;
- piccalilli or mustard pickle, with mixed vegetables in a thickened sauce with turmeric and/or mustard;
- fruit pickle, with one fruit in a sweetened spiced vinegar.

– Vegetable Pickle

Onions and shallots are popular and cauliflower, runner beans and cucumber can be pickled singly or used in a mixed pickle with onions and marrow. Beetroot and red cabbage are usually pickled on their own. Nasturtium seeds make a cheap substitute for imported pickled capers. The vegetables should be young and fresh. Wash them quickly if necessary and drain thoroughly. Prepare according to kind as shown in Table 3.

BRINING

In order to reduce the water content of the prepared vegetables, they are either submerged in a basin of brine or layered with dry salt before pickling. Dry salt is more drastic than brine and is usually reserved for vegetables with a high water content such as cucumbers and marrows. The salt used should be kitchen salt, not table salt which has an additive to prevent caking. Brine for pickling is a 10% salt solution and, for small quantities of vegetables, 100g. (4oz.) salt dissolved in 1 l. (2pt) cold water will be adequate. For dry salting, allow 100 to 125g. (3 to 4oz.) salt for each 1 kg. (2 lb.) vegetables. With vacuum packed salt it is easy to use too much, so it is advisable to weigh it. Brining times are given in Table 3, overleaf.

When brining period is completed, the vegetables are put in a colander, quickly rinsed in cold water and thoroughly drained. They are then packed into jars, firmly but not too tightly, leaving a 25mm. (1in.) headspace. In a mixed pack the effect is improved if the various ingredients are arranged attractively. Add the spiced vinegar either hot or cold so that it covers the pickle by 15mm. ($\frac{1}{2}$in.) thus leaving a small head-space under the lid.

Cover at once. The cover should be vinegar resistant and reasonably air-tight. Vinegar evaporates readily and if an inadequate cover is used, the pickle will dry out. Label the jar with the details of the pickle and date made and store in a cool, preferably dark place.

Pickled cabbage is ready to eat in a week or so and deteriorates after 3 months, becoming progressively softer and less attractive. Other pickles are better if left for a month before eating.

– Pickled Gherkins

Leave in brine for 3 days, then drain and pack into jars. Cover with hot spiced vinegar, seal and leave in a warm place for 24hr. Drain off the vinegar, boil it and pour again over the gherkins, seal and leave for a further 24 hours. Repeat this until the gherkins have a good green colour, then top up with extra vinegar and seal.

Modern commercial pickles tend to be mild and sweet compared with home recipes. A little sugar (10g. per 500ml.) can be added to spiced vinegar for most pickles if liked. If a sweeter product is required, to ensure keeping, the pickle will have to be put into fruit bottling jars, stood in water, heated to simmering point and held for 20 to 30 min., depending on the size of the jar. Seal the jar as for bottled fruit.

– Piccalilli and Mustard Pickle

The vegetables used are the same as for mixed pickle (see Table 3) and they are similarly prepared and brined. To make the sauce for 2·5kg. (6 lb.) vegetables take:

    10g. ($\frac{1}{2}$oz.) turmeric
    15g. ($\frac{3}{4}$oz.) dry mustard
    7g. (1$\frac{1}{2}$tsp.) ground ginger
    35g. (1$\frac{1}{2}$oz.) flour
    250g. (9oz.) white sugar
    1·5 l. (3pt) white vinegar.

Put most of the vinegar into a large saucepan and stir in the spices and sugar. Heat and add the rinsed brined vegetables. Cook gently until the desired texture is reached: but do not allow it to become mashed. Remove saucepan from the heat. In a separate basin blend the flour with the remaining vinegar and stir into the contents of the saucepan. Return pan to the heat and bring to the boil stirring gently. Allow to boil for 2 to 3 min. and then pour into pots, leaving small headspace and cover at once. There should be ample sauce to cover the vegetables in the jar.

For an entirely mustard pickle, increase the mustard to 25g. (1oz.) and omit the turmeric. The quantity of sugar can be reduced if a sourer pickle is preferred. Cornflour gives a smoother sauce but tends to crack or divide during long storage.

– Fruit Pickle

Suitable fruits are pears, peaches, apricots, cherries, damsons and crab apples. They should be of good quality and a little under ripe. Hard pears pickle well. For a yield of 4kg. (8lb.) prepared fruit allow:

    2kg. (4 lb.) sugar
    1 l. (2pts) vinegar
    rind of half a lemon
    10g. ($\frac{1}{2}$oz.) whole cloves
    10g. ($\frac{1}{2}$oz.) allspice
    5g. ($\frac{1}{4}$oz.) root ginger
    5g. ($\frac{1}{4}$oz.) stick cinnamon

Prepare the fruit. Peel pears, cut in half and remove core. Small halved pears make an attractive pickle but if larger, quarter or slice. Dip peaches in boiling water for $\frac{1}{2}$min. then into cold water, peel, cut in half and remove stones.

3 Preparation and brining of vegetables for pickling

VEGETABLE	PREPARATION	BRINE OR DRY SALT	SALTING TIME (HR)	VINEGAR HOT OR COLD
Cauliflower	Remove leaves. Break curd into florets. Remove any blossom fragments.	brine	24	cold
Cucumber	Do not peel. Cut into 10 to 15mm. ($\frac{1}{2}$in.) cubes for mixed pickle.	dry salt	24	cold
	Slice finely for pickling on its own.	brine		
Beetroot	Cook and skin before pickling. Baby beets are used whole and larger beets are sliced or cubed. Avoid tight pack. Add $\frac{1}{2}$ to 1 tsp. salt per jar. Seal securely. To give variety, add a little grated horseradish.	none	—	boiling
Gherkins	Use fresh, firm and small.	brine	72	boiling (see text)
Marrows	Use young. Peel, remove seeds. Cut in 15mm. ($\frac{1}{2}$in.) cubes. Too uninteresting to use alone (see Chutneys).	dry salt	24	cold
Nasturtium seeds	Pick on a dry day. Pack into small jars.	brine	12	cold
Onions	Small use whole, large use sliced. Less tearful if peeled and prepared after 12 hours brining and then replaced in fresh brine. Carefully remove any blemished parts at neck of onion.	brine	48	cold
Pickling Cabbage, Red	Use very fresh and red. Discard outer leaves. Slice finely, removing large stems of leaves. Use within 3 months as crispness is lost.	dry salt	24	cold
Runner Beans	Use young. Remove strings, and cut across width into diamond-shaped pieces.	brine	24	cold
Shallots	Whole. Can be skinned after 12hr brining as for onions.	brine	48	cold
Mixed pickle	Usually tiny onions or shallots. Cauliflower, runner beans, cucumber or marrow. Start onions day before.	brine brine	48 24	cold

Quarter or slice large peaches. Wipe apricots, halve and remove stones. Preferably remove stones of cherries but this is not essential. Wipe and prick damsons but do not remove stones. Use crab apples whole unpeeled. Pour vinegar into a large saucepan, add and dissolve the sugar. Bruise the spices and with the finely peeled lemon rind tie together loosely in a muslin bag and put this in the saucepan. Add the fruit and cook gently until it is tender. A certain amount of cooking is

necessary to maintain the colour of the fruit, so very ripe fruit is not suitable.

Remove the fruit with a perforated spoon and pack it into jars. It will tend to sink so the jars can be packed to the brim. Pour any syrup in the jars back into the saucepan and boil until considerably reduced. Try a little on a cold plate to test for consistency which should be like thin honey. Fill up the jars with hot syrup, taking care not to leave air spaces between the pieces of fruit.

The vinegar syrup should cover the fruit comfortably and there should be a small headspace above the vinegar. Cover at once.

These sweet fruit pickles are delicious with any cold meat and particularly with pork or gammon, either cold or hot. They are useful in or as an accompaniment to many savoury dishes.

Surplus syrup should be kept in a sealed jar and will be useful for topping up the pickle as the fruit absorbs the syrup during storage. It also makes a good gargle or a toffee if boiled with a little butter.

Chutneys

Pickles demand high quality fruit and vegetables but chutney can make use of damaged and imperfect produce, such as windfall apples and green tomatoes. Any damaged parts must be discarded and decayed, stale ingredients cannot be used. A skeleton recipe yielding 2.3kg. (5lb.) chutney will show how to use up spare fruit:

2kg. (4$\frac{1}{2}$ lb.) of any suitable acid fruit or mixture of fruit and marrow (prepared weight)
500g. (1 lb.) onions
250g. ($\frac{1}{2}$ lb.) dried fruit (optional) sultanas recommended
500g. (1 lb.) sugar or golden syrup; brown sugar for a rich colour, white sugar for a bright colour
10g. ($\frac{1}{3}$oz.) salt
20g. (1oz.) ground spices to taste (cinnamon, ginger, cloves, mace, allspice, etc.); use red spice for ripe tomatoes, i.e. paprika and a pinch of cayenne
500–750ml. (1–1$\frac{1}{2}$pt), brown vinegar; white vinegar for ripe tomato

Enamel, stainless steel or bright aluminium saucepans are recommended.

Peel, chop the onions finely and cook gently in a little water until really tender. In the meantime, prepare the fruit and mince, chop or cut it up roughly. Add it, with most of the vinegar, the salt, dried fruit and spices to the softened onions. Allow to simmer very steadily until cooked down to an even consistency. Stir from time to time with a wooden spoon. Dissolve the sugar in the rest of the vinegar and add to the chutney. Cook fairly briskly until consistency correct. Put a small teaspoonful of chutney on a cold plate and leave to cool. It is ready when it has no liquid running free from the sample. With ripe tomato a little liquid is permissible but apple chutney should stand firm. Fill jars full and cover at once. A vinegar-proof cover which seals well is necessary to prevent loss of quality on storage. Note contents of chutney on label so that it can be repeated.

Old chutney recipes required 3 months or more to mature. Present taste is for a milder flavour which can be ready to eat in a week or so but will improve if given long storage.

When trying an unknown chutney recipe from an old or oriental recipe book it is best to make a small trial batch. If it proves to be too 'hot' it can be toned down by re-boiling with stiff apple pulp and perhaps more sugar and a little extra vinegar.

– *Mild Apple Chutney*
For a yield of 3·5 (8 lb.).
3kg. (6 lb.) prepared apples
1kg. (2 lb.) prepared onions
45g. (1$\frac{1}{2}$oz.) salt
1kg (2 lb.) sugar
1·5 l. (2pt) vinegar

30g. (1oz.) ground ginger
15g. (½oz.) ground cinnamon
Good pinch cayenne pepper
450g. (1 lb.) golden syrup

Peel and chop or mince the onions, check the weight and cook in 250ml. (½pt) water. Peel and core the apples, weigh them, chop finely and add to the onion. When tender, add salt, spices and half the vinegar and continue cooking until thick. Dissolve the sugar in the rest of the vinegar, and add to the chutney. Stir in the syrup. Cook until firm with no free liquid. Pour into jars avoiding air bubbles, seal at once. Ready for use in a week.

– ***Ripe Tomato Chutney***

The good colour of this chutney depends largely on the redness of the tomatoes and is helped by the use of white sugar and white distilled vinegar.

5kg. (11 lb.) ripe red tomatoes
500g. (1 lb.) onions (optional)
700g. (1½ lb.) granulated sugar
500ml. (1pt) distilled spiced vinegar
10g. (¼oz.) paprika
Pinch of cayenne pepper
40g. (1½oz.) salt

Remove the skins of the tomatoes by dipping the fruit into boiling water for ½min. and then into cold water before skinning. Cut the tomatoes in quarters and remove the small pale 'core' at the stalk end as this does not cook down well. Peel and chop or, preferably, mince the onions, if used. Put the tomatoes and onions in a large pan and cook down to a thick pulp. Add half the vinegar and the spices and continue cooking until thick. Finally add the sugar dissolved in the remaining vinegar and cook until the right consistency when a little is cooled on a plate. Remember that ripe tomato chutney will never be quite as firm as apple chutney. Bottle while hot and cover at once.

– ***Green Tomato Chutney***

2kg. (4½ lb.) firm green tomatoes
500g. (1 lb.) apples
250g. (½ lb.) raisins or sultanas
500g. (1 lb.) brown sugar
600ml. (1pt) vinegar
500g. (1 lb.) shallots or onions
6 to 8 chillies
10g. (¼oz.) ground ginger
15g. (½oz.) salt

Cut up the tomatoes – do not attempt to peel them. Peel and cut up the apples and shallots (or onions). Put them all in a saucepan with the vinegar, ground ginger and salt. Chop the raisins, if large; bruise the chillies and tie them loosely in a piece of muslin before adding. Cook all together until thick, stir in the sugar and continue boiling with occasional stirring until the correct consistency. Take out the bag of chillies, pot the chutney and cover at once.

Sauces

Because ripe tomato sauce is more liquid than a similar chutney, there is a risk that it may not keep in storage. To overcome this, the loosely covered bottles of sauce are heated for 30 min. in fast simmering water and then sealed securely. This heat processing is not necessary for sauces made with more acid fruits.

Sauce recipes are similar to those for chutney. In preparation, onions are peeled but the skin is left on apples and tomatoes. Chop the fruit and onions roughly and cook them down with all the remaining ingredients except the sugar. When tender, rub through a nylon or stainless steel sieve, taking care to sieve thoroughly, otherwise a thin sauce will result. Return the pulp to the pan, stir in the sugar and boil gently until a small sample cooled on a plate gives the required consistency – flowing but not too freely. Pour into sauce bottles and seal at once.

– ***Plum Sauce***

A good alternative to commercially prepared savoury sauces.

2kg. (4½ lb.) plums
250g. (½ lb.) onions
125g. (¼ lb.) dried fruit, sultanas or currants
30g. (1oz.) salt
10g. (¼oz.) root ginger
10g. (¼oz.) whole allspice
4 chillies
8 peppercorns
5ml. (1tsp.) mustard
1 l. (2 pt) vinegar

Bruise the whole spices and tie them loosely in a bag. Peel the onions and cut them up with the plums. Put all ingredients except the sugar in a saucepan and cook until tender. Remove the bag of spices and sieve the rest carefully. Return the pulp to the pan, stir in the sugar and simmer gently until consistency correct. Bottle and seal at once. Leave for 4 weeks before use.

– ***Ripe Tomato Sauce***

3kg. (6½ lb.) ripe red tomatoes
250g. (½ lb.) granulated sugar
10g. (½oz.) salt
5ml. (1tsp.) paprika
Pinch of cayenne pepper
300ml. (½pt) distilled spiced vinegar

Slice the tomatoes and cook gently until they are thoroughly softened. Rub them through a nylon or stainless steel sieve and return the pulp to the saucepan with the salt, paprika, cayenne pepper and half the vinegar. Cook until it thickens, then add the sugar dissolved in the rest of the vinegar and continue cooking with occasional stirring until a cooled sample of the sauce has a thick creamy texture. Bottle at once, seal lightly and stand the bottles in simmering water for ½ hour. Remove them and immediately seal securely. This delicious mild sauce does not need maturing before use but it stores well.

Jams and Jellies

The characteristic feature of these delectable preserves is their *set* which gives a spreadable texture, neither too soft, nor too stiff. Set depends on pectin, acid and sugar.

PECTIN is a natural gum-like constituent of the cell walls of fruit and is at its maximum setting quality in slightly under ripe to firm ripe fruit. It is present in an insoluble form in very under ripe fruit and loses its setting power in over ripe fruit so the condition of the produce is critical. The quantity and quality of pectin varies; black currants and apples are good sources whereas strawberries and cherries are weaker. The recipes given later are based on a constant yield for which a constant weight of sugar is used but fruit weight is variable depending on its pectin content. It will be seen that almost twice as many strawberries as black currants are needed to give the same yield of jam. To save money or make more economical use of scarce fruit, a proportion of cooking apples can be used to improve the set. Providing the proportion of apples does not exceed a quarter of the total fruit, the flavour will not be unduly weakened. Another alternative is to add the strained extract from cooked apples or gooseberries, etc. or to use commercially prepared pectin which is on sale at most chemists and grocers. However, jam made entirely from one kind of fruit will naturally have the most character.

ACID is required in conjunction with pectin and sugar and fortunately it is present in the right proportion in most fruits. It is necessary to add some for strawberry jam and a greater quantity for cherry jam. To add acid to 2kg. (4 lb.) fruit, either 2tbsp. of lemon juice or ½ level tsp. of citric acid or tartaric acid can be used. Where pectin and acid are both weak, the addition of 150ml. (¼pt) red currant, gooseberry or apple juice is recommended for 2kg. (4 lb.) fruit.

SUGAR is the major ingredient in jam and jelly and must be in the right proportion to balance the pectin and acid. It is not always realized that low pectin fruits will set less sugar than high pectin ones. A common mistake is to endeavour to correct unset strawberry jam by reboiling it with more sugar. In fact it needs more fruit to balance the sugar already used. As a general guide, in a well balanced recipe the sugar should be approximately 60% of the final yield i.e. 6kg. or 6lb. sugar will give 10kg. or 10 lb. jam. This proportion of sugar together with a good set and correct cover and storage will produce a jam that will store well without mould or fermentation.

Some jams will give a good set with a yield of double the weight of sugar used. The economy of this is attractive but special care is needed in covering and storage. Preserving or granulated sugar can be used for jam-making. For unrefined sugar a slightly increased weight should be used. The resulting preserve may be enjoyed but it is not characteristic of traditional jam. Honey alone is not suitable although it can be used to replace about ⅙ of the sugar.

JAM PAN Although not essential for jam-making a preserving or jam pan is better designed for the job than most saucepans are. There are two types of preserving pan, one is wide and shallow, and the other deep and narrow. Whichever type is preferred it is important to choose a suitable size and a good quality. If the quantity of jam usually made is 5kg. (10 lb.) then the pan should hold 8 l. (15pt). A small pan limits the rate of boiling which wastes time and does not improve the quality of the preserve. Jam pans are made of stainless steel, aluminium or enamel and any of these materials can be recommended if the quality is good. A strong base is essential to prevent burning. Jam pans will last a lifetime and longer, so it is worth making a good purchase. Formerly copper pans were much used and they made preserves of excellent colour but unfortunately much of the Vitamin C (ascorbic acid) in the fruit was lost. Copper pans nowadays feature as ornaments and if there is an urge to return one to its original use, it must be well cleaned with cut lemon and a scourer before making jam in it. With a good quality pan, comparatively little stirring is necessary during jam-making but it is useful to have a long handled wooden spoon with a squared-off bowl, or a long wooden spatula. These prevent the fruit or jam from sticking to the base of the pan much more efficiently than a rounded spoon.

JAM JARS There are two kinds. Those with plain necks should have a fitting disc which is pressed flat on the surface of the jam as soon as it is

Tests for setting: sugar boiling thermometer used in conjunction with plate test.

made or commercial pectin. If no methylated spirit is available, whisky, brandy, etc. can be used instead – and will provide the jam-maker with a bracing nip after the end of the experiment! There is no point in testing for the presence of pectin with fruits of well known setting quality but it is worthwhile for little known fruits or, say, strawberries which are soft. The pectin test must be done before the addition of sugar.

ADDING THE SUGAR

The quicker the jam is made once the sugar is added the better its quality, and, as warmed sugar dissolves rather more quickly than cold sugar, there is a marginal advantage in warming it. However, whether added warm or cold, the sugar should be stirred into the fruit pulp until it is completely dissolved. The addition of the sugar raises the level of the jam but with an adequate sized pan it should still be less than half full. Increase the heat to give a good rolling boil and stir occasionally to prevent burning. With stone fruit, the stones are easy to remove at this stage and they should be lifted out with a perforated spoon or skimmer to avoid wasting the preserve.

TESTS FOR SETTING

With a good reduction in volume before adding the sugar the final boiling should not be long. When the jam begins to make a 'plopping' sound, it is time to test for set. Take a clean, cold plate and on it place 1 tsp. of jam from the pan. Leave in a draughty place to cool and then draw a finger through the jam. If it is ready, a skin will be seen on the surface and the jam will stay parted. In this case remove the pan at once from the heat. If the jam sample is still runny, continue boiling for 3 to 5 minutes and re-test. This is a good test but it is important to do it quickly and therefore the plate must be cold and the sample small and quickly cooled. For those who have a reliable sugar boiling thermometer, the boiling out temperature for jam is 105°C (220°F), and this can be used in conjunction with the plate test.

FINISHING THE JAM

Most jams produce a certain amount of scum which is caused by air and syrup being caught in fruit fibres during turbulent boiling. If there is very little, it can be dispersed into the jam by steady stirring with a wooden spoon and this is helped by the addition of a little butter or margarine, preferably unsalted (about 15g. (½oz.) for 4kg. (8 lb.)). Usually it is removed. To do this, first of all draw as much scum as possible to one side of the pan and lift it off with a metal spoon and then collect the remaining fragments. Scum has a weak flavour, as it is largely air bubbles, but it can be used in steamed puddings, etc. Jam should be skimmed as quickly as possible and then poured into pots without delay. Jam jars must be clean and dry inside. Most people prefer to warm them before pouring in the hot jam, which should come right to the top of the jar. For filling, a 600ml. (1pt) jug with a good pouring lip should enable the operator to fill the jar without a spill and this saves time later when sticky jars have to be washed. The plain-necked jam jars have a fitting disc which should be pressed flat on the surface of the jam as soon as it is potted. The top cover can be put on at the same time but it is usual to add this the next day when the jam has shrunk a little on cooling. One side of the cover should be damped and that side put upwards over the jam pot. Either a rubber band or string can be used to hold the cover in position. When the

Filling clean, dry jam jars, completes the process. (Right) wax discs and elastic bands for sealing the jars.

cover is dry, trim round it neatly with scissors.

Those jam jars with sloping ridges at the neck should have an appropriate twist-top fixed on at once. It is essential to put twist-tops on while the preserve is really hot *i.e.* not less than 90°C (180°F).

Jam jars should be labelled, giving any details about the fruit or method that might be useful later, and stored in a cool, preferably dark place. Ventilation is not necessary in the store for twist-top jars, but those with cellulose or paper covers need a little circulation of air and a relatively dry atmosphere.

– *Apricot Jam*

For a yield of 2.5kg. (5 lb.).

  1.5kg. (3 lb.) fresh apricots

  1.5kg. (3 lb.) sugar

  300ml. (½pt) water

Select firm ripe fruit, wash, drain and cut in half. Put the fruit in the jam pan with the water and heat gently. Crack about 15 stones and take out the kernels. Dip the kernels in boiling water for ½min. to loosen the skins. Add the skinned, halved kernels to the fruit in the pan. Continue the gentle cooking until the fruit is tender and well broken down, and the original level reduced by one third. If doubtful about the quality of the fruit, test for pectin.

Add the sugar and stir until it has dissolved. Increase the heat to give a brisk boil, stirring occasionally to prevent burning. Test for set and when ready, skim, pour into pots and cover at once. A quick boil is recommended for jam once the sugar has been dissolved but with apricots it is wise to reduce the rate of boiling as setting point is reached. Some apricots are rather fibrous and the jam holds a lot of air if boiled very fast. This entrapped foam spoils the appearance of the jam and there is a poor yield if it is all removed as scum.

– *Black Currant Jam*

For a yield of 2.5kg. (5 lb.).

  1kg. (2 lb.) black currants

  1.5kg. (3 lb.) sugar

  1 l. (1 pt) water

Choose good sized fruit, remove stalks and wash the currants if necessary. Put the fruit and water in the jam pan and simmer until the skins are very

potted. Those with sloping ridges at the neck have an appropriate twist-top fixed on at once after the jam is potted.

Either type is satisfactory but in centrally heated homes the twist-top prevents shrinkage of the jam which occurs under the cellulose or paper type of covers. With high yielding jams i.e. where the sugar content is less than 60%, twist-tops are recommended for covering.

Jams

PREPARING AND SOFTENING THE FRUIT

Select the fruit at the right state of ripeness, remove leaves or stalks and discard badly damaged portions and any insects. Frozen fruit can be made into jam without previous thawing. Allow a little extra weight of fruit (about $\frac{1}{10}$ extra) *or* reduce sugar by $\frac{1}{10}$ to offset loss of pectin with frozen blackberries, gooseberries and strawberries. Check the weight of the fruit, whether fresh or frozen. Wash fresh fruit gently if necessary and drain it in a colander. Put the fruit into the jam pan and add acid and water as required. Fresh soft fruits like strawberries, raspberries, etc. do not require any water as the juice will soon flow when gently heated. Frozen soft fruit must be put into a moistened pan to prevent sticking while still frozen. Firmer fruits require water whether fresh or frozen and the quantity is usually indicated in recipes. However, the quantity needed may vary according to the size of the pan and the toughness of the fruit so it is quite safe to use a little extra. This softening of the fruit should be gentle and thorough and, at the end, the quantity in the pan should be reduced to a little over half the original level.

TESTING FOR PECTIN

If there is doubt about the setting quality, the presence of pectin can be checked at this stage. Take 1 tsp. of juice from the jam pan and put it into a little jar or glass. Allow it to cool and add 3 tsp. methylated spirit. Shake the jar gently and leave it for 1 min. Then pour the contents slowly into another jar. If pectin is present a firm clot will have formed; 2 weaker clots indicate less pectin, and if there is no real clotting at all it is a waste of time to continue without adding either extra fruit of good setting quality or some home-

tender. The main fault of this jam is tough skins and to ensure tenderness it is essential to soften them very thoroughly before adding the sugar. The level of fruit in the pan should be reduced by a good third during this process. Add the sugar and stir until it has dissolved. Then boil briskly until setting point is reached. Black currant jam does not usually make scum. If a little butter 12g. ($\frac{1}{2}$oz.) is stirred in the scum will disperse and the quality of the jam will be improved. Pour into jars and cover at once.

– **Black Cherry Jam**

Continental cherry jam is usually made from black cherries.

For a yield of 1.3kg. (3 lb. 4 oz.).

   1kg. (2$\frac{1}{4}$ lb.) black cherries
   juice of 2 lemons
   800g. (2 lb.) sugar

Take ripe, but not over ripe fruit, remove the stones, and save any juice that drips out. Put the prepared fruit and the juice into a bowl and gently stir in the sugar. Cover the bowl and leave for several hours or overnight. Turn the contents of the bowl into a jam pan, add the lemon juice and cook until the syrup is well thickened. Remove the scum, pot and cover. A rather better consistency can be obtained if the stones are placed in a piece of muslin and soaked and cooked with the preserve. Squeeze the bag firmly into the pan just before the jam is finished. This recipe makes a soft setting jam.

– **Plum Jam**

This recipe is suitable for damsons, greengages and plums.

For a yield of 2.5kg. (5 lb.).

   1.5kg. (3 lb.) fruit
   1.5kg. (3 lb.) sugar
   300ml to 1 l. ($\frac{1}{2}$ to 1$\frac{1}{2}$pt) water

Choose firm ripe fruit and wash if necessary. Cut out any bruises. Large plums can be cut in half to hasten the softening process but this is not necessary. Put the fruit in the jam pan with water regulating the quantity according to the firmness of the fruit. It is better to use too much water as the excess can be boiled off, rather than too little with the risk of tough fruit or a burnt pan. When the fruit has simmered until pulped and the quantity has reduced by one third, add the sugar and stir until it is dissolved. Increase the heat and boil jam briskly, removing the stones with a perforated spoon. Test for set and when ready, skim, pour into pots and cover at once.

– **Raspberry Jam**

This recipe is also suitable for loganberry jam.

For a yield of 2.5kg. (5 lb.).

   1.5kg. (3 lb.) fruit
   1.5kg. (3 lb.) sugar

Select ripe, but not over ripe fruit. Look it over to remove leaves, stalks, spoilt fruit and maggots. Put the fruit in the jam pan and heat gently until the juice runs. Allow to reduce a little, add the sugar, stir until it is dissolved and then boil briskly until the setting point is reached. With a good quality fruit 1.25kg. will be sufficient to set 1.5kg. sugar and in this case the final boiling time will be only 4 to 5 min. Skim, pour into pots and cover at once.

– **Strawberry Jam**

   1.75kg. (3$\frac{1}{2}$ lb.) prepared strawberries
   1.5kg (3 lb.) sugar
   40ml. lemon juice (1 lemon)

Select firm, red fruit and wash quickly if necessary. Remove the hulls and check the weight

before putting the fruit into the jam pan. Large fruit may be cut in half to shorten the cooking time. Add the lemon juice and cook gently until the fruit is broken and reduced. Stir in the sugar and boil steadily until the setting point is reached. Remove the scum and allow the jam to cool for 10 min., then pour into unheated jars and cover. During the short pause before potting the jam cools slightly and becomes less fluid so that the pieces of fruit are held evenly in suspension when the jam is potted.

– **Strawberry Conserve**

   Equal weight of hulled strawberries and granulated sugar.

Layer the prepared strawberries in a bowl with *half* the sugar and leave for 12 to 24 hr. Put the fruit and syrup into the jam pan and boil gently for 20min., stir in the rest of the sugar and boil until the setting point is reached. Remove the scum and leave 10 min. before potting, then cover at once. A conserve contains whole fruit in thick syrup but does not have a jam-like set.

Jellies

Jams contain fruit, whereas jellies are made from the strained fruit extract. Because of this more fruit is required to produce a given quantity of jelly than would be needed to make the same weight of jam. When fruit has to be purchased, jelly making can be expensive, but many wild fruits are suitable such as blackberries, crab apples and rowanberries. The fruit must have good setting quality and, of cultivated fruits, black and red currants, damsons and gooseberries are recommended.

PREPARING AND SOFTENING THE FRUIT

The condition of the fruit must be slightly under ripe to just ripe, as for jam. The preparation is similar except that for jelly-making there is no need to remove all the stalks on currants or to 'top and tail' gooseberries. Water is added to the fruit which is softened by gentle simmering and occasional pressing with a wooden spoon or vegetable presser.

TESTING FOR PECTIN

When the fruit is well cooked down it is wise to take a pectin test (p. 184) before straining. If the resulting clot is weak, the fruit can be simmered for a little longer and then re-tested, or some cooking apple can be cooked down and added to the fruit. The addition of prepared apple in the proportion of a quarter of the weight of the original fruit will usually give sufficient pectin to make a satisfactory clot.

STRAINING FOR EXTRACT

Sparkling clarity is a characteristic of a well-made, light-coloured jelly. The material used for straining the extract affects clarity and felt or flannel gives a better result than linen or muslin. A suspended bag is traditionally used for straining but a piece of material securely tied to the legs of an upturned stool makes an adequate substitute. Place a bowl under the bag or cloth and pour hot water through the material to make it damp. This is important as fruit juice does not drip readily through dry cloth. Empty the bowl, replace it and then pour the contents of the jam pan into the cloth and leave it to drip for 45 to 60min. Resist any impulse to squeeze or press the cloth as pressure spoils clarity.

   With very good setting fruit, such as black currants, it is possible to make a second extraction. After the fruit has dripped for about 15min.

Straining for extract through material securely tied to the legs of an upturned chair.

the pulp is returned to the jam pan with half the original quantity of water, simmered for about 30min. and then re-strained. The 2 extracts can be made up separately but it is usually more satisfactory to mix them.

ADDING THE SUGAR

Measure the extract and return it to the jam pan; if the quantity is small, to a clean saucepan.

   Calculate the sugar required as follows:

	Sugar per l. extract	Sugar per pt extract
Very strong clot	1kg.	1$\frac{1}{4}$ lb.
Good average clot	800g.	1 lb.
Fair clot	600g.	$\frac{3}{4}$ lb.

For most jellies the quantity of sugar used is for a good average clot. With fruit such as black and red currants which are rich in pectin, a bigger yield and better texture is achieved by using the higher proportion of sugar recommended for a very strong clot. Blackberries may give a less firm pectin clot in which case the quantity of sugar for a fair clot will produce a good quality jelly. As a general guide the thicker the consistency of the extract the better is its setting power.

   Heat the extract, add the appropriate quantity of sugar and when it has dissolved, allow the jelly to boil steadily until setting point is reached. A very fast boil may spoil the clarity of the final jelly.

TESTS FOR SETTING

The tests given for jam can be used. It is essential to work quickly as jelly can begin to set in the pan if there is a delay. Draw the pan off the heat while testing for set.

FINISHING THE JELLY

Remove all scum and pour the jelly gently into pots to avoid trapping air bubbles. Cover and leave the jars undisturbed for 24hr. Label and store as for jam.

   It is traditional to use straight-sided jars for jelly but this is not necessary. However jars of 225g. ($\frac{1}{2}$ lb.) capacity are recommended. Jelly tends to liquify once it has been opened and therefore there is less risk of this with small jars which are used up quickly.

– *Apple Jelly*

Select cooking or crab apples with a good flavour. Windfall or damaged apples can be used providing the diseased or bruised parts are discarded. Cut up the apples but do not remove peel or cores. Put the fruit into the jam pan with just enough water to cover and simmer until tender. Test for pectin (p. 184) and if the resulting clot is satisfactory, strain the juice through a scalded cloth. Leave for 1hr to drip, then measure the juice; allow 800g. of granulated sugar per litre (1 lb. per pt). Return the extract to the jam pan and boil it for 5min. Stir in the sugar until it is dissolved and then boil steadily until setting point is reached. Quickly remove scum and pour the jelly gently into small jars, cover and leave for 24hr before moving it. Label and store as for jam.

If the apples lack flavour, the jelly can be made interesting by adding thinly peeled lemon rind, mint leaves, a few cloves or a small piece of root ginger or cinnamon stick. Whichever of these flavourings is used, it should be put in with the fruit at the beginning.

– *Blackberry Jelly*

3kg. (7 lb.) blackberries
sugar
Juice of 3 lemons
900ml. (1½pt) water

If using wild fruit, avoid any from dusty roadsides. Choose firm ripe fruit and wash it quickly if necessary. Put it into the jam pan with the water and lemon juice and let it simmer until tender. When soft and well cooked down, take a pectin test – if the clot is reasonably good, strain the juice through a scalded cloth. After 1hr measure the juice, return it to the pan and let it boil for 5 to 10min. before adding the sugar allowing 600 to 800g. per litre (½ to 1 lb. per pt), according to the strength of the pectin clot. Stir until the sugar has dissolved, then let the jelly boil steadily until setting point is reached. Continue as for apple jelly above.

If the blackberries are ripe, a better set will be produced by using 2kg. (4½ lb.), berries and 1kg (2¼ lb.) prepared apple and omitting the lemon juice.

– *Red Currant Jelly*

This jelly is usually served with meat and game. It should be well-flavoured, a deep ruby red colour and firm in set. Ideally it can be made of neat red currant juice but the jelly sets very quickly and can present difficulties to the inexperienced.

For 2kg. (4½ lb.) red currants it is advisable to simmer the fruit in 1 litre (1½ pt) of water before straining and proceeding as for blackberry jelly. The pectin clot should be firm, indicating that 800g. to 1kg. sugar can be added per litre of extract. If more than 800g. of sugar is added per litre (1 lb. per pt) do not boil the extract before putting in the sugar.

Where there is a surplus of white currants, they can be added to red currants when jelly-making. A jelly made entirely of white currants has a pleasant sharp flavour but its fawn colour is unattractive. Mixed with red currants the resultant colour is bright.

Fruit Syrups

Fruit syrups have a double advantage as they add glamour to plain desserts and are economical because they make use of fruit too ripe for other uses. Black currant syrup is well known for its ascorbic acid (vitamin C) content but black-

berries, loganberries, raspberries and strawberries make delicious syrups too.

There are many ways of making syrups but the following method is recommended for home use. In jam-making the natural pectin in firm fruit is needed to produce a good consistency but with syrups pectin is not required. Therefore it is important to use fully ripe fruit which will release its juice readily without any risk of setting. Dirty, stale or mouldy fruit must be discarded but otherwise the riper the fruit the better for syrup-making. It is hardly worth making syrup with less than 450g. (1 lb.) fruit.

Put the fruit in a heat-resistant bowl that will fit comfortably over a saucepan. Press the fruit with a vegetable presser, if available, or a wooden spoon. For blackberries add 300ml. (½pt) water to 2.3kg. (5 lb.) fruit and for black currants add 600ml. (1pt) water per 900g. (2 lb.) fruit. Half fill the saucepan with water and place the bowl on top. Heat the water to a gentle boil and leave until the fruit juice is running freely, pressing the fruit from time to time. The heating will take about 1 hr for 1.8 to 2.7kg. (4 to 6 lb.) fruit. If black currant skins are very firm, the fruit and water can be heated directly in a saucepan, stirring all the time, and allowed to boil for 1min. only. The gentle heating over boiling water preserves the fresh flavour better than direct heat. Other methods for extracting the juice are with an electrical juice-extractor or in a steamer made specially for the purpose.

When the juice is flowing, the fruit must be strained through a scalded bag as for jelly. Unless a very clear syrup is desired, a linen cloth can be used for straining and it can be pressed or squeezed lightly to give the maximum yield of juice. Measure the juice and add 600g. sugar per litre (12oz. per pt). Preferably stir in the sugar without heating the juice, but if heating is necessary keep it to the minimum to avoid a cooked flavour. The quantity of sugar may seem excessive but it strengthens the fruit flavour so that syrups can be diluted with 4 parts of water, etc. when used. If only a little sugar is added, the resulting product would have to be used un-diluted. Once the sugar has dissolved the syrup is ready for use; but to preserve it, it must either be frozen, in for example the ice cube tray and the cubes subsequently bagged for use as required, or bottled. Clean non-returnable mineral water bottles are a suitable size and type for bottling syrup which should be poured in leaving a 3 to 4cm. (1 to 1½in.) head-space. Screw the caps *loosely* on the bottles and stand them in a deep saucepan of water. A pan with a false bottom is ideal but several layers of newspaper will make a good substitute. It is recommended to support the bottles with 'collars' of newspaper to prevent them from falling over. The water should come to the level of the bottle tops. Put a lid on the saucepan and heat the water to simmering 88°C (190°F) and hold for 20min. Remove the bottles and immediately tighten the screw caps. When cool, label the bottles and keep in a cool, dark store.

Syrups can be drunk diluted 1 part to 4 parts water, soda water or other minerals. When making milk shakes, add the syrup slowly to the cold milk, stirring or whisking all the time. Syrups are delicious neat on ice cream, junket, milk puddings and steamed puddings. They can be used with or without wine to soak trifle sponge

cakes, to enrich fruit salads or diluted to mix with arrowroot or gelatine to glaze fruit flans.

Continental *sirop* is a sweeter product in which the added sugar is sufficient to preserve the syrup without heat processing.

Fruit Flavoured Vinegars

These link with syrups as they also require very ripe fruit and the kinds of fruit used are the same. Steep 500g. (1 lb.) fruit in 700ml. (1pt) vinegar for 3 to 5 days, stirring and pressing occasionally. Malt vinegar is generally used, but for a bright fruit vinegar, such as raspberry, distilled vinegar may be preferred. It is important to cover the bowl of fruit as flies are much attracted. After steeping, strain and measure the extract. Put it into a saucepan and add 800g. granulated sugar to each litre of extract (1 lb. sugar to 1pt extract). Stir to dissolve the sugar, then boil for 10 min. Pour into bottles as for syrup and screw on the caps firmly. No further processing is necessary.

The traditional uses for fruit vinegar were as a gargle to ease a sore throat or as an accompaniment for 'boiled batter' a steamed pudding now rarely served. Modern interest in 'sweet-sour' dishes gives a new scope for these fragrant piquant vinegars which enhance pork, bacon and many savoury dishes.

Salting Vegetables

Salt has been used for preservation for over 2000 years but mainly for meat. Here are 2 old fashioned but still useful recipes for salting vegetables.

– *Beans*

Runner and French beans can be used but they must be young and fresh. Small French beans can be left whole but larger beans should be sliced. Runner beans are always sliced. A large jar of glass, stoneware or earthenware makes a useful container. The proportion of salt is 350g. (1 lb.) salt to 1kg. (3 lb.) beans. Table salt should not be used but either vacuum pack kitchen salt or block salt is suitable. Although absolutely accurate weighing is unnecessary, it is important to keep to the right proportions. First place a layer of salt in the bottom of the container, then a layer of prepared beans and another layer of salt and so on, always finishing with a layer of salt. Put a cover on the container and leave it for 1 or 2 days, by which time brine will have formed and the level will have dropped, so that more beans and salt can be added. When the jar is really filled, put on a permanent cover. A double layer of poly-thene tied on will suffice. Plastic lids, glass stoppers and corks are excellent but a metal cover

Salting beans: alternate layers of salt and beans packed in jars.

will become corroded. Earthenware jars should be stood on wooden or plastic boards – not on a concrete floor. To use the beans, take out the quantity required, and, if the level of the brine does not cover the remaining beans, put in enough salt to cover them. Replace the lid. Put the beans in a colander in a bowl of water and wash them very thoroughly with several changes of water. Finally soak them for 2 hr in warm water and cook them in unsalted boiling water until tender, which will be 20 to 30 min. Overnight soaking is not recommended.

Provided young and fresh beans are used the final product will be very acceptable and this method enables those without freezers to avoid waste.

Dry salting is not used for other vegetables.

– Sauerkraut

Where there is a surplus of cabbages, sauerkraut is well worth making, but before embarking on the recipe, it is advisable to ensure that suitable equipment and premises are available. A fairly large bowl or tub must be kept at a temperature of 20° to 27°C (70° to 80°F) for 2 to 3 weeks while the cabbage ferments and this process might not be popular in, for example, the family airing cupboard.

Finely shred the fresh cabbage hearts and mix with salt using 30g. (1oz.) per 1kg. (2 lb.) cabbage. Pack the salted shreds firmly in a sufficiently large tub or container, spread a clean cloth over the top and add a lid which fits inside the container. Put a clean brick or stone on the lid to hold it down to exclude the air. Keep the container at the recommended temperature so that fermentation proceeds steadily. In 2 to 3 days, the brine should cover the lid. Remove the scum from the brine every few days, and, if the level of brine drops, add freshly made brine using 25g. (1oz.) salt to 1 litre (2pt.) water. After 2 to 3 weeks the sauerkraut is ready for use. To preserve it, strain the brine and bring it to the boil. Add the cabbage and, when simmering, pour it into bottling jars. Adjust lids loosely, stand jars in a false-bottomed pan containing hot water. Bring to the boil, boil for 25 min., remove jars and seal lids securely at once. Allow to cool, then label and store.

Drying Fruit, Vegetables and Herbs

Today there are many sophisticated dehydrated foods on the market but the drying technique is simple and has been practised for centuries.

– Fruits

Apples, pears, plums and grapes are all suitable for drying. Sound apples can be stored, but windfall apples have a limited life unless preserved, and when there is a glut, drying is an easy method of coping with quantities. Fruit should be in good ripe condition and a dark fleshy cultivar of plum is recommended. Wash the fruit quickly if necessary. Peel apples, remove the core with an apple corer and cut the fruit into rings 0.5 to 1cm. (¼in.) thick; discard any blemished parts. Peel pears, remove core and cut into 4 or 8 pieces. Immediately put prepared apple or pear pieces into salted water, 10g. (¼oz.) salt per litre (pt) water and leave for about 10min., then shake well before drying. Spread the fruit on clean muslin over mesh trays such as cake coolers. It is essential for air to circulate all round the fruit so avoid packing it too closely. Apple rings should be strung on clean canes or sticks and hung in a

suitable place. String is not recommended, as it sags and the apple rings slide together leaving no space between them. Hold the fruit in a gentle temperature of 50°C (120°F) which can be allowed to rise to 60°F (140°F) as drying proceeds. It is particularly important to heat plums and grapes gently at first as they may burst if the process is hurried. Once they are drying well, the heat can rise to 65°C (150°F). When drying apple rings under ideal conditions, they should be ready in about 5hr but plums will take double this time

Apple rings strung on cane.

or more, and with intermittent drying the process is slower. To test apple or pear, squeeze 4 or 5 pieces in the hand, release the grip, and, if ready, the individual pieces will spring apart. Continue the drying process if they still cling together. Dried apple feels very much like chamois leather. A correctly dried plum will not exude juice when squeezed, and a grape will resemble a raisin. To store dried fruit, leave it at room temperature for 12hr and then pack in boxes lined with waxed paper. Empty cereal cartons are very suitable. On no account put dried fruit in sealed containers as it may become mouldy.

To use dried fruit, soak it in ample water for 24hr or longer, then gently heat it in the same water until it is plump and tender. Add sweetening when cooking is nearly complete, since sugar added earlier can harden the fruit. Dried grapes are generally used as raisins and therefore need no soaking but remember to remove the pips.

– Vegetables

Although many vegetables can be dried, probably only two are worthwhile today, onions and field mushrooms. For those who wish to dry marrowfat peas or beans of the haricot type, it is important to select the right cultivars and these will be found in the lists published by seed merchants specializing in vegetables. The vines can be uprooted when the crop is ready, hung up in bundles to dry and the peas or beans podded in the autumn for storage. It is important to hang the vines in a place inaccessible to mice.

Drying usefully prolongs the life of onions that will not store well. Remove the outer skin and slice the onions about ·5cm. (¼in.) thick. Plunge the slices into boiling water for ½min., drain and spread on a muslin covered rack in a temperature of 50°C (120°F) rising as drying proceeds to 70°C (160°F). The pieces of onion must be dried until crisp, then left at room temperature for up to a day before packing into jars with tight fitting lids. A tablespoon of dried onion can replace a medium size fresh onion in stews and casseroles and there is no need to soak it before use as it will soften during the long cooking.

Cultivated mushrooms are always available but field mushrooms have a short season. They are tender and well flavoured so it is well worthwhile to dry some when they are plentiful in autumn. They must be freshly picked, peeled, if necessary, and the stalks removed. They can be dried on trays as for onions or threaded with a

coarse needle on to fine string with a knot to hold each cap in place. The string can be tied above a cooker or other warm place. The heat should not exceed 50°C (120°F) and drying must continue until the mushroom is shrunken and crisp. Allow to stand at room temperature for a day and then pack into containers with close fitting lids. Dried mushrooms are usually put into stews or soup but if they are to be served with a grill, they must be soaked for 24hr, drained and sautéed in butter in a covered pan.

Mushroom caps held in place on strings by knots.

– Herbs

These are the most usual dried preserve to find at home although nowadays freezing is sometimes preferred.

Herbs should be picked just before flowering. Early morning gathering ensures that the leaves are fresh and not wilted by a day's heat.

SMALL-LEAVED HERBS

Plants such as thyme are picked and tied into bunches, quickly washed and inverted to dry in a warm place. If there is dust, a collar of clean paper will keep the leaves clean. When they are crisply dry, they can be rubbed off the stalk.

LARGE LEAVED HERBS

The leaves of mint for example are removed from the stalk and dried on a muslin covered rack in a warm place. Drying takes from 1 to 4hr depending on the heat. It will be noticed that herbs treated this way become very yellow on storage. The green colour can be deepened and retained by dipping the leaves into boiling water for ½ to 1min. The leaves are then drained and, after this preliminary treatment, they are dried in a warm place until crisp.

When herbs have been dried they are usually crushed with a rolling pin or sieved. Mint to be used for mint sauce can be left fairly coarse but herbs required for omelette seasoning should be much finer. Parsley is rather a special case as its green colour is important when used for garnishing or in sauce. A half-minute dip in boiling water darkens the green but fixes it. To retain the natural lighter green colour the sprigs can be put into an oven at 200°C (400°F) for just 1min. and then dried off until crisp at lower heat.

All dried herbs should be stored in securely sealed jars. Small quantities are recommended and jars should be well packed. A loose, half-filled pack soon loses its fresh aroma. Dark glass or metal containers help to retain the herb's colour. Label clearly and store in a cool place.

Dried herbs are not usually soaked before use as the small fragments loose their crispness in cooking.

Cooking

Vegetable Cookery

Good vegetable cookery depends as much on the prime quality of the produce as on the skill of the cook. Nevertheless, poor cookery can ruin the best of food. Economically-minded gardeners have a tendency to let some vegetables become over-mature before they are used and this is particularly the case with peas and beans: French, broad and runner. It is better to lose a little in yield to gain much in quality. When a vegetable is ready for use, it should be gathered, prepared and cooked (or frozen) without delay. If it cannot be used at once, the produce should be kept cool and lightly covered to prevent wilting. The salad crisper or vegetable compartment in a refrigerator maintains vegetable quality for a few days or alternatively a clean, capacious polythene bag can be used but it should not be sealed. However the fresher the vegetable, the better its quality both for palatability and nutritionally, so from plot to pot is a good rule.

WASHING

Leafy green vegetables need careful washing in cold water. This is most conveniently done after removing the coarse and damaged outer leaves and thick stalks. If 5 to 10ml. (1 to 2tsp.) of salt is added to 600ml. (1pt) water the weak brine will help to draw out any insects present. If too much salt is added, insects will be killed in the heart of the vegetable and may not be detected. Vegetables should not be left in soak for more than 20 to 30min. as soluble nutrients begin to diffuse and the plant's texture softens. Drain vegetables in a colander or strainer before cooking.

Earthy root vegetables, celery, etc. should be scrubbed with a brush and then thoroughly rinsed in cold water before peeling or other preparation. Peas and beans and sweet corn grown at home require washing only if they are soiled.

Vegetables can be cooked by a variety of methods, to make a main dish or to accompany other food. There are many cookery books devoted to the subject from *haute cuisine* to cottage economy. The main cooking processes are outlined first and later potatoes are dealt with in more detail because of their universality, popularity and versatility.

Boiling Vegetables

This is the traditional English way of cooking vegetables. In former years, they were cooked awash in water with a pinch of bicarbonate of soda and the final product was often a tired mound of unearthly green. Nowadays, colour, texture and nutritional value are improved by cooking in a closed pan with as little salted water as is necessary to prevent them from burning. Cooking times are shorter and, for most vegetables, they are served with a little crispness in the texture.

PREPARATION

Leafy vegetables are often shredded before cooking but cabbage can be cooked in sections, if preferred. A cross-cut in the end of brussels sprouts stalks and a wedge removed from cauliflower stems will enable heat to penetrate evenly. Cauliflower can, of course, be divided into sprigs for quick cooking. Root vegetables can be cooked whole and this is necessary with beetroot to prevent colour loss, but for quicker cooking and fuel economy, carrots, turnips, swedes are often diced or sliced. Parsnips are usually cooked whole: they are delicious if parboiled for 5 to

10min. and then finished in the oven round a joint of beef. Sliced runner beans and broad beans need about a teacupful of water per 450g. (1 lb.), but petits pois require half that quantity, sliced marrow, about 2tbsp., and washed spinach none at all as the water already on it will suffice.

COOKING

Take a saucepan of suitable size to hold the vegetable comfortably and add the required quantity of salted water, 5ml. (1tsp.) of salt per 600ml. (1pt) water. It is usual to add 1tsp. of sugar when cooking peas, 1tbsp. of vinegar for red cabbage, and a sliver of bacon for broad beans. Beetroot may need 600ml. of water per 450g. (1pt per lb.). Place the lid on the saucepan and bring the water to the boil. Quickly add the vegetables, replace the lid and, when the water reboils, reduce the heat to maintain a steady boil, not a gallop. Cooking times are short: peas about 3min.; shredded cabbage 4 to 8min. depending on thickness of shreds and degree of crispness required, young marrow 8 to 10min., runner, French and broad beans about 10min., diced roots 10 to 15min. Whole beetroot will take from 40min. for young, medium size ones to 1½hr for old stored beets. Overcooking ruins vegetables and it is a good idea to set the timer on the cooker as a reminder. Always test whether the vegetables are done before dishing up. Strain through a colander, reserving the water for use in gravy or sauce, and then finish the vegetable as required. Tossing in melted butter is a quick method but a sauce is traditional for marrow, broad beans or cauliflower.

A few vegetables merit special note. For cauliflower, more cooking water should be used and the curd should be placed in the boiling water for the first 5min. and then reversed so that the stalk-end cooks evenly. The whiteness of the curd is preserved by the initial 'blanching'. When it is just cooked turn the cauliflower straight into a colander to drain and then straight into the serving dish. This will ensure the cauliflower being right side up for coating with sauce. Asparagus should be tied into bundles of uniform thickness so that the thicker stalks can have a longer cooking time. In the absence of special equipment for cooking asparagus, the bundles can be stood in a jug in a deep saucepan with a lid. Boiling water should cover the stalks and the heads will cook more gently in steam. Untie the bundles and serve on toast with melted butter or Hollandaise sauce served separately. After preparation, globe artichokes should be gently bound with twine to keep them in shape during cooking. Test by pulling off a leaf after about 45min. Remove the twine and carefully pull out the choke (the centre leaves). Make sure that none of it is left. Serve hot with separate melted butter, or cold with French dressing or vinaigrette, some of which can be poured into the cavity of the choke. Sweet corn should be cooked in unsalted water. Courgettes can be boiled but are better if blanched in boiling water for about 3 to 5min. and then finished by cooking gently in butter in a closed saucepan or casserole.

Baking Vegetables

Leafy green vegetables do not lend themselves to baking but most other vegetables can be cooked in the oven and this can be economical. Potatoes cooked in the oven are a commonplace but it is not always realized that beetroot and onions can

be baked in their skins in a moderate oven. Prepared root vegetables, cut into pieces, or sliced marrow can be cooked in the oven in hot fat. A mixture of vegetables, roots, celery, beans, peas can be cooked in a casserole in a moderate oven. Put 3 to 4 tbsp. of water in the casserole, add the vegetables and some fat. Season well and cover with the lid. Cook in a moderate oven. Root vegetables, unless very young, will be improved by blanching in boiling water for 2min. before casseroling in the oven. Peas will be ready in about 20min., beans about 25 to 30min. and roots about an hour. Leeks are usually boiled but casserole well.

Frying Vegetables

Very few vegetables, apart from potatoes, are fried. The main exceptions are onion rings, mushrooms and tomatoes and the 2 last are more often grilled. However, a very wide range can be cooked in a sauté pan with very tasty results. Apart from the usual vegetables, courgettes, aubergines and celeriac sauté well. Green vegetables are unattractive. Use a strong pan with a closely fitting lid. Heat sufficient fat to cover the base of the pan and add the prepared vegetables and seasoning. Put the lid on the saucepan, lower the heat and let cooking proceed gently. From time to time, grasp the handle of the pan in one hand and the lid in the other, and shake the contents gently but thoroughly. The vegetables tend to shrink considerably so an ample quantity should be prepared initially. When cooked, the vegetables will not deteriorate if there is a delay in serving. Serve with the liquid that will have collected in the saucepan. Mixtures of vegetables prepared this way can be very attractive as, for example, ratatouille which is a mixture of aubergine, courgette, tomatoes, and a little green pepper cooked gently in fat with sliced pre-fried onion and seasoning. A recipe like this leads on to vegetable innovations depending on the crops available.

Salads

In this brief review of methods of cooking vegetables, much has necessarily been curtailed but, in conclusion, it must be remembered that the most nutritious, the simplest and, perhaps, the most attractive way to serve vegetables is in a salad. Lettuce, cress, cucumber, radish, spring onions, celery, beetroot and tomatoes are familiar. It is not always remembered that cooked vegetables and many raw grated roots can add considerable interest. Jerusalem artichoke discolours quickly but a little grated on a mixed salad immediately before serving gives a delicious nutty flavour. The mock capers which are the fruit of the nasturtium will give a fiery touch. The scope for extending family menus is wide.

Potato Recipes
New Boiled Potatoes

Select a well-matched sample to ensure uniform cooking. Scrape off the skins, wash the potatoes and put them into a lidded saucepan containing sufficient boiling water to cover them. Add salt to taste, usually 5ml. (1tsp.) per 600ml. (1pt) water. Boil gently until tender, usually about 20min. A fine skewer can be used to test whether they are tender. Drain off the water and replace the pan over low heat to dry the potatoes. It is customary to add a sprig of mint to new potatoes and the best fresh flavour is obtained if this is added for the last 5min. of the cooking time or put into the pan for the drying period. It is removed before serving. Toss the potatoes in melted butter with some finely chopped parsley and serve.

New potatoes can be lightly scrubbed and cooked in their skins. Skins are easily rubbed off after cooking – or can be left on and eaten.

– Old Boiled Potatoes

Peel the potatoes finely, remove any blemishes and, if necessary cut to even size pieces. Put into cold, salted water to cover and boil gently with the lid on the pan. Fast boiling will break down most potatoes and give a wet, mushy result. When tender, drain off the cooking water and retain it for gravy making. Replace the pan on the heat to dry off the potatoes. The lid should be left on the pan at an angle to let the steam escape. Alternatively a clean cloth can be put in the pan under the closed lid and this will absorb the steam and give a good floury finish to the potatoes. Toss the potatoes in butter and serve garnished with small sprigs of parsley. As with new potatoes, old ones can be scrubbed and boiled in their skins which can be left on or removed before serving – an easy but finger-burning process.

– Mashed Potatoes

Take hot, floury cooked potatoes and mash them well with a fork or masher. Add a little milk (2 to 4 tbsp. per 450g. or 1 lb.) and beat well. Warmed milk gives a better result than cold. Also beat in extra seasoning and, perhaps, a little ground mace. When smooth add a nut of butter or some thick cream and give a final beat before piling the potatoes into the hot serving dish. Mark lines from the peak of the pile downwards with a fork, garnish with a little parsley and serve.

– Potato Croquettes

These can be prepared from hot mashed potato (as above) omitting the milk and adding 1 egg yolk to 450g. (1 lb.) potatoes. Spread the mixture on a damp plate and, when quite cold, cut into portions and shape as required on a lightly floured board. Dip the portions in beaten egg and then in breadcrumbs and fry, preferably in deep fat, until golden brown. Drain well and serve on a dish paper. If a shallow fat is used, the croquettes must be turned for even browning.

– Jacket Potatoes

Allow 1 good size potato per person, avoiding those with blemishes. Scrub each potato thoroughly and make a cut along one side. Rub each potato with a buttery paper and sprinkle lightly with salt, if liked. Each potato can be wrapped in foil if a soft skin is required. Put the potatoes on a central oven rack and cook in a moderate heat for 1 to 2 hr depending on the size of the potatoes. A small metal stand on which 4 potatoes can be impaled during cooking reduces cooking time somewhat. Immediately before serving, press the potato gently to expel the steam through the cut made originally. This makes the potato floury. Insert a small nut of butter into the slit and serve at once. The whole potato should be eaten.

– Roast Potatoes

Peel old potatoes and cut into even size pieces about 6cm. (2½ in.) across. Put into boiling salted water and cook for 5min. Strain the potatoes into a colander and rinse them under the cold tap. They will dry quickly because they are hot. Cook at 180°C (350°F), Gas 4, either round the joint or in a separate, previously heated container with 1cm. (½in.) of cooking oil, lard or dripping. After 45min. turn the potatoes and if they lack colour

increase the heat to 220°C (425°F), Gas 7 for a final 30min. To serve, drain on clean absorbent paper, sprinkle with salt and serve in an open dish as a lid makes the potatoes soft. To get a crusty surface the potatoes can be lightly dredged with flour before roasting.

– Sauté Potatoes

Choose waxy potatoes, peel and dry them and slice thinly. Put the slices into a frying basket – not too many at a time – and fry in oil at 170°C (340°F) for 4 to 5 min. Shake the basket from time to time to keep the slices separate. When they begin to rise, lift up the basket, reheat the oil to 195°C (390°F) and return the basket to the pan. The slices should puff up but do not remove them until they are golden brown. Drain quickly, sprinkle with salt and serve.

– Creamed Potatoes

This homely dish can be made from raw or cooked sliced potatoes. Butter an ovenproof dish and fill with layers of potato, adding salt and pepper to each layer. Avoid packing too solidly as milk has to be added, about 200ml. (⅓pt) per 450g. potatoes. Put small flakes of butter or margarine over the top layer and bake uncovered in a moderate oven for ¾ to 1hr for cooked potatoes, or 1½hr if raw. Serve from the dish. Mace, nutmeg, curry powder, horseradish, chopped parsley or grated onion can be added.

– Chipped Potatoes

Choose a suitable cultivar (see table), peel and cut into chips, 5 to 8cm. (2 to 3in.) long and about 1cm. (½in.) in section. Soak the chips in cold water for up to 1hr if possible, drain and dry thoroughly on a clean cloth or kitchen tissue. Put the chips into a frying basket and fry in oil or fat at 170°C (340°F). Lower the basket gently into the hot fat as there can be considerable frothing and shake the basket during cooking which should continue until the chips look pearly or translucent but they should not colour. Take out the basket and, at this stage, the chips can be left for several hours. Reheat the fat to 190° to 195°C (380° to 390°F) and continue frying the chips until they are golden brown. Drain, sprinkle with salt and serve.

Fat can overheat and ignite so it is wise to have a heavy cloth to clamp over the flames. Never carry a burning pan, smother the fire where it is.

– Potato Salad

Choose a suitable cultivar (see table), peel or scrape, and boil in salted water taking care not to overcook. While still warm, dice the potatoes and mix with French dressing and grated onion or chopped chives. Scatter with chopped parsley and serve at once or when quite cold. If the salad is to be made from cold cooked potatoes, dice them and heat them in a bowl over boiling water, adding the other ingredients when heated. Cold potatoes do not absorb the dressing and the result is uninteresting.

Some recommended potato cultivars

METHOD OF COOKING	RECOMMENDED CULTIVARS	
	Early (May to August)	Maincrop (August to May)
Boiling	Maris Peer Arran Pilot	King Edward Maris Piper Pentland Hawk Pentland Crown Majestic
Mashed Croquettes Creamed (oven)		As above
Baked in jacket		King Edward Desirée Majestic
Roast with meat		Desirée Maris Piper King Edward
Chipped Sauté	Red Craigs Royal Maris Peer Ulster Sceptre	Majestic Maris Piper Desirée
Salad	Maris Peer Red Craigs Royal Arran Pilot	August to December Maris Piper Pentland Crown January onwards Pentland Ivory Pentland Hawk

These cultivars are selected from a list produced by the Potato Marketing Board, 50 Hans Crescent, Knightsbridge, London SW1X 0NB.

Fruit Cookery

Fresh dessert fruit is a general favourite but at times some different form is required and many typical old English puddings derive their character from fruit as do many of the lighter desserts which are now more in favour.

The range of fruits suitable for cookery is wide but it is useful to remember that, when a particular fruit is in short supply, up to one quarter of the required weight can be replaced by rhubarb. This humble, so-called fruit has pleasant qualities of its own but it can also be used to add bulk to other fruits without overriding their flavour. With vegetables, potatoes tend to dominate the scene and in the same way apples have pride of place with fruit because of their availability, choice of cultivar and keeping qualities.

Most fruit dishes belong to the dessert course but apples are equally at home with savoury dishes, particularly pork, curry and cheese. An outline of fruit cookery methods follows and further recipes can be found in general cookery books and those dealing specifically with fruit of which there are many.

– Stewed Fruit
This represents the simplest form of cooking and sadly it is unlikely to rouse a surge of enthusiasm. This need not be so if it is made as a compôte in which the shape of the fruit is better retained.

First of all make a syrup by adding 125g. (4oz.) sugar to 150ml. ($\frac{1}{4}$pt) warm water in a saucepan. Stir until the sugar is dissolved and then bring the syrup to a gentle boil. Carefully add about 450g. (1 lb.) fruit and let it simmer until tender. When ready, turn into the serving dish and use hot or cold. If, when the fruit is cooked, the syrup is thinner than liked, strain out the fruit and re-boil the syrup until it has reduced to the required consistency then pour it over the fruit.

– Fruit Pulp
This is a useful base for fruit crumble or charlottes. The texture should be fairly firm and therefore minimum water should be used and the fruit can be mashed with a wooden spoon as it cooks and sweetened after cooking. The addition of the sugar moistens the pulp so there is very little chance that it will be too firm. The softening of the fruit can be done in a covered casserole in the oven if more convenient.

– Fruit Purée
This is made by sieving fruit pulp. The fruit pulp should be sweetened before sieving otherwise the fruity flavour of the purée will be weak. A nylon or stainless steel sieve must be used to prevent discoloration of the fruit. Purées are used for soufflés, cheesecake, ice cream, etc. and specifically for traditional fruit fool.

– Fruit Fool
This is made of equal parts of firm, sweetened purée of any soft fruit and whipped cream or, economically, evaporated milk. To whip evaporated milk satisfactorily, it is best to boil the unopened tin in a saucepan of water for 30min. and then to cool it overnight in the refrigerator before use. For gooseberry, black currant and blackberry fools, the fruit must be cooked first but for strawberry or raspberry, sweetening, mashing and sieving is sufficient. If gooseberry or strawberry fool is very pale in colour, a few drops of colouring diluted in a small teaspoonful of cream can be added. Cool and serve with sponge finger biscuits.

– Liquidized Fruit
This can be prepared from most fruits to produce a pulp. These are useful for immediate use but uncooked light coloured fruit pulp will discolor quickly. Lemon juice will arrest colour change but will be detectable – ascorbic acid (vitamin C) tablets are preferable. They can be obtained at chemists and are simple to use. Allow 300mg. for 450g. (1 lb.) fruit, crush the tablets, dissolve them in 1tbsp. of water and stir into the liquidized pulp. Liquidizing breaks down the fruit thoroughly but tough skins and seeds will remain.

– Baked Fruit
This is usually confined to apples. Choose a good cooker, 'Bramley's Seedling' for example, and select 1 medium to large apple per person. Wash the fruit and remove the core. Cut through the skin around the centre or equator of the apple to allow for expansion on cooking. Put each apple on an individual greased baking dish or cook all on 1 large dish. Fill the core cavity with dates or sultanas or mincemeat or brown sugar and put a knob of butter on top. Bake in the centre of a moderate oven, 170°C (325°F) Gas 3 for 40 to 50min. When the apples are cooked they will puff up and should be served as soon as possible. They shrink sadly if left. Serve sugar, preferably demerara, and cream separately. There are many variants of this popular and time-hallowed dish, particularly in the stuffing. For a savoury course, a skinned raw sausage is tasty. Sometimes peeled apples are used but this makes rather a drastic difference and a final apricot glaze is recommended.

– Apple Fritters
These are simple to make but tend to keep the cook very busy all through the meal time as they are better eaten as soon as they are made and the demand for them is usually hard to satisfy. Prepare medium-sized cooking apples by peeling, coring and cutting into 1cm. ($\frac{1}{2}$in.) slices. Dip each slice into fritter batter and fry at once in deep fat. It is easy to manipulate the slices if they are on a skewer during coating. When golden brown, drain, sprinkle with caster sugar mixed, if liked, with a little ground cinnamon or ginger, and serve at once. Fritters can be fried in shallow fat but must be turned. Bananas and pineapple slices also make excellent fritters but these fruits are outside the scope of this book. Fortunately canned fruit is not limited geographically!

Pies and Puddings
Shortcrust pastry is used extensively with fruit for double-crust, plate pies or single-crust pies made in a pie-dish, or for fruit turnovers. In the past, it was usual to use raw fruit and sugar in all of these but lightly cooked sweetened fruit is often preferred now. This is probably due to the modern preference for very lightly browned pastry.

– Apple Dumplings
A shortcrust pastry using 225g. (8oz.) of flour should be sufficient to cover 4 or 5 medium apples. Select firm apples, peel and core them. Divide the pastry into 4 or 5 portions which should be rolled fairly thinly into circles large enough to cover each apple. Stand an apple at each centre. The core hole is usually filled with sugar, and a clove or piece of quince added. Damp the edges of the pastry and neatly enfold the apple working in any fullness at the top. Turn the completely sealed dumpling upside down and place on a baking sheet. Brush over with beaten egg white, dredge lightly with caster sugar and bake at 220°C (425°F), Gas 7 in the centre of the oven. After 10 to 15min. reduce the temperature to complete the cooking of the apple. The total cooking time is about 25 to 30min. Apple dumplings are delicious hot or cold.

– Fruit Flan
Flan pastry can be used for dumplings and flans are one of the most popular ways of serving fruit, particularly fruits that display well. The base can be either pastry or sponge. It is important that the glaze over the fruit should follow the contours of the fruit and not submerge it. A plain flan need have no further decoration although cream rosettes can embellish the dish. A layer of cheesecake under the fruit is another variant.

– Summer Pudding
A simple and adaptable recipe which is a general favourite. Grease a pudding basin rather liberally with butter or margarine and then line carefully with day-old bread. The bread should be cut into slices 1cm. ($\frac{1}{2}$in.) thick and the crusts removed. It is essential to line the basin completely and it is often easier to do this if the slices of bread are cut across diagonally. The centre of the basin is then filled with sweetened cooked fruit according to season. Lightly stewed raspberries, red and black currants are a 'high' summer mixture, but gooseberries, cherries, blackberries, strawberries, etc. can be included and here a little rhubarb will give bulk unobtrusively. The fruit should not be too moist, any excess syrup should be reserved for serving with the pudding later. Place a bread lid on the pudding, put a plate on top and a weight. The basin should be stood on a plate to catch the drips that will ooze out. Leave for 24hr in a cool place then carefully turn out the pudding on to a serving dish. The fruit juice will have coloured the bread but if there are a few white patches the reserved syrup can be poured on. Serve with cream. This pudding can be made with sponge cake to line the basin but the result is rather sweet.

– Charlotte
Although apple charlotte is traditional, a variety of fruit may be used.

450g. (1 lb.) fruit
75g. (3oz.) fresh breadcrumbs
45g. (1$\frac{1}{2}$oz.) demerara sugar
25g. (1oz.) butter/chopped suet
grated rind of $\frac{1}{2}$ lemon

Use some of the butter/suet to grease a pie-dish and line it with breadcrumbs. Use the fruit raw. Apples should be peeled cored and sliced. Put the ingredients in layers in the pie-dish, pressing them down firmly and cover with the remaining breadcrumbs and knobs of butter or grated suet. Bake for 30 to 45min. – the longer time if suet is used – in a moderate oven until the fruit is soft and the top browned. Serve with custard or cream.

– Fresh Fruit Salad
It is perhaps good to finish with a reminder of the general appeal and good nutritional value of a fresh fruit salad. For this a basic sugar, or honey, and water syrup is made and allowed to cool. A little lemon peel added while making the syrup, or lemon juice added afterwards, heightens the flavour. Dessert fruits are added whole or sliced. White fruits will discolor unless they are submerged in the syrup until they are served. A plate that fits inside the serving dish can be used to keep the fruit immersed.

A dash of white wine or a suitable liqueur added to the syrup gives a festive touch.

Frozen foods

Frozen foods are now very much a part of our daily diet and the consumption of commercially prepared foods increases annually. An estimated 2000 million frozen fish fingers are consumed each year in Britain alone, which illustrates the size of the market. The production of frozen foods was originally the province of the food processing industry, but the development of efficient home freezers over the last few decades has brought the process into many kitchens. Currently almost 1 British home in 5 has a freezer and they are even more common in some European countries, particularly Scandinavia where they are found in over 60% of homes. Freezer owners soon realize that, in addition to the convenience of a supply of commercially frozen food, there is economy and satisfaction in preserving their own produce. A wide range of foods can be frozen at home and many of the fruits and vegetables grown in temperate climates freeze very well.

Unlike most of the methods detailed in Preserves, freezing has little effect on the characteristics and condition of the produce. Providing the original quality is good and the freezing process is carried out correctly, most frozen food will remain similar to fresh and be nutritionally good and very acceptable. Keen gardeners have a considerable advantage as they can harvest and freeze their produce in prime condition and much of the quality will be retained in the frozen food. For best results it is essential to freeze fruit and vegetables in fresh, good condition rather than use the end of crops, as freezing will not improve poor quality produce.

Micro-organisms and enzymes

Freezing is an efficient and satisfactory method of preserving fruit and vegetables as the low temperature slows down the processes which cause foods to spoil. Just as cold slows us down, chilling, refrigeration and freezer temperatures slow down and eventually stop the food spoilage activities of the natural food enzymes and micro-organisms. The table below shows how these activities are gradually stopped by lowering the temperature of a food.

PATHOGENIC BACTERIA The first column shows that those bacteria that cause food poisoning or similar diseases, are not active at freezer temperature and cannot grow on frozen foods and cause illness.

SPOILAGE MICRO-ORGANISMS The second column illustrates their activity at low temperatures – these are the bacteria, yeasts and moulds which will attack badly stored or preserved foods and make them unattractive but not harmful to health. These too are unable to grow at the temperature of the home freezer, so frozen food is free from microbial spoilage. The reason for recommended storage times for frozen foods has nothing to do with the growth of micro-organisms, as stored frozen food cannot go 'bad'.

However we must not ignore these organisms during the 'before' and 'after' stages of freezing foods, that is the preparation and thawing or utilization of the foods. All foods, including fruits and vegetables, contain a natural population of micro-organisms which are present at the time of harvesting. These may be the harmless spoilage type or harmful pathogenic organisms and frozen food must be treated hygienically and with care during all handling. Good quality, rot-free food should be prepared in clean conditions and frozen as soon as possible because many of the organisms will multiply at kitchen or even refrigerator temperatures. Freezing may kill some of the organisms, but many remain dormant and ready to multiply as soon as the food begins to thaw. Vegetables are usually cooked from frozen, but most fruits are thawed before consumption and will be at least as perishable as the fresh equivalent. Indeed thawed frozen foods can be *more* susceptible to microbial spoilage as the freezing process ruptures the food cells and releases nutritious juice or 'drip' which encourages micro-organisms to grow if other conditions are right. For this reason it is advisable, whenever possible, to thaw foods in a refrigerator.

ENZYMES Prolonged storage might however result in the food 'going off' due to the activities of the substances mentioned in the third column of the chart, the enzymes. Enzymes are chemical substances, not living things like micro-organisms, which are naturally present in all foods. They act as intermediates in the processes which go on in the cells of foods; for example, many enzymes are involved in the ripening and maturing of fruits and vegetables. If their actions are not stopped in a food they will continue the ripening process past the peak at which we prefer to consume fruit and vegetables and go on to reduce the quality by softening, colour changes, etc. Unlike micro-organisms, which are completely dormant at freezer temperatures, the enzymes remain slowly active and very gradually reduce the quality of frozen foods. It is for this reason that frozen storage times are given to the foods.

In preparing fruit and vegetables for freezing we can help to prolong storage times by treating the produce in certain ways to slow down the enzyme action even further. These treatments will be discussed in more detail in the sections on freezing methods for fruit and vegetables.

Advantages

The range and choice of foods available in a home with a freezer can be much extended as a great variety of foods can be frozen. Stocks can include basic garden produce, baked foods and complete meals in convenient portions for the family.

Whether or not a freezer can help save money by reducing food bills is open to doubt if calculations include the running costs, capital outlay, depreciation on the freezer itself and items such as packaging materials. Obviously the home gardener has a considerable advantage over the town housewife purchasing ready frozen foods, or even bulk supplies of fresh produce for freezing as frozen garden produce is 'free'. The freezer can be used to save money by preserving gluts of seasonal fruit and vegetables and the gardener can enjoy short season crops, such as raspberries, throughout the year.

Undoubtedly the major advantage of owning a freezer is the convenience of having a stock of good quality preserved food easily and quickly available. For the working wife shopping trips can be reduced and meals can be planned and prepared ahead by batch cooking and served in a short time when required. These advantages also apply to other groups, for example, the elderly who can be 'stocked up' by visiting relatives, and those living alone can have a supply of food for unexpected visitors. The fact that most foods are prepared before freezing means shorter times for meal preparation, for example, runner beans are cleaned, sliced and blanched in bulk when they are harvested and have only to be cooked from frozen for a shortened time before serving.

Basic principles of refrigeration.

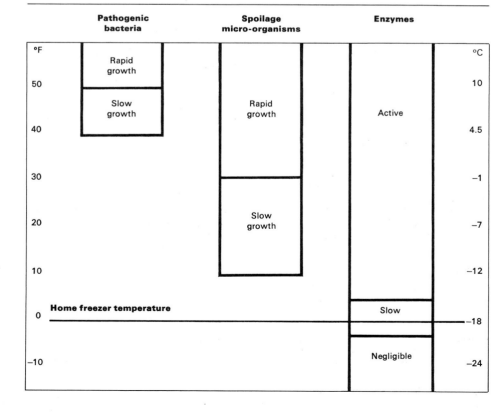

Choice and siting

SIZE

The biggest mistake made when buying a home freezer for the first time is to under-estimate how much the freezer will be used. Most people have an ice-box or frozen food compartment in their refrigerator and think some extra space would be useful to keep a larger stock of frozen food and even freeze some of their own produce. Once the many advantages of owning a freezer become apparent, usage is increased and the new purchase is often too small. A careful estimate of probable use, taking into account the likelihood of freezing large quantities of garden produce, should be made before purchase. It is generally recommended that 90 to 110 l. (3 to 4 cu. ft) of freezer space should be allowed for each member of the family, so that a 350 to 450 l. (12 to 16 cu. ft) freezer would be suitable for a family of four.

A constraint on the size of the freezer may be available space, especially in smaller, modern homes. Exactly where the large, heavy freezer will go should be another consideration before the final choice. Ideally a freezer should be situated in a fairly cool (10 to 15°C/50 to 60°F) place, to avoid prolonged running of the motor, but the site should not be damp because of the risk of the cabinet rusting. The kitchen is a convenient location for easy access to the food, but a spare bedroom, study or hallway may be used for large freezers. There is often room for the freezer in the cellar, garage, scullery or an outhouse, but if these sites are damp the freezer should be placed on wooden blocks to allow good air circulation and prevent condensation.

FREEZER CAPACITY

Most freezers work on similar principles to refrigerators with a network of pipes circulating a liquid refrigerant around the cabinet. The main and most important difference is that freezers have the capacity actually to freeze food. Refrigerators have frozen food compartments where already frozen food can be stored for certain times, depending on the temperature. This is indicated by the star-marking system.

Temperature	Storage time
* −6°C (21°F)	1 week
** −12°C (10°F)	1 month
*** −18°C (0°F)	3 months

The star system has recently been extended to show freezing capacity and most home freezers, whether chest, upright or fridge-freezer types now have this symbol.

FREEZER MODELS

The pipes carrying the refrigerant around the freezer should be in close contact with the stored food around the freezing compartment or under the shelves. Heat from the food then turns the liquid into vapour which is carried away through the system to a condenser. This condenser dissipates the heat into the atmosphere and the refrigerant is compressed to the liquid form and circulated again.

Freezers vary in types of condenser used and chest models usually have skin condensers. In this system the refrigerant tubes are located under the outer casing and pass the heat out to the air. This type can be identified by the fact that the surface feels warm to the touch and this has the advantage of minimizing surface condensation. Most

upright and some chest freezers have a condenser at the back of the casing, which functions like a car radiator and perhaps has a fan to accelerate the removal of heat. This type must be sited with good ventilation for the air vent. It must not be covered or set close against a wall, as good air circulation is essential to allow the heat to escape.

A new design of upright freezer is the fan-assisted type. In these models, the refrigeration unit is located at the top and air is cooled by the refrigerant. This cold air is then circulated by a fan, similar to those in the new fan-assisted ovens, and draws heat from the food. These can be more efficient as food cooling is accelerated and larger quantities of food can be frozen at any one time.

Apart from the mechanical differences the 3 main types of freezer differ in other respects, such as space required, ease of use and running economy. The upright and fridge-freezer types take up far less floor space and fit conveniently in most kitchens, but they may be more expensive to purchase and run. The running costs are perhaps higher because cold air is heavy and tends to drop out of upright freezers when the door is opened, so that warm air drawn in from the room has to be cooled. Also the distance between the shelves may be inadequate for storing larger items, but both these difficulties can be overcome by careful freezer management. The chest types, with the lid on the top, take up considerably more floor space, but cold is not lost when they are opened as the cold air stays inside the body of the freezer. Chest freezers are more difficult to pack and organize than upright types as food may be lost in the depths of the cabinet and stacking uneven packs can cause problems. Special baskets will help to keep the freezer stocks in order and chest freezers will accommodate large packs more easily than upright types with limiting shelves.

Packaging

A most important aspect of preparing food for home freezing is packaging. Food should never be left unwrapped in a freezer for long periods for a number of reasons. Firstly, the air inside a freezer is very drying and soon draws moisture out of unprotected foods and leaves them unacceptably dehydrated. Secondly, prolonged frozen storage in contact with air will allow enzymes which oxidize food substances to work and cause unwanted changes in the food, such as breakdown of nutrients and colour changes. Apart from these effects on individual foods, a selection of unwrapped foods stacked in a closed freezer will exchange flavours and aromas and all the foods may end up tasting and smelling of the food with the strongest characteristics. This is particularly true of strongly flavoured foods such as beetroot and onions, which require special care in packaging. Micro-organisms can also be transferred between foods with poor or non-existent wrapping and, although they do not multiply at freezer temperatures, these may cause spoilage or a health hazard when the food is thawed. An example of this is raw meat contaminating foods which are not heated before serving, where food-poisoning organisms from the meat might grow on the cold food during poor thawing.

Packaging is obviously necessary to keep small pieces of food such as peas and beans together in the freezer, but it is also useful in producing convenient size packs in portions rather than the

whole crop in one solid block. Packs containing 1 to 4 or more portions will be useful at various times, depending on family size and meal habits. Many fruits, such as raspberries and strawberries, have delicate structures and are best frozen in rigid containers to protect them from damage in the freezer. Other fruits, especially pale coloured types, are packed in sugar syrups to give added protection from enzymic colour changes and these need good packaging to prevent leakage.

All these protective functions of packaging for frozen foods can be achieved by using strong moisture- and vapour-proof materials. These materials should not be toxic or taint the food and should be easy to use and seal. They also have to withstand freezer temperatures without splitting or cracking and a large variety of purpose-made wraps and containers are available from freezer centres, stationers and mail order suppliers. Packaging can be an expensive item if small amounts of each of the various types are purchased, but some savings can be made by considering the foods to be frozen and the sizes of packs required. Then suitable packing in 1 or 2 sizes can be bought in bulk and will last over several seasons if stored in a clean, dry place.

POLYTHENE BAGS are perhaps still the cheapest wrap and can be used to pack a large variety of foods for freezing. Cheap, thin bags should not be used as they may allow transfer of flavours and loss of moisture and they may harden and split in the freezer. The minimum thickness suitable for freezing is 120 gauge, but 150 to 250 gauge bags are recommended for re-use, heavy items or large packs. Flat bags are suitable for freezing but gusseted bags make neat rectangular packs which are easy to stack and take up less space than the banana-shaped packs made by ungusseted bags. A good shape can be achieved by shaping the bag inside a cardboard box of suitable size until the pack is frozen and solid. The bags can be purchased in various colours or with coloured stripes or markings which are a useful aid to freezer management if different types of foods are packed in different coloured bags. All vegetables can be packed in green bags and all fruit in red, or the individual packs in plain bags can be kept together in large coloured sacks.

HIGH-DENSITY POLYTHENE BAGS will withstand boiling as well as freezing and are useful for packing vegetables to produce portioned 'boil-in-the-bag' packs similar to commercial ones. The vegetables are prepared and packed, then sealed in the bags with the special ties provided, or with an electric heat sealer. When required all the vegetables for a meal can be cooked from frozen in one saucepan and served from the bags, which saves washing up pans.

FREEZER FILMS Kitchen 'cling films' are rather too thin and weak for use in the freezer, but special freezer films are now on the market. These are fairly easy to use and give a tight pack on solid, round items such as small swedes and grapefruit, and are also useful for baked fruit pies and tarts. An alternative wrap for similar items is aluminium foil, but this is rather expensive for regular freezer use as heavy duty (0.025mm.) grade is advisable to prevent splitting and damage by other packs.

RIGID CONTAINERS are the easiest type to stack in the freezer, but their relatively high cost means they are generally only used for more delicate foods or fruits packed in syrup. Plastic containers

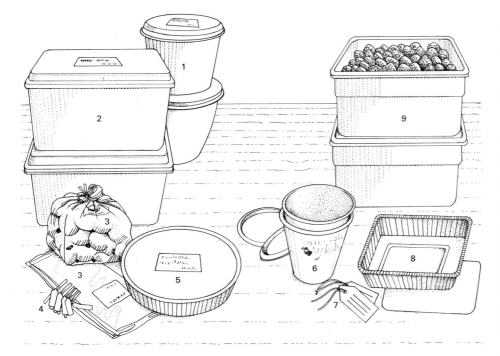

Suitable containers and labels for packaging
produce in the freezer. On the left are bought
containers, on the right commercial packs:
1 wax containers
2 plastic containers
3 plastic bags with printed labels

4 wire ties with labels
5 foil container with label
6 yoghurt cartons
7 luggage labels
8 foil pack
9 ice cream containers

have the advantage of excellent seals and good
resistance to freezing. Most types and makes are
suitable, although cheaper brands may become
brittle after much use. Savings can again be made
with bulk orders to freezer suppliers for sets of
containers of useful sizes and shapes.
WAXED PAPER CONTAINERS can be substituted for
plastic packs and are considerably cheaper.
Round and square types of various capacities are
available, but the round tubs use freezer space
less economically than square ones. These cartons
can be used for vegetables and fruits packed dry,
in sugar or in syrup, and are easy to seal. They
can be lined with polythene bags to avoid staining
so that they can be re-used.
ALUMINIUM FOIL CONTAINERS A wide range of
dishes and trays with and without lids is available. These again are expensive but packs of
selected sizes and shapes are useful for occasional
items. They are especially valuable for fruit pies,
tarts and puddings which can be heated and
served straight from the freezer in the dishes.
Acid fruits will corrode aluminium and only the
special type with a protective lacquer coating
should be used for freezing these.
GLASS CONTAINERS Most are not suitable for
freezing and thawing as they are liable to crack.
Special toughened brands can be used, but most
households do not have enough glass plates and
dishes to leave any idle in the freezer. Plate pies
and tarts can be frozen, removed from the dish
and wrapped to release the dish for everyday use,
then the pie can be cooked and served on the
original dish when required. Glass jam jars can be
used for the popular uncooked freezer jam
recipes, as these are sufficiently strong to withstand freezing if treated carefully.
COMMERCIAL CONTAINERS Instead of buying
special containers for freezing it is possible to re-
use many commercial food packs, such as plastic
ice cream, margarine and yoghurt cartons. These
usually have good seals and will tolerate freezing
and thawing, but should be *thoroughly* cleaned.
Containers from non-food products should *not*
be used as they may not be made from materials
suitable for packing foods.

Packing
EXCLUDING AIR From the wide range of freezer
packaging materials the home gardener can freeze
his produce economically, using a selection of
polythene bags, waxed cartons and 'free' ex-food
containers, with perhaps a few plastic and foil
containers for special items. When packing the
foods as much air as possible must be removed
from the packs to prevent unwanted oxidative
changes. Also trapped air is a very efficient
insulator and will slow down the freezing rate of
the food. This can be prevented by squeezing the
bag or container carefully to drive out the air or
by drawing the air out with a drinking straw or a
special pump. Exceptions to this rule are the more
fluid foods like fruits packed in syrup and purées,
which will expand as they freeze and should be
packed with a little headspace.

Sealing
All types of pack should be carefully sealed to
stop re-entry of air or loss of moisture in the
freezer. Plastic containers have efficient seals, but
other packs may need tape or ties. Freezer tape
should be used as the adhesive on ordinary tapes
will not seal in the freezer; special dispensers,
similar to those used by butchers, can be obtained
to make bag sealing easier. String or bell wire can
be used on polythene bags provided it does not
cut into the bag, but rubber bands may perish at
freezer temperatures. Bags are perhaps most
easily sealed with plastic- or paper-coated wire
ties which can be fastened around the twisted and
doubled-over neck of the bag to give a good seal.
Polythene bags and the 'boil-in-the-bag' types can
be heat sealed under a protective layer of tissue
paper, using the edge of a cool iron, or with a
purpose-made electric heat sealer.

Labelling
Once the packs are sealed they should be labelled
as one food can look much like another if frozen
in the same wraps. Small luggage labels are cheap
and can be attached to the containers with tape or
tie when sealing, or self-adhesive freezer labels
can be used. Perhaps the easiest labels to use for
bags are the flag-ties with combined label and
paper-coated wire tie. Most inks tend to fade in
the freezer so a waxed crayon or thick felt-tip pen
should be used to write suitable information on
the label. This information should include type of
food, size of portion, treatment and date frozen
or, more conveniently, a 'use by' date. Gardeners
may like to include the name of the cultivar on
fruit and vegetable labels to assess their suitability
for freezing.

Suitable Fruits and Vegetables
All fruits and vegetables *can* be frozen, but the
quality and suitability for certain uses of some
produce will be affected by freezing. Also those in
supply all the year round and which store well
unfrozen are just not worth freezing. Most
vegetables freeze entirely satisfactorily, except
those normally eaten raw, which lose crispness on
freezing. Examples of these are salad vegetables
and celery, although frozen celery can be used in
stews and casseroles where the texture is not so
important. Root vegetables such as carrots,
turnips, swedes and potatoes have long seasons
and store well for several months. However, baby
carrots, new potatoes and stew packs are convenient items to have in the freezer in small
amounts for special occasions and speedy meal
preparations.
   The same criteria of texture and availability
apply to fruits. Bananas and grapes give poor
results unless frozen in fruit salads. Dessert citrus
fruits can be frozen whole for short periods, but
are in sufficiently good supply and keep well
enough without freezing. Crab apple, medlar and
quince are best preserved as jellies and not frozen.
   The choice of cultivars is important when
considering what to grow for freezing at home,
just as commercial processors specify certain
crops from their growers. Most seed catalogues
mark cultivars that freeze well and a list of tested
cultivars is given overleaf.

Preparing Vegetables
The major criticisms of home frozen vegetables
are tasteless or tainted products with poor
textures. These faults are usually due to one or
both of 2 factors: poor quality fresh produce or
inadequate pre-freezing treatment. Both can be
easily rectified so that home grown and frozen
produce can be enjoyed with satisfaction throughout the year. It is *essential* that young produce in
prime condition is used for freezing. The tough,
tail-end of the crop will be no more acceptable
after freezing than before, so produce should be
shared between fresh consumption and freezing
all through the season. Deterioration of flavour
and colour in vegetables may be due to in-

Suitable fruits and vegetables for home freezing

VEGETABLES

Beans, broad	Aquadulce Claudia, Masterpiece Green Longpod, Meteor
Beans, dwarf French	Masterpiece, Phenix Claudia, The Prince, Tendergreen
Beans, runner	Achievement, Kelvedon Marvel, White Emergo
Beetroot	Boltardy, Cylindra
Brussels Sprouts	Citadel, Peer Gynt
Carrot	Amsterdam Forcing, Chantenay Red Cored, Little Finger, Nantes – Champion Scarlet Horn
Cauliflower	Autumn Giant – Majestic, Mechelse – Classic, Snowball
Celeriac	Globus
Courgettes	Early Gem
Peas	Dark Skinned Perfection, Gradus, Onward, Pioneer, Show Perfection, Sugar Dwarf de Grace
Potatoes	Majestic *for chips*
Rhubarb	Cawood Castle, Timperley Early, Hawke's Champagne
Spinach	Longstanding Round
Sweetcorn	Canada Cross, Earliking, First of All, Kelvedon Glory, Northern Belle
Tomato	Ailsa Craig, Moneymaker, Gardener's Delight (small fruited). *Use firm ripe fruit*

FRUITS

Apples	*For pulp:* Bramley's Seedling, Woolbrook Russet *For slices:* Bramley's Seedling, Grenadier, Lane's Prince Albert
Apricots	Moorpark
Blackberries	*Large ripe berries:* Himalaya, Bedford Giant
Black currants	Baldwin, Boskoop Giant, Westwick Choice, Seabrook's Black (*acid*), Wellington XXX
Blueberries	Jersey
Cherries	*Any dark red:* Morello (*acid*), Governor Wood
Gooseberries	*All firm:* Keepsake, Careless, Leveller Whinham's Industry (*red*), Golden Drop (*dessert*)
Loganberries	*Thornless: use fully ripe and dark red*
Mulberries	*Use fully ripe. Eliminate core by pulping and sieving*
Peaches	Hale's Early (*free stone*)
Pears	*Not recommended.* Clapp's Favourite, Gorham, Louise Bonne, Williams' Bon Chrétien, Doyenné du Comice
Plums	*Not recommended whole. Freeze halved in syrup, or stewed. Avoid large fruit.* Shropshire Prune Damson, Belle de Louvain, Jefferson's Gage (*tough skin*), Pond's Seedling
Raspberries	Malling Admiral, Malling Orion, Malling Jewel, Malling Promise, Lloyd George (*dark*), Norfolk Giant (*acid*), Glen Cova
Strawberries	Cambridge Vigour (*keeps its shape*), Cambridge Prizewinner, Cambridge Rival (*dark, better for jam*), Cambridge Favourite (*weak flavour*), Royal Sovereign

adequate packaging, but it is more likely to be caused by lack of blanching or scalding before freezing. This is the process used by all commercial frozen vegetable producers to stop the actions of food enzymes which give rise to unwanted changes during frozen storage. The fact that commercial processors blanch vegetables highlights the need for treatment of home produce and experimental work has emphasized that blanching prolongs the frozen storage life of vegetables. Without prior blanching, flavour taints and colour changes are noticeable in frozen Brussels sprouts after only 3 days and in broad beans after 3 weeks, but both will store well for 1 year if blanched before freezing. However, some frozen vegetables such as carrots and spinach will store for a year without blanching because they are less susceptible to enzyme changes.

Blanching

The main principle behind blanching is heating the vegetables sufficiently and for a long enough time to destroy the enzymes right through the food. Therefore larger pieces of food, such as maize cobs, will require longer heat treatment than small pieces, such as peas or runner beans, to ensure central penetration of heat. Apart from destruction of enzymes the heat of blanching also reduces the number of micro-organisms present and makes the vegetables less liable to microbial spoilage. It also drives air from within the cells and so helps to stop oxidative changes.

BLANCHING TIMES for specific vegetables are given in Table 1, and it is very important to blanch for the *exact* times given. Under-blanching means that the centre of the food may still be subject to enzyme changes. Over-blanching is equivalent to cooking the food so that when it is cooked again before serving it may be tasteless and soft-textured.

EQUIPMENT needed for blanching should be assembled before picking the vegetables, so that the produce can be prepared, blanched and frozen in as short a time as possible. Most of the equipment can be found in the kitchen, except perhaps a container to hold the vegetables while they are blanching. Special light-weight metal blanching baskets can be purchased or the basket from a chip fryer or a salad basket may be adequate. The requirements are that the container mesh holds the vegetables in, even small pieces like peas, yet allows the boiling water to circulate evenly and freely. A cheaper alternative to a metal basket is a deep bag such as a nylon wine straining bag or a clean nylon stocking. These hold the food securely, allow good water circulation and have the added advantage of taking less heat from the boiling water than bulky metal baskets.

A large, lidded saucepan is required which will hold 1.8 l. (3pt) of water and the container of vegetables and leave room for frothing. The pan may become stained after prolonged use so an old pan can be kept specifically for blanching. Other requirements are a large bowl and ice or running cold water to cool the vegetables, and a colander and straining spoon to drain them. An accurate timer and, ideally, a certain amount of peace and quiet to ensure precise timings are also essential.

THE METHOD Once the vegetables are harvested they should be prepared as if for cooking and divided up into 225g. (½lb.) portions ready for blanching. The amount of water in the pan is not absolutely critical, but too little will not circulate well and may not cover the vegetables, while too much may be difficult to keep boiling and to control. It has been found that 25g. (1 level tbsp.) of salt in the blanching water helps retain a good colour in the vegetables. The water must be boiling well when the vegetables are submerged and *must* return to the boil within 1 minute so that they are not cooked. For this reason a good heat source is required and the lid should be kept on the pan. Blanching is timed from the moment the water returns to the boil. As soon as the blanching time is over, the vegetables are emptied from the container into the colander and cooled in iced or gently running water for the same time as they were blanched. The vegetables are then drained, but not dried, and packed ready for freezing. With practice, 1 batch of vegetables can be blanched while the previous one is being cooled to speed up the operation. The same blanching water can be used 6 or 7 times provided the quantity is kept fairly constant.

Vegetables can be packed in polythene bags or waxed or plastic containers in suitable portions, or in 'free-flowing' bulk packs like fruit for easy separation when required. The packs should be sealed and frozen quickly to preserve quality.

Most vegetables can be blanched in water before freezing, but some are sautéd or partially fried to destroy the enzymes. These and any vegetables requiring special preparation methods are noted in Table 1.

Table 1 Preparing vegetables for home freezing

VEGETABLE	PREPARATION	BLANCH-ING TIME (MIN.)	SUGGESTED COOKING METHODS
Artichoke, Chinese	Lift and wash immediately. Leave whole.	1–2	Parboil and sauté or steam and fry.
Artichoke, Globe whole	Wash thoroughly. Discard outer leaves, cut off bud, trim base.	8–10	Boil or steam (40–45min.).
hearts (fonds)	Remove all leaves, keep under cold water. Add 50ml. (2tbsp.) lemon juice to blanching water to prevent darkening.	4–5	Boil or steam (20–50min.).
Artichoke, Jerusalem	Peel and cube or slice. Keep under cold water.	1–2	Boil (15min.) and serve or purée.
Asparagus	Wash, remove woody base and grade sizes. Tie in bundles.	2–4	Boil or steam (15–20min.) with heads above water.
Asparagus pea	Pick when young and tender, 3cm. (1in.) long. Top and tail.	1	Simmer or steam (5–10min.).
Aubergine (egg plant)	Cut in half lengthways or peel and slice or cube.	5 / 3–4	Fry, sauté, bake or casserole.
Beans, broad	Pod and grade to size. Discard large, starchy beans.	3	
Beans, dwarf French	Use only small ones. Top and tail.	2–3	Boil (3–5min.) or steam (5–10min.).
Beans, runner	String and cut off ends. Cut into chunks 1cm. (½in.) wide.	2–3	
Beans, soya	Wash, blanch, squeeze from pods and pack.	4–5	Boil (5–10min.).
Beet, leaf	Wash, trim green leaves and blanch in small amounts.	2–3	Boil (5–10min.) or steam (10–20min.).
	Stems or midribs can be trimmed and treated like asparagus.	2–4	Boil (15–20min.) or steam (20–30min.).
Beetroot	Choose small ones (3cm./1in.). Peel after blanching and cooling. (Larger beetroot may be cooked, cooled and sliced.)	5–15	Salads or pickle.
Broccoli, sprouting Calabrese	Remove coarse outer leaves. Cut into small sprigs and grade sizes.	3–4	Boil (5–10min.) or steam (15–20min.).
Brussels sprouts	Use small, compact sprouts. Trim off outside leaves and make a cut in stem base.	3–4	Boil (5min.) or steam (10min.).
Cabbage, white, Savoy, red, Chinese	Use only fresh, firm cabbage. Trim and cut into 1–3cm. (½–1in.) slices.	1–2	Boil (3–5min.) or steam (5–10min.).
Calabrese	See broccoli		
Capsicum (sweet, red and green peppers)	Select firm peppers. Cut in half lengthways, remove stalk and seeds. Slice or dice.	3	In stews, casseroles and ratatouille.
Cardoon	Wash well, cut stems into 10cm. (4in.) lengths and blanch in water with added lemon juice.	5	Simmer in stock (60min.) or cook as celery.
Carrots	Select small, even carrots. Skin after blanching, pack whole. Large carrots should be sliced or diced (useful in stew packs).	5	Boil (5min.) or steam (10min.).

VEGETABLE	PREPARATION	BLANCH-ING TIME (MIN.)	SUGGESTED COOKING METHODS
Cauliflower	Choose compact heads and break into florets about 5cm. (2in.) across.	3	Boil (5min.) or steam (10min.).
Celeriac	Scrub root, peel and grade or dice or slice (useful in stew packs).	1	Use in stews or simmer until tender (15–20min.).
Celery	Not suitable for salad use. Clean, string and cut into chunks (3cm./1in. long).	2	As celeriac.
Chicory	Not suitable for salads. Wash thoroughly, trim off outside leaves. Blanch whole or separate into spears.	2–5	As celeriac.
Corn, on-the-cob	See sweet corn		
Courgettes	Cut when small (10–15cm./4–6in.). Freeze whole, halved or in thick slices.	1–3	Boil (10–15min.) or steam (15–20min.) or sauté in butter.
Cucumber, ridge	Peel, chop, drain and freeze raw.	–	In recipes, e.g. soups.
Egg plant	See aubergine		
Endive	See chicory		
Fennel	Trim top stems and base. Halve or quarter.	5–10	As endive.
Good King Henry (Mercury or perennial goosefoot)	Wash and trim green leaves.	2	Use as for beet or spinach.
Herbs	1. Wash sprigs, pack and freeze. Crumble from frozen to use. 2. Chop leaves finely and pack in small containers. 3. Chop finely and add water (vinegar for mint). Freeze in ice-cube trays. Blanching improves the colour of herbs frozen by methods 2 and 3.	5secs.	In recipes, stuffings and sauces.
Horseradish	Scrub roots well and peel. Slice thinly or grate.		For sauce.
Kale	See beet, seakale.		
Kohlrabi (turnip cabbage)	For small (3cm./1in.) bulbs, twigs, scrub and blanch whole. Larger ones should be peeled and diced.	3 / 2	Boil (15–30min.) or braise (30–50min.).
Leeks	Leaves may be blanched and used as 'greens'. Cut off green parts and wash thoroughly. Blanch whole or sliced.	2 / 3	Boil (5min.). Boil (5–10min.).
Lettuce	Not suitable for salads. Trim outside leaves and wash hearts thoroughly.	2	Braise or use in soups or stews.
Macedoine	Prepare peas, carrot cubes, French beans and sweet corn and blanch separately. After cooling make up assorted packs.		Boil (3–5min.) or steam (5–10min.) or use in recipes.
Maize	See sweetcorn.		

VEGETABLE	PREPARATION	BLANCH-ING TIME (MIN.)	SUGGESTED COOKING METHODS
Marrow	Use only small ones (see courgettes) or slice or dice.	1	Sauté in butter or purée.
Mushrooms	Not really recommended, as widely available. *Do not* blanch; wash well and freeze while damp or sauté in butter before freezing.		Grilled or in recipes.
Onions	Peel small onions (useful in stew packs). Peel and chop larger ones. Onion rings pan-fried in batter can be frozen.	2 1	Fry from frozen. Casseroles, stews and other recipes.
Parsley, Hamburg	Trim and peel roots. Dice.	2	Use as for celeriac or parsnip.
Parsnips	As for Hamburg parsley (useful in stew packs).	2	As Celeriac.
Peas, green	Select young, sweet peas; shell.	1–2	Boil (2–3min.) or steam (5–7min.).
Mangetout (sugar pea)	Select young pods, top and tail; break larger ones in pieces.	2	Simmer in a little water with mint if liked.
Petit pois	Select young pods. Blanch in pods, cool and shake out peas; discard pods.	2	Boil (2–3min.) or steam (5min.). Toss in butter and mint.
Peppers	See capsicum.		
Potatoes, chipped (French fried)	Use a good cultivar. Prepare even sized chips and soak in cold water for 1hr. Drain and blanch in deep fat or oil, cool and freeze.	2	Deep fry from frozen.
Potatoes, new	Select small, even-sized potatoes of a good cultivar. Scrape and slightly under-cook in salted water. Drain, cool and freeze.		Reheat gently in a little salted water with a knob of butter and a sprig of mint.
Pumpkin (squash)	Select mature, fine-textured specimens. Wash, cut into chunks and remove seeds. Steam until tender. Remove pulp from rind, cool and freeze.		For pies, soups, jam or as marrow.
Purées, vegetable	Select mature vegetables, cook by any preferred method and sieve. Cool quickly and freeze.		Reheat slowly in a double pan or use as soup base.
Salsify	Scrub roots and blanch whole. Remove skins and cool in air, not water.	2	Toss in butter or serve in a white sauce.
Scorzonera	As salsify.		
Shallot	As onion.		
Sorrel	Pick and treat as spinach.	2	Use as spinach.
Spinach beet	Wash well and treat as beet.	2	Use as for beet or spinach.
Spinach	Pick fresh young leaves and wash very thoroughly. Remove spine, blanch whole leaves and squeeze out excess water.	2	Reheat slowly with no added water and toss in butter, or use in recipes.
Squash	See pumpkin.		

VEGETABLE	PREPARATION	BLANCH-ING TIME (MIN.)	SUGGESTED COOKING METHODS
Stew pack	A mixture of root vegetables for example, carrots, swedes, turnips, onions and parsnips. Blanch separately.		Use in recipes.
Succotash	Sweet corn and broad beans mixed. Blanch separately.		Boil (3–5min.) or steam (5–10min.).
Swede	Trim, peel and dice (useful in stew packs), or pulp.	2	Boil (5–10min.) or steam (10–15min.).
Sweet corn	Use well developed cobs. Remove husk and silk.	4–6	Thaw before cooking. Boil (10–15min.) or steam (15–20min.).
Sweet corn grains	Blanch on cob, remove kernels with knife.	4–6	Boil (5–10min.) or steam (10–15min.).
Tomatoes	Too soft for salads, but small ones can be frozen whole or puréed for cooking. Scald to remove skins and freeze whole or halved.		Cook from frozen or in recipes.
Turnips	See swede.		
Turnip tops	As spinach.		

Table 2 Preparing fruits for home freezing

FRUIT	PREPARATION	SPECIAL POINTS
Apple pulp	Peel, core and slice. Cook in minimum water until tender and mash. Cool before freezing.	Use a good cooking cultivar. Add sugar on thawing if required.
Apple purée	As for pulp, but sieve before packing.	As for pulp.
Apple slices	Peel, core and cut into even slices. Blanch for 1–2min. until pliable and cool quickly *or* soak in lightly salted water and pack tightly.	Use a good cooking cultivar. Submerge in salt water during preparation to prevent darkening. Dry sugar or a weak syrup can be added to the pack.
Apricots	Wipe clean and freeze whole or halved in syrup with ascorbic acid or poach in syrup before freezing. Pulp as for apple. For preserves freeze whole coated in dry sugar.	Keep fruit submerged in syrup with paper. May be sweetened. Store for three months only.
Bilberries	Freeze in syrup or dry sugar, or plain for preserves.	Useful for pies. Pack in rigid containers.
Blackberries	As bilberries.	
Blueberries	As bilberries.	
Boysenberries	Pick when almost black. Freeze in dry sugar or syrup.	Use rigid containers for protection.
Cape gooseberries (golden berries)	Remove husks. Pack whole in syrup, or stew.	Use as a dessert.
Cherries, sweet	Use ripe red or black cherries, stone them and freeze in syrup.	Added ascorbic acid preserves colour. Keep fruit submerged.
Cherries, red and acid	Use bright red fruit, wash, drain and remove stones. Freeze whole in dry sugar, syrup or crush in sugar.	Use in pies.
Chinese gooseberries	Best not frozen. Cut in half crossways and scoop out flesh. Sweeten.	Add lemon juice to prevent discoloration.
Cloudberries	As bilberries.	
Cranberries	Use firm good fruit. Wash and drain. Freeze dry, in syrup, puréed or as a sauce.	
Currants, black	Freeze plain on sprigs for cooking or preserves. Pulp or purée for pies and sauces.	Remove from sprigs with a fork while still frozen.
Currants, red, white	As black currants or in syrup as a dessert.	
Damsons	Freeze whole plain, pulped or as pie fillings.	Use whole fruit within 6 months or stones may cause a taint.
Elderberries	Use good sized berries and remove stalks. Blanch for ½min. and pack plain for cooking.	Useful combined with apple or blackberry.
Figs, green	Select ripe fruit, wash and cut off stems. Peel if desired and freeze whole, halved or sliced in syrup.	Add ascorbic acid to preserve colour.
Gooseberries	Top, tail and freeze plain for preserves. Stew or purée with added sugar for pie fillings, etc.	Usually used for cooking.
Grapes, black or green	These become soft on thawing but can be used in a fruit salad. Freeze in syrup. Remove seeds before freezing.	Add ascorbic acid to preserve colour.
Greengages	As plums.	Better bottled for puddings.
Japanese wineberries (Chinese blackberry)	Pick when wine-red and treat as for boysenberries.	
Loganberries	Handle carefully. Pulp and purée freeze well.	Use rigid containers.
Lowberries	As loganberries.	
Melons	Cut in half, remove seeds and peel. Freeze as cubes or balls in syrup.	Eat before fully thawed. Useful in fruit cocktails.
Mulberries	Fully ripe, large berries can be frozen in syrup. Purée or pulp freezes well.	
Nectarberries	As loganberries.	
Nectarines	As peaches.	
Peaches	Select firm ripe peaches. Scald to remove skins. Cut in half and remove stone, or slice. Freeze submerged in heavy syrup.	Prepare quickly to avoid discoloration. Add ascorbic acid to preserve colour.
Pears, cooking	Peel and core. Cook until nearly tender and freeze.	
Pears, dessert	Peel, core and halve or slice. Firm types can be poached for 1min. in boiling syrup to preserve colour. Ascorbic acid can be added to softer fruit. Pack in cold syrup.	Keep submerged in syrup with crumpled paper.
Plums	Select firm fruit. Freeze whole plain for preserves or halved in syrup. Pulp for pie fillings can be frozen.	Not really recommended.
Raspberries	As loganberries.	
Rhubarb	Young pink rhubarb can be cut into 3–5cm. (1–2in.) lengths and blanched for 1min. Cool and freeze plain, in dry sugar or syrup. Stewed or pulped fruit will freeze well.	
Strawberries	As loganberries.	
Veitchberries	As loganberries.	
Worcesterberries	As black currants.	

Preparing Fruit

A supply of home-grown soft fruits out of season is perhaps one of the major attractions of a home freezer. Most fruits are relatively easy to prepare for freezing and give excellent results if care is taken to avoid enzyme action and oxidation, which cause colour, flavour and aroma changes. In some fruits these enzyme changes can be controlled by heat treatments such as blanching, stewing or poaching in sugar syrup. The texture and flavour of some delicate fruits would be unacceptably altered by any form of heating and these are usually protected by immersing in sugar syrup, coating in dry sugar or by tight packaging.

For best results fruit should be picked in good, clean condition on a dry day and frozen as rapidly as possible. This is particularly important for soft fruits which have a high water content and are harvested during hot weather. If these are not frozen quickly, or at least kept cool, they will soon wilt and give a poor product. In general, fruits need more careful handling to avoid physical damage than vegetables and are more susceptible to colour changes during preparation and frozen storage.

Choice of Freezing Methods

The method chosen largely depends on the type of fruit and the subsequent use. Suitable methods for each fruit are given in Table 2.

– Sugar syrups

Packing in sugar syrups is an effective way of freezing many fruits as they are protected from enzyme changes and discoloration by the barrier of syrup, which also speeds up the rate of freezing of the fruit. The strength of syrup made depends on family taste, the delicacy of the fruit flavour and what the fruit will be used for. Usually, heavy syrups are used for dessert fruits and weaker ones for fruit to be cooked. An acceptable syrup for freezing many fruits is made from 500g. (1 lb.) sugar dissolved in 1 l. (2pt) of water and this will be enough to pack about 2kg. (6 lb.) of fruit. Syrup should be prepared in advance so that it may be cooled or chilled before use. A large batch may be made and stored in the refrigerator for 7 to 10 days. The measured amount of water should be heated in a clean, bright pan and the sugar stirred in to dissolve it. The syrup is then brought to the boil and boiled for 2min. before cooling. The pan must be bright to keep the syrup clear. The boiling removes dissolved oxygen from the water which would otherwise oxidize the fruit. CONTAINERS. Fruit in syrup is best packed in rigid containers, especially soft fruits, which need protection from damage, and light-coloured fruits which must be completely submerged to prevent darkening. The proportion of syrup to fruit in a pack is not critical, but average quantities are 300g. (10oz.) fruit to 200ml. (6 fl. oz.) syrup in a 500g. (1 lb.) pack. Whatever size container is used, some headspace must be left to allow room for expansion on freezing.

The cold syrup should be measured into the containers beforehand so that the fruit can be dropped in as soon as it is prepared. The fruit pieces can be kept under the surface of the syrup with a piece of crumpled greaseproof paper, pushed down with the lid. The fruit should be frozen as soon as it has been packed, sealed and labelled.

ANTI-OXIDANTS An added precaution when freezing light-coloured fruits is incorporating lemon juice or ascorbic acid (vitamin C) in the syrup. These substances are anti-oxidants and will help keep the colour of the fruit during preparation and storage. Lemon juice is effective, but the strong flavour may mask the flavour of the fruit, and ascorbic acid is preferable. Ascorbic acid can be bought from the chemist as 100mg. vitamin C tablets. A standard pack, 500g. (1 lb.), needs three 100mg. tablets and the tablets should be crushed and added to the syrup just before use. Apart from keeping the fruit colour the tablets boost the vitamin C content of the fruit.

Syrup, with or without added ascorbic acid, gives adequate protection from enzyme changes and oxidation for many fruits, especially those to be consumed cold. Heat treatments can be used to destroy enzymes in fruits which are little affected by heating or will be subsequently cooked. Blanching, as described for vegetables, may be used for firm fruits, such as apple slices. More delicately flavoured fruits, like pears, may be poached in a light syrup for a few minutes. Many fruits, for instance gooseberries and rhubarb, may be stewed down and sweetened for serving hot or for pie fillings, as the heating kills the enzymes and reduces the bulk for storing.

– Dry sugar

Dark-coloured dessert fruits to be served 'fresh' may be packed in a dry sugar coating which will give a protective glaze to the fruit without changing the fresh characteristics. The fruit enzymes are not destroyed but the glaze stops oxidation and colour changes to some extent. The fresh fruit is spread out on a sheet of greaseproof paper and dampened slightly by sprinkling on a small amount of water. Caster sugar can then be scattered or sieved over the fruit to give an even coating. Usually 250g. (4oz.) of sugar is adequate to cover 1kg. (1 lb.) of fruit and more can be added if required when the fruit is thawed.

– Free-flow pack

Dry sugar treatment is ideal to produce large 'free-flowing' packs of fruit for family use. After coating with sugar the fruit is spread on plastic or metal trays and 'open' frozen without any covering on the trays. As soon as the fruit is frozen it should be packed, sealed and labelled in the normal way. This method of freezing allows portions to be removed from large packs when required without having to thaw the whole pack.

– Plain packing

Free-flowing packs can also be made with fruit frozen without any treatment or added sugar. This method is really only suitable for dark fruits, like blackberries and black currants, and fruits for cooking, such as gooseberries and Seville oranges, as the fruit is only protected by the packaging. Plain packing is quite adequate for fruit frozen for subsequent jam-making and bulk packs can be prepared in recipe quantities, allowing a little extra fruit to compensate for pectin loss (see p. 183).

Fruit prepared in dry sugar or plain for cooking can be packed in polythene bags but shallow, rigid containers are best for soft dessert fruits which might otherwise be damaged. Stewed fruits, pulps and purées can be put into polythene bags but the packs should be shaped in rigid containers until frozen for easier stacking in the freezer.

Storage and Later Use

As soon as produce has been prepared, packed and labelled it should be cooled and frozen rapidly to ensure good quality. Freezing will be faster if food is put close to the tubes circulating the coolant, and in chest freezers there is often a special freezing compartment. Most freezers are fitted with a fast- or super-freeze switch which should be turned on a few hours in advance of loading. The freezer and already frozen food will then be as cold as possible, giving a reservoir of 'cold' to chill the fresh food as it is loaded. Most home freezers do not have the refrigeration capacity to freeze more than one-tenth of a normal load of food in any 24 hr, although the new fan-assisted freezers will freeze larger amounts. On average 300g. of food can be packed into 1 l. of freezer space (18 to 20 lb. per cu. ft), so a 500 l. freezer will freeze 15kg. of food in 24hrs (10 cu. ft freezer will freeze 18 to 20 lb.) Load size should not exceed the capacity of the freezer or the produce will freeze too slowly and quality may be affected.

Once the produce is frozen it should be stacked neatly to make the maximum use of space. A system of loading the food, such as coloured bags, separate shelves or baskets for each type, will make freezer management and location of food when required much easier. It is advisable to keep a stock record of food as it is loaded into the freezer and cross off items as they are removed. This need not be complicated, but it is very useful to know what types and sizes of packs are in the freezer.

– Defrosting

For maximum efficiency, freezers should be defrosted regularly and ice should not be allowed to build up to more than 1cm. ($\frac{1}{2}$in.) thick around the cabinet walls. Chest freezers should only need defrosting annually but upright types may require attention more frequently. The freezer should be switched off and the food removed and well wrapped to keep it cool. A bowl of hot water placed on a towel (to absorb thawed ice) in the bottom of the closed freezer will speed up the process.

After about ten minutes the ice should be loose enough to remove in large pieces. Replenish the hot water until all ice has been removed, then wash the freezer walls with warm water containing 10gm. ($\frac{1}{2}$tbsp.) of bicarbonate of soda per litre. Dry the interior, switch on the freezer and replace the food, which should soon be cooled down to –18°C (0°F) again.

– Storage time

Storage times for foods in the home freezer are based on food kept at a constant temperature of –18°C (0°F). Higher or fluctuating temperatures reduce the storage life and quality of frozen foods and it is well worth investing in a freezer thermometer to ensure that carefully frozen produce is stored at the correct temperature. It is also a good idea to tape over the power point for the freezer to avoid accidental loss of power, and to ensure that the freezer is left on when going away from home for long periods. Depending on the size and load in the freezer, it should not be too much affected by power cuts, provided the freezer is *not* opened. The food in a medium-sized, full freezer will remain frozen for at least 24hr and be perfectly safe.

Provided the freezer is managed correctly and is working efficiently, home frozen produce should retain high quality for the following periods:

Vegetables

blanched	12 months
sautéd or fried	6 months
chipped potatoes	4 to 6 months

Fruits

in syrup (with or without ascorbic acid)	12 months
in dry sugar	12 months
plain	12 months
stewed	12 months
puréed	10 months
whole on stone	3 to 6 months

These times are approximate and depend on such factors as type of fruit or vegetable, condition and storage. There is little advantage in longer storage for crops that can be replaced annually and it is a good idea to have a short break before the next season so that the fresh, new crop is fully appreciated.

– Eating Frozen Foods

The quality of carefully preserved and stored produce can be ruined by incorrect handling when it is removed from the freezer for use. Suitable cooking methods for frozen vegetables are detailed in Table 1 – most have been par-cooked (e.g. by blanching) *before* freezing and therefore need *shorter* final cooking times to avoid soft and tasteless products. Most can be cooked from frozen, and blanched vegetables can be cooked in boiling, salted water allowing 300ml. of water to 500g. of vegetables (½pt per lb.), or steamed. Sautéed vegetables should be reheated gently in a thick pan or casserole in the oven. 'Boil-in-the-bag' packs can be heated through in a saucepan of boiling water.

Fruit packs, purées or pulps to be eaten cold should be thawed slowly in the unopened pack, preferably in a refrigerator overnight. This keeps the fruit in good condition and it should be served while still chilled for a good texture. If required at short notice, the fruit can be thawed at room temperature: a 500g. (1 lb.) pack takes 4 to 6 hours, or by immersing the pack in cold, running water, but the quality will suffer. Light-coloured fruits must be kept submerged in syrup whilst they thaw or they will darken quickly. Darkening of fruits to be cooked or used in preserves can be minimized by cooking straight from the freezer.

The remarks and methods set out above are intended as guidelines for the beginner. As experience is gained modifications of methods will be developed and family preferences formed. If a particular fruit or vegetable is not mentioned it is always worth trying a small portion, especially for the new types and cultivars which are coming on to the market for the home grower.

Wine-making is not a method of preserving fruit and vegetables in the strictest sense, as the aim of all preservation methods should be to prevent decomposition or fermentation of the food. However, making wine at home can be a fascinating and satisfying hobby which makes full use of garden surpluses, bulk purchases from the greengrocer or food gathered for free from the hedgerows.

The basic principle of wine-making is the fermentation of naturally occurring sugars in the fruit and vegetables to ethyl alcohol (ethanol) by special wine yeasts.

$$C_6H_{12}O_6 \xrightarrow{\text{yeast}} 2C_2H_5OH + 2CO_2$$

glucose *yeast* alcohol   carbon dioxide

The characteristics of the wine, such as flavour, colour and aroma, are derived from the starting material or substrate and the yeast during the wine-making process. Commercial wines are made from grapes, but the home wine-maker has a far wider choice of substrate, and palatable wines can be made from many of the temperate fruits and vegetables. A flow chart giving basic recipes for fruit, flower and vegetable wines is given on p. 201 and examples of recipes are included.

Before dealing with methods of making wine at home some words of warning are necessary. Firstly, home made wine *must not be sold* as no excise duty has been paid on it. Secondly it is illegal (and potentially dangerous) to distil homemade wines by any method. Naturally fermented ethyl alcohol is the only potable alcohol and others, such as methyl alcohol, should *not* be used to fortify wines. Only 'B.P.' (*British Pharmacopoeia*) grade chemicals, available from wine-making suppliers, should be used in fermentations. If any doubt exists do *not* add the substances to your wines.

Wine-making is a fascinating hobby, but wine-makers have been known to become over-enthusiastic and fill their houses, garages and sheds with frothing fermentations and volumes of maturing wine – moderation in production and consumption of strong homebrews is advised for the beginner!

Stages in Wine-making

There are 4 stages in wine-making which need special attention and different equipment.
– *Juice extraction* The raw materials and other ingredients are prepared to produce a fermentable liquid or *must* containing sugars, flavour, colour and nutritious nitrogenous compounds for the yeasts to act upon.
– *Preliminary fermentation* Yeast is added to the must and gives a vigorous fermentation as the number of yeast cells increases and much of the debris and cell tissue from the substrate are removed.
– *Completion of fermentation and clarification* This stage must be carried out in a special fermentation vessel so that the yeast can work in the absence of air (anaerobically), to convert efficiently all the sugar present to the required alcohol.
– *Storage* Storage of the finished wine is very important to the production of a mature wine. Throughout all these stages the wine must be kept free from spoilage organisms and pests by

sterilizing the ingredients and equipment as far as possible.

Raw Materials

The essential raw materials for wine-making are: a substrate, water, sugar and yeast. Most fruits, grains and some flowers and vegetables are suitable starting materials for wines. Good quality produce, free from rot and mould, should be used either fresh or from the freezer.
– *The substrate* The flavour, aroma and sugars provided by the substrate ensure a good fermentation and final product.
– *Water* Water is required to extract these constituents from the substrates.
– *Extra sugar* In addition to the natural substrate sugar, extra sugar is usually necessary to produce a strong wine which will store well.
– *Yeast* Since this is the 'worker' in the fermentation, a good wine yeast will add extra character to the wine.
– *Acid and tannin* Certain additional ingredients will help to give a well-balanced wine, and these include acid and tannin, which are present in such fruits as oranges and tannin-rich red fruits. Bland materials like root vegetables and flowers may need added acid and tannin to give astringency and 'bite' to the wine.
– *Nutrients* Some substrates may also be deficient in the nutrients, particularly nitrogenous matter, which yeasts need to ferment the must to completion; such deficiencies can be overcome by adding commercial preparations of nutrients.
– *Enzymes* Other refinements to wine-making which can be purchased from wine-making suppliers are enzymes to destroy pectin or starch in the substrate which might cause cloudiness in the finished wine.

Equipment and Processes

Wine can be made with a small amount of equipment which can be supplemented as experience is gained. Most of the basic utensils can be found in the kitchen or around the house but the equipment must be made from suitable material which will not react with or taint the acid must or wine. Glass, china and some plastic vessels and equipment can be used and stainless steel, aluminium, tin or enamelware, provided it is free from cracks and chips, is also suitable. Containers previously used for horticultural products, disinfectants, etc. should be avoided, as should earthenware crocks that have soft lead glazes.
– *For Juice Extraction*
Kitchen scales, sharp stainless steel knives, scissors, a large saucepan, bucket, funnel and straining muslin are all that is required to prepare and extract the juice from many sources. The juice can then be seeded with the yeast and the preliminary fermentation carried out in a covered bucket or similar vessel at about 21°C (70°F).
– *For Preliminary Fermentation*
After 3 to 7 days, when the vigorous fermentation has died down, the liquid should be strained into a suitable fermentation vessel. Ideally, narrow-necked containers should be used as these are easily sealed to prevent air entering the fermentation – the best types are the glass jars used for commercial ciders, vinegars and sherries, and sold by wine-making suppliers.

The seals used can vary from special airlocks to children's balloons or polythene sheets tied down

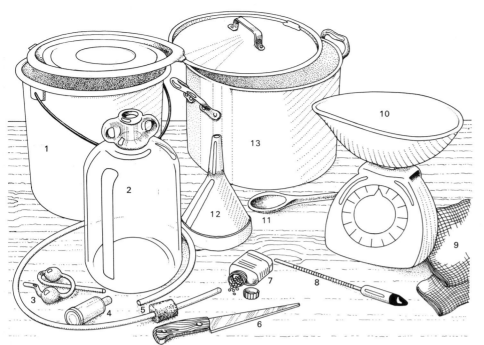

Basic equipment for wine-making:
1 plastic bucket
2 demi-john
3 glass airlock
4 plastic airlock
5 plastic tube and cork
6 knife

7 bottle of Campden tablets
8 hydrometer
9 muslin
10 kitchen scales
11 wooden spoon
12 plastic funnel
13 heavy saucepan

fairly tightly over wide-necked crocks. Well worth buying are the glass or plastic airlocks sold by winemaker's suppliers. Whatever airlock is used it must allow the carbon dioxide gas produced by the fermentation to escape slowly under pressure and stop air and pests, such as the vinegar fly, getting into the wine.

Once the fermentation is set up, it should be left in a warm room at 16 to 18°C (60 to 65°F) until gas bubbles are no longer formed and yeast activity has finished. This should take about 2 months for a good fermentation with the correct ingredients and yeast. The suspended yeast cells, which make the wine cloudy, should then gradually sink to form a deposit under a clear wine.

– For Racking
At this stage the wine should be syphoned or racked from the deposit or *lees*, using plastic or rubber tubing. If this is not done, taints may be produced from the dead yeast cells, oxidation or bacterial action. The racked wine should be stored to allow further clarification and to ensure that all fermentation has stopped, then racked at least once more before bottling.

– For Storage
Initially any type of bottle can be used although special 'punted' wine bottles are available.

It is worthwhile investing in new corks, but if old corks are used they must be sterilized first to prevent contamination of the new wine. Various types of corks are available apart from the traditional straight-sided ones which should be driven fully home. The shouldered corks with cork or plastic caps are popular for home use, as are the plastic type which can be used again and again. All corks, except waxed, pre-sterilized ones, should be sterilized and softened in boiling

water for easier fitting. On no account should screw caps or crown corks be used in case fermentation continues with the subsequent build-up of pressure which will eventually shatter the bottle.

The stable bottled wine should be stored at 10 to 13°C (50 to 55°F) to produce a smooth, palatable wine with character.

A Basic Wine
The simple steps and equipment so far detailed should be sufficient to produce an acceptable wine at the first attempt both from the ingredients shown in the flow chart and from basic recipes such as this sultana recipe.

  1kg. (1 lb.) washed sultanas
  1.25kg. (2½lb.) white sugar
  10g. (⅓oz.) dried baker's yeast
  4 l. (7pt) water

Put the sultanas in a polythene bucket. Boil the sugar in the water for 2 min. and, while boiling, pour it over the sultanas. Allow to cool and add the yeast. Cover with sheet polythene tied down tightly. Each day for 7 days crush the 'cake' of sultanas which fermentation drives to the surface. Strain through fine muslin and wring out tightly. Put the strained wine into a fermentation jar, top up with boiled, cooled water and fit an airlock. Allow to ferment in a warm room until no gas bubbles are formed. Rack the clear wine from the yeast deposit. Herbs or flavourings can be added at this stage to produce, for example, a vermouth-type wine. Rack again and store.

The sultana recipe is very simple and requires a minimum of ingredients and equipment. However a better product would probably result from a little more attention, such as the addition of nutrients for the yeast, using a special wine yeast

or adding acid or tannin to the bland starting material.

Another important consideration is the need for sterility in the wine-making process to prevent infection of the wine by micro-organisms which might cause spoilage. These factors and other refinements to home wine-making are discussed in greater depth in the following sections.

The Method
– *Juice Extraction and Preparation of Must*
COLD EXTRACTION The first method of juice extraction, cold extraction, is sometimes used for fruit wines. The simplest technique is to crush by hand (or foot!) and soak the fruit, although this may not release all the available juice and must constituents. Aids to this method are the commercially available pectin destroying enzymes such as Rohament P, Pektolase or Pectinol, which help to break down the fruit and release the juice with maximum colour and flavour. Heat destroys these enzymes and the recommended amount should be sprinkled on to cold, pulped fruit and left to act for 24 hours at room temperature. To speed up the process, food liquidizers or special juice extractors can be used.

HEAT EXTRACTION This method, used for vegetable, flower and some fruit wines, is more efficient, but subtle flavour components may be lost or changed if heating is too vigorous. Flower and herb recipes and the basic sultana recipe use heat extraction in the simplest form – pouring boiling water over the substrate. Gentler heat extraction methods include simmering the material in water, preferably in a double saucepan, or using a 'Fruit Master' or similar domestic juice extractor.

One problem with wine-making is the pectin present in many fruits. This, with sugar and acid, is the setting agent of jams and can cause troublesome gels and hazes in wines. Heat extraction methods bring out more pectin than cold methods and also inactivate the natural pectin-destroying enzymes of the fruit, so treatment of the cooled extracts with one of the commercial enzymes mentioned above is advisable to ensure a clear wine. Another problem may be similar hazes caused by starch released from vegetables during extraction. These can also be prevented using commercial enzymes known as amylases.

STERILIZATION After extraction, the juice can be partially cleared of cell debris by straining through muslin or a special nylon wine-straining bag. It can be fermented at this stage, but, for a good product, it is advisable to ensure a pure fermentation from only the added yeast by sterilizing the juice to remove natural, but unwanted, micro-organisms from the starting material. Hot extraction achieves this to some extent, but the juice is best treated with Campden fruit-preserving tablets. These contain sodium metabisulphite and release sulphur dioxide, in acid conditions, which destroys spoilage yeasts and bacteria. For 5 l. (1 gall.) of wine 2 to 3 tablets should be crushed with a wooden spoon, dissolved in a small amount of water and stirred into the acid must. It should then be left for 24 hours before the fermenting yeasts are added or these may be killed by residual sulphur dioxide. The tablets can also be used to sterilize apparatus, bottles, corks, etc. by rinsing the equipment with a solution containing 4 tablets and 5g. (½tsp.)

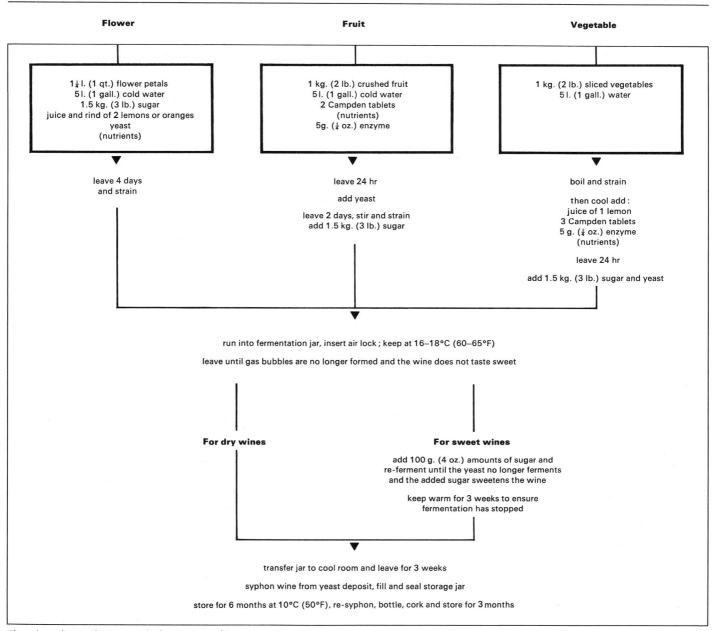

Flow chart showing basic steps for home winemaking.

citric acid (BP grade) per litre (2pt), thus ensuring that no spoilage organisms enter from these sources and the fermentation remains pure.

– *Preliminary Fermentation*
The amount that juice extraction overlaps this next stage of wine-making depends on the recipe. In the basic sultana recipe the vigorous action of the yeast in the preliminary fermentation is actually combined with heat extraction and crushing by hand. This method is often used for flower and some fruit wines where the starting material is bulky and is best done in a covered bucket or bowl.

In wines where the juice is extracted, strained from the debris, purified and added to the other ingredients, the preliminary fermentation can be done in the fermentation vessel, covered and partially filled to allow room for frothing. This is particularly appropriate for heat- or enzyme-extracted juices for some fruit and vegetable wines like the potato recipe, p. 202.

– *Completion of Fermentation and Clarification*
The most important part of wine-making is the actual fermentation of the sugar to alcohol. Provided the yeast has suitable conditions, this should continue to completion and need little attention.

Once the frothing preliminary fermentation has finished the wine needs 'cleaning up' operations such as straining to remove substrate debris and topping up. When the wine is funnelled into the fermentation vessel it should be topped up with surplus must or syrup of the same sugar concentration. Then an airlock should be fitted to keep the fermentation anaerobic, but allow gas out of the jar. A glass or plastic airlock is fitted into a rubber bung or waxed cork to give a tight fit in the neck of the vessel, and filled with a liquid through which the carbon dioxide can bubble out but which prevents the entry of air and flies. This liquid should be sterile in case the vessel 'sucks back' and boiled water or preferably Campden solution to kill invading spoilage organisms should be used.

The fermentation vessel is then left at a temperature of 16 to 18°C (60 to 65°F) until gas bubbles no longer form. At this stage, if the recipe calculations were correct, the wine should be dry or contain only enough residual sugar to make it palatably sweet. If the yeast has worked more efficiently than anticipated and produced a dry wine where sweet was required, the fermentation can be continued to the limit of the yeast alcohol tolerance by adding small amounts of extra sugar (100g./4oz.) until fermentation ceases and the added sugar sweetens the wine to taste.

The wine should then be left for 3 to 4 weeks to make sure that all fermentation has stopped, when it can be transferred to a cool room, 10 to 13°C (50 to 55°F), for a further 3 weeks to allow the yeast cells to settle into a firm deposit with the clear wine above.

– *Racking*
The wine is next syphoned or racked from the lees using a plastic or rubber tube to transfer it into another sterilized fermentation jar. The operation

is made easier by fitting a 'hockey-stick' shaped glass tube into the bottom of the flexible tubing so that the syphoning action does not disturb the deposit. The jar should be tilted slightly to collect as much clear wine as possible.

The new vessel should be topped up to the neck with other wine, spirit, or boiled water, *not* syrup at this stage or the fermentation may begin again. The airlock is refitted and the wine stored for 6 months to clear further. It can then be racked again and, as fermentation should be complete, bottled ready for storage.

– Storage
The clarification procedure detailed above is all part of the stabilizing and storage processes for wine, but once it is perfectly stable it can be bottled to allow further mellowing of flavour.

The bottles should be sterilized by rinsing with acid Campden solution and filled to within 2cm. (¾in.) of the cork. Wine bottles should *always* be sealed with corks as these will blow out safely if in-bottle fermentation occurs. Corking bottles can often be difficult as a tightly-fitting cork will tend to compress the headspace air and give resistance. A simple method of overcoming this, if a corking machine is not available, is to feed a piece of clean string down the side of the neck, push the cork in and slowly withdraw the string which will make a channel for the air to escape.

The wine should then be labelled and stored in a cool, dark place in a suitable rack to keep the bottles on their sides. This keeps the corks moist and prevents them drying out and allowing air into the wine. Most wines should be kept for at least 3 months before drinking.

Refinements
– Potato Wine
2.5kg. (5 lb.) small, old potatoes
1.5kg. (3 lb.) demerara sugar
30g. (1oz.) root ginger
10g. (⅓oz.) dried yeast
4 l. (7pt) water
2 oranges
2 lemons
yeast nutrients
30ml. (1tbsp.) strong tea

Scrub the potatoes clean, bring to the boil in the water and simmer gently until tender. Strain through muslin and add the orange and lemon zest and bruised ginger to the liquid. Boil for a further 15min., then pour onto the sugar and stir until dissolved. Add the yeast, nutrients and citrus juices and pour into a sterilized fermentation jar, filling the jar up to the shoulder. Stand the jar on a tray in a warm room to ferment. When froth no longer forms, clean the jar, top up with surplus liquid or cold boiled water and fit an airlock. Leave until gas bubbles cease, rack, bottle and store.

Apart from the essential starting material, sugar, yeast and water, the potato wine has additional ingredients which have been briefly mentioned. This section discusses ingredients in greater detail to show the many variations possible on basic recipes.

Water
Water is an essential ingredient in most wine recipes either to aid juice extraction or to dilute the must and other ingredients to a readily fermentable liquid. Tap water is usually perfectly satisfactory, but the calcium in very hard water may react with pectin in the substrate to give troublesome stiff gels of calcium pectate. Chlorinated water can give a flat flavour to the finished wine as the chlorine oxidizes flavour components. In both these cases the water should be boiled to deposit the calcium salts or drive off the chlorine. In any event boiling the water helps to keep the fermentation sterile, and cold, boiled water should be used for topping-up fermentations.

Sugar
Starting materials for home-made wines have varying amounts of naturally-occurring sugars, but most need added sugar so that a high enough alcohol concentration is reached and the wine will keep. A useful piece of equipment to allow manipulation of the sugar and alcohol levels and to ensure consistent results is the hydrometer.

This instrument relies on the fact that sugar dissolved in water increases the density or gravity. As a standard point the gravity of water is taken as 1000 and other liquids are measured against this, the readings obtained being known as specific gravities or SG. The more sugar is added the greater the SG and a reading on the hydrometer enables calculation of sugar content and potential alcohol if all the sugar is fermented, by reference to the table. As the wine ferments the reading will drop until all the sugar has been used, the wine is 'dry' and the SG is 1000 or slightly lower.

Specific Gravity Table

SPECIFIC GRAVITY	APPROXIMATE AMOUNT OF SUGAR IN		POTENTIAL ALCOHOL % BY VOLUME
	5 l. (g.)	1 gall. (oz.)	
1010	65	2	0.9
1020	220	7	2.3
1030	385	12	3.7
1040	535	17	5.1
1050	660	21	6.5
1060	790	25	7.8
1070	920	29	9.2
1080	1040	33	11.3
1090	1200	38	12.0
1100	1325	42	13.4
1120	1580	50	16.3
1130	1705	54	17.7

Special wine-making hydrometers can be purchased with this data printed on the glass tube to give a direct reading.

The extracted juice should be tested with the hydrometer to measure the approximate amount of sugar naturally present. Then extra sugar is added depending on the type of wine required:

	Total sugar per 5 l. (1gall.)	Approx SG
dry wine	1.2kg. (2½ lb.)	1085
medium wine	1.6kg. (3 lb..)	1100
sweet wine	1.8kg. (3½ lb.)	1125

The yeast will be capable of fermenting all of the sugar added to the dry recipe to alcohol, but some sugar should be left in the sweet recipe as the yeast produces the maximum tolerable amount of alcohol and leaves the remaining sugar to sweeten the wine. Very rarely should larger amounts of sugar be used as the finished wine will contain too much unfermented sugar and be very syrupy.

White sugar or sucrose is the cheapest and most frequently used sugar. Yeasts contain an enzyme called invertase which can split this into the fermentable sugars glucose and fructose. Some wine-makers prefer to use 'invert' sugar in which this reaction has already been carried out by chemical action, as fermentation may proceed more quickly. If invert sugar is used, slightly more (5%) should be added to recipes specifying white sugar.

Other sugar sources can be used, for example the brown or demerara sugars used in the potato and similarly bland wines which are improved by the flavour and colour of these sugars. Honey also imparts its own characteristics and produces mead type wines, but is rather an expensive source of sugar for those other than bee-keepers. If it is used the recipe quantity of white sugar should be replaced with approximately 1¼ times the amount of honey.

Whatever type of sugar is used it is always best to add too little initially and sweeten the wine gradually until the yeast cannot tolerate any more alcohol and fermentation stops. The wine can then be sweetened to taste. If too much sugar is added at first and the yeast is unable to ferment it all, the resulting syrupy liquid can be difficult to make into a palatable wine.

Yeasts
The inability of yeasts to ferment massive amounts of sugar leads on to the choice of yeast for wine-making. Although the beginner may find dried or fresh baker's yeast perfectly adequate to produce an acceptable wine, much better results can be obtained using some of the commercially available wine yeasts. This is because different types of yeast are particularly suited to different situations – baker's yeast is adapted to producing good bread, brewer's yeast produces good beer and wine yeasts undoubtedly produce the best wines. These wine yeasts have a higher tolerance of alcohol than the other types and can therefore produce a stronger wine (up to 18% alcohol by volume). They also produce other substances which give some character to wines, for example a Burgundy yeast will give a Burgundy-type wine when used to ferment suitable ingredients. They have the further advantage of settling into a firmer deposit than other types of yeast, so that the finished wine can be more easily separated from the yeast cells.

The wine yeasts are available in the form of living cultures, as liquids, tablets or dried. All must be grown up to an actively multiplying culture before adding to the must, just as baker's yeast is 'encouraged' by mixing with warm milk and sugar before adding to dough. The wine yeast is grown up into a starter culture using heated sterilized fruit juice or a starter mixture such as malt extract, granulated sugar and lemon juice in water. The wine yeast is added to a bottle of sterile starter and left to grow in a warm place for about 48 hours before adding it to the must. Most commercial yeast packs have clear instructions on reconstitution and it is best to follow these as the individual yeasts may vary in requirements.

Whatever yeast is used it should be added in the recommended quantity to cool starting material or juice, which has been left 24 hours to allow the sterilizing sulphur dioxide to disperse and which contains a suitable amount of sugar.

Nutrients

As already mentioned, the yeast needs certain nutrient substances other than sugar in order to ferment efficiently and produce the expected amount of alcohol. Many fruit juices, especially grape juice, contain a sufficient amount of these nitrogenous materials and vitamins, but other substrates, especially flower wines, may need an added dose to ensure that the fermentation is completed. Commercial preparations are available and it is perhaps simplest for the beginner to purchase these and use as rec-ommended. Alternatively, nutrients can be provided by adding 10ml. (2tsp.) plain malt extract to 5 l. (1 gall.) of wine or the essential nutrients can be purchased from the chemist and added at these rates:

ammonium sulphate (BP)
1g. per 5 l. (1gall.)
vitamin B₁ tablets
1g. per 5 l. (1gall.) fruit wine
2g. per 5 l. (1gall.) vegetable wine
3g. per 5 l. (1gall.) flower wine

Acid

Apart from the sweetness and flavour com-ponents from the starting material and wine yeast, a smooth, palatable wine needs a certain amount of acidity and tannin to balance the flavour and give it character.

The final amount of acid in the wine depends on the substrate used and the fermentation. Acid fruits usually provide sufficient natural acid to give a good wine, but vegetables and flowers may need added acid. Acid is sometimes lost during the fermentation and may need to be replaced, especially in sweet wines which require acid to balance the sweetness.

Some idea of the acidity of must is given by testing it with pH papers available from wine-making suppliers. A reading of 3 to 4 will give the necessary acidity and keeping quality in the final wine, but musts with readings higher than this should be adjusted using citrus juices: 1 to 2 oranges or lemons to 5 l. (1 gall.) or citric acid (BP) at 10 to 15g. (¼ to ½oz.) to 5 l. (1gall.).

Tannin

Addition of acid is perhaps a refinement of wine-making, but without sufficient acid the final wine may be disappointingly insipid and uninteresting. The same applies to wines that are low in tannin. This substance is naturally present in the skins and stems of fruits, and some vegetables, but flower and grain wines are much improved by adding it. For the beginner, the simplest and cheapest source is probably cold, strong tea added to the must at the rate of 20ml. (1tbsp.) to 4.5 l. (1gall.). Other sources are a few oak leaves, pear peelings or commercial grape tannin.

Fruit Wine

A good wine, with sufficient natural acid and tannin to compare with the potato recipe with added acid and tannin, is the black currant recipe given below. This will give a red wine of good character and illustrates many of the principles discussed, including heat and enzyme extraction.

– Black Currant Wine

1kg. (2¼ lb.) black currants
1kg. (2¼ lb. white sugar
15g. (½ oz.) pectin-destroying enzyme
wine yeast
water

Remove the fruit from the stems by pulling the bunches through a fork and place in the centre compartment of a double saucepan or in a 'Fruit Master'. Simmer until the juice begins to run from the berries. Pour the pulp into a large mixing bowl or plastic bucket and add 2 l. (4pt) of water. When cool, sprinkle on the enzyme, mix well and leave for 3 days, stirring the mixture several times a day. Strain through muslin or a bag. Dissolve the sugar in the juice, add the yeast and make the volume up to 5 l. (1gall.) with boiled water in the fermentation vessel. Fit an airlock and allow to ferment in a warm room until no gas bubbles form. Rack, bottle in dark bottles to preserve the colour and store.

Flower Wine

Compared to the naturally balanced blackcurrant wine, flower wines often need more attention, as the recipe for elderflower wine shows.

– Elderflower Wine

500ml. (¾pt) elderflowers
1.5kg. (3 lb.) white sugar
250g. (½ lb.) raisins
juice and zest of 2 oranges and 2 lemons
5ml. (1tsp.) grape tannin
5 l. (1gall.) water
wine yeast

Trim the flowers from the stems, measure by pressing down lightly in a measuring jug and place in a bucket. Boil the water and pour while still boiling over the flowers. Add the sugar, chopped raisins and citrus juice and rind. When cool add the yeast, grape tannin and nutrients. Tie down with sheet polythene and leave to ferment in a warm room for 4 to 5 days. Strain into a fermentation vessel, top up if necessary, fit an airlock and leave to ferment. Rack, bottle and store.

There are many other published recipes which have been calculated and tested to give good wines, but much of the pleasure of home wine-making is in the informed manipulation of ingredients to give your 'own' brand of wine.

Faults

If the basic steps and sterilization procedures are carefully carried out few faults should develop in home-made wines. However, if the worst hap-pens, it may be possible to rescue the wine. There are 4 main categories of fault: 'stuck' fermen-tations, hazes and colour faults, flavour faults and spoilage due to micro-organisms.

– 'Stuck' fermentations

A fermentation is 'stuck' if the yeast stops working and leaves an unpalatable amount of sugar because conditions are no longer ideal in the fermentation vessel. This may be because the recipe contained too much sugar and the yeast has converted as much as it can to a high level of alcohol. This situation can sometimes be rectified by splitting the liquor, diluting the sugar with more juice and restarting the fermentation with fresh yeast. If the sugar level was not too high initially the yeast may be limited by low nutrient or acid levels and will ferment again if more are added, or the temperature may be incorrect.

– Hazes

A hazy wine may be due to pectin or starch in suspension because the must was not enzyme treated initially. To make sure the haze is caused by pectin, a pectin test as used in jam-making (p. 184) can be carried out, or a starch haze is indicated by an intense blue colour with dilute iodine. Both should be removed by treatment with the appropriate enzyme. Another fault can be coloured hazes due to contamination by contact with unsuitable metals – these may be cured by addition of a small amount of lemon juice or citric acid. Other hazes or cloudy wines can sometimes be cleared by filtering through several thicknesses of muslin or special filter papers. If the haze remains finings can be used to precipitate out the suspended material. Com-mercial finings, such as the fine clay Bentonite, can be used as recommended by the manufac-turers. They all work by coagulating the protein-aceous matter causing the haze and should be mixed thoroughly with the wine and left to act for at least a month before the cleared wine is racked from the deposit.

– Colour

Darkening of white wines is usually due to oxidation occurring at some stage when the wine has been inadvertently left in contact with air. This may be corrected by bleaching with sulphur dioxide or an anti-oxidant such as ascorbic acid (vitamin C). Red wines should be fermented and stored in darkened bottles as nothing can be done if their colour is dulled by over-exposure to light.

– Flavour

Flavour problems are sometimes caused by poor recipes, although many taints are due to micro-bial action. Over-sweetness, over-acidity and low alcohol content can best be remedied by blending out the faults with other wines. A wine low in flavour or 'thin' can be blended with another with more 'body', and an insipid, flat or medicinal wine may be improved by adding extra tannin or acid.

– Spoilage by micro-organisms

Microbial faults are all due to invasion of the wine during fermentation or bulk storage by spoilage micro-organisms and imply a lack of adequate sterilization. The faulty wine should be treated with 1–2 Campden tablets to 4·5 l. (1gall.) to halt the invasion. If the trouble is a vinegary taste, there is too much air in contact with the wine allowing acetic acid bacteria to grow and produce acetic acid from the alcohol. Jars should be sulphited, topped up and set to ferment again. The vinegar flavour may be masked by this or by blending with a sweet wine, but if the fault has gone too far and produced wine vinegar the 'wine' can only be used as a condiment and in cooking. Other spoilage organisms which grow in the presence of air are the *film yeasts* which spread across the surface of the wine and convert it to water. These should be removed by filtering and fresh wine yeast added to start the fermen-tation again if this is possible. A thick, syrupy or 'ropy' wine is due to lactic acid bacteria using the sugar to make complex slimy substances. This should be stopped by adding Campden tablets, filtering and fermenting with fresh yeast.

These faults are rare and home wine-making is an interesting and rewarding hobby.

Index